CLASSIC MUSIC

Expression, Form, and Style

Leonard G. Ratner

Professor of Music
Stanford University

SCHIRMER BOOKS
A Division of Macmillan Publishing Co., Inc.
NEW YORK

COLLIER MACMILLAN PUBLISHERS
LONDON

Schirmer Books
A Division of Macmillan Publishing Co., Inc.
866 Third Avenue, New York, N.Y. 10022

Collier Macmillan Canada, Ltd.

Library of Congress Catalog Card Number: 76-57808

Printed in the United States of America

printing number

1 2 3 4 5 6 7 8 9 10

Library of Congress Cataloging in Publication Data

Ratner, Leonard G
    Classic music.

    Bibliography: p.
    Includes index.
    1. Music—History and criticism—18th century.
2. Classicism in music. I. Title.
ML195.R38   780'.903'3   76-57808
ISBN 0-02-872020-2

To Ingeborg

Contents

Abbreviations

AM	Acta Musicologica
AMW	Archiv für Musikwissenschaft
AMZ	Allgemeine musikalische Zeitung
HAM	Historical Anthology of Music
JAMS	Journal of the American Musicological Society
JMT	Journal of Music Theory
MGG	Musik in Geschichte und Gegenwart
ML	Music and Letters
MMR	The Monthly Musical Record
MQ	The Musical Quarterly
MR	Music Review
NMA	W. A. Mozart, Neue Ausgabe sämtlicher Werke
PAMS	Papers, American Musicological Society
RBM	Revue belge de musicologie
RISM	Repértoire international des sources musicales (International Inventory of Musical Sources)
SIM	Sammelbände der internationalen Musikgesellschaft
StM	Studien zur Musikwissenschaft

Preface

The music of Haydn, Mozart, and Beethoven and their contemporaries has a familiar and friendly ring. It speaks to us clearly and directly. We are moved by the powerful eloquence of its masterpieces, and we delight in the trimness and fluency of its minor works.

Much has been written about this music and its makers. Library shelves are crowded with histories, biographies, surveys, bibliographies, and genre studies. Yet something eludes us among this extensive literature; that is, a full-scale explication of the stylistic premises of classic music, a guide to the principles according to which this music was composed.

This book undertakes to define these principles. It offers a set of criteria, drawn from musical analysis and theoretical treatises of the late 18th century, that can serve as guidelines for the investigation of classic music.

The music central to this study, circa 1770–1800, is vast in quantity. The *Breitkopf Thematic Catalogue*, 1762–1787, lists thematic incipits of close to 10,000 compositions; thousands of 18th-century composers are listed in the *RISM* catalogue. Scanning the thematic catalogues of Haydn, Mozart, Beethoven, Gluck, the Bach sons, Boccherini, and Viotti will give some idea of the magnitude of production by a single composer.

The problems of recovery, authentication, and editing this enormous repertory are overwhelming. But its very size becomes an advantage for style analysis. Since most of this music had to be composed quickly, for immediate use, composers relied on familiar and universally accepted formulas for its organization and handling of detail. Wherever we sample this music, we find it runs true to type.

This consistency bespeaks a *language* understood throughout Europe and parts of the New World. Moreover, to speak of 18th-century music as a language is not simply to use a figure of speech. Structural parallels between music and oratory follow a clear path through music theory of the 17th and 18th centuries. Just as there were rules for organizing an oratorical discourse, so were there explicit prescriptions for building a musical progression. Both language and music had their vocabulary, syntax, and arrangement of formal structures, subsumed under the title *Rhetoric*. The skilled composer, the well-trained performer, the perceptive listener had command of musical rhetoric, much as a literate person today deals with the grammar of language. The expertise of the composer was shown in his ability to manipulate his ideas flexibly and felicitously within the rhetorical system.

The exposition of 18th-century musical rhetoric is found in theoretical and critical treatises. These are compendia of the practice of the time, instructive for the student and amateur of that age; for us, they point to what was current *then*, illuminating our present view of the music. Coordinated with analysis of the music itself, the data gleaned from these writings make it possible to determine the basic criteria of expression, rhetoric, structure, performance, and style that govern classic music.

The term *classic* is used in this book principally for purposes of chronology, although it has a number of meanings. Any perfected style in art can be called classic in the harmonious relationship of its elements and the refinement of its techniques. Clarity, balance, focus, universality in its own time and thereafter, great works that stand as "classics": these meanings can be applied to the music of the last quarter of the 18th century. But, as we shall see, other meanings of *classic* — objectivity, austerity, noble simplicity, purity of style, lack of disturbing irregularities or mixtures — do not apply. If we were to rename this period according to late 18th-century views, it would be called the *galant* style, possibly qualified as *late Franco-Italian galant*. For 18th-century musicians, the term *galant* was applied to all music not directly associated with the strict church style or imitating it. For them, *galant* had a much broader meaning than our image of mid-18th-century music characterized by extensive local and superficial elaboration. Of all terms used to designate this period, *Viennese classic* is most limiting because it shortens our perspective. While Vienna became very important quite late in the century and remained so in the early 19th century, there is hardly a mention of Vienna throughout 18th-century comments on style. The music there drew upon elements of Italian, French, and German styles, and Vienna's most important role was to provide a locale for a magnificent synthesis of styles in the mature works of Haydn, Mozart, and Beethoven. We can best savor the subtleties and the brilliance of this synthesis by seeing how it came about through *the fusion of elements* drawn from common 18th-century musical practice. This calls for a perspective that includes the entire range of expression, form, and style in 18th-century music.

Many features of the classic style originated in the early 18th century and formed a stream of continuity that maintained its flow long after the classic era had become history. Just as these features were already present in the early part of the century, so were elements of the older style, the baroque, very much alive in classic music. The division between the two styles has been considered marked and decisive, but it tends to be overstressed. The change in stylistic emphasis was due to an overlap of two streams of stylistic continuity rather than a sharp change of direction. Baroque and classic music were based upon the same criteria, a common set of premises, despite their obvious differences; they used one language, and their differences represented sublanguages of a universal 18th-century musical speech.

This book allows the student to approach the music and musical precepts of the 18th century in much the same way a listener of that time would have done. The first attraction to the music would be to its melodic materials, the topics of the musical discourse, its vocabulary. They are examined in detail in Part I, "Expression." Each of the following sections probes deeper into the core of the music: its syntax is examined in Part II, "Rhetoric"; its formal structure in Part III, "Form"; and its overall style in Part IV, "Stylistic Perspectives." The rhetorical principles discussed here have been used by the author in his teaching of music literature and theory at Stanford University. The volume is addressed to students, performers, and listeners, whose appreciation of the scope of classic music can be increased by insights into how it was put together.

Acknowledgments

My gratitude and appreciation go to the many students, colleagues, and friends who gave strong and positive response to the ideas incorporated in this book. Their encouragement, their many comments and criticisms during its writing were most helpful. My thanks go also to the staff members of the music sections in the following libraries for making available eighteenth-century sources, materials which give this book its special perspective: The Stanford University Libraries, The University of California Library, The Frank V. De Bellis Collection of the San Francisco State University, The Newberry Library, Chicago, The New York Public Library, The Library of Congress, Washington, The British Library, London, The Bibliothèque Nationale, Paris, The Bibliothèque Royale, Brussels, The Staatsbibliothek, Munich, The Nationalbibliothek, Vienna, The Library of the Gesellschaft für Musikfreunde, Vienna, The Royal Library, Copenhagen.

I Expression

Expression was an ever-present concern in 18th-century musical thought and practice. In its most general sense, expression referred to ways in which the listener's feelings could be stirred. The term covered a wide range of concepts and procedures, from frank pictorialism to subtle evocation of mood. Critical and theoretical writings of the 18th century contain much material on musical expression. Some comments are subjective, as those of Rousseau, 1768;[1] others, as Kirnberger's, 1771-1779,[2] aim for objective pinpointing of expressive content. This latter approach bespeaks the rationalism of the time; it reflects the encyclopedic view that endeavored to bring all observable phenomena into a hierarchical order, thus making them understandable and manageable. Apart from individual interpretations, 18th-century preoccupation with expression indicates the strong presence projected by this aspect of the musical art. Expression, however defined or regarded, was an essential quality; without it no piece was fit to be heard.

Composers' own comments tell of their concern with expression; even more important is the weight of evidence in their music as it ranges from pictorial imagery to metaphor and affective states. Therefore, the first two chapters deal specifically with ideas of expression and how they were embodied by various musical procedures in the 18th century. Chapter 1 examines general ideas of expression in 18th-century music and their significance for musical communication. Chapter 2 surveys materials which composers, performers, and listeners at that time associated with various moods, attitudes, and images; these constituted the *topics* upon which a persuasive musical discourse could be built.

NOTES

1. Rousseau, *Dictionnaire*, article on "Expression", pp. 207-213.
2. Kirnberger, *Kunst*, on intervals, Part II, pp. 103-104; on meters, Part II, pp. 118-136.

1

1 Ideas of Expression

These concertos are a happy medium between what is too easy and too difficult; they are very brilliant, pleasing to the ear, and natural, without being too vapid. There are passages here and there from which connoisseurs alone can derive satisfaction; but these passages are written in such a way that the less learned cannot fail to be pleased, though not knowing why.[1]

With these words, from a letter to his father, Mozart characterized the piano concertos in F major, K. 413, A major, K. 414, and C major, K. 415, that he wrote in 1782 and 1783 for performance in Vienna. Thanks to the musical language of the times—clear, simple, flexible, spoken everywhere in Europe—Mozart could reach everyone in his audience, connoisseur and amateur.

But the message involved more than the music itself. All artistic expression, including music, was dedicated to *stirring the feelings*; this was a constant theme in critical writings. Dies, 1810, an early biographer of Haydn, says that the master's ultimate aim was to "touch the heart in various ways."[2] Heinrich Christoph Koch, whose *Lexikon*, 1802, is the most complete and authoritative source of musical information of its time, says "the principal object of music is to stir the feelings."[3] Daniel Gottlob Türk, in his *Klavierschule*, 1789, the most important treatise on late 18th-century performance practice, says that "the expression of the ruling sentiment" is "the highest goal of music."[4]

The address to the feelings could take many forms. Feelings could be stirred in a general way by a sensitive or fiery performance. Jean-Jacques Rousseau, a champion of Italian music, was strongly drawn to frank and open sentiment and to its bold expression. He says in his *Dictionnaire*, 1768:

It amounts to little simply to read the notes exactly; it is necessary to enter into all the ideas of the composer, to feel and render the fire of his expression. . . .[5]

Koch, 1802, refers to nuances of performance that bring the expressive qualities of the music to life:

Every sentiment is distinguished by its characteristic modifications of tones, and this distinction is what gives meaning and life to a series of tones in performance, and without which it is nothing but an insignificant bustle of tones.[6]

More specifically, feelings were suggested or symbolized by musical figures linked to poetry or pantomime. Music took its cues from the vocal music of church and theater, which had distinct advantages over instrumental chamber

3

music. Johann Mattheson, in his work on musical style and technique, *Der vollkommene Capellmeister*, 1739, says:

> The first distinction between vocal music and instrumental music . . . is that the first is the mother, the second the daughter. . . .[7]

More than a half-century later Koch, 1802, makes the same point:

> It remains an established fact that vocal music retains a marked and undeniable advantage over pure instrumental music.[8]

Music could suggest the sentiment expressed in a text; this was embodied in the *doctrine of affections*, a governing principle for early 18th-century music and an important, though somewhat less formalized, factor in classic music.[9]

Feelings and passions were classified in various codes; Sir John Hawkins, in his monumental *General History of the Science and Practice of Music*, 1776, quotes from an English translation of René Descartes' *Musicae Compendium*, 1653:

> We say in the generall that a slow measure doth excite in us gentle and sluggish motions, such as a kind of languor, sadness, fear, pride, and other heavy and dull passions; and a more nimble and swift measure doth proportionately excite more nimble and sprightly passions, such as joy, anger, courage, &. the same may also be sayd of the double kind of percussion, viz. that a quadrate, or such as is perpetually resolved into equals, is slower and duller than a tertiate, or such as doth consist of three equal parts. The reason whereof is, because this doth more possesse and employ the sense, inasmuch as therein are more, namely 3, members to be adverted, while in the other there are only 2.[10]

Mattheson, 1739, characterizes dances according to their qualities of feeling.[11] Christian Gottfried Krause, a member of the Berlin musical circle to which Johann-Joachim Quantz belonged, gives a long list of affections in his *Von der musikalischen Poesie*, 1752. The following are samples:

Joy, lively clear, free tones; flowing, rather rapid style

Hope, proud, exultant music

Fear, groaning, trembling, broken tones

Doubt, irregular, broken syllables

Yearning, simple, languid tones

Malediction, tremolo, many dissonances[12]

Johann Philipp Kirnberger, the pupil of J. S. Bach, assigns expressive qualities to intervals in *Die Kunst des reinen Satzes*, 1771–1779. Some of these are:

Rising
augmented prime, anxious
minor second, sad
major second, pleasant, also pathetic (feelingful)

augmented second, languishing

minor third, sad, melancholy

major third, gay

perfect fifth, spirited

minor seventh, tender, sad, undecided

Falling

minor second, pleasant

major third, pathetic, also melancholy

augmented fifth, frightening (only when it appears in the bass)

octave, very restful[13]

Koch, 1802, recommends wide, slowly moving intervals within a chord to convey high, exalted feelings; conjunct intervals can express pleasant, ingratiating sentiments.[14] These conventions are exemplified on many pages of Mozart's operas. "Finch'han dal vino" from Act I, *Don Giovanni*, 1787, holds to one exuberant figure throughout to convey the idea of intoxication; "Or sai chi l'onore" and "Ah, chi mi dice mai" use widely spaced, slowly moving intervals to suggest the towering anger of Donna Anna and Donna Elvira, respectively. Don Ottavio, in "Il mio tesoro," Act II, expresses a gentler passion with one of the most ingratiating tunes ever written by Mozart, built principally of stepwise motion.

The doctrine of affections applied specifically to vocal music, where a text gave the clue for expression. Johann David Heinichen, in his *Der General-Bass in der Composition*, 1728, one of the principal sources for late baroque techniques of composition, recommends that for an aria the composer select some significant phrase in the poetry and invent a musical figure, a motto, to symbolize the affect. Ex. 1-1 illustrates two affections taken from the same text. Ex. 1-1a shows the *fugitive* aspect of fortune, expressing the frantic affect by means of a rushing figure. Ex. 1-1b suggests the painful aspect of fortune implied in the word *distress* through a pathetic melody whose changes of direction picture fortune's shifts.

Ex. 1-1. *Figures appropriate for affects.* Heinichen, *General-Bass*, 1728, pp. 43-46.

Text: "Whoever has fortune as an enemy will always find himself in distress."

a. Elusive Fortune

Ex. 1-1, cont'd.

b. Capricious, distressful Fortune

Chi hà nemica la for tu na   fi

More than a century later Pierre Baillot, in his celebrated *L'art du violon*, 1834, cites 46 examples of what he calls "accents" (expressive attitudes). His excerpts are taken from the music of Tartini, Haydn, Mozart, Beethoven, Boccherini, and others. A sampling is presented in Ex. 1-2.

Ex. 1-2. *Accents.* Baillot, *L'art du violon*, 1834, p. 196ff.

a. *Accent naïf.* Beethoven, Quartet in C Major, Op. 59, No. 3, 1806, 2nd movt.

b. *Accent vif et léger.* Mozart, *The Magic Flute*, 1791, overture.

c. *Accent de mélancolie.* Tartini, Sonata, Op. 3.

d. *Accent véhément.* Boccherini, Quartet No. 1, 1761.

These stylized attitudes toward musical expression reflected the formalities of 18th-century life. Status, place, and protocol were carefully defined by signs, badges, and rules of conduct.[15] Specific types of music and expressive qualities were proper for various locales, occasions, or situations. Distinctions between church, chamber, and theater styles were valid for the entire century. Meinrad Spiess, in *Tractatus Musicus*, 1746, says:

De Stylo Ecclesiastico, oder Kirchen-Stylo
  Among the three styles, the ecclesiastical merits the first rank because its aim and its very reason for being is to encourage and motivate the praise and honor of God; therefore, it is worked out with care, skill and diligence. . . .
De Stylo Cammerali, oder Cammer-Styl
  Chamber music, also called *galanterie-music*, takes its name from the rooms and salons of the nobility, where it is usually performed. Whoever looks for delight, artifice, invention, art, taste, affection (tendresse) will find them all in the so-called Concerti Grossi, Sonatas da Camera, etc. in which one cannot fail entirely to be pleased to hear all the high, middle, and low voices concert with each other, imitate each other, and compete for attention, all with neatness and zest.
De Stylo Theatrali
  If the present-day theatrical or operatic style is not a twin to the chamber style, at least it is a closely-related blood kinsman. Often the difference lies only in the place where the style is used, in comedies on the stage, or in salons; still, distinctions can be made not only as to the place of performance, but as to entirely different types of composition as well. . . .[16]

Degrees of dignity are described by Johann Adolf Scheibe in *Der critische Musikus*, 1745. He distinguishes between the *high, middle,* and *low* styles. He says that the *high style* must be stately and emphatic; the harmony must be full, the ideas fully carried through, the melody rich in invention, fresh, lively, and elevated. It should be used only for heroes, kings, and other great men and noble spirits; magnanimity, majesty, love of power, magnificence, pride, astonishment, anger, fear, madness, revenge, doubt, and other similar qualities and passions can only be expressed in the high style.

The *middle style*, according to Scheibe, is ingenious, pleasant, and flowing; it must please the listener rather than excite him or lead him to reflection. The melody must be clear, lively, flowing, and well turned; harmony must serve only to make the melody clearer and must never dominate (this refers to texture, rather than chord progression). Joy, delight, love, devotion, modesty, and patience are best imitated in this style.

The *low style* avoids all clever elaborations; it permits no extensions and should be used in short pieces. It represents nature in its simplest form, and is used for low-born persons and for objects and situations associated with them. Its characteristic embodiment is the shepherd; some others are beggars, slaves, poor prisoners, and farmers.[17]

The evidence that a piece of music was expected to move the passions of the soul by expressing a ruling sentiment is impressive. It is found in treatises, journals, and letters, and in the close correspondence between a given text and its musical setting. In vocal music, the connection between feeling and figure was explicit. In instrumental music—which imitated opera, church music, and ballet—this connection could only be implied, but it was unquestionably present.

NOTES

1. Anderson, *The Letters of Mozart*, 2nd ed., p. 833.
2. Gotwals, *Joseph Haydn*, p. 125.
3. Koch, *Lexikon*, p. 894.
4. Türk, *Klavierschule*, p. 347.
5. Rousseau, *Dictionnaire*, p. 206.
6. Koch, *Lexikon*, p. 1729.
7. Mattheson, *Capellmeister*, p. 204.
8. Koch, *Lexikon*, p. 794.
9. See Bukofzer, *Music in the Baroque Era*, p. 388ff., for a discussion of the *Affektenlehre*, or doctrine of affections.
10. Hawkins, *History*, p. 626.
11. Mattheson, *Capellmeister*, p. 224ff.
12. Krause, *Poesie*, p. 92ff.
13. Kirnberger, *Kunst*, II, pt. 2, pp. 103, 104.
14. Koch, *Lexikon*, pp. 896, 897.
15. See Walter H. Bruford, *Germany in the Eighteenth Century*, Cambridge University Press, London, 1935, p. 45ff., and Arthur Pryor Watts, *A History of Western Civilization*, 2 vols., Prentice-Hall, New York, 1939-1940, p. 311ff., for accounts of social classes in the 18th century.
16. Spiess, *Tractatus*, p. 161ff.
17. Scheibe, *Critische Musikus*, p. 126ff.

2 Topics

From its contacts with worship, poetry, drama, entertainment, dance, ceremony, the military, the hunt, and the life of the lower classes, music in the early 18th century developed a thesaurus of *characteristic figures*, which formed a rich legacy for classic composers. Some of these figures were associated with various feelings and affections; others had a picturesque flavor. They are designated here as *topics* — subjects for musical discourse. Topics appear as fully worked-out pieces, i.e., *types*, or as figures and progressions within a piece, i.e., *styles*. The distinction between types and styles is flexible; minuets and marches represent complete types of composition, but they also furnish styles for other pieces.

TYPES

Dances

The protocol and formality of 18th-century life were reflected in dances: the minuet, sarabande, and gavotte were of the *high* style, elegant and courtly; the bourrée and gigue, pleasant and often lively, represented the *middle* style, while contredanses and Ländler were of the *low* style, rustic and buoyant. Minuets and polonaises grew livelier toward the end of the century, reflecting both a more frivolous life style and the restlessness of the times.

Dances, by virtue of their rhythm and pace, represented feeling. Their trim and compact forms served as models for composition. They were written by the thousands by classic composers; Mozart composed more than 300 minuets and contredanses; Beethoven and Haydn produced a comparable number. Books of dances were issued periodically for the fashionable world much as popular music is published today. Dances were used to teach composition[1] and to instruct in performance;[2] they furnished material for opera and chamber music, for arias, sonatas, concertos, symphonies, serenades, and even invaded church music (see Ch. 10). Kirnberger, in *Recueil*, 1783, emphasizes the importance of dance music as a basis for elaborate compositions and especially for the understanding of the rhythmic nature of various types of fugues.[3] Joseph Riepel, in his *Anfangsgründe*, 1752, says that the working out of a minuet is no different than that of a concerto, aria, or symphony.[4] Koch, 1793, makes the same point.[5] Mozart used dances to teach composition.[6] Dance rhythms virtually saturate classic music; therefore, one of the principal points of attention for the student, listener, and performer is the recognition of specific dance patterns that can provide important clues to the expressive quality of a composition. The following survey covers the principal dances current during the classic era.

Minuet and Related Types. The most popular dance in the classic era was the *minuet*.[7] Originally it was associated with the elegant world of court and salon. It was described as noble, charming, lively, expressing moderate cheerfulness by

9

virtue of its rather quick triple time.[8] In classic music, compositions entitled *minuet* or *menuetto* covered a wide range of expression, from the frankly humorous to the deeply pathetic. Ex. 2-1 represents the elegant vein of this dance; Ex. 2-2a has a popular rustic flavor; Ex. 2-2b expresses a deeply pathetic mood; Ex. 2-2c, while entitled *menuetto*, exemplifies the breathless and headlong manner of Beethoven's later scherzos.

Ex. 2-1. *Minuet.*

a. Koch, *Versuch*, III, 1793, p. 64.

b. J.C. Bach, Symphony in E♭, Op. 9, No. 2, 1775.

Ex. 2-2. *Expressive range in minuets.*

a. Haydn, Symphony No. 102 in B♭ major, 1794, menuetto.

b. Mozart, Quintet in G minor, K. 516, 1787.

Edwards

c. Beethoven, Symphony No. 1 in C major, Op. 21, 1800, menuetto.

Charles Burney, in his *History of Music*, 1789, has many references to "minuet time" in his comments on Handel's music.[9] The minuet, as a style, was used in first movements, slow movements, and finales, as in the first movement of Mozart's Symphony No. 39 in E♭ major, K. 543, 1788, and the first movement of Beethoven's Symphony No. 8, Op. 93, 1812.

Dances related to the minuet included the *passepied*, described in Jean le Rond d'Alembert's *Élémens de musique*, 1766, as a rather lively minuet, and the *sarabande*, which he characterizes as a slow minuet.[10] Ex. 2-3 illustrates the passepied set typically in 3/8 meter; this topic was also used by Haydn in the finale of his Sonata in G major, H.V. XVI, No. 6, before 1766.

Ex. 2-3. *Passepied.* Löhlein, *Clavier-Schule*, 5th ed., 1791, p. 174.

As a dance the sarabande disappeared toward the end of the 18th century, yet its characteristic style was retained. The essential feature was the emphasis on the second beat of its triple measure. With its slow tempo, this halt gave the sarabande a deliberate, serious character which represented the high style (Ex. 2-4; see also Haydn's D major Sonata, H.V. XVI, No. 37, circa 1779–1780, second movement).

Ex. 2-4.   *Sarabande style.* Mozart, Symphony No. 41 in C major, K. 551, 1788, 2nd movt.

Popular dances in triple time often masqueraded as minuets. *Waltzes, Ländler, allemandes, Schleifer* (sliding dances), and *Swabian allemandes* had a quicker tempo, more buoyant manner, and simpler quality reflecting the middle and low styles (see Ex. 2-5). Haydn used the Swabian allemande style, with a constant play of cross rhythms, in the menuetto of his Quartet in F major, Op. 77, No. 2, 1799, to create a broadly humorous effect.

Ex. 2-5.   *Swabian allemande.* Christmann, *Elementarbuch*, 1782, examples, p. 15.

Polonaise.   The *polonaise*, a dance in triple meter, was rather serious and deliberate in style in the early 18th century. Its characteristic feature was a momentary pause within the measure, upon a syncopation or upon the last beat of the measure.[11] It fell out of favor in mid-century but returned in classic times as a quick dance with many 16th-notes (see Ex. 2-6). Koch, in the *Lexikon*, 1802, says:

> Recently it appears that the dance (polonaise) and the taste for its melodies have overcome their previous neglect.[12]

Haydn juggled polonaise figures with amazing dexterity in the finale of his F major Quartet, Op. 77, No. 2, 1799, shifting the already misplaced accents and trimming the figures to irregular lengths, again with delightfully humorous effects (see Ex. 5-6).

Ex. 2-6. *Polonaise.* Beethoven, Serenade in D major, Op. 8, 1796-1797.

Allegretto alla Polacca

Bourrée.   The *bourrée* was rather lively in manner and in duple meter, calling for lightness in performance.[13] While the term *bourrée* does not appear in classic music as a title for a movement, the style was frequently used. The bourrée has a short upbeat and an articulation after the third beat of the measure. Exs. 2-7 and 2-8 illustrate its use in early and late 18th-century music.

Ex. 2-7. *Bourrée type.* J. S. Bach, Partita in B minor, ca. 1720.

Ex. 2-8. *Bourrée style.* Mozart, Concerto for Clavier and Orchestra in G major, K. 453, 1784, finale.

Allegretto

Contredanse.   Rousseau describes this popular dance, 1768:

The melodies of contredanses are most often in duple time; they should be well-articulated, brilliant, and gay, and still should be quite simple; since they must be heard many times, they will become intolerable if they are over-ornate. In every genre, the simplest things are those that tire least.[14]

If we quicken the pace of the bourrée, the music will be in the style of the contredanse, also called the *angloise.*[15] Ex. 2-9 is a contredanse used as a teaching piece.

Ex. 2-9. *Contredanse.* Christmann, *Elementarbuch,* 1782, examples, p. 13.

Contredanses were standard items in ballet suites, e.g., Mozart, *Les petits riens*, K. 299b, 1778; they were composed in sets for dances and balls. The effervescent contredanse style was a favorite topic for finales (see Ex. 2-10).

Ex. 2-10. *Contredanse.* Mozart, Quintet in E♭ major, K. 614, 1791, finale.

Gavotte. The *gavotte* was a rather lively dance in duple time,[16] distinguished by a cesura after the second quarter-note of the measure. The principal charm of this dance lay in the retention of this rhythmic pattern, which accommodated a melody of elegance, poise, and self-containment. Koch, 1793, quotes a gavotte by his teacher Scheinpflug (Ex. 2-11).

Ex. 2-11.   *Gavotte.* Koch, *Versuch*, III, 1793, p. 41.

Gavotte style was used at times in slow movements (Ex. 2-12). *Romanzas*, with their *amoroso* character and ingratiating melody, were often set in gavotte time,[17] as in the slow movement of Mozart's *Eine kleine Nachtmusik*, K. 525, 1787. The distinctive rhythm of the gavotte was also adapted to neatly turned melodies in quicker tempo (Ex. 2-13).

Ex. 2-12.   *Gavotte style.* Mozart, Quintet in E♭ major, K. 614, 1791, 2nd movt.

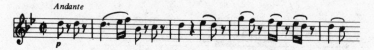

Ex. 2-13. *Quicker gavotte tempo.* Mozart, Sonata for Clavier and Violin in A major, K. 526, 1787, finale.

Gigue. The *gigue* was a quick dance, gay and lively, generally in 6/8 meter.[18] The distinctions made in the early 18th century among the *gigue, giga, canarie, forlane, loure* — all related dances — disappeared in classic times. Few pieces were entitled *gigue* in classic music, but the style remained in finales, and occasionally in first movements (see Ex. 2-14).

Ex. 2-14. *Gigue* style. Haydn, Symphony No. 101 in D major, 1794, 1st movt.

Mozart's "Little Gigue" in G major, K. 574, 1789, is deliberately modeled upon the earlier 18th-century imitative gigues that often closed dance suites and partitas. This little work, a tribute to J. S. Bach, has none of the high exuberance of classic gigue finales. Its chromatic, twisting subject and its tightly woven counterpoint retain only the vestiges of the gigue manner (see Ex. 2-15).

Ex. 2-15. Mozart, "Little Gigue" in G major, K. 574, 1789.

Siciliano. Like the gigue, the *siciliano* was set in 6/8 time, but it was performed in slow tempo, in a rather languishing manner. Its principal feature is the dotted pattern ♪♩. Türk, 1789, said that it should *not* be played staccato, to express its gentleness.[19]

Ex. 2-16.   *Siciliano style.* Mozart, Quartet in D minor, K. 421, 1783, finale.

Rousseau, 1768, classifies the siciliano as a dance melody,[20] although it was generally considered a *style* for songs and pastoral instrumental pieces (see Ex. 2-16). It was traditional in music for the Nativity; J. S. Bach used the style in the *Christmas Oratorio*, BWV 248, 1734, and Handel in the *Messiah*, 1741. Mozart evokes a pathetic mood in the music presented in Ex. 2-16, as he does in another movement using siciliano rhythm, Concerto in A major, K. 488, 1786, second movement.

The March

The *march* had both dance and ceremonial meaning in the 18th century. As an *entrée*,[21] it served to open ballet performances, ceremonies, and stage presentations. It was sometimes included among sets of dances in suites, as for example in Suites VII, IX, XII, and XXIV from the *Little Music Book* of Leopold Mozart, 1762. Its natural habitats were the parade ground and battlefield, where its moderately quick duple meter, dotted rhythms, and bold manner quickened the spirit. If the minuet, the queen of 18th-century dances, symbolized the social life of the elegant world, the march reminded the listener of authority, of the cavalier and the manly virtues ascribed to him.

Ex. 2-17 illustrates the march *type*, used as a teaching piece. Many first movements, especially in symphonies and concertos, have march rhythms. One of the most familiar examples is the first movement of Mozart's *Jupiter* Symphony, K. 551, 1788. French violin music after the Revolution—concertos, quartets, trios, duets—used a broadly scaled march style for first movements.[22]

Ex. 2-17.   *March type.* Christmann, *Elementarbuch*, 1782, examples, p. 24.

The march and the bourrée shared a common tempo and meter—a quick 4/4. Quantz, 1752, refers to marches in bourrée rhythm.[23] Ex. 2-18 illustrates this combination; the dotted rhythms come from the march; the sprightly manner and the upbeat rhythm are those of the bourrée.

Ex. 2-18.   *Mixture of bourrée and march.* Mozart, Sonata for Clavier and Violin in F major, K. 376, 1781, finale.

Incorporation of Dances into Classic Music

Dances were incorporated into classic music in three general ways: social, theatrical, and speculative.

1. *Social dances.* In social dances, the music conforms to choreography; the melody is simple, and the sections are brief and symmetrical in form.

2. *Theatrical dances.* Theatrical dances could conform to the patterns of social dances or become freer and more extended, as in the "Dance of the Furies" from Gluck's *Don Juan*, 1761 (see Ex. 21-12). Koch comments on the distinction between social dance and theatrical dance as embodied in *ballet*, 1802:

> One distinguishes by this word the theatrical dance from those social dances whose one and only object is to provide pleasure for the dancers. Included under the name ballet are those theatrical dances whose apparent object is to please the spectator by a series of steps and leaps that are more highly regulated and artificial than those of the social dances; as fine art such dances deserve no further mention. The true ballet presents an interesting action by means of dance and pantomime, and often is called the pantomimic ballet, classified into serious and comic. Like drama, it has plan, plot, and dénouement. The music consists of an unbroken series of various styles and genres of pieces, in which the expression of the sentiments is defined by the content and progress of the plot. Here the art of gesture should be as intimately unified with music as poetry is with music in opera.[24]

Theatrical dances had some *mimetic* content. Mattheson, 1739, gives a detailed account of the "Geberden-Kunst," the art of gesture.[25] Krause, 1752, says that the poet and musician should provide the singer with opportunities for posture and pantomime.[26] Kirnberger, 1774-1779, relates the note values in dances to various kinds of movement, step, and gesture.[27] Concerning the pantomimic style, Schubart, in his *Ideen zu einer Aesthetik der Tonkunst*, written circa 1784-1785, says:

> This is actually the interpreter of the music. . . . It is partially dramatic, partly social. The composer of dances must have almost as much skill as the great opera composers. Indeed, the exalted, the awe-inspiring, the Shakespearean lie within his sphere. . . . He must be as well versed in the tragic as in the comic. . . .[28]

For Jérôme-Joseph de Momigny, *Cours complet*, 1806, the ideal performer should have the qualities that belong to the perfect actor.[29]

3. *Speculative treatment of dance material.* This phrase refers to the use of dance rhythms as subjects for discourse in sonatas, symphonies, and concertos, as well as in church and theater music. Koch, 1793, says:

> Dance melodies, when they are not specifically intended for dancing, may contain more than 8 measures even in the first reprise.[30] [See Ch. 12.]

In speculative treatment of dance topics, the typical dance rhythms are employed, but the length of sections does not conform to choreographic patterns of symmetry. Dance topics saturate the concert and theater music of the classic style; there is hardly a major work in this era that does not borrow heavily from the dance.

Typically, dances entered the international repertory from regional sources. Thus the minuet came from Poitou, the bourrée from Auvergne, the polonaise from Poland. Occasionally, exotic dances found their way into theater and chamber music, as the Spanish *fandango* in Mozart's *Marriage of Figaro*, 1785–1786, Act III, the *chaconne* in Gluck's *Don Juan*, 1761, the *tarantella* in the finale of Beethoven's D major Quartet, Op. 18, No. 3, circa 1798–1800. Most of the dances of the baroque eventually disappeared except for a few such as the minuet, gavotte, angloise, bourrée, and polonaise,[31] and these acquired a more popular and simple style.

STYLES

Military and Hunt Music

Military and hunt music was familiar throughout the 18th century. Noble houses had their own court guards, parading to the fanfare of trumpets accompanied by the tattoo of drums; German towns had their *Stadtpfeiffer* (town bands) that performed for festivals, birthdays, weddings, and trade fairs; the hunt was a favorite diversion of the nobility; horn signals echoed and re-echoed throughout the countryside.[32]

Fanfares and hunting signals were imitated by strings, woodwinds, and keyboard instruments. Mozart used a hunting fanfare as the opening theme of the first movement of his E♭ major Quintet, K. 614, 1791 (Ex. 2-19). This passage is an imitation of the type of fanfare described by Koch, 1802, as "horn duet in lively tempo, set in 6/8 time."[33]

Ex. 2-19. *Hunting fanfare.* Mozart, Quintet in E♭ major, K. 614, 1791, 1st movt.

From Ratner, *Music: The Listener's Art.* Copyright 1957, 1966, 1977 by McGraw-Hill Book Company. Used by kind permission of the publisher.

The horn figure could be turned to a poignant or lyric vein; Beethoven used it to represent the *Lebewohl*, the final call or parting signal, in his E♭ major Sonata, Op. 81a, 1808. The same mood pervades the second movement of Mozart's

Eb major Sonata, K. 570, 1789. The key of Eb was a favorite of brass instruments; thus the imitation of horn signals in both these works includes pitch and key as well as figure; both composers return repeatedly to the opening signal to recall the nostalgic affection.

Military and hunt figures also furnished material for humor, as in the delightful parade march of "Non piu andrai" from Mozart's *Marriage of Figaro*, K. 492, 1785–1786, Act I, where Figaro tells Cherubino what is in store for him as a soldier. Haydn parodied horn fifths in the first movement of his Eb major Sonata, H.V. XVI, No. 52, 1794, where he has the piano imitating a musical clock imitating a fanfare. The double meaning of the word *horns*—a military instrument and the horns placed on the head of a deceived husband or lover—was familiar in comic opera. In "Se a caso" and "Se vuol ballare" from Mozart's *Marriage of Figaro*, Act I, 1785–1786, the intent of the Count to seduce Susanna is suggested by horn figures.

The Singing Style

References to the *singing style* are found in Koch, 1802,[34] and Daube, 1797.[35] The term indicates music in a lyric vein, with a moderate tempo and a melodic line featuring relatively slow note values and a rather narrow range. Presumably any of the familiar dance rhythms could be used. Ex. 2-20 is set as a bourrée.

Ex. 2-20.   *Singing style.* Gluck, *Orfeo,* 1762, Act III, "Ach wohin ohne Euridyke" ("I have lost my Euridice").

Andante con moto

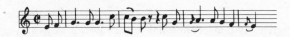

The term *singing allegro* is presently used to designate a song-like melody set in quick tempo; it is accompanied by steadily repeated rapid notes or by broken chord figures, as in the first four measures of the finale of Mozart's *Jupiter* Symphony, K. 551, 1788.

The Brilliant Style

The term *brilliant*, used by Daube, 1797, Türk, 1789, and Koch, 1802[36] refers to the use of rapid passages for virtuoso display or intense feeling. Earlier Italian composers—Alessandro Scarlatti, Arcangelo Corelli, and Antonio Vivaldi among them—codified the brilliant style by systematic repetitions and sequences. Ex. 1-1a illustrates the brilliant style in an aria. Burney, 1789, quotes a number of examples of brilliant passages sung by the great virtuosos of the 18th century.[37]

In Ex. 2-21 the brilliant style is shared by the five performers in a precise, exhilarating give-and-take. The mechanical arrangement is clear; each brilliant turn is *one* measure in length; the figures are taken by successively lower-pitched instruments. The ensemble becomes a "clockwork," imitating the toy mechanisms which fascinated the 18th-century mind.

Ex. 2-21. *Brilliant style.* Mozart, Quintet for Clarinet and Strings in A major, K. 581, 1789, 1st movt.

Edwards

The French Overture

The French overture, a distinctive style of ceremonial music, uses a slow and heavy march tempo with dotted rhythmic figures.[38] In the courts and theaters of France under Louis XIV it accompanied the entrance of the royal spectators and the performers. Later it was adopted throughout Europe as the opening piece for many theatrical performances, for instrumental suites, and for some symphonies, when the occasion called for a serious, elevated tone. To emphasize its air of punctilious ceremony, dotted notes were performed longer than the notation indicated, short notes as briefly as possible.[39] In classic music, the French overture style appears in slow introductions to symphonies (see Ex. 2-22). Mozart also set it as the principal affect in the unfinished fantasia K. 396, 1782.[40]

Ex. 2-22. *French overture style.* Mozart, Symphony in E♭ major, K. 543, 1788, introduction.

Musette, Pastorale

Musette and *pastorale* refer to rustic music played on the *bagpipe, cornemuse,* or *musette*. The principal feature is the sustained bass—the bourdon or drone—on a single tone or a fifth.[41] The melody proceeds either as a naive, pastoral tune or as a melodic flourish. Musette effects abound in classic music; Clementi and Haydn were criticized for taking up this "burlesquerie."[42] Measures 90-103 of the first movement of Mozart's C major Quintet, K. 515, 1787, illustrate the two elements of this style—the drone bass using a fifth and the melodic flourish. A few measures later Mozart will turn this effect upside down, putting the flourish into the lower instruments, while he extracts a bourrée-like figure from the drone fifth as a counter-melody in the upper voices, a striking example of the speculative treatment of a simple topic. This movement, the broadest in scale in all of Mozart's chamber music, is remarkable for its constant references to the musette style and elaborations upon it; they occupy 120 of its 360 measures.

Haydn placed a very simple melody over a drone bass in the finale of his Symphony No. 104 in D major, 1795, although the melody itself shows some rhythmic oddness (see Ex. 5-7). Much of the breadth of the first movement of Beethoven's F major Quartet, Op. 59, No. 1, 1806, is due to the extensive use of musette style (see Ch. 24).

Turkish Music

Turkish effects in western European music were by-products of the long military and diplomatic confrontation of western nations with the Turks. The Turks had a colorful military style called *janissary music*, using drums, triangle, winds, and cymbals. Classic composers imitated this style yet modified it to accommodate to western taste.[43] Mozart's *alla Turca* from his A major Sonata, K. 331, 1778, the overture to his *Abduction from the Seraglio*, 1781-1782, and the "Turkish March" from Beethoven's *The Ruins of Athens*, Op. 114, 1822, are specific references to the Turkish military style. The march in B♭ in the finale of Beethoven's Symphony No. 9 in D minor, 1822-1824 (see Ex. 9-7), and the first movement of Mozart's A minor Sonata, K. 310, 1778, suggest this style without specific references in their titles. We hear momentary hints of the Turkish style in the first movement of the E♭ major Sonata, H.V. XVI, No. 52, 1794, by Haydn, mm. 29-30.

Storm and Stress

The term *Storm and Stress*, taken from the title of a drama, *Sturm und Drang*, 1776, by Klinger, has been adopted by music historians to refer to some early manifestations of romanticism—the expression of subjective and intense personal feelings.[44] Koch, 1802, refers to "stürmende Leidenschaften," (stormy passions).[45] Storm and Stress uses driving rhythms, full texture, minor mode harmonies, chromaticism, sharp dissonances, and an impassioned style of declamation. Haydn's music in the 1770s has some of these qualities, as in his F minor Quartet, Op. 20, No. 5, 1772; Storm and Stress is also present in his later symphonies (see Ex. 9-10). The music of Beethoven, Cherubini, and many of their contemporaries takes the stormy manner as one of its principal focal points of expression, a counterpart to the intensity in the writings of Goethe and Schiller.

Sensibility, Empfindsamkeit

Sensibility and *Empfindsamkeit* apply to an intimate, personal style, often sentimental in quality. Classic musical criticism constantly refers to *Empfindun-
gen*, feelings and sentiments.[46] C. P. E. Bach was the principal representative of
this style. His keyboard music has rapid changes in mood, broken figures,
interrupted continuity, elaborate ornamentation, pregnant pauses, shifting, uncertain, often dissonant harmony—all qualities suggesting intense personal involvement, forerunners of romantic expression, and directly opposed to the stat-
uesque unity of baroque music.

The keyboard works of Mozart, Haydn, and their contemporaries contain
many hints of this style. Ex. 2-23 begins with a plaintive melody, broken by sighing figures. From m. 5 onward, each measure has a different figure; chromaticism saturates the stop-and-start continuity. This style, with the sudden changes
of mood and the subtle variations in tempo that it invites, is typically a keyboard
genre. Yet Mozart was able to induce a sensibility effect in the first part of the introduction to his *Prague* Symphony, 1786, by using short, contrasted figures,
with sudden shifts of instrumental color, range, dynamics, and harmony (see Ex.
6-18). Beethoven captured the pathetic sentimental value of this style in the
Maliconia of his Bb major Quartet, Op. 18, No. 6, circa 1798–1800, principally
by means of harmonic color.

Ex. 2-23. *Sensibility style.* Mozart, Fantasia in D minor, K. 397, 1782.

The Strict Style; the Learned Style

The types and styles already discussed were subsumed under the general rubric *galant, or free, style*, associated with theater and chamber music. In contrast, the *strict and learned styles* were associated with the church. Koch, 1802, summarizes the *strict* style:

The *strict* style, which is also called the *bound* style or the fugal style, . . . is distinguished from the free style principally

1. by a serious conduct of the melody, using few elaborations. The melody retains its serious character partly through frequent closely-bound progressions which do not allow ornamentation and breaking-up of the melody into small fragments, . . . partly through the strict adherence to the main subject and figures derived from it.

2. through the frequent use of bound dissonances (suspensions). . . .

3. through the fact that the main subject is never lost sight of, as it is heard in one voice or another; this ensures that each voice partakes of the character of a principal part and shares directly in the expression of the sentiment of the piece.
    Because of these characteristics, the strict style is best suited for church music. . . . the fugue is the principal product of this style. . . .[47]

For comparison, here is Koch's description of the *galant*, or *free*, style:

The *free*, or unbound style, which is also called the *galant* style, is distinguished from the preceding [strict]

1. through many elaborations of the melody, and divisions of the principal melodic tones, through more obvious breaks and pauses in the melody, and through more changes in the rhythmic elements, and especially in the lining up of melodic figures that do not have a close relationship with each other, etc.

2. through a less interwoven harmony

3. through the fact that the remaining voices simply serve to accompany the main voice and do not take part in the expression of the sentiment of the piece, etc.

All kinds of individual sections of large vocal works, such as arias, choruses, and such; all ballet and dance music, as well as introductions, concertos, and sonatas that are not in the style of the fugue, are included among the compositions in the free style.[48]

In *Versuch*, I, 1782, Koch specifies the principal technical distinction between the two styles; in the free style, *dissonance need not be prepared.*[49]

The strict style sets firm rules for harmonic and melodic progression, creating a smooth connection of slowly moving melodies and harmonies; its simplest and most traditional form was the *alla breve* progression in whole- and half-notes.[50] *Stile legato* means *bound style*, which refers to this kind of connection. *Learned style* signifies imitation, fugal or canonic, and contrapuntal composition, generally. The finale of Beethoven's Quartet in A major, Op. 18, No. 5, 1800, begins as a quick contredanse, but the voices enter in imitation, suggesting the learned style; later there is an extended section in which the *alla breve* style is worked over in various ways (see Ex. 2-24). The juxtaposition of these contrasted topics

Ex. 2-24. *Learned style and alla breve.* Beethoven, Quartet in A major, Op. 18, No. 5, 1800, finale.

Eulenburg No. 20

gives this movement a pictorial flavor clearly understood by 18th-century listeners—perhaps the merrymaking of an improvised rustic comedy, interrupted by a procession of priests. In a letter to Hoffmeister, April 8, 1802, Beethoven writes about composing a Mass in which the "Credo" would be given "great notes weighing a pound each,"[51] an obvious reference to *alla breve*.

Fantasia

The *fantasia* style is recognized by one or more of the following features—elaborate figuration, shifting harmonies, chromatic conjunct bass lines, sudden contrasts, full textures or disembodied melodic figures—in short, a sense of improvisation and loose structural links between figures and phrases. Thus toward the end of the second movement of Haydn's D minor Quartet, Op. 76, No. 2, 1798, the leisurely minuet rhythm is interrupted for an extended fantasia-like section.

In 18th-century opera, the fantasia style is used to evoke the supernatural—the *ombra*, representing ghosts, gods, moral values, punishments—and to bring forth feelings of awe and terror. Mozart incorporates elements of the church style—*alla breve, stile legato*—in the introduction to his overture to *Don Giovanni*, K. 527, 1787, and later recalls this music in the duel, Act I, and the "supper" scene, Act II. Beethoven may well have had the *ombra* in mind in the introduction to his Symphony No. 4 in Bb major, Op. 60, 1806.

PICTORIALISM; WORD-PAINTING

Given the wealth of available topics, 18th-century composers at times could easily take a further step and become frankly pictorial in their music. Pictorialism and word-painting in music represent efforts to imitate or symbolize specific ideas from poetry or other types of literature. *Pictorialism*, generally associated with instrumental music, conveys some idea of an action or scene. *Word-painting* is the matching of a word of phrase in a text to a musical figure. Both procedures had been honored for centuries in madrigals, descriptive French clavecin music, battle pieces, etc.

Koch includes an entry for "Simphonies à programme" in the *Lexikon*,[52] he mentions Dittersdorf (*The Four Ages*, *The Fall of Phaeton*), Rosetti (*Telemachus*), and Haydn (*The Seven Last Words*, circa 1786). He questions the validity of such relationships between literature and music. Concerning these, he comments in the article "Malerey" (pictorialism):

When certain sounds and motions out of inanimate Nature, such as the rolling of thunder, the tumult of the sea, the rustle of the wind and such, are imitated in music, this is called tone painting. Some such similarities exist between natural phenomena and musical tones and one can transfer them to music; but music betrays its nature when it takes over such descriptions, since its one and only object is to depict the feelings of the heart, and not the picture of inanimate things. Most devices for tone painting are objectionable, even though they allow the imagination free play, since they divert the attention from the principal content to accessory things, and therefore deprive the feelings of that which will maintain them musically. . . . However, occasionally there are instances in which such tone paintings are immediately related to the state of the soul or where it can express the stirring of feelings.[53]

Haydn's *The Creation*, 1798, is celebrated for its many touches of pictorialism, especially when natural phenomena and fauna are the subject of the text. Haydn also introduced descriptive material into his works from time to time — the finale of his Symphony No. 82, the *Bear*, 1786; the second movement of his Symphony No. 100, the *Military*, 1794. In his Symphony No. 103 in E♭ major, 1795, he may have been thinking of the Battle of Vienna, 1683, between the Viennese and the Turks. Apart from the military drum roll at the beginning, followed by the imitation of plainsong as a prayer, the second movement, with its alternation of exotic and military versions of the same theme, suggests a confrontation of the two forces; included is an episode which is unmistakably a battle, with furious rushes, drum tattoos, and cries of the wounded. John Stoye in *The Siege of Vienna* relates an incident during the siege:

On July 31st, The Christian forces listened to their own bands making excellent music, so they said, with drum and pipe. In the Turkish camp, the Sultan's special envoy, Ali Aga, took his leave of the Grand Vizier before returning to Belgrade and the Turkish musicians were also commanded to strike up. The accounts of the besiegers and the besieged serve to show that the enemy's music roused scorn on both sides.[54]

Perhaps Haydn had heard of this incident as a boy and remembered it in later life to use it as a framework for this movement. Momigny, 1806, in his analysis of the first movement of this symphony, suggests a pictorial interpretation, a pastoral scene with thunder, prayers, dances, conversations.[55]

USE OF TOPICS

Many if not most of the topics described above were current throughout the 18th century. Their use, however, differed considerably in baroque and classic music. Baroque music tended to develop one idea, affection, or topic throughout a piece, to maintain unity through consistency. But mixtures and contrasts became increasingly frequent until, in classic music, they were the rule. Burney's comment, 1789, on J. C. Bach could apply to classic music generally:

> Bach seems to have been the first composer who observed the law of *contrast* as a *principle* . . . [he] seldom failed, after a rapid and noisy passage to introduce one that was slow and soothing.[56]

Lack of contrast was noted by Burney in the music of Tartini:

> He certainly repeats his passages, and adheres to his original *motivo* or theme too much, for the favorite desultory style of the present times. . . .[57]

Koch, in his *Journal der Tonkunst,* 1795, complains of the recent tendency to mix the styles of the serious and comic operas;[58] in the same article, he censures the mixture of the learned and the galant styles.[59] John Marsh, an English composer and conductor of the late 18th century, in *Hints to Young Composers,* 1800, criticizes partisans of the "new": "admiring the brilliancy of the modern symphony [they] think that the ancient music is dull; . . . deficient in light and shade. . . . [60] He credits Haydn with rescuing the new style from the trivialities that threatened to erase the dignities of the older style:

> . . . the modern style would have also failed in its turn (as it was about this time [1784] degenerating into a light, trivial and uniform character) had not the great Haydn by his wonderful contrivance, by the variety and eccentricity of his modulation, by his judicious dispersion of light and shade, and happy manner of blending simple and intelligible air with abstruse and complicated harmony, greatly improved the latter species of composition; insomuch that, instead of being able, as was before the case, to anticipate in great measure the second part of any movement, from its uniform relation to the foregoing, it is on the contrary, in his works, impossible to conceive what will follow, and a perpetual interest is kept up, in much longer pieces than any of the same kind ever before composed.[61]

The Rev. William Jones took a strong stand in his *Treatise on the Art of Music,* 1784, for the older style:

> Had it not been for the CONCERTS of ANCIENT MUSIC, some of the finest Compositions, and the rational and manly Entertainment arising from

the superior manner in which they have been performed, would probably have been lost to this country. The Stream of Fashion would have carried on its surface what is light and frothy; while that which is more solid and valuable would have sunk to the bottom.[62]

We are now divided into parties for the old and the new Music, in which there is undoubtedly a great diversity of Style and a attention to different effects. . . . I confess that my feelings give their testimony to the Style which is now called ancient. . . . I quote Corelli, Purcell, Geminiani, and Handel. . . .[63]

Handel and Corelli are distinct in their ideas, and clear in the design of their accents and measures. . . . As for Haydn and Boccherini, who merit a first place among the moderns for *invention*, they are sometimes so desultory and unaccountable in their way of treating a subject, that they must be reckoned among the wild warblers of the wood: and they seem to differ from some pieces of Handel as the talk and laughter of the Tea-table (where, perhaps, neither Wit nor Invention are wanting) differs from the Oratory of the Bar and the Pulpit.[64]

For the English the polarization of old and new was especially sharp, since they entertained and celebrated the two most famous composers of their times, Handel and Haydn.

Mozart was the greatest master at mixing and coordinating topics, often in the shortest space and with startling contrast. The allegro of the first movement of his *Prague* Symphony, K. 504, 1786, is a panorama of topics, old and new, in which a change of subject occurs every few measures. The introduction is linked to the allegro by the subtlest of means. We hardly sense at first the change of tempo from adagio to allegro; the syncopation on two levels—the quarter- and eighth-notes in the first violins against the *alla zoppa* ("limping") quarter- and half-notes in the lower strings—clouds the rhythm; the singing melody is buried in the lower instruments while the harmony falters toward G, thanks to the C♮. All this lends added brilliance to the fanfares that conclude the first period of the allegro, finally giving sharp profile to the key, melody, and rhythm. Once again the tentative first phrase is heard, and again the music coalesces into a brilliant style, with lively contrapuntal give-and-take. Such quicksilver changes take place throughout the movement, creating a large-scale rhythm of varied moods, exhilarating and effervescent. Ex. 2-25 lists the topics in this movement.

Ex. 2-25. *Topics*. Mozart, *Prague* Symphony, K. 504, 1786, 1st movt.

		Measures
1.	Singing style, *alla breve*	37–40
2.	Brilliant style, learned	41–42
3.	Fanfare I	43–44
4.	Singing style, learned	45–48
5.	*Alla breve*, brilliant style	49–50
6.	Brilliant style, learned	51–54
7.	Brilliant style, modified *stile legato*	55–62
8.	Fanfare II	53–65

Ex. 2-25, cont'd.

9.	Brilliant style	66–68
10.	Cadential flourish (new material)	69–70
11.	Singing style	71–74
12.	*Alla breve*, brilliant style	75–76
13.	Learned, brilliant, *alla breve*	77–87
14.	Storm and Stress	88–94
15.	Singing style, later set in learned style	95–120

NOTES

1. Koch, *Versuch*, III, p. 39ff.; Riepel, *Anfangsgründe, Grundregeln,* passim.
2. Christmann, *Elementarbuch,* passim; Kirnberger, *Recueil;* Türk, *Klavierschule,* appendix.
3. Kirnberger, *Recueil*, preface, p. 2.
4. Riepel, *Anfangsgründe*, p. 1.
5. Koch, *Versuch*, III, p. 129.
6. Anderson, *The Letters of Mozart*, p. 796.
7. Of the 136 pieces in L. Mozart's *Little Music Book*, 1762, 45 are minuets.
8. Rousseau, *Dictionnaire*, p. 277; Türk, *Klavierschule*, p. 401. Descriptions of the minuet and other dances listed in this chapter appear in many dictionaries and treatises, including Bossler, *Elementarbuch*, Alembert, *Élémens*, Sulzer, *Allgemeine Theorie*, and Momigny, *Cours complet.*
9. Burney, *History*, pp. 741, 765, 771, passim.
10. Alembert, *Élémens*, p. 209; Rousseau, *Dictionnaire*, pp. 366, 423.
11. Marpurg, *Kritische Briefe*, II, pp. 43–44.
12. Koch, *Lexikon*, pp. 1158–1159.
13. Rousseau, *Dictionnaire*, p. 58; Türk, *Klavierschule*, p. 400.
14. Rousseau, *Dictionnaire*, p. 122; see also Koch, *Versuch*, III, p. 47.
15. Türk, *Klavierschule*, p. 399; Koch, *Versuch*, III, p. 47.
16. Alembert, *Élémens*, p. 210; Türk, *Klavierschule*, p. 401.
17. Türk, *Klavierschule*, p. 398.
18. Ibid., p. 401.
19. Ibid., p. 402; see also Koch, *Lexikon*, p. 1382.
20. Rousseau, *Dictionnaire*, p. 432.
21. Türk, *Klavierschule*, p. 400.
22. See Schwarz, "Beethoven and the French Violin School," *MQ*, October 1958, p. 431ff.
23. Quantz, *Versuch*, p. 271.
24. Koch, *Lexikon*, p. 213.
25. Mattheson, *Capellmeister*, I, ch. VI.
26. Krause, *Poesie*, p. 185.
27. Kirnberger, *Kunst*, II, pt. 1, p. 106.
28. Schubart, *Ideen*, p. 350.
29. Momigny, *Cours complet*, p. 678.
30. Koch, *Versuch*, III, p. 130.
31. Koch, *Lexikon*, in the entries for older dances—allemande, courante, passepied, sarabande, canarie—says that they are no longer in fashion.

32. See Ringer, "The Chasse as a Musical Topic in the 18th Century," *JAMS*, VI, 1953, pp. 148-159.
33. Koch, *Lexikon*, p. 554.
34. Ibid., p. 1390.
35. Daube, *Melodie*, p. 10.
36. Ibid., p. 10; Türk, *Klavierschule*, p. 115; Koch, *Lexikon*, p. 272.
37. Burney, *History*, pp. 831-838.
38. Koch, *Lexikon*, pp. 1126-1132; Rousseau, *Dictionnaire*, p. 356.
39. Türk, *Klavierschule*, p. 361.
40. The movement was later completed by Maximilian Stadler.
41. Rousseau, *Dictionnaire*, p. 305; Koch, *Lexikon*, pp. 270, 992.
42. *AMZ*, 1798, p. 87.
43. Koch, *Lexikon*, pp. 775, 776.
44. See Geiringer, *Haydn*, ch. 14, for comment on the Storm and Stress.
45. Koch, *Lexikon*, p. 1391.
46. Ibid., p. 533.
47. Ibid., pp. 1451-1452.
48. Ibid., p. 1453.
49. Koch, *Versuch*, I, p. 155.
50. Kirnberger, *Kunst*, I, p. 190.
51. Anderson, *Letters of Beethoven*, p. 73.
52. Koch, *Lexikon*, p. 1384.
53. Ibid., p. 924.
54. John Stoye, *The Siege of Vienna*, Holt, Rinehart and Winston, New York, 1965, p. 170.
55. Momigny, *Cours complet*. p. 600ff.
56. Burney, *History*, p. 866.
57. Ibid., p. 449.
58. Koch, *Journal*, p. 102.
59. Ibid., p. 95.
60. Marsh, *Hints*, p. 1.
61. Ibid.
62. Jones, *Treatise*, p. ii.
63. Ibid., p. iii.
64. Ibid., p. 49.

Conclusion to Part I

The foregoing survey of affect and topic has focused attention upon important objectives in 18th-century musical expression—to touch the feelings through appropriate choice of figure and to stir the imagination through topical references. The theater was the principal source for these expressive aspects, with its projection of feeling specifically through word and gesture, and its imagery of storytelling. Classic music inherited its expressive attitudes from the baroque era, but modified the formalized sustained unity of baroque expression by means of frequent contrasts to create a kaleidoscopic, sharply etched, subtly nuanced, and sensitive expressive palette, with a considerable admixture of humor.

Apart from the clearly defined affects and topics described above, there are many passages in classic music that show less sharply defined expressive or topical profile—running passages, connective figures, spun-out melodic lines. Still, the vivid climate of feeling, with its theatrical overtones, that permeates all classic music lends expressive color to such passages, giving each the quality of a meaningful gesture. Moreover, the frequent well-marked contrasts of topic and mood in classic music bring about striking changes in posture and gesture that add expressive substance to even the most casual or routine figures, creating an ever-moving series of highlights and shadows. For analysis, the recognition of these expressive qualities, explicit or implicit, is illuminating, often providing a clue to a striking aspect of structure; for performance, such recognition is essential, since it points to the poetic implications of the music.

II Rhetoric

The language arts—poetry, drama, and oratory—in addition to providing music with expressive and topical notions, gave music important clues for framing these expressive values. These are found in the parallels between linguistic and musical rhetoric that were extensively studied in the 18th century. Musicians acknowledged their debt to language as they borrowed concepts from rhetoric to designate various aspects of musical composition. Hawkins, 1776, expresses a widespread view as he compares music and rhetoric:

> The art of invention is made one of the heads among the precepts of rhetoric, to which music in this and sundry instances bears a near resemblance; the end of persuasion, or affecting the passions, being common to both. This faculty consists in the enumeration of common places, which are revolved over in the mind, and requires both an ample store of knowledge in the subject upon which it is exercised, and a power of applying that knowledge as occasion may require.[1]

To be persuasive, both linguistic and musical rhetoric had first to establish *coherence* and then promote *eloquence*. This was done by defining the various components of discourse, indicating their functions, and demonstrating ways in which they might be persuasively arranged. Many 18th-century theorists looked upon phrase structure, chord progression, rhythmic scansion, melodic construction, texture, and performance as the *rhetoric of music*.[2] Part II of this book will proceed along these lines, linking rhetoric and music at the many points where the relationships between the two are relevant.

NOTES

1. Hawkins, *History*, pp. XXX–XXXI.
2. Forkel, *Allgemeine Geschichte*, I, pp. 66–68. See Lenneberg, "Johann Mattheson on Affect and Rhetoric in Music," *JMT*, II, Nos. 1 and 2, 1958, pp. 47–84 and 193–236.

3 Periodicity

As we listen to classic music, we sense that its motion is focused toward points of arrival, on every scale of magnitude, from the figure to the complete movement. This clear and direct sense of arrival is designated here as *periodicity*. Periodicity represents the tendency of classic music to move toward goals, toward points of punctuation. The most important of these is the *period*, which marks the end of a complete statement.

The period was the most important concept adapted by music from traditional rhetoric. Its importance in the 18th century arose from (1) the *firmness* of its basic features—a solid opening, an area of continuation, and a conclusive ending; (2) a *flexibility* that allowed countless options in length and internal arrangement; (3) its *adaptability* to typical 18th-century musical procedures—cadences, rhythmic action, melodic patterns.

As a musicorhetorical effect, the period had already been described by Zarlino, 1558, who defined it as a point of arrival:

> Wherefore the cadence is of equal value in music as the period in oration; thus it may truly be called a period of cantilena . . . one must not employ it unless one arrives at a period or clause in prose or poetry. . . .[1]

Traditional rhetoric extended the meaning of *period* to include the *entire statement* terminated by such a point of punctuation. Thus a period in language is a *complete* statement, a sentence whose sense is fully grasped only when it has come to a close; the listener's attention is held until the final word. Likewise, in music, a passage is not sensed as being a period until some sort of conclusive cadence is reached.

The length of a period in 18th-century music cannot be prescribed. The first eight measures of Mozart's Sonata in A major, K. 331, 1778 (see Ex. 3-1), form a

Ex. 3-1. *Symmetrical period.* Mozart, Sonata in A major, K. 331, 1778, 1st movt.

1778, 1st movt.　　　　　　　　　　phrase I　　　　　　　　　　half cadence

Andante grazioso

Ex. 3-1, cont'd.

phrase II   authentic cadence

neat little period, while the great cadenza for cembalo solo in Bach's Branden-burg Concerto No. 5, 1721, is an enormous period that reaches its cadence only after 49 measures. These options in musical practice resulted in some confusion among theorists concerning the definition of the period. We read in Sulzer's *Allgemeine Theorie der schönen Künste,* 1771–1774:

> The names used to designate the smaller and larger sections of a melody are still somewhat indefinite. One speaks of *Perioden, Abschnitten, Einschnitten, Rhythmen, Cäsuren,* etc., in such a way that one word will have two meanings and two words will have the same meaning.[2]

Koch, 1802, echoes this complaint.[3]

Accepting the traditional rhetorical definition of a period—the completion of a line of discourse at a final point of punctuation—then the most decisive element in musical periodic structure is its *final cadence.* Lesser cadences are intermediate stations along the way, helping to clarify and focus the motion and to build an expectation for the ultimate point of arrival.

CADENCES

A listener attuned to 18th-century musical rhetoric accepts the *authentic cadence*—the progression of dominant to tonic with both chords in root position—as a firm and proper conclusion to a period. The *half cadence*—a pause upon the dominant—is a momentary interruption of movement, a comma or semicolon. A *deceptive cadence*—the tonic replaced by some other harmony after the dominant—is a question, delay, or digression. An *inconclusive cadence*—tonic or dominant inverted—is a signal for further action. Cadences, thus, are controlling and shaping factors in the motion of the period toward its conclusion; each has a lesser or greater effect of periodicity according to its impression of finality.

Cadences were thoroughly explained in 18th-century musical theory. Each theorist had his own nomenclature. Giorgio Antoniotto, in *L'arte armonica,* 1760, lists the cadences as follows:

> It has been repeated that musick is composed by way of diverse sorts of cadences. These divers sorts of cadences are to be considered in some gradual

order. The principal cadences, the perfect and imperfect, consonant and fundamental, must be placed in the first order; to which may be added the suspended cadences, and the deceptive or false cadences; the flying cadences may follow as second in the same order. . . . Inverted cadences are called "broken" cadences. . . . The perfect cadences are the more pleasant after an harmonic progression which is done by a continuation of broken, flying, and other divers cadences. . . .[4]

Riepel, 1755, uses the terms *Grundabsatz* (tonic cadence) and *Aenderungs-absatz* (alternate or dominant cadence) to designate the *authentic* and *half cadences*, the two most important punctuations in period structure.[5] Rousseau, 1768, borrows terms from Rameau, 1722, listing *perfect, imperfect* or *irregular, interrupted,* and *broken* cadences.[6]

Generally, a period was terminated by the authentic cadence; a strong half cadence, especially when it introduced a new key, could serve the same purpose (see Ex. 3-9); when an authentic cadence ended the first phrase, the effect was that of a colon or semicolon.

SYMMETRY

Dance and poetry added another parameter to musical period structure in the 17th and 18th centuries — the *symmetrical grouping* of short phrases, two, three, or four measures in length, clearly articulated by lesser points of punctuation. Complementary arrangements of melodic figures, rhythms, and harmonic progressions reinforced the impression of balance. In addition to the greater effect of stability thus produced, symmetry increased the degree of immediate intelligibility to the listener who quickly grasped paired statements — $2 + 2$ and $4 + 4$ measure groups — as *units* and was undoubtedly more comfortable in following the continuity of the music.

François Chastellux, in his *Essai sur l'union de la poésie et de la musique*, 1765, credits the Italians with developing this kind of phrase structure:

They [the Italians] saw very well that they could not invent a melody unless they held to a simple and unique idea and gave this idea proper expression in form and proportion. This observation led them to discover the musical period. A minuet, a gigue have their definite measures; melodies form phrases, and these phrases have their regular and proportional elements. . . . Although our small French pieces, minuets, gigues, etc. appear to be like those of the Italians, one must not assume that they are periodic. It is not enough for a melody to have a certain number of measures. . . . When the expression of the melody is to be periodic, a certain unity must be present, a balance in the members out of which the melody grows, a rounding-off of the melody, which hold the attention to the very end. Most older French melodies are almost nothing but rows of tones, which have neither rule nor aim.[7]

Daube, 1773, refers to this trend:

Wherein arises the symmetry of architecture? In the beautiful relationship of the various masses of the component parts. . . . Beautiful symmetry is found today in painting, sculpture, dance, poetry, and literature, and all others that represent beauty and creativity. We also know this in music, but our forefathers had little knowledge thereof.[8]

Mattheson, 1739,[9] Riepel, 1752,[10] Marpurg, 1761,[11] and many others explain phrase and period structure in terms of balanced members and regular articulations.

Symmetry appears in classic music on every level of structure, from paired motives, phrases, periods, to larger sections of a movement. On the period level, symmetry was represented by musical sentences that varied in length from 4 to 16 measures. They had precise hierarchical arrangements among their cadences. They were divided in the middle by a half cadence or a light authentic cadence; they ended with a strong authentic cadence; *each half* or *phrase* incorporated lighter points of punctuation. Ex. 3-1 illustrates such a period; its structural balance creates a sense of clarity and order. The two phrases of a symmetrical period were designated as "subject and predicate" by Koch, 1787;[12] as "antecedent and consequent" by Jones, 1784;[13] and as "question and answer" by Portmann, 1789.[14]

Short symmetrical periods—composed as dances and songs—appeared by the thousands in the 18th-century. They were used in teaching composition and performance;[15] they represented the principal structural plan for the themes of rondos and variations; and they often were incorporated into larger works.

Symmetry works best when the complementary members are short. The thrust and counterthrust of brief figures or phrases can be crisp and energetic. When the members became much longer, as in early 19th-century music—8 to 16 measures—it was difficult for symmetry to maintain its buoyancy. Gottfried Weber, 1830, warned against carrying symmetry too far:

The further the symmetry of the rhythm is carried, the more plain, even, and obvious the music will be . . . therefore, this rounding-off should not be overdone.[16]

Another function of symmetry was to organize groups of figures within a period that might have a complex and irregular structure, as in Ex. 3-9. Baroque music frequently began a period with a symmetrical arrangement (see the gigue from J. S. Bach's Partita for Violin in D minor, circa 1720, and then continued with material that broke the complementary arrangement.

Anton Reicha, in his *Traité de mélodie*, 1814, said that earlier melodies lose their symmetry after three or four measures, while Cimarosa, Haydn, Mozart, and others have trained the hearer to expect rhythmic symmetry, which makes the music incomparably more felicitous.[17] The first movement of Mozart's C major Sonata, K. 545, 1788, may have been a conscious emulation of the earlier type; after four measures of singing melody, the music breaks into a powerful sequence that drives toward a half cadence eight measures distant.

The two chief aspects of 18th-century musical period structure—a firm point of arrival and complementary internal arrangements—provided classic composers with rhetorical resources that they could manipulate with more effectiveness and greater variety than was possible at any other time in the history of western music. Without these two resources, the classic style as we know it could not have achieved its unique fusion of elegance and eloquence.

DISTURBANCES OF SYMMETRY; PERIOD EXTENSIONS

Symmetry in phrase structure is susceptible to disturbance. Even the simplest eight-measure period carries an imperfection; given an alternation of strong and weak measures, as _1_ 2 _3_ 4 _5_ 6 _7_ 8, a purely symmetrical arrangement cannot provide a firm point of arrival: its final measure is accentually weak! Thus the period must undergo some _compression_ of action to give the eighth measure the value of a strong beat; or the cadence must come upon the ninth measure. In either case, symmetry is disturbed.

Compression, extension, and other modifications of symmetry are the counterparts of various kinds of sentence structure; each adds in its way to the demands made upon the listener for heightened attention.

Disturbances within the Normal Pattern

Within the standard eight-measure framework of a normal period, it is possible to modify the order of events to create some sense of imbalance or irregularity. Chief among these is a compression of action.

Compression of Action.   In order to provide for the periodic cadence within the eight-measure limits, some _compression of action_ must take place. Ex. 3-2 gives a rudimentary melodic line that illustrates perfect symmetry by repetition. Ex. 3-3 shows the compression necessary to make room for the cadence; Ex. 3-4 is a period in which compression takes place. In both Exs. 3-3 and 3-4 the compression is achieved by a quicker rate of chord change, i.e., a faster harmonic rhythm.

Ex. 3-2.   _Symmetrical phrases in a period._

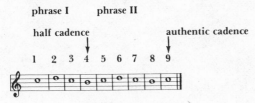

Ex. 3-3.   _Compression._

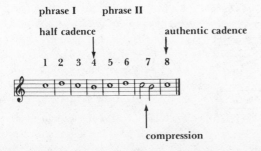

Ex. 3-4. *Compression.* Mozart, Sonata in D major, K. 284, 1775, 3rd movt.

From Mozart, *Sonatas and Fantasias for the Piano* (Nathan Broder, ed.). Copyright 1956, 1960 by Theodore Presser Company, Bryn Mawr. Used by kind permission of the publisher.

Tacterstickung (suppression of a measure), in which the final measure of a phrase becomes the first measure of the next, is mentioned by theorists as a device for compression.[18] The period in Ex. 3-5 is seven measures long, m. 4 acting both as a point of *arrival* and a point of *departure*. *Tacterstickung* is often used as a connective device between periods; its principal function is to maintain momentum.

Ex. 3-5. *Tacterstickung.* Koch, *Versuch*, III, 1787, p. 456.

Rearrangement of Functions.   Rhetorical discourse has three basic functions: *opening, continuation*, and *completion* (see p. 91). Classic music has well-defined procedures to represent these functions. Opening statements generally use some kind of symmetrical pattern as a firm point of departure; continuations tend to be more flexible; conclusions are the firmest statements, anchoring the structure.

Exs. 3-6 and 3-7 show rearrangements of normal functions. Each pause in mm. 1-3 of Ex. 3-6 is a clear and emphatic articulation. Ordinarily, a half cadence would appear at m. 4 but the preceding pauses would reduce its punctuating effect. Hence, while m. 4 is actually a half cadence, the dissonance in the melody, the weak position of the bass, and the sustained tones in all voices disguise the effect of punctuation. Measure 4, presumably the end of phrase I, introduces the legato style of the latter half of the period, building to a broad authentic cadence in m. 8. The fragmentary beginning, three measures long, built from terse cadential gestures, is answered by a broadly scaled line—five measures long. Punctuation is *overstated* in the beginning and *understated* at the half cadence—a rearrangement of normal cadential functions. The rhetorical effect is a powerful movement to the climax in the *sixth* measure and an intensified effect of periodic movement to the broad cadence.

Ex. 3-6.   *Rearrangement of functions.* Beethoven, Sonata in E♭ major, Op. 7, ca. 1796-1797, 2nd movt.

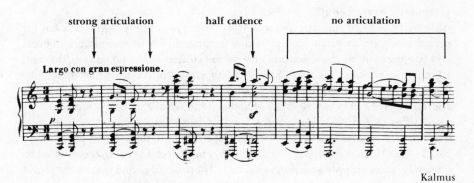

Kalmus

In Ex. 3-7, Mozart subverts the role of the authentic cadence. He dearly loved to turn things topsy-turvy, and in the excerpt given, the cadence is placed at the *beginning* of the period, not the end, as if it were a final cadence for the minuet. The half cadence in m. 4 of the trio loses much of its clarity and almost all of its emphasis because of the steady eighth-note motion in the melody. Throughout this trio, in fact, the cadence never seems to find its proper place; it is used for everything *but* a point of arrival, and this seems to be the point of the trio—to put the cadence out of countenance.

Ex. 3-7. *Displacement of cadence.* Mozart, Symphony No. 41 in C major, K. 551, 1788, menuetto.

Philharmonia

Irregular Phrase Lengths

Although the eight-measure symmetrical pattern was the recognized norm for period structure in small pieces,[19] other arrangements were available. Three- and five-measure phrases, six-measure periods (often in the polonaise), 10- and 12-measure periods—all these are found in classic music to frame dance-like topics. Riepel, *Anfangsgründe*, 1752, and *Grundregeln*, 1755, Koch, *Versuch* II and III, 1787, 1793, and Reicha, *Mélodie*, 1814, deal extensively with such irregularities (see p. 73). Haydn was fond of beginning a period with an *odd number* of measures; the first movement of his Sonata in E minor, H.V. XVI, No. 34, 1783, has a grouping of three, two, and three. Listeners accustomed to the solidly square duple groupings that usually opened a period must have found these odd arrangements intriguing, and perhaps a bit elusive.

Extensions

Internal disturbances of symmetry throw greater weight upon the cadence to complete the effect of periodicity. Even stronger focus on the cadence can be developed by delaying it. This gives rise to *extensions* of the period; these include added phrases, deceptive or inconclusive cadences, melodic action at the cadence point, internal digressions or extensions, and reinforcement of the cadence.

The first eight measures of Ex. 3-8 embody a perfect symmetry—I–V, V–I—with counterstatement of the melodic figures—a b a b. This reciprocal action lacks a strong point of arrival and requires four additional measures to complete the period.

Ex. 3-8. *Added phrase to provide for the cadence.* Haydn, Sonata in E♭ major, H.V. XVI, No. 49, 1789-1790, 1st movt.

Adapted from Haydn, *Sämtliche Klaviersonaten* (Christa Landon, ed.). Copyright 1964 by Universal Edition A. G. Wien. Used by kind permission of the publisher.

Reciprocal Action. *Reciprocal action*, the pairing of figures, essential to symmetry, can also lead to extensions if it is carried far enough. In Ex. 3-9 the period opens with a sing-song regularity, but the continued repetition through seven measures obliterates the balance of normal period structure; the period then drives forward powerfully to a broadly scaled half cadence, adding eight measures of extension.

Ex. 3-9. *Extension by means of continued reciprocal action.* Haydn, Sonata in C major, H.V. XVI, No. 35, ca. 1780, 1st movt.

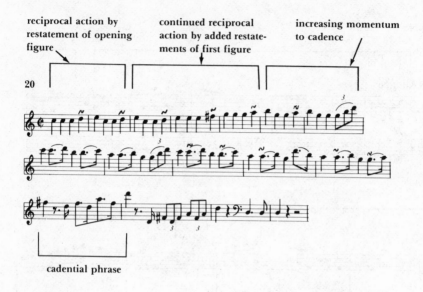

At the climax of the first movement of his *Eroica* Symphony, Op. 55, 1803, mm. 631–662, one of the greatest moments in all his music, Beethoven gives his opening theme a perfectly symmetrical form for the first time in the movement; four times the melody alternates in four-measure phrases between tonic and dominant. Yet at the final dominant response it cannot make its cadence and must break the symmetry, compressing action to come to a close. This period is a great peroration to the searching action that propels this movement.

Deceptive Cadence.   Arrival is deferred by a *deceptive cadence* — by substituting some chord other than the tonic in the authentic cadence. When the cadence is thus delayed, the periodicity is raised to a higher level of intensity and the expression can take on greater eloquence.

In Ex. 3-10 a deceptive cadence involving *interchange of mode* (see pp. 56–60) appears at m. 28. The period begins symmetrically, in a singing style, but by the time the third statement appears, at m. 22, the symmetry has lost some of its firmness, yielding to a feeling of uncertainty and thereby setting the stage for the sudden contrast of m. 28. The cadence that was *indicated* in m. 27 is finally *achieved* at m. 43, after the shock waves of the contrast play themselves out and a wealth of musical interest has been added to this period that began very gently.

Inconclusive Cadence.   The effect of arrival in an otherwise normal period is weakened by an *inconclusive cadence* — dominant or tonic harmony *inverted*. Ex. 3-11 begins as a symmetrical period, but the first inversion of tonic harmony in m. 8 does not act as a period. Four measures are added with strong cadential

Ex. 3-10.   *Extension by means of deceptive cadence.* Beethoven, Concerto for Violin and Orchestra in D major, Op. 61, 1806, 1st movt.

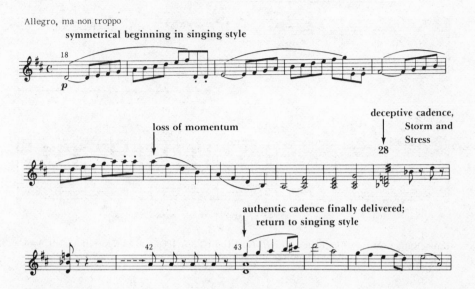

From Ratner, *Music: The Listener's Art.* Copyright 1957, 1966, 1977 by McGraw-Hill Book Company. Used by kind permission of the publisher.

reinforcement; then the violent strokes of alternating tonic and dominant chords drive home the sense of arrival. But the force of the gesture becomes an agent for continuation, maintaining and augmenting the momentum of the driving rhythm and the great upward sweep of the melody. The pulsating bass, the Storm and Stress manner, and the broadly scaled melody all drive the action past the normal cadential point. This represents a style intensively cultivated in early 19th-century music.

Ex. 3-11.   *Extension by means of an inconclusive cadence.* Beethoven, Quartet in C minor, Op. 18, No. 4, ca. 1798-1800, 1st movt.

Ex. 3-11, cont'd.

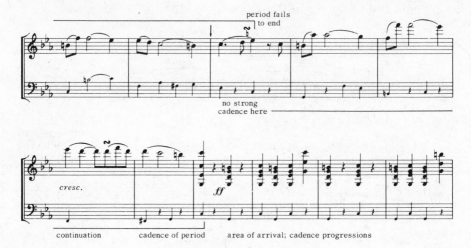

From Ratner, *Music: The Listener's Art.* Copyright 1957, 1966, 1977 by McGraw-Hill Book Company. Used by kind permission of the publisher.

Internal Digressions. If the harmony *digresses* at some point within the period, it leaves no space within the normal cycle for the final cadence. An extension is required. In Ex. 3-12, after a symmetrical beginning, the harmony moves afield at m. 66. This not only initiates an extension but prepares for a magnificent cadential effect. When the digression interferes, we sense a tightening of action that explodes into a soaring flight which comes to rest only when the tonic arrives. Hunting gigue, learned style, brilliant style, and fanfare succeed each other in a scintillating display.

Ex. 3-12. *Extension by means of internal harmonic digression.* Mozart, Quintet in Eb major, K. 614, 1791, 1st movt.

cadence begins here

end of cadence
extremely emphatic
point of arrival

From Ratner, *Music: The Listener's Art.* Copyright 1957, 1966, 1977 by McGraw-Hill Book Company. Used by kind permission of the publisher.

Melodic Action.   *Melodic action* can reduce the effect of arrival even when the harmony clearly makes an authentic cadence. In Ex. 3-13 the cadential effect is clear and emphatic in the bass, yet the action of the upper voices reduces the effect of periodicity and maintains momentum. The flowing conjunct motion of the melodic material joins two periods. The closing gesture in the three upper voices occurs in m. 44, just as the violoncello begins a new statement. An overlap is created by dispersing the effect of closure among different voices at different times; mm. 43-44 thus act both for arrival and departure. This procedure is often used in classic works of broad scope, where full stops would interrupt the ongoing discourse.

Ex. 3-13.   *Extension by means of melodic activity at the cadence.* Mozart, Quartet in C major, K. 465, 1785, 1st movt.

cadence
of period

45

part-writing continues the movement

From Ratner, *Music: The Listener's Art.* Copyright 1957, 1966, 1977 by McGraw-Hill Book Company. Used by kind permission of the publisher.

Cadential Reinforcement.   The most powerful effect of arrival is created when the *cadential action* itself is *reinforced and extended,* forming an *area* of arrival. This generally takes place toward the end of a large section of a movement, and represents periodicity on the largest structural scale. The technique is found in Italian music throughout the century and is a standard device in opera to drive home the affect of the text. Thus the resolve of Anna and Ottavio to seek revenge in Act I of Mozart's *Don Giovanni,* 1787, in the duet "Fuggi, crudele, fuggi," is underscored by a series of strong cadences in D minor, culminating in an extended play on the D minor chord.

One of the most broadly scaled periods in classic music begins Mozart's Quintet in C major, K. 515, 1787. This period, 57 measures long, incorporates symmetries, imbalances, overlaps, harmonic digressions, and deceptive cadences, each of which contributes to the momentum that finally reaches its climax in a triumphant cadence, whose reinforcement, in turn, gives rise to a new phase of action. Ex. 4-8 sketches the harmony of this period, while pp. 78–80 describe some of its rhythmic and topical manipulations.

Among classic theorists Koch, in his *Versuch,* 1782–1793, investigated period structure and periodic extension most carefully and thoroughly. He also introduced the term *Hauptperiode* (principal period), corresponding to an entire section of a movement.[20] August Kollmann, in *An Essay on Musical Harmony,* 1796, refers to "one of those fancy periods [of Haydn] of some extended length in which the composer seems to lose himself in the modulation for the purpose of making the ear attentive to the resolution."[21] Reicha, in *Mélodie,* 1814, quotes a period from Haydn's Symphony No. 44 in E minor, H.V. I, No. 44, circa 1771, which encompasses 42 measures, the entire second part of the Adagio.[22]

In analysis of classic period structure, the clearest points of reference are authentic cadences. These should be determined first, however widely they may be spaced. Then the action between such cadential points should be observed, beginning with the opening symmetries, then noting digressions, extensions, and intermediate cadences. The purpose of the action within a period is both to articulate and to maintain momentum; therefore, we often encounter cadences that are strong and clear, but lack a sense of finality, and thus the music can press forward. Cadential overlaps are especially crucial in sustaining motion; the period ends, but at the same instant—at the arrival at the tonic—a new period begins.

While the concept of the period was present throughout 18th-century music, each era, in its most typical usage, embodied the concept differently. Late baroque music would often begin a period with a short symmetrical phrase and then spin out by means of sequences, arriving at a strong cadence to regain firm rhythmic-harmonic footing. Mid-century music, in what is often referred to as *rococo* style, was characterized by short, symmetrical periods, in which melodic figures were short and highly ornamented; punctuations were equally spaced, often well marked; cadences were clear but not particularly strong. This chapter has illustrated the broad symmetries, the extended periods, and the powerful cadences which are critically important to both the expressive eloquence and the structural scope of classic music.

NOTES

1. Zarlino, *Istitutioni*, p. 221.
2. Sulzer, *Allgemeine Theorie*, II, p. 35.
3. Koch, *Lexikon*, p. 1150.
4. Antoniotto, *L'arte armonica*, p. 101.
5. Riepel, *Grundregeln*, p. 39ff.
6. Rousseau, *Dictionnaire*, p. 62ff.
7. Chastellux, *Essai sur l'union*, p. 16-17.
8. Daube, *Dilettant*, p. 81.
9. Mattheson, *Capellmeister*, p. 224.
10. Riepel, *Anfangsgründe*, passim.
11. Marpurg, *Kritische Briefe*, II, p. 4.
12. Koch, *Versuch*, II, pp. 351, 352.
13. Jones, *Treatise*, p. 48.
14. Portmann, *Lehrbuch*, p. 37.
15. See p. 9 of the present work.
16. Weber, *Versuch*, II, p. 103.
17. Reicha, *Mélodie*, p. 70.
18. Koch, *Versuch*, II, p. 453ff.; Reicha, *Mélodie*, "Supposition," p. 23.
19. Koch, *Versuch*, III, pp. 54, 57.
20. Ibid., p. 305.
21. Kollmann, *Harmony*, p. 84.
22. Reicha, *Mélodie*, plates, p. 22.

4 Harmony

For classic music, harmony is the broadest theater of action. Harmony governs the form of an entire movement through the classic sense for *key*. Whatever may take place in the course of a movement, it must begin and end in the same key. Events are planned so that the harmony follows an unbroken path from beginning to end, with progressions linked by means of their cadential relationships.

While the vocabulary of classic harmony does not differ essentially from that of baroque or romantic music, a great difference exists in classic harmonic rhetoric — the ways in which the chords and cadences are arranged and the impression of key thus given. No other style in the history of western music places such emphasis upon key or explores with such imagination and verve the ways in which key can be affirmed. The definition of key is a structural event of the first magnitude in classic music, a satisfying and often triumphant reinforcement of periodicity on every level of structure.

THE KEY SYSTEM

The tonic key can rule the harmony of a movement in one of the following ways:

1. By a circular, or "solar," arrangement
2. By a contrasting, or "polar," arrangement

The circular arrangement of keys was employed chiefly in early 18th-century music, in concertos, fugues, fantasias. It represents a modification by cadential reinforcement of the older system of church modes, in which the tonic was a "sun" surrounded by a constellation of closely related degrees (Ex. 4-1).

Ex. 4-1. *Circular, or "solar," system of keys.*

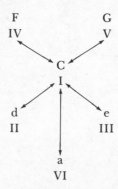

The most thorough explanation of this system is given by Riepel in his *Grund-regeln*, 1755. He shows how these related degrees could be arranged in a move-ment in different ways by permutation. Ex. 4-2a gives a table of the possible order of keys and 5 of the 120 harmonic plans possible in this system. Ex. 4-2b il-lustrates the key schemes listed in the upper left-hand box. It should be under-stood that each scheme begins and ends in C major.

Ex. 4-2. *Permutation applied to key schemes.* Riepel, *Grundregeln*, 1755, pp. 112, 113.

a. Table of key schemes

g a e d f	a d f g e	e d f g a	d f a g e	f g a e d
g a e f d	a d f e g	e d f a g	d f a e g	f g a d e
g a f d e	a d e g f	e d a f g	d f e g a	f g d a e
g a f e d	a d e f g	e d a g f	d f c a g	f g d e a
g a d e f	a d g f e	e d g a f	d f g e a	f g e d a
g a d f e	a d g e f	e d g f a	d f g a e	f g e a d
g e d f a	a e d f g	e g d f a	d a e f g	f e a g d
g e d a f	a e d g f	e g d a f	d a e g f	f e a d g
g e a d f	a e g f d	e g a d f	d a g e f	f e d a g
g e a f d	a e g d f	e g a f d	d a g f e	f e d g a
g e f a d	a e f d g	e g f d a	d a f g e	f e g a d
g e f d a	a e f g d	e g f a d	d a f e g	f e g d a
g f a e d	a g e d f	e f g a d	d g f e a	f d a g e
g f a d e	a g e f d	e f g f a e	d g f a e	f d a e g
g f d e a	a g f e d	e f d a g	d g a e f	f d g a e
g f d a e	a g f d e	e f d g a	d g a f e	f d g e a
g f e d a	a g d e f	e f a d g	d g e a f	f d e g a
g f e a d	a g d f e	e f a g d	d g e f a	f d e a g
g d e a f	a f d g e	e a d g f	d e g f a	f a e d g
g d e f a	a f d e g	e a d f g	d e g a f	f a c g d
g d a f e	a f e g d	e a f g d	d e a g i	f a g d e
g d a e f	a f e d g	e a f d g	d e a f g	f a g e d
g d f a e	a f g d e	e a g f d	d e f g a	f a d e g
g d f e a	a f g e d	e a g d f	d e f a g	f a d g e

b. Sketch of key schemes

Riepel explains the relationship of the satellite keys in this "solar" harmonic system, adding a touch of colloquial humor as he draws an analogy between key relationships and social hierarchy:

If C is the tonic

C = *Meyer* (landowner, farmer-master)

G = *Oberknecht* (chief servant)

a = *Obermagd* (chief maid)

e = *Untermagd* (second or kitchen maid)

F = *Taglohner* (day laborer)

d = *Unterläufferin* (female interloper, possibly, or a female worker in the salt factory)

c = *schwarze Gredel* (black Margaret—a local nickname for a Swedish queen whose swarthy complexion made her look like a man)[1]

Note that only the first four keys belong to the "household" of C major; the others may enter but do not play as important a part in this overall key scheme, which is typical of baroque fugues and concertos. Each of the minor keys has a feminine name, a notion held by Riepel (and shared by others) that the minor key is "feminine."[2] Ex. 4-3 demonstrates *one* possible arrangement of these keys in a movement; the solar arrangement is maintained by several returns to the *Meyer*, the tonic; within the piece, it "must never be lost to the eye or the ear."[3]

Ex. 4-3. *Key scheme.* Riepel, *Grundregeln*, 1755, p. 66.

Solar arrangement promotes unity of key by subordinating related degrees to the tonic and by occasional returns to the home key. This layout lends itself to discursive, exploratory treatment of a theme, as in fugues and concertos. Classic composers used this older plan when they wrote fugues; Mozart's Fugue in C minor, K. 426, 1782, an imitation of the learned style of the baroque, visits related degrees, with several returns to the home key, C minor.

"Polar" arrangement sets the dominant *against* the tonic (in minor key movements, the relative major is the opposing key). This opposition is potentially dramatic, as the dominant takes over from the tonic in the first part of a movement and the tonic eventually reasserts itself in the second part. Baroque dances, with their choreographic, even dramatic content used this plan, as did many baroque arias, matching the shift of meaning in the text to the shift to the dominant.

The polar arrangement dominated classic structure in sonatas, arias, many rondo and variation themes, concertos, and some fugues. As harmonic layouts shifted from the discursive solar arrangement to the dramatic polar, the rate of chord change began to slow, and progressions began to show greater symmetry, with stronger focus upon the harmonic goal at the end of a period. Thus the polar arrangement contributed to the strong sense of periodicity characteristic of classic structure.

HARMONIC FUNCTIONS; CADENTIAL FORMULAS

A key is defined, or impressed upon the listener, by *funtional harmonic relationships*. Functional harmony uses certain tones in a scale to create cadences. The essence of the cadence-creating process is the interaction of the tonic note with the *tritone* formed by 4 and 7 of the major scale. The sounding of 4 and 7 together or consecutively creates an interval of tension; such a tension is resolved when 7 proceeds to 1. Rhetorically, 1 stands as a point of departure to begin the process; 4 moves away from 1; 7 pulls back toward 1, thus reversing the action; 1 then becomes a point of arrival and can also stand as a new point of departure. In a chain of such progressions 1 can serve as a link that can bind the harmonic action of an entire composition. The 1-4-7-1 progression is designated here as a *cadential formula*. Regardless of the number of parts—one, two, three, or more—it is the constant mutual interaction of these tones that gives functional harmony its powerful key-defining thrust. Ex. 4-4 illustrates these functions, first isolating them, then showing their use in simple two-part progressions, where the two voices *share* the functional tones, and finally showing them in a chain of cadential formulas.

Ex. 4-4.   *Cadential formulas.*

a. *Basic formula: 1-4-7-1 cycles.*

1   4   7   1

Ex. 4-4, cont'd.

b. *Basic formula distributed among two voices.*

c. *Chain of cadential formulas.*

Koch, 1787, in speaking of leading tones, names the seventh and fourth degrees as determining the identity of a key:

> the major seventh of the scale which generally presumes an immediate progression to the octave . . .
>
> the fourth degree when it is the seventh of the chord on the fifth degree, demands an immediate progression to the third . . .
>
> all incidental altered tones of the key . . . [This refers to what is now termed *tonicization.*][4]

Daube, in his three treatises, classifies chords and intervals as belonging to one of three groups: (1) the *first* chord, corresponding to the tonic; (2) the *second* chord, corresponding to an F-A-C-D chord in C (subdominant function); and (3) the *third* chord corresponding to the dominant seventh.[5] Rameau, in *Traité de l'harmonie*, 1722, and later works, was the first to base a harmonic theory upon the *polarity* of I to both V and IV.

DEFINITION OF KEY

Cadential formulas define a key on three increasingly strong levels of rhetorical emphasis:

1. *Indication* of a key. A tonic chord or a single cadential formula, usually at the beginning of a phrase, indicates a key, sets a harmonic direction. A change of key is also generally indicated by one or more cadential formulas.

2. *Establishment* of a key. Establishment is achieved by a series of cadential formulas that fix the key in the mind of the listener. In Ex. 4-4c the key is firmly established by the seventh interval.

3. *Confirmation* of a key. This completes the cycle of harmonic action by one or more authentic cadences, satisfying the harmonic requirements for periodicity.

Tonal centers have been approached by leading tones ever since the 14th century, but 18th-century harmony is distinguished from the harmony of other eras by (1) the virtual saturation of the total harmonic flow by cadential formulas, and (2) the clarity and emphasis with which keys are defined. This constitutes affirmative action and stands in contrast to the occasional cadences in Renaissance music and the growing tendency to cloud cadential action in the 19th century. Furthermore, classic key definition is distinguished from that of baroque by slower rates of chord change, more palpable and broader symmetries, and sharper and more intense focus upon harmonic goals, all of which build a dramatic staging of key.

The stages of key definition correspond closely to the course taken in rhetorical argument — to present an idea or thesis, then to explore and develop it, and finally to confirm it. Ex. 4-5 illustrates the three stages of key definition. The brackets in Ex. 4-5 mark the cadential formulas in the first period, mm. 1-8. The first four measures focus on the tonic, with a symmetrical arrangement in the alternation of tonic and dominant harmony. A drive to the cadence develops in mm. 5-8. The second period provides a large-scale balance to the first. Measures 10-14 loosen the cadential focus momentarily to prepare, in mm. 15-16, for a final cadence. Now the home key has been strongly confirmed, and the music may be launched toward the dominant.

Ex. 4-5. *Degrees of rhetorical emphasis in definition of key.* Haydn, Sonata in Eb major, H.V. XVI, No. 28, ca. 1773, 1st movt.

a. Indication of Eb by alternation of I and V.
b. Establishment of Eb by authentic cadence somewhat lightened by emphasis on Db in mm. 6-7.
c. Confirmation of Eb in the second period by another authentic cadence; restatement of the cadential cycle provides confirming weight.

Ex. 4-5, cont'd.

c.

From Haydn, *Sämtliche Klaviersonaten* (Christa Landon, ed.). Copyright 1964 by Universal Edition A. G. Wien. Used by kind permission of the publisher.

MODULATION

Tritone action, in addition to defining keys, is the principal agent in modulation for functional harmony. A new key is defined in the same manner as a home key. Koch's rating of the strength of modulation is made on the basis of the degree of rhetorical emphasis; "incidental" (a single alteration or two), "passing" (a phrase in the new key), "formal" (close in the new key).[6] Ex. 4-6 reduces the process of modulation to its simplest terms. It is from Charles Dibdin's *Music Epitomized*, 1822, a small handbook written for amateurs. Note that the examples are given in two voices, and that each modulation involves the tritone of the succeeding key.

Ex. 4-6. Dibdin, *Music Epitomized*, 1822, p. 30.

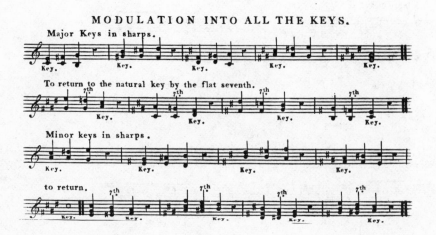

MODULATION INTO ALL THE KEYS.

Shift of key focus can range from the slightest hint of a new tonic to a broad-scale establishment with repeated cadential formulas. Ex. 3-6 hints at a shift to the dominant in m. 3, but strong indications of C major, the tonic, supervene in mm. 4-6, and a broad cadence in C major confirms the tonic. In Ex. 3-4, the tritone of the new key is introduced as an indication in m. 6, and in mm. 7-8 the new key is confirmed. In Ex. 3-9, we hear the tritone of the new key in the fourth measure, followed by a series of cadential formulas to stage the establishment of the new key. Here, a powerful thrust is developed to set off the ensuing singing melody.

For all 18th-century music, the most important modulation is the shift from the tonic to the dominant; it predominates in most dances, arias, sonata movements, many concerto movements, even some fugues. As classic music developed techniques for extending periods and for reinforcing rhetorical functions, this opposition of V and I became an event of high dramatic importance in large-scale classic form.

THE MAJOR MODE

Even to the casual listener, the marked orientation of classic harmony to the major mode is unmistakable. To some extent this bias is expressive, reflecting late 18th-century taste for humor, the more cheerful affections, and the lower styles. Yet works of great scope and serious intent manifest this preference. Christmann, 1782, expresses a generally held view:

> The major mode corresponds more to the sentiment of joy, because it lifts the spirit through its sharpness and its bright sound. The minor mode is better for the expression of sadness. Its tones are not so sharp, so bright; they are more dull, shaky and hollow; thus they depress the spirit.[7]

The superiority of the major mode was considered as derived from the *chord of nature*, as exemplified in the overtone series and the divisions of a monochord. Rousseau, 1768, says:

> The major mode is engendered directly by the resonance of the *corps sonore* which produces the major third from its fundamental; but the minor mode is not given by Nature; it is discovered only by analogy and inversion.[8]

Kirnberger, 1771–1779, says that the minor mode, because of its less natural quality, is less complete and settling than the major, and therefore "is appropriate for the expression of sad, doubtful sentiments, for hesitation and indecision."[9] From these comments and others, the rhetorical implications are clear: the minor mode provides less than the major in periodic definition and confirmation of key.

The cadential assertiveness of the major mode is one of the principal reasons for its higher rank in classic music. Rousseau (as well as others) points out that its tonic triad reinforces the harmonic series, an advantage not offered by the minor triad. The major diatonic scale contains the tritone between 4 and 7, therefore it has the power to make functional cadences. The minor mode has no leading tone in its diatonic form; hence it must borrow a leading tone from the major, thereby becoming a chromatic scale. Progressions in the major mode have the authority that supports periodic rhetoric. This may explain the shift to greater use of major keys during the 18th century. Earlier styles, in the Renaissance and early baroque, exploit the fluid, shifting nuances of minor-mode harmonies in various subtle ways. In later baroque music, the pull of the cadence begins to reach back into the phrase; eventually its thrust starts with the opening chords; hence the more fragile minor mode gave way to the peremptory major. In classic harmony, the minor mode is sometimes raised to a position of central authority as a ruling key, but otherwise remains subordinate to the major.

INTERCHANGE OF MODE

Within the bright climate created by the major mode in classic music, minor harmony can introduce a colorful and often dramatic contrast. When, for example, a C minor chord replaces the C major in a cadential formula, a "deepening" or "darkening" effect occurs in the harmony. Whenever harmony from a minor key is introduced into its *parallel* major, *interchange of mode* takes place.

The *color* value of interchange of mode is its most striking characteristic, immediately perceivable as an expressive nuance or turn. When used momentarily, interchange throws the brightness of the major into high relief. In Orpheus's great aria "I have lost my Euridice" from Gluck's *Orfeo*, 1762 (see Ex. 2-20), the harmony shifts from C major to C minor at the words "deadly silence." The Countess in Mozart's *Marriage of Figaro*, 1785–1786, remembers her happier days in the aria "Dove sono," Act III, and when she sings of pain and tears, the harmony shifts to minor for a few measures, the only such nuance in this sad and poignant song. But for classic music the color value of the minor mode in a major key context serves to highlight an even more important process than an expressive nuance: it can expand harmonic functions, either within a key or for purposes of modulation. Since the minor mode in functional harmony has the same cadential functions as the major, the harmony may proceed to a major or minor tonic from a given tritone.

Ex. 4-7 illustrates the range of keys linked to C major through interchange of mode in the resolution of dominant harmonies. Interchange of mode can be introduced either as a momentary nuance or as a broad-scale digression. In Ex. 3-6, the Ab in m. 7 is a momentary nuance that adds a pathetic touch to the broad cadence. In Ex. 4-8, interchange of mode takes place at m. 21, following the half cadence that is presumably the midpoint of the period. This initiates a broad harmonic digression that makes its way back to I, with a touch of IV at m. 43. The cadence at m. 46 is deceptive, and another broad digression to the minor region is initiated, this time moving to Db major, the Neapolitan key, which finally leads to a brilliant concluding flourish, mm. 55–57. The interchange of mode in the tonic chord at m. 21 thus generates a far-reaching harmonic action that does not play itself out until some 36 measures later. This surprising harmonic twist opens the way for a greatly enriched topical content. Part I of the period, to m. 20, alternates a military figure in the bass with a singing motive in the treble. Part II of the period, in addition to darkening the mood to a pathetic vein with the shift to minor, introduces a parodistic effect by putting the military figure in the treble and the singing figure in the bass. Then, as the harmony circles back toward the tonic, we hear closely spaced imitations, two different kinds of musette, and a grandly scaled ceremonial cadence to close the far-reaching trajectory of this period.

Ex. 4-7. *Interchange of mode relationships.*

> G minor–Bb major
> C major — C minor–Eb major
> F minor–Ab major
> Db major

Ex. 4-8. *Interchange of mode as digression within a period.* Mozart, Quintet in C major, K. 515, 1787, 1st movt.

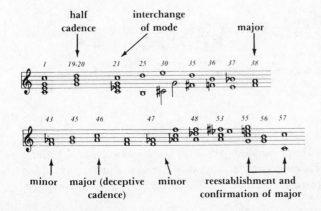

The first eight measures of the second movement of Mozart's F major Sonata, K. 332, 1778, are remarkable for the intensity achieved by the compression of harmonic events—establishment of the tonic major, interchange of mode at m. 5, strong thrust toward the dominant including a deceptive cadence in m. 7, and a broad cadence in the dominant major in m. 8. Here the interchange of mode is the agent by which the modulation from V to I is accomplished; the minor mode acts as a foil to both keys, not only by virtue of its minor sound but also by the powerfully expressive declamation in m. 7 with its saturation of accented dissonances, a dramatic climax emerging out of the singing style that rules this piece.

Interchange of mode can explain so-called third-related progressions sometimes heard in classic music. Beethoven, in the first movement of the *Waldstein* Sonata, 1803-1804, and in the *Leonore* Overture No. 3, 1806, proceeds from C major, the first key, to E major as the second key, instead of the conventional dominant key, G major. In both compositions, C major can be heard retrospectively as the minor VI of E major. Exs. 4-9 and 4-10 sketch the sections of both works where these progressions occur. In both of these works, the drumming out of C major in the opening themes provides a firm and powerful springboard for the leap to the distant key; the headlong nature of the ruling subjects indicates the direction the music will take.

Ex. 4-9. *Interchange of mode.* Beethoven, *Waldstein* Sonata, Op. 53, 1803-1804, 1st movt.

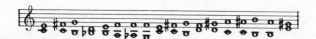

Note. First a bass descent to G; then a rise, eventually to E.

Ex. 4-10. *Interchange of mode.* Beethoven, *Leonore* Overture No. 3, Op. 72a, 1806.

Note. First a tremendous impact of C, 65 measures, with tonic pedal points, I-V alternations; then a bold, instant shift to F♯; mm. 37-121 build an enormous cadence to E.

Cherubini, after hearing the *Leonore* Overture No. 3, commented, "Well, to be honest, I must confess that I could not tell what key it was in from beginning to end."[10] Beethoven was criticized for "strange modulations, and aversion to the standard harmonic progressions" in *AMZ*, 1799.[11] Most of Beethoven's "strange modulations" are applications of interchange of mode, introduced often abruptly and massively to create a strong effect of surprise or shock, as in Ex. 3-10.

Minor-mode episodes often appear as shadings of the major in rondos, arias, baroque concertos, and sonatas. Ex. 4-11 illustrates this usage in a Bach sonata.

Ex. 4-11. *Momentary use of interchange of mode.* J. S. Bach, Sonata for Solo Violin No. 3, ca. 1720, fuga.

61

Interchange of mode received considerable attention in theoretical writings in connection with key schemes. Koch, 1787 and 1802, says:

> This procedure by which a piece in a major mode incorporates an entire period in its parallel minor . . . occurs in all types of compositions. . . .[12]
>
> The frequent and bold modulations by which the newer works of the art are distinguished from the older . . . is one of the features by which the art of music has made such progress in the last third of the century, along with period structure. . . . Haydn, for example, composes Menuettos in which he modulates to very distant keys. . . .[13]

(See the menuetto of the Symphony No. 103 in E♭ major, 1795, where Haydn moves abruptly from E♭ major to C♭ major via E♭ minor.)

The tonic minor had a place in the solar system of keys; Riepel's *schwarze Gredel* (see p. 50) appears in a number of his examples. For classic times, Ex. 4-12, from Galeazzi, deomonstrates how firmly this procedure was locked into the available harmonic schemes. Galeazzi lists similar relationships for all major and minor keys.

Ex. 4-12. Galeazzi, *Elementi*, II, 1796, pp. 266-267.

> "Of the correspondence of all the keys most commonly used in music for modulation:
> A♭ 3 [triad] major [the home key]
> A♭ 3 [triad] minor [N.B., the tonic minor]
> E♭ 3 [triad] major
> D♭ 3 [triad] major
> C 3 [triad] minor
> F 3 [triad] minor . . ."

Since some form of mean-tone tuning was still practiced in the late 18th century, the distinction between major and minor keys was further qualified by the degree of "purity" incorporated in the tuning of a given scale. Koch, 1802, gives Kirnberger's table of interval proportions as a standard for tuning; each scale has minute differences, in contradistinction to the present-day equal temperament in which all half steps are of equal size.[14] Koch quotes from Sulzer on this point:

> It is certain that the purest keys are poorly suited for the expression of pathetic feelings, yet are best used for amusement, for noisy and warlike, for pleasant, charming, humorous, for straightforward serious feelings. The less pure keys, according to their degree of impurity, are more effective for mixed feelings, and the greater the major or minor effects are, the more telling the expression. . . .[15]

The differences in mean-tone tuning lend credence to classifications of keys according to their expressive implications.[16]

CONJUNCT BASS PROGRESSIONS

Apart from cadential formulas, progressions based on *conjunct voice-leading* appear from time to time in classic music. Conjunct voice-leading is the simplest and most intelligible kind of melodic action. It reflects an easy and natural vocal declamation, from plainsong to 20th-century music. A stepwise line of tones in any voice (but best in the bass) gives direction to a harmonic progression. Generally, these progressions appear in the course of a period to maintain continuity, but they are also available at the beginnings of periods, as alternatives to the reciprocal action of I, IV, and V. Examples of these progressions are:

1. Diatonic ascending bass line, Ex. 20-1
2. Diatonic descending bass line, Ex. 7-6b
3. Chromatic ascending bass line, Ex. 18-7
4. Chromatic descending bass line, Ex. 18-6
5. Sequence, Ex. 7-4b
6. Descending parallel sixth chords, Ex. 7-7

Conjunct bass progressions may include cadential formulas which reinforce the stepwise thrust. The sequence by rising or falling fifths consists of alternating conjunct lines in the bass. All of these patterns of voice-leading stem from a simple progression in *alla breve* style, upon a stepwise *cantus firmus*. Expressively, descending bass lines are often used in passages of serious or pathetic import, as in the opening of Mozart's Quartet in D minor, K. 421, 1783, and in his Fantasia in C minor, K. 475, 1785.

Conjunct bass patterns figure prominently in manuals of composition and performance. Along with cadences, they represent the codification of harmonic rhetoric that characterizes 18th-century harmonic concepts, and by traversing all the chords of a key, they help to define it. By the turn of the 18th century the *rule of the octave* had become a standard type of formula by which a bass line rising or falling an octave was furnished with a set of chords. The final chapter of C. P. E. Bach's *Versuch*, 1753,[17] includes many diatonic and chromatic conjunct bass lines; one of the most systematic treatments of this subject appears in Jones's *Treatise*, 1784, where many types of sequence and stepwise bass, diatonic and chromatic, are illustrated.[18] John Callcott's *A Musical Grammar*, 1817, another English work intended primarily for amateurs and drawing heavily from the leading 18th-century theorists—Koch, Kirnberger, Rousseau, Marpurg, and others—gives the list of standardized sequences presented in Ex. 4-13.

Ex. 4-13.   *Sequences.* Callcott, *Musical Grammar*, 1817, p. 164.

I.   Dominant Motion by FOURTHS.

Rising *Fourths* and falling *Fifths*

Descending Melody.

Rising *Fifths* and falling *Fourths*.

Ascending Melody.

II.   Mediant Motion by THIRDS.

Rising *Thirds* and falling *Fourths*.

Descending Melody.

Rising *Fourths* and falling *Thirds*.

Ascending Melody.

III.   Gradual Motion by SECONDS.

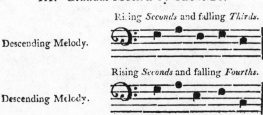

Rising *Seconds* and falling *Thirds*.

Descending Melody.

Rising *Seconds* and falling *Fourths*.

Descending Melody.

DISSONANCE TREATMENT

Each era in western music treats dissonance in a characteristic way, with specific relationships between consonance and dissonance—places where dissonance may be used, how it may be introduced and resolved. Dissonance, an important resource for achieving expressive emphasis, provides a significant clue to the nature of a musical style.

For the classic style, the most striking dissonance is the *appoggiatura*, an *unprepared accented dissonance*. The appoggiatura is an arresting sound that creates an intense expressive nuance, and a grateful release as it resolves by step into the chord. It is the chief dissonance of the free, or galant, style.

Classic period structure, with its strong accents spaced regularly within a slowly moving harmony and a rather transparent texture, invites appoggiaturas frequently, as in mm. 4, 6, and 8 of Ex. 3-6 and mm. 3, 7, and 10 of Ex. 3-8.

Distinctions between the *strict* and *free* styles included the treatment of dissonance. Approach to a dissonant chord in the free style is described by Koch, 1787:

> In the free or galant style the following dissonances and the chords stemming from their inversions can appear without preparation:
>
> 1. The dominant seventh chord. . . .
> 2. The minor seventh with the diminished fifth and the minor third. . . .
> 3. The diminished seventh chord.
>
> To these are added the diminished and augmented fifths, with inversions, the augmented and diminished fourths; the augmented sixth, and the perfect fourth in the six-four chord. . . .[19]

Türk describes the treatment of the appoggiatura:

> The appoggiatura has the privilege—except in the strict style—to enter freely without preparation. . . .[20]

Mozart's music has a high saturation of appoggiaturas; they constitute one of the chief ingredients of his musical speech and show specifically the degree of Italian influence in his music. He is incredibly resourceful in his treatment of the figure, going so far as to put it into a parodistic context. Note the strangeness of effect in Ex. 4-14 where the bass echoes the figure of the melody, another of Mozart's subtle reversals of normal order.

Ex. 4-14.   *Appoggiaturas in treble and bass parts.* Mozart, Sonata in F major, K. 533, 1788, 1st movt.

Allegro

In addition to the appoggiatura, the *suspension,* the chief dissonance of Renaissance and baroque harmony, continues to play an important role in classic music. It is a tone held over from a preceding chord, then led (resolved) to the proper chord tone. When the *stile legato* appears as a topic, suspensions are generally used, as in the finale of Mozart's Quartet in G major, K. 387, 1782 (see also Ex. 7-6). In the free style, suspensions can be struck with the chord to take on the sharpness of the appoggiatura. Ex. 4-15 has a concentration of accented dissonances—repeated suspensions, appoggiaturas—to add poignancy to the Countess's reminiscences.

Ex. 4-15. *Expressive use of appoggiaturas.* Mozart, *The Marriage of Figaro,* 1785-1786, Act II, "Porgi amor."

The above comments on suspension and appoggiatura apply as well to dissonant chords—sevenths, ninths, diminished triads, augmented sixth chords. These could be treated in traditional bound style with careful preparation, or they could be unprepared to deliver a more striking expressive impact. Beethoven begins the Symphony No. 1, Op. 21, in C major, 1800, with a V⁷ of F major, the subdominant of the home key, and the Quartet in C major, Op. 59 No. 3, 1806, with a diminished seventh chord. In each case, the boldness of the gesture immediately draws the listener's attention by creating a harmonic problem.

The qualities in classic harmony that enabled the appoggiatura to play a prominent role also led to another striking treatment of dissonance—the *simultaneous sounding of two harmonies*. Typically, this procedure takes two forms:

1. A double or triple appoggiatura over the bass note
2. Passing harmonies over a pedal point

Occasionally in Beethoven we have the simultaneous sounding of two superimposed chords (Symphony No. 6 in F major, Op. 68, 1807–1808, finale, m. 5). The double or triple appoggiatura is generally found at a cadence to emphasize the arrival effect, and thus it serves a rhetorical and expressive purpose. The procedure in Ex. 3–6 is typical of classic usage in this respect.

In pedal points one voice, usually the bass, remains upon a tonic or dominant tone for a number of measures, while the other voices move through a series of chords, generally connected by stepwise motion or in parallel chords of the sixth. A pedal point should be anchored at both ends by the harmony represented by the bass note, inasmuch as the intervening harmony is in reality a highly charged elaboration. Ex. 4–16 contains a double pedal point, in bass and soprano, bracketing a chromatic rise in the middle voices in parallel sixth chords that initiates a powerful drive toward the tonic.

Ex. 4-16. *Dominant pedal point.* Mozart, Sonata in D major, K. 576, 1789, 1st movt.

From Mozart, *Sonatas and Fantasias for the Piano* (Nathan Broder, ed.). Copyright 1956, 1960 by Theodore Presser Company, Bryn Mawr. Used by kind permission of the publisher.

Two extraordinary uses of pedal points are found in (1) Mozart, overture to
Don Giovanni, 1787, mm. 23-26, where a tonic pedal point is placed *above*
slowly rising chromatic ⁶₃ chords, and (2) Beethoven, F major Quartet, Op. 59,
No. 1, 1806, mm. 53-58 and 300-306, where a dominant pedal point in the second violin cuts through descending chromatic sixth chords (see Ex. 24-7a). Both
of these passages, consequently, have extremely biting dissonances; in the
Mozart overture, this effect intensifies the *ombra* mood which is one of the principal affects of the opera; in the Beethoven quartet, the dissonances set the stage
for a grateful resolution to a rich and glowing C major sound. Rhetorically,
pedal points on the *tonic* represent statement and conclusion; those on the *dominant* build cadential drive. Pedal points, both on tonic and dominant, contribute substantially to the breadth of the first movement of Mozart's C major
Quintet, K. 515, 1787 (see p. 21).

The essential harmonic vocabulary remained the same through the 18th
century; details of voice-leading, doubling, and progression did not change. Yet
the expressive and rhetorical aspects of harmony assumed a decidedly different
character in classic music. Harmonic progressions in late baroque music, con-
trolled by the active bass part, had *quick* rates of chord change; symmetry, while
present to some extent in these progressions, was not a governing factor. The
clearer symmetries of classic music made it possible to achieve simple but attractive musical effects with *slow* regular changes of chord within relatively simple
cadential formulas. The two approaches to harmonic rhythm are demonstrated
by the menuetto and trio from Mozart's *Eine kleine Nachtmusik*, K. 525, 1787
(Ex. 4-17). Ex. 4-17a is in the style of the court minuet; note the suggestion of
cross rhythm (hemiolia) in mm. 6 and 7. Ex. 4-17b is a German waltz, a Ländler, and maintains a regular rhythm throughout. Mozart, Haydn, and their contemporaries, having grown up with mid-18th-century idioms, found many opportunities to recall earlier styles in their mature works.

Slow, regular chord changes, along with fuller textures, made it possible for
classic composers to create expressive nuances purely through the sound of a
given chord. The rich sound of four strings on the F♯ major chord in the second

Ex. 4-17. *Continuo bass, quick rate of chord change; punctuating bass, slow
rate of chord change.* Mozart, *Eine kleine Nachtmusik*, K. 525, 1787.

a. *Continuo bass.* Menuetto.

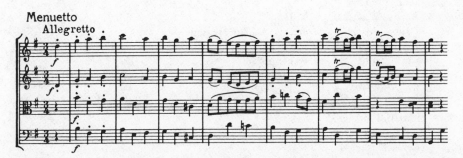

Ex. 4-17, cont'd.

b. *Punctuating bass.* Trio.

Eulenburg No. 28

movement of Haydn's D major Quartet, Op. 76, No. 5, 1797, exemplifies this aspect of classic harmony; without the sustained chords, the simple triadic melody would lack the glow that illuminates this movement.

Volumes could be filled with commentary on 18th-century speculation on the nature of harmony. Much of this speculation, dealing with ratios, the nature of harmony, the origin of major and minor chords, nomenclature of chords and scales, reflects the kinship that music has had with other intellectual disciplines —mathematics, philosophy—and, in the quadrivium, a parity with astronomy, arithmetic, and geometry.

NOTES

1. Riepel, *Grundregeln,* p. 66–69.
2. Ibid., p. 66.
3. Ibid., p. 67.
4. Koch, *Versuch,* II, p. 157ff.
5. Daube, *Generalbass, Dilettant, Melodie,* passim.
6. Koch, *Lexikon,* p. 202.
7. Christmann, *Elementarbuch,* p. 266f.
8. Rousseau, *Dictionnaire,* p. 285.
9. Kirnberger, *Kunst,* II, pt. 1, p. 70.
10. Frederick J. Crowest, *Cherubini,* 1760–1842, Sampson, Low, & Marston, London, n.d., p. 100.
11. *AMZ,* 1799, p. 570.
12. Koch, *Versuch,* II, p. 198.

13. Koch, *Lexikon,* p. 197.
14. Ibid., p. 1559ff.
15. Ibid., p. 1553.
16. Kirnberger, *Kunst,* II, pt. 1, p. 70ff.; Schubart, *Ideen,* p. 377ff.; Galeazzi, *Elementi,* II, p. 293ff.
17. C. P. E. Bach, *Versuch,* II, ch. 7.
18. Jones, *Treatise,* ch. 7.
19. Koch, *Versuch,* II, p. 155.
20. Türk, *Klavierschule,* p. 201.

5 Rhythm

Rhythm in 18th-century music contributes to *expression* with typical dance and march patterns (see Ch. 2) and by choice of meter and tempo. It helps to organize *rhetoric* by locating stressed and unstressed moments and by the play of regular and irregular groupings of beats, measures, and phrases. This chapter covers rhythmic theories and rhythmic analysis.

METER

Early 18th-century music used a wide range of metric signs, from 4/2 and 6/2 to 3/16 and 6/16. Classic time signatures were generally similar to those used today—2/2 (C), 4/4 (C), 2/4, 3/4, 3/8, 6/8. Despite this drastic simplification, the metric subtleties of the earlier style must have been known to classic composers, especially in their formative years.

These subtleties involved the relationship of meter and expression. Kirnberger, whose *Kunst des reinen Satzes*, 1771-1779, forms a link between the practice of J. S. Bach and the classic composers, gives considerable attention to *measure* and the proper choice of *meter* for different expressive values. He says:

> The *alla breve* measure is proper for serious and pathetic matters and therefore is used in motets and other serious church music. The great 4/4 measure has a very emphatic and serious pace, and is proper for splendid choruses, for fugues in church music and especially for music which demands stateliness and gravity. The 3/2 measure is heavy and very grave, provided that only a few shorter notes are included. The 4/4 measure is suited best for a lively and rousing effect that has a somewhat emphatic quality. The 2/4 measure is lively also, but lighter, and thus can be used to express playful feelings. The 4/8 measure is volatile, and its liveliness has nothing of the energy of the 4/4 measure. The character of the 3/4 measure appears gentle and elegant, especially when it uses simple quarter notes. The 3/8 measure has a kind of bold liveliness.
>
> These general characters are more sharply defined by the principal note values used, and by the rules which govern the progression of smaller and larger intervals. The character of a 3/4 measure changes greatly when only quarter notes are used, and when mostly small intervals form the progression as when frequent leaps appear. . . .

At least it should be clear from my remarks on the various meters that such variety should help to express the nuances of the passions.[1]

Kirnberger recommends that a performer analyze the music he is about to play, since it was a common practice to omit barlines when copying music in shorter meters. He was still influenced by the doctrine of the affections and the mathematical finesse of proportional notation. His view of metrical notation reflects the typical baroque practice of holding to a single expressive stance throughout a piece.

Classic music mixed and contrasted expressive or topical content within a movement. Therefore meter was reduced to signs representing common denominators covering any differences in style. Momentary changes in meter were managed by the performer. According to Kirnberger, 1779, the first eight measures in Ex. 5-1 would clearly be in 3/4, while the next eight measures might have been notated in 6/4.

Despite the differences in early and late practice, 18th-century music theory recognized two *basic* types of meter — duple and triple.[2]

Ex. 5-1. *Metrical notation.* Mozart, Symphony No. 39 in E♭ major, K. 543, 1788, menuetto and trio.

(Ländler with waltz accompaniment)

Ex. 5-1, cont'd.

(6/4 *stile legato;* stepwise bass)

Philharmonia

QUANTITAS INTRINSECA

Quantitas intrinseca refers to the differences in accent within duple or triple groups of notes. Accented notes were designated as "good" and unaccented as "bad." The remarks of Ernst Wilhelm Wolf, in his *Musikalischer Unterricht,* 1788, are representative of a general view:

One says of two notes that have the same length, such as ♩♩ that the heavier note, designated with a ˅, is *intrinsically and extrinsically* long . . . the lighter note, however, designed here with a –, is only *extrinsically* long, and intrinsically short.[3]

While this view of meter corresponds to our present ideas, the distinction between strong and weak had more profound implications in the 18th century. Superior regard for the heavier note was carried over into performance to incorporate subtleties of accentual nuance—to delineate the characteristic rhythmic patterns of dance and poetry with a nicety that would be lost if the meter were purely quantitative (see Ch. 11).

SCANSION

Poetic Modes

Quantitas intrinseca, which defines the accentual relationship between groups of two or three notes, represents the primary level of *rhythmic scansion. Scansion,* sometimes designated as *rhythmopoeia*[4] denotes groups of notes, figures, measures, and phrases formed into rhythmic units.

Poetic modes were applied to music for purposes of scansion. Spiess, 1746, drawing upon both Mattheson and Mizler, 1739-1754, gives illustrations of poetic feet, with recommendation for setting them to music of various affective content. Koch, 1802, also lists the poetic modes. (See Ex. 5-2.) Koch includes samples of text that correspond to musical feet; for trochaic meter, he cites "Künsté" and "spiēlĕn," for anapest "Dăs Gĕstād," for creticus "Ēdlĕ Thāt." These correspond to their normal spoken accent.[5]

Mattheson, 1739, shows how a chorale melody (representing the ecclesiastical style) may be transformed into a galant dance melody simply by changing its rhythmic character. Typical patterns of the minuet, gavotte, bourrée, polonaise, and anglaise are superimposed upon six chorale melodies, two of which are given in Ex. 5-3.

Ex. 5-2. *Poetic feet in music.* a. Mattheson-Mizler-Spiess (from Spiess, *Tractatus,* 1746, p. 165). b. Koch, *Lexikon,* 1802, p. 953ff.

a.

b.

Spondaeus — serious, thoughtful pieces		Trochäus
Pyrrhicius — lively and military melodies		Iambus
Iambus — rather cheerful		Spondäus
Trochaeus — naive, not serious; mixed with iambic in minuets		Pyrrichius

Ex. 5-2, cont'd.

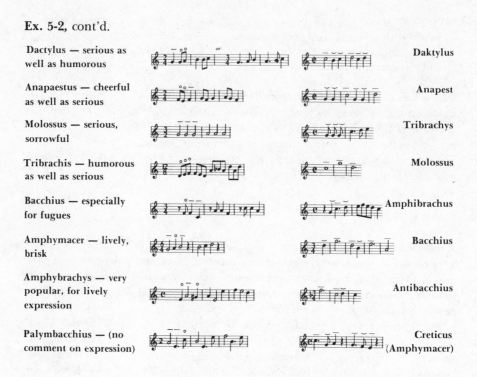

Dactylus — serious as well as humorous — Daktylus

Anapaestus — cheerful as well as serious — Anapest

Molossus — serious, sorrowful — Tribrachys

Tribrachis — humorous as well as serious — Molossus

Bacchius — especially for fugues — Amphibrachus

Amphymacer — lively, brisk — Bacchius

Amphybrachys — very popular, for lively expression — Antibacchius

Palymbacchius — (no comment on expression) — Creticus (Amphymacer)

Ex. 5-3. *Transformation of melodies.* Mattheson, *Capellmeister,* 1739, p. 161.

In larger rhythmic groups, the normal pattern maintained the *quantitas intrinseca*. Alternate measures and measure groups would be strong and weak, as in Ex. 3-1, where mm. 2, 4, 6, and 8 are sensed as weak and 1, 3, 5, and 7 as strong. Measure group 1-2 is strong in relation to 3-4, and 1-4 is strong while 5-8 is weak. Mattheson designates this symmetry as "geometrical."[6]

Quantitatively, theorists designated *phrases* according to the number of measures contained; Koch, 1802, refers to "Zweier," "Dreier," and "Vierer," basing his analysis upon Riepel.[7] Ex. 5-4 illustrates Riepel's system of measure scansion, based upon measure count. Many of the examples in Reicha's *Mélodie*, 1813, illustrate uneven measure groupings within phrases and periods.

Ex. 5-4.   *Scansion of measure.* Riepel, *Anfangsgründe*, 1754, p. 33.

RHYTHMIC ARRANGEMENTS

Absolute symmetry—a perfect balance among rhythmic, melodic, and harmonic units—eventually loses its force when carried too far. As pointed out in Ch. 3, the normal eight-measure group has to undergo some internal compression in order to provide a periodic strong point in m. 8. Even Ex. 3-1, with its neat balance, undergoes a compression of harmonic action in m. 7 and displaces the cadence to the weak part of m. 8, so that the four beats of mm. 7–8 suggest a 1 2 3 1 arrangement above the established two measures.

Manipulation of rhythmic groups is one of the chief resources in classic music for intensifying large-scale rhythmic action and for directing thrust to the periodic cadence. The analyses to follow demonstrate this type of action on various levels—beats, phrases, and phrase groups.

Groups of Beats.   This includes rearrangement of accents within and across the measure, generally embodied in displacement of longer notes or irregular length of figures, sometimes known as *imbroglio*. In Ex. 5-5 Koch quotes a Haydn quartet to illustrate this technique. Upon the basic 3/4 meter, the melodic figures superimpose 4/4, 3/2, and 6/4 scansions, a comedy of witty "errors." Another disturbance of normal rhythm was the *alla zoppa*, the "limping" rhythm, consisting of a long note between two short ones, the first short note being on a strong beat: ♪ ♩ ♪.[8]

Ex. 5-5.   *Imbroglio.* Koch, *Lexikon*, 1802, pp. 775-777 (quoting Haydn, Quartet in G major, Op. 9, No. 5, H.V. III, No. 21, before 1769, menuetto).

Note. Numbers indicate the scansion of each voice.

In Ex. 5-6 the melodic figures of the first violin, the principal agent in the capricious action, take the characteristic shifts of stress of the polonaise and complicate them further, so that notes of length or stress delineate irregular groupings. While symmetry is felt between the first two phrases and somewhere in the middle of the period, it remains imbedded in the shifting patterns. If the question-answer implications of the first four measures were carried out, the period would have had a normal eight-measure span. As it stands, the period incorporates a four-measure extension that heightens the "stomping" effect of arrival in m. 13, where the sforzando tonic harmony on the first beat momentarily brings all rhythmic factors into line.

Ex. 5-6. *Imbroglio.* Haydn, Quartet in F major, Op. 77, No. 2, 1799, finale.

Payne

In Ex. 5–7, the opening tune in rustic low style appears to be normal, beginning at m. 3. The half cadence is answered four measures later by an authentic
cadence; melodic members balance perfectly. If we have the *alla breve* beat
firmly in mind at the beginning, we can easily scan the tune as a series of strong
and weak beats, alternating regularly, forming geometrical units of 2 + 2 or
4 + 4. Yet the drone at the beginning provides no metric definition; if we can
imagine ourselves hearing the piece for the first time, taking our metric cues
from accents of long and short notes, we might make the following scansion:

$$2 / 1\ 2 / 1\ 2\ 3 / 1\ 2\ 3 / 1\ 2 / 1\ 2\ 3 / 1\ 2$$

When the theme is repeated, starting at m.11, this strong hint of irregularity is
reconciled with the firm duple meter that underlies the movement itself. Actually, the period is 10 measures long; the drone is by no means perfunctory; its lack
of metric character opens the door to the rhythmic ambiguity.

Ex. 5-7. Haydn, Symphony No. 104 in D major, the *London*, 1795, finale.

The finale of Beethoven's E minor Quartet, Op. 59, No. 2, 1805-1806 (Ex. 5-8), is remarkable for its effect of rhythmic stretto carried to the point that weak beats are suppressed in a momentary spondee meter. The heavy opening march style does not betray any irregularity until the middle of m. 7, when the harmony tries to correct its *false* beginning in C major by a belated shift to E minor. At this point, m. 7, the *five-beat* group is delineated and the tug-of-war between C major and E minor begins, to be resolved finally for E minor at m. 51. Small wonder that C major has to reassert itself with powerful spondees at mm. 21-22, and later at mm. 34-35.

Ex. 5-8.   Beethoven, Quartet in E minor, Op. 59, No. 2, 1805-1806, finale.

Eulenburg No. 29

Measure Groups.   Measures group themselves into discernible rhythmic units (see p. 73), creating a scansion on a broad level of structure. At first glance, Ex. 5-9 seems to exemplify a normal eight-measure formula. But if we scan it, we cannot distinguish two four-measure phrases that complement each other. Measure 4, which represents the completion of phrase I, also acts to begin the next. Presumably the period will contain seven measures, if phrase II is four measures long (see discussion of *Tacterstickung*, p. 38). But this is not the case; Haydn adds one measure to phrase II, so that we have phrase lengths of three and five measures, respectively, with m. 7 acting to broaden the cadence and throwing emphasis upon m. 8. This delicate minuet, with its somewhat naive musette style, takes on considerable cadential force, especially since the musette drone, lasting through six measures, becomes a powerful subdominant lever for the arrival at the dominant, and the sing-song becomes eloquent.

Ex. 5-9.   Haydn, Sonata in E♭ major, H.V. XVI, No. 49, 1789-1790.

Ex. 5-9, cont'd.

From Haydn, *Sämtliche Klaviersonaten* (Christa Landon, ed.). Copyright 1964 by Universal Edition A. G. Wien. Used by kind permission of the publisher.

The beginning of the menuetto of Mozart's C major Quintet K.515, 1787, comprises a 10-measure period. In Ex. 5-10 we can distinguish two phrases; the first is four measures long, the second is six. Grouping measures, we have a large duple "measure" followed by a large triple "measure," a palpable disturbance of symmetry. But, on this same level, there is an even greater rhythmic disturbance. The long note, D, that is heard after two measures (m. 3) has the rhetorical value of an accent of length, and can thus be felt as a downbeat; four measures later the note D again acts as an accented note, even stronger in its effect because it is a beat longer than the preceding D; counting ahead, we arrive at the cadence of the period three measures later; when the reprise is repeated, the first long D is heard again, this time after *three* measures. Thus against the automatic duple measure scansion ordinarily employed in dance music we have *two* counterscansions, one reinforcing the duple, the other contradicting it.

Ex. 5-10.   Mozart, Quintet in C major, K. 515, 1787.

Edwards

Throughout this entire minuet, such fluctuations pervade the measure rhythms, aided by the conjunct flow of legato melody, which itself can be manipulated easily to different lengths. Eventually, this rhythmic instability is further intensified at the beginning of the trio. It is then answered by one of Mozart's most grateful moments — a delicious Ländler tune imbedded within the trio, totally satisfying in its perfect symmetry (m. 64 and, later, m. 106).

On a much broader scale, the first movement of this quintet gives an impression of balance and symmetry, thanks to the wide swing of long phrase units that flow smoothly together. This movement has a breadth and grandeur of conception unmatched in chamber music before Beethoven; far-ranging harmonic digressions, sweeping melodic trajectories, and bold part-writing share in building the scale of this movement. Rhythmic groupings shift between regular and irregular, and, paradoxically, the irregular groups contribute much to the overall sense of balance, the magnificent poise that pervades this work. The opening 20 measures demonstrate this point:

1. The five-measure phrase that opens the work is not symmetrical — a bold military figure of three measures, answered by a singing-sigh figure of two measures. Quite possibly the first measure is the added member, yet because of the stance taken by the violoncello, this note is the true signature of the movement, its most characteristic and essential measure. This phrase moves from I to V.

2. The second phrase, also five measures long, answers with V to I, a symmetrical counterstatement.

3. The third phrase continues the pattern, but in its fifth measure, m. 15, a *Tacterstickung* supervenes, to begin a six-measure phrase that compresses the harmonic action and drives to a cadence, mm. 19–20; the measure of silence, m. 20, completes the six-measure group.

4. This section stands as the antecedent member of a period; the consequent member, beginning at m. 21, counterstates the opening figure, but in the minor (see Ch. 4 on interchange of mode), and extends the period enormously, to reach its cadence in m. 57 (see Ex. 4–8).

The scansion of mm. 1–20 is:

```
1 2 3 4 5   1 2 3 4 5   1 2 3 4 5
└─┘ └─┘     └─┘ └─┘     └─┘ └─┘

                        1 2 3 4 5 6
                        └─┘ └─┘ └─┘
                         1   2   3
```

Phrase Groups.   Throughout the course of an extended movement, opening and closing statements impress themselves strongly upon the attention; hence they have greater accent, greater *quantitas intrinseca*. This also applies to well-defined thematic statements. Continuations and digressions have less firmness and stability; hence they act as lighter rhythmic elements. The development section of the first movement of Mozart's C major Quintet organizes phrase groups into an extended heavy-light-heavy relationship. These phrase groups may be scanned as follows, beginning after the double bar:

Phrase groups
Number of phrases   4   /   5   / 2 /   3

Phrases

	heavy	light		heavy
Number of measures	4 4 4 6 /	3 3 3 3 3 /	4 4 /	4 4 4

The four-measure phrases that begin this section compress the original five-measure phrases that opened the movement by overlapping the violoncello and violin figures; these four-measure phrases are balanced at the end of the development by another group of four-measure phrases. Both groups frame a section in which a series of imitations on a three-measure alla breve subject is carried out upon a circle of descending fifths, beginning on E (see p. 225f. on the importance of this key relationship in the development section of the sonata form). The systematic compression to three-measure groups and the subsequent expansion to fours adds much force to the wide-ranging trajectory of action of the harmony of this development section. At some point in the composition of this piece, Mozart must have become aware of the scansion outlined above and seen to it that the plan was carried out fully to realize its structural potential.

Subtleties of rhythmic grouping represent a play between centrifugal and centripetal forces, analogous to the interaction of functions in cadential harmony. This rhythmic and harmonic tug-of-war, arising from the thrust of intense feeling, generates the drive that animates the great works of the classic masters.

NOTES

1. Kirnberger, *Kunst,* II, pt. 1, pp. 133–134.
2. Rousseau, *Dictionnaire,* p. 282; Türk, *Klavierschule,* p. 89.
3. E. W. Wolf, *Unterricht,* p. 25; also Walther, *Lexikon,* p. 507.
4. Mattheson, *Capellmeister,* p. 160.
5. Koch, *Lexikon,* p. 953.
6. Mattheson, *Capellmeister,* p. 224.
7. Koch, *Lexikon,* pp. 14, 478, 1688, 1770.
8. Rousseau, *Dictionnaire,* p. 30; Koch, *Lexikon,* p. 130.

6 Melody

For all listeners, the most gratifying moments in classic music — a winning gesture, a delightful tune, an eloquent phrase — are furnished by melody. Melody alone can indicate the configuration of the basic harmonic and rhythmic action, delineating a cadential progression, taking on a characteristic rhythmic imprint, organizing the scansion, and shaping the phrase, much as a cartoon or sketch can give the viewer the essential elements of a graphic message. Thus classic melody is a central gathering point for elements of expression and rhetoric.

IDEAS OF MELODY: DEFINITIONS

The glimpses we have into the workshops of the classic composers — the sketches of Beethoven, the unfinished works of Mozart — show that they planned much of their music by means of a leading melodic line. Mozart commented to Michael Kelly, the Irish tenor who, in 1786, sang in the first performance of *The Marriage of Figaro*, 1785-1786:

> Melody is the essence of music. I compare a good melodist to a fine racer, and counterpointists to hack horses. . . .[1]

Music theory of the later 18th century was heavily oriented to melody. Rousseau, 1768, says:

> If music only depicts through melody and draws all its power from it, it follows that all music that does not sing, no matter how harmonious it may be, is only an imitation, and can neither move nor depict with its beautiful chords; it soon tires the ear and always leaves the heart cold.[2]

Daube, 1797,[3] and Koch, 1802,[4] both say that the melody should rule and the harmony should serve. Mattheson, one of the strongest champions of the superiority of melody over harmony, provides an exhaustive treatment of melodic rhetoric in the first half of his *Capellmeister*, 1739, before he turns his attention to contrapuntal composition. These distinctions between melody and harmony-counterpoint lie in the preference for a single leading line as distinguished from a number of active voices or a full chordal sound.

The term *melody* itself had a number of meanings in the 18th century.

1. *A line of tones*. The simplest and most general meaning, differentiating melody from harmony, i.e., tones heard simultaneously.

2. *Characteristic types of music*. Koch lists the gavotte, bourrée, minuet, polonaise, contredanse, and march among the customary dance melo-

dies, and the choral and figured melodies (songs) among the familiar melody types for odes and other kinds of lyric poetry. Mattheson mentions many similar items.

3. *The part given to the principal voice, the Hauptstimme.*[5]

4. *A line of tones that is unified by key, rhythmic pattern, punctuation, and contour.*

5. *Classifications of melody according to its several functions in texture and structure.*

Terms used to designate various aspects of melody include:

Air, a measured melody (Jones, *Treatise*, 1784, p. 41)

Cantilena, the principal theme of a piece (Momigny, *Cours complet*, 1806, p. 671)

Chant, inflection of the voice; melody par excellence, as a sung line of tones (Momigny, *Cours complet*, 1806, p. 671)

Dessein, theme (Momigny, *Cours complet*, 1806, p. 676; Reicha, *Mélodie*, 1813, p. 31)

Figure, short characteristic pattern (Daube, *Melodie*, 1797, pp. 8-9; Koch, *Lexikon*, 1802, p. 569ff.)

Gedanke, musical idea (Quantz, *Versuch*, 1752, p. 253)

Gesang, vocal melody; phrase; principal melodic line of a piece (Wolf, *Unterricht*, 1788, p. 28; Daube, *Melodie* 1797, p. 11; Koch, *Lexikon*, 1802, p. 662)

Glieder, figures, sections of a melodic line (Koch, *Lexikon*, 1802, p. 943)

Hauptmelodie, Hauptsatz, principal idea or theme of a piece, setting its style or manner (Koch, *Lexikon*, 1802, p. 746)

Modulation, the conduct of melody in a piece (Rousseau, *Dictionnaire*, 1768, p. 295; Koch, *Lexikon*, 1802, p. 972)

Motif, motivo, subject, *dessein*, principal idea (Rousseau, *Dictionnaire*, 1768, p. 302; Paisiello, *Regole*, 1782, p. 38; Momigny, *Cours complet*, 1806, p. 686)

Strain, section or reprise of a composition (Jones, *Treatise*, 1784, p. 42)

Subject, theme or a fugue, a principal idea, a leading strain (Avison, *Musical Expression*, 1752, p. 22; Jones, *Treatise*, 1782, p. 42; Callcott, *Musical Grammar*, 1817, p. 283)

Tune, an entire piece; a complete melody (Callcott, *Musical Grammar*, 1817, p. 85)

Melody is built first with *simple coherent* materials, upon which various degrees of *elaboration* are incorporated for *eloquence*.

SIMPLE MELODY

Clear distinctions were made between *simple* and *figured* melody. Simple melody consisted of a line of chord tones sung by one voice; it was built from conjunct intervals and small leaps, using quarter-, half-, or whole-notes. As a *topic*, simple melody appears in the alla breve, or strict, style. Figured melody was built from figures and motives which elaborated the tones of the simple melody. It was linked specifically to the free, or galant, style. (See p. 23 for Koch's description of the strict and free styles. Many other theorists describe the differences between the two styles.)[6]

Manuals of composition are filled with examples using simple melody; the most celebrated was Fux's *Gradus ad Parnassum*, 1725, in which the rules of counterpoint in the strict style were codified. The masters of the classic style were trained in this discipline, and they did not forget their lessons. *Alla breve* melodies appear frequently in their music, as if they recalled some of their better exercises in the strict style and put them to later use (see Ex. 2-24).

FIGURED MELODY

Apart from its use as a topic, simple melody served a more important purpose — *to provide a framework for figured melody*. Elaboration by means of divisions and *agréments* had for centuries been the principal means by which melody was given life and character. Classic composers built their elegant melodic lines in the same manner, by ornamenting a simple melodic skeleton. They drew upon a rich vocabulary of melodic figures, codified and labeled in dictionaries, manuals, and lexikons. Ex. 6-1 gives a sampling from these sources.

Ex. 6-1.   *Melodic figures.*

a. *Tirata, Läufer,* scale.

b. *Doppelschlag,* turn.

c. *Groppo,* turning figure.

Ex. 6-1, cont'd.

d. *Durchgang*, passing note.

e. *Halbcirckel*, half circle.

f. *Messanza*, mixture of figures.

g. *Mordent*, lower-neighbor note.

h. *Nexus*, series of rising or falling thirds.

i. *Pettera, bombo, Schwärmer*, repeated tones.

j. *Ribattuta*, trill-like figure beginning with main note, accelerating into a trill.

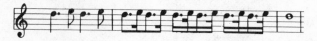

k. *Appoggiatura, Vorschlag*, accented dissonance struck against the harmony.

l. *Retardatio*, series of syncopations, generally with an oblique change of harmony.

m. *Alla zoppa*, short-long, "limping" figure.

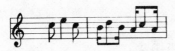

Riepel, in *Anfangsgründe*, 1752, p. 39, illustrates four basic types of melodic figure:

1. *Singer*, longer tones
2. *Springer*, leaps and arpeggios
3. *Läuffer*, running scales
4. *Schwärmer*, quick repeated tones

Most of the figures illustrated above represent what Quantz, 1752, designated as "arbitrary" elaborations,[7] in which a simple melody or interval is ornamented. These elaborations were distinguished from "essential" elaborations,[8] or *agré-ments*, in which an appoggiatura, trill, or turn was required at a certain point in a melodic line, with or without a sign to indicate the elaboration. Arbitrary elaborations formed part of the continuity of the melodic line; essential elaborations were used principally for accentual nuance.[9]

In addition to the melodic figures illustrated in Ex. 6-1, arpeggio figures of many types were available. Ex. 6-2 gives 11 samples of figured melody drawn from a single structural melody. Ex. 6-3 shows how such elaborations can be used as melodic components in phrases.

Ex. 6-2.   *Elaboration of a simple melody.* Koch, *Lexikon*, 1802, p. 569.

Ex. 6-2, cont'd.

Ex. 6-3. *Rearrangement of figures.* Portmann, *Lehrbuch,* 1789, examples, pp. 22, 23.

shortened

lengthened

Concerning figured melody, Jones, 1784, says:

> But the most natural fund of variety, for the promotion of the Air of a com-
> position, is the Art of dividing upon its harmony, or running a course of
> quicker notes upon the ground of a subject; an Art of so much consequence
> to Music, that it was formerly considered and treated as a Branch by itself.[10]

Jones gives a plain melody that moves in quarter-notes with the bass, and shows
how it may be elaborated. His examples imply a structural line in *alla breve* style
(see Ex. 6-4). Hundreds of examples of this process of elaboration can be found
in treatises, from the simplest divisions of an elementary counterpoint exercise to
the complex ornamentations of the Italian violin style, as demonstrated by Tartini, 1771.[11] The reverse procedure was also used by theorists—to expose the
structural line under a florid melody, as in Ex. 6-5. Additional reductions are
given in Ex. 6-6; note that the structural melody consistently moves stepwise,
implying simple cadential formulas.

Ex. 6-4.   *Melodic elaboration.* Jones, *Treatise,* 1784, examples, p. 30.

Structural line

Ex. CXXXVI.   The Plain Notes

Ex. 6-4, cont'd.

Ex. 6-5. *Reduction of a figured melody.* Momigny, *Cours complet,* III, 1806, p. 96.

a. Florid melody.

b. Reduction.

c. Further reduction to structural lines of melody and bass [ed.].

Ex. 6-6. *Melodies and their reductions.*

a. Mozart, Concerto for Clarinet and Orchestra in A major, K. 622, 1791, finale.

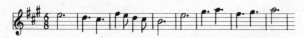

Reduction.

b. Haydn, Quartet in C major, Op. 20, No. 2, 1772, finale.

Reductions.

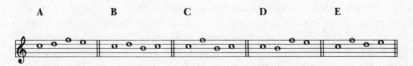

Basic structural melodies are relatively few, simple, and neutral in expressive quality. Elaborations are uncountable and embody topic, affect, and expressive nuance; they also contribute to periodicity as they create tensions against structural tones. To illustrate this, Ex. 6-7 lists some structural melodies built on variants of I-IV-V-I and I-V-V-I progressions. The first of these (C, D, F, E) is the famous *cantus firmus* that opens the finale of Mozart's *Jupiter* Symphony, 1788. Ex. 6-8 quotes several other melodies by Mozart built on this same *cantus firmus.*

Ex. 6-7. *Variants of a structural melody; elaborations.*

Ex. 6-8.   *Melodies built on Ex. 6-7, A.*

a. Mozart, Symphony in G minor, K. 550, 1788, 2nd movt.

b. Mozart, Sonata for Piano and Violin in B♭ major, K. 378, 1779, 1st movt.

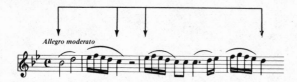

c. Mozart, Concerto for Clavier and Orchestra in C major, K. 467, 1785, 2nd movt.

One further aspect of melodic invention merits attention, namely the similarity among figures used by different composers and by the same composer in different works. A glance through the *Breitkopf Thematic Catalogue*, 1762–1787, reprinted 1966, shows many such similarities, especially in incipits with the following rhythmic patterns:

One further aspect of melodic invention merits attention, namely the similarity among figures used by different composers and by the same composer in different works. A glance through the *Breitkopf Thematic Catalogue*, 1762–1787, reprinted 1966, shows many such similarities, especially in incipits with the following rhythmic patterns:

Matheson, 1739, says that melodic invention arises from experience and attentive listening so that suitable combinations can be made from one's own store of figures, turns, and passages.[12] Avison, 1752, also speaks to this point:

> This may be seen by certain particular favorite passages that are to be found in almost all the compositions of our greatest masters. I know it is a received opinion among the *connoisseurs* in music, that the best *Subjects* for *Fugues*, or *Airs*, are pretty much exhausted, and perhaps their observations may be right: nevertheless, the skillful composer will so artfully vary and conduct them, that they will seem not only natural, but also new.[13]

The variation and conduct of melody to which Avison refers is *melodic rhetoric* — the arrangement of familiar melodic figures into phrases and periods that have a distinctive character.

MELODIC RHETORIC, DISTRIBUTION OF MELODIC FIGURES

The basic unit of melody for all 18th-century music was the *figure*. Melodic rhetoric, the distribtuion of melodic figures, received much attention throughout the entire century from such theorists as Mattheson, Heinichen, Spiess, Riepel, Daube, Koch, Portmann, Momigny, and Reicha. Some theorists borrowed terms from traditional rhetoric to identify melodic figures and their grammatical relationships; others described these procedures more simply. Following is a list of terms used to describe melodic relationships, compiled from theoretical works. As in language, these terms refer to various parts of the musical discourse — opening, continuation, and conclusion.

Abruptio, breaking off of a final note

Anadiplosis, repetition of a figure after a punctuation

Anaphora, repetition

Antistrophe, the second part of a melodic section

Antithesis, an opposing idea

Aposiopesis, breaking off of a thought; general pause

Apostrophe, digression to another topic

Confirmatio, reinforcement of an idea

Confutatio, resolution of an idea

Contrast (self-explanatory)

Dispositio, arrangement of ideas

Distributio, breaking up of an idea

Dubitatio, uncertainty; broken, unexpected turn

Ellipsis, rest instead of a note

Epiphora, repetition of a phrase after intervening material as an ending to a line (rhyme)

Epistrophe, repetition of an idea

Exordium, introduction

Gradatio, climax, sequence

Narratio, statement

Parenthesis, insertion, interpolation

Periphrasis, circumlocution, use of many notes where one will do

Peroratio, conclusion

Propositio, statement or restatement

Repercussio, restatement or counterstatement (not repetition)

Repetitio, repetition

Variatio, variation

Versetzung, restatement of a figure on another degree

Wiederschlag, counterstatement or restatement

Wiederkehr, restatement

Zergliederung, breaking up of a figure or idea

The two examples to follow demonstrate the application of rhetorical principles to extended musical passages. Ex. 6-9 from Mattheson, 1739, shows the application of the traditional nomenclature—exordium, narratio, propositio, confirmatio, confutatio, peroratio—to an Italian bravura aria; Ex. 6-10, from Koch, 1793, takes a typical instrumental work of the galant style and shows how an eight-measure dance melody can be extended by rhetorical devices to a length of 32 measures.

Ex. 6-9.   *Melodic rhetoric.* Mattheson, *Capellmeister,* 1739, p. 237ff.

Exordium, introduction.

Narratio, statement.

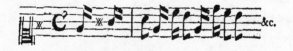

Propositio simplex, simple [counter]statement.

Propositio variata, varied [counter]statement.

Propositio composita, compound statement.

Confirmatio, reinforcement.

a) *Peroratio*, conclusion.   **c)** *Apostrophe*, digression.

        b) *Transitus*, transition.   **d)** *Repercussio*, answer.

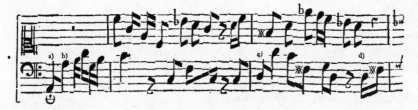

        e) *Confutatio*, resolution.

Wiederschlag, restatement by means of *amplificatio* and *argumentatio*, extension and reinforcement.

Ex. 6-9, cont'd.

Wiederschlag with refractio, contrary motion.

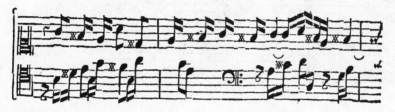

Confutatio, resolution.

Da Capo.

Matteson's example, taken from an aria by Marcello, displays the typical baroque method of using a single principal figure and its variants to carry out the phases of the rhetorical discourse. On the contrary, in Ex. 6-10 there are more than a half-dozen different figures, a distribution typical of later 18th-century melodic rhetoric. The following comments summarize Koch's explanations of his techniques for melodic extension:

1. Similar restatement of a motif on another harmony, mm. 2, 15, 28
2. Reinforcement of a full cadence by varied repetition of the cadence formula, m. 4
3. Repetition of a motif, taking another level of the same harmony, m. 7
4. Extension of a section by repeating established metrical formulas, mm. 8-9
5. Parenthesis, insertion of new material, m. 12
6. Progression, i.e. sequence, mm. 18-21
7. Reinforcement of a half-cadence by repetition, m. 23
8. Closing section strengthened by additional cadential formulas, m. 25
9. Spinning out a rapidly moving figure, m. 27
10. Transposition, i.e., modulating sequence, mm. 28-30[14]

Koch's treatment of melodic construction, which he calls "mechanical," covers every scale of structure, from figures to complete movements.

Ex. 6-10.   *Melodic extension.* Koch, *Versuch*, III, 1793, p. 226ff.

a. Original eight-measure melody.

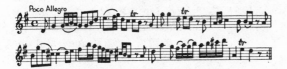

b. Koch's extension of original melody.

Another work devoted to the *mechanical* aspects of melodic construction is Daube's *Anleitung zur Erfindung der Melodie*. Its date of publication, 1797, and its place of issue, Vienna, qualify this work as a summary of galant melody in the time of Haydn and Mozart. Daube's treatment is not as thoroughgoing as those of Riepel, 1754, 1755, Koch, 1787, 1793, and, later, Reicha, 1814, but his insights are acute and his examples ring true for the style of his era. The excerpts in Ex. 6-11 illustrate Daube's method. In Ex. 6-11a the harmony and the rhythm each tread a straight and narrow line; cadences and phrases are rigidly regular. However, the melodic figures give no evidence of such thoroughgoing symmetry; their order is 1 2 3 4 1 2 1 1 4 3 1 2 1 2 4 1. An element of the unexpected, of caprice, pervades the melodic order and imparts a charm that it would otherwise lack. Of all classic composers, Haydn was greatest master of this kind of melodic legerdemain, as demonstrated in Ex. 5-6.

Ex. 6-11.   *Melodic construction.* Daube, *Melodie,* 1797, pp. 9-10.

a. "Through frequent repetition and transposition of each figure, a melody of one or two measures can be extended to a length of one hundred or more measures, whose length will not be annoying to the listener—the following example illustrates this:"

b. "The singing, the brilliant, along with the mixed style, are illustrated below:"

Koch's and Daube's methods of extending phrases and periods represent the late 18th-century version of the technique of *parody* that had been applied in western music since early medieval times — addition and elaboration upon a *cantus firmus* or a previously composed piece. The reduction of part of the finale from the Haydn D major Quartet, Op. 76, No. 5, 1797, that is given in Ex. 6-12 shows how the process might be reversed. The principal melodic components are retained; the scansion is trimmed to four-measure phrases, yet the form retains the proportions of the movement itself — eight measures of tonic and 34 of dominant in the reduction as against 20 measures of tonic and 100 of dominant in the original. The brief motives, simple and straightforward, lend themselves to a wide range of rhetorical combinations. The reduction given here may assist the listener to grasp the unique patterns, connections, and extensions that characterize the continuity of this movement, and their derivation from standard formulas.

Ex. 6-12.   *Reduction* of Haydn, Quartet in D major, Op. 76, No. 5, 1797, finale.

Beethoven, in the first movement of his E minor Quartet, Op. 59, No. 2, 1806, appears to have carried out a similar procedure, interpolating extra measures and rests between "substantive" figures and phrases. This "parenthesizing" contributes to the somewhat irregular flow of the movement, with bits of singing melody alternating with spun-out figures and strategically placed rests.

Melodic Ars Combinatoria

The play of notes and figures was recognized in 18th-century music theory as a basic method of teaching melodic construction. It was a musical application of the *Ars Combinatoria*,[15] a mathematical process that received much attention throughout the 17th and 18th centuries. Briefly, it deals with the number of different ways in which a given quantity of objects may be arranged according to a given set of conditions. For example, the numbers 1, 2, 3, and 4, taken two at a time, can make 12 different combinations:

12 13 14 21 23 24 31 32 34 41 42 43

Such arrangements, applied to tones of the scale and to short figures, appear in many theoretical works from Mersenne, *Harmonie universelle*, 1636, and Kircher, *Musurgia Universalis*, 1650, to Riepel, *Grundregeln*, 1755, and Langlé, *Traité de la basse sous le chant*, circa 1798.

A very thoroughgoing treatment of melodic arrangments is found in a manuscript treatise *Anleitung zur musikalischen Composition* by Christian Gottlob Ziegler, dated at Quedlinburg in 1739. Ziegler's approach to style is the same as that of Heinichen and Mattheson, to whom he refers frequently, while his musical examples are in the vein of Telemann, to whom he also refers. From p. 81 to p. 128 Ziegler gives several hundred permutations and variations of the C major triad, showing how one can invent motives in different rhythms, shapes, and styles; several of these are quoted in Ex. 6-13.

Ex. 6-13. *Melodic arrangements.* Ziegler, *Anleitung zur musikalischen Composition*, 1739, p. 84.

Riepel, 1755, begins the formal consideration of melody by discussing mathematical permutations. He then applies permutations to musical tones in series of three or four notes; the four-note permutations are given in Ex. 6-14.

Ex. 6-14. *Melodic arrangements.* Riepel, *Grundregeln*, 1755, p. 27.

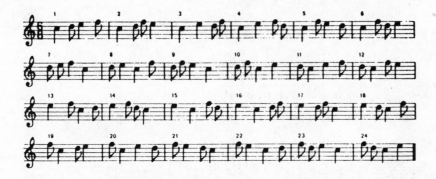

Given these mechanical methods of melodic construction, it was inevitable that they would be applied to games. From 1757 to 1813 some dozen or more musical games based upon the *Ars Combinatoria* were published, including games by Haydn, Mozart and Kirnberger. The earliest and most famous of the publications was Kirnberger's *Der allezeit fertige Polonoisen- und Menuetten- componist*, which had a wide circulation after its publication in 1757, appearing in several editions and in various languages. Polonaises and minuets were put together by throwing dice. The numbers on the dice corresponded to musical figures provided by the composer for each measure of the two periods of the polonaise and of the minuet. Eleven figures were available for each measure, so that the total number of polonaises that could result was 11^{14}, and for the minuet and its trio there could be 11^{32} versions.

Kirnberger must have begun with the idea of characteristic dance styles, a favorite topic in his teaching of composition. He laid out the proper number of measures, located the proper harmonies, and then drew upon his bag of melodic tricks to provide characteristic melodic figures for each dance. He saw to it that each figure assigned to a given measure would make good connection with the figures for adjacent measures.

The musical content of the short pieces thus constructed is not distinguished; they are solid and sturdy because their harmonic, rhythmic, and melodic components are fashioned from useful musical stuff; they do not necessarily betray their mechanical origins. Thematic correspondences or restatements of motives need not figure in their coherence (see Ex. 12-3). Some of these pieces could well find a place in a light serenade or divertimento. Ex. 6-15 reproduces Kirnberger's table of numbers for the dice (*Würfel*) throws, a melody extracted from the list of figures (note the *Versetzung*, or transposition, in m. 4), and the first page of figures for the polonaise.

Ex. 6-15. Kirnberger, *Polonoisen- und Menuettencomponist*, 1757, pp. 7, I.

a. Numerical chart and sample polonaise

			for the first part								
with one die	1	2	3	4	5	6					
with two dice	2	3	4	5	6	7	8	9	10	11	12
1st throw	70	10	42	62	44	72	114	123	131	138	144
2nd throw	34	24	6	8	56	30	112	116	147	151	153
3rd throw	68	50	60	40	7	4	126	137	143	118	146
4th throw	18	46	2	12	79	28	87	110	113	124	128
5th throw	32	14	52	16	48	22	89	91	101	141	150
6th throw	58	26	66	38	54	64	88	98	115	127	154

b. Page I of Kirnberger's polonaise figures.

These games were taken seriously as a manifestation of the *Ars Combinatoria*. Kirnberger himself prefaces his game with a carefully reasoned discussion, explaining the rationale of his work. He says:

It is possible for this method to be useful in the composition of larger pieces, for example symphonies. Those who truly understand musical composition will at least not be displeased by the manifold elaborations upon the same harmony over a single bass line. A beginning student of composition can derive advantage from the store of variations of the musical figures.[16]

Riepel, 1755, speaks in a similar vein:

The unique ars permutatoria, by which one can invent many more than 99 themes in one day, is at least 99 times more healthy for musical composition than the aforesaid mathematical measurements (of tones).[17]

Kirnberger's game is reviewed seriously in Marpurg's *Historisch-kritische Beyträge*,[18] and *AMZ*, vol. 15,[19] contains an extended article on this subject.

Now and then, we run across situations in which permutation and combination appear to have been applied deliberately. Ex. 3-7 shows a permutation of phrase members. Ex. 6-16, from the *alla tedesca* in Beethoven's Bb major Quartet, Op. 130, 1825, shows how Beethoven has permuted the figures of the original melody near the end of the movement. The scattered form, after the automatic regularity of the normal version, has an odd, humorous effect, befitting the somewhat precious treatment that Beethoven gave to the familiar topic of the movement, a German waltz, through finicky dynamics, phrasing, and over-elegant, often capricious scoring.

Ex. 6-16. *Permutation of theme.* Beethoven, Quartet in Bb major, Op. 130, 1825, *alla tedesca.*

a. Normal arrangement.

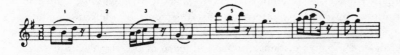

b. Permutation.

To demonstrate how a permutation of two tones in a melody can change its character drastically, Ex. 6-17 offers two versions of a melody from the menuetto of Mozart's *Eine kleine Nachtmusik*. Two notes of each phrase have been reversed (permuted) in the first version; the result, an unbroken conjunct line, forms a melody that could be found in any of the thousands of *Redoutenmenuetten* churned out at this time, a totally undistinguished tune. Mozart's tune, the second version, breaks the conjunct line, gives an elegant turn to phrase I by suggesting a hemiolia, and in phrase II realizes this hemiolia by clearly changing the meter to 3/2 in mm. 6 and 7; a powerful drive to the cadence is thus created. Further, Mozart creates an effect of syncopation in the already sprung rhythm by putting an expressive accent, a trill, upon what would be the weak beat of the momentary duple time. Thus we sense three different levels of rhythmic displacement: (1) between beats, (2) between measures, (3) between phrases—an *imbroglio* that transforms the entire period, achieved minimally by the deft permutation of *two* tones.

Ex. 6-17. Mozart, *Eine kleine Nachtmusik*, K. 525, 1787, menuetto.

a. Scale-line melody modified from original.

b. Original melody with leaps and hemiolia rhythms.

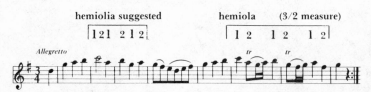

Combinatory processes were not confined to melodic arrangments. Cadences, chord positions, invertible counterpoint, arrangements of thematic material within a piece, plan of key (see Exs. 4-2 and 4-3), the standard forms of the classic style—all of these give evidence of the influence of the *Ars Combinatoria*, where elements may be arranged in different ways or substituted for each other.

Finally, to make a proper assessment of the *Ars Combinatoria* and the musical games which arose from it, we should draw the line clearly between *construction* and *invention*. This is not a way to compose important music. The skilled composer makes his selections from the store of figures in his own mind, and his interlocking combinations and permutations are infinitely more complex than those set down for the dilettante. But for the student of composition the *Ars Combinatoria* was a way to spark the imagination, to expose possibilities for the invention of musical figures and their arrangement.

Theme; Subject

The length and inner arrangement of a *Hauptsatz* (subject or principal theme) were prescribed only in short pieces oriented to dance forms. The main and accessory ideas of a longer piece were determined by the composer. Often these do have a high degree of tunefulness and a self-sufficiency of structure arising from the completion of a symmetrical pattern, as in the opening Allegro of Haydn's *Drumroll* Symphony, No. 103, 1795.

In other works, a subject may be put together as a patchwork of small figures, as in the first movement of Mozart's *Prague* Symphony, K.504, 1786; or it may begin as a symmetrical tune, then spin itself out discursively, as in the first movement of Mozart's C major Quintet, K.515, 1787. While short, complete themes in classic music, as in the first movement of Mozart's A major Sonata, K.331, 1778 (Ex. 3-1), are both tuneful and satisfying, melodic appeal in classic music, generally speaking, arises from a gratifying turn of figure or a happy connection of motives, not necessarily from complete tunes.

Ex. 3-1 achieves a perfection, on a small scale, of melodic *coherence* and unity. Yet only a relatively small fraction of classic melody was shaped in this manner. Coherence, as a basic factor in classic melodic unity, arose from one or more of the following conditions:

1. *A compatibility of figures, whether similar or not.* This is the principle of the melodic *Ars Combinatoria*; one figure could be substituted for another, provided it was compatible in style.

2. *Counterstatements of melodic figures.* Coherence is promoted by repetitions and variations of melodic figures and by judicious melodic contrast. Similarities and contrasts of melodic figures represent the most palpable aspect of melodic coherence and unity. Indeed, the identification and relationship of melodic material have been among the chief parameters employed by scholars who have studied the classic style (see Ch. 13).

Koch extended his original eight-measure melody (in Ex. 6-10 to 32 measures largely by counterstatements of figures; of the 24 additional measures, 18 involve such counterstatements. Melodic counterstatment can promote coherence within a normal period, as in Ex. 3-1; it can be used as a springboard for extending the period, as in the example by Koch and in the opening of Mozart's *Jupiter* Symphony, 1788, where striking stylistic contrasts among short figures create a sense of compression that explodes into a broad extension, the layout being

coups d'archet	singing style		march	
a	b	a b c	c c c etc.	

Counterstatement also plays a vital unifying role in the latter part of a movement, as it recalls and rhymes the material heard at first.

3. *Contour established by the structural line.* Since simple or structural melodies tend to progress stepwise, often for three, four, or more degrees consecutively in one direction, a figured melody pegged to this motion will have a long-range sense of direction; hence it will possess a coherence based upon this rise or fall. Ex. 6-6 illustrates this procedure. Notwithstanding the elaborate tracery of the figured melody, the overall melodic coherence rests upon the stepwise structural line.

4. *Contour established by the figured melody.* This is one of the chief methods by which a melodic line acquires a long-range unity; it is a powerful device for intensifying expressive quality, provided the melody seems directed to some point of *apex* or *climax*, that is, a point of furthest *rise* or *fall*, as in Ex. 3–4; it may stand as the climax of a period, as in Ex. 3–10, where A is the apex of the melodic rise; it can organize the melodic action over an entire group of periods, as in the first movement of Mozart's C major Quintet, K.515, 1787, mm. 152–205, where the high F in m. 199 represents the highest crest of the rising waves of melodic action, covering a span of 53 measures. Such a deliberate, wave-like upward surge toward a melodic apex, covering an extended section in a composition, is a universal configuration. We hear it in the *Alleluya* of Pérotin (*ars antiqua*, 13th century), in Josquin, in Lassus; it is a basic feature of J. S. Bach's music (Prelude I from *The Well-tempered Clavier,* where the high A in m. 5 is the point from which a slow melodic descent is made to the end of the prelude), in Wagner (Prelude to *Tristan*) and in Bartók (*Music for Strings, Percussion, and Celesta*, first movement, where the high E♭ represents the climax of the movement).

5. *Felicity of motive connection.* Felicity of motive connection places familiar materials into apt, often unexpected relationships; the end of a figure may be the link to the next so that a new line of discourse is taken; a turn in a phrase may be surprising but logical. Felicity conveys a sense of eloquence, of freshness, and of inevitability in the melodic line. Mozart was especially gifted in this area. The richness and variety of his melodic material and his ability to link a chain of many different figures with exquisite timing were unequaled. The first 15 measures of the introduction to his *Prague* Symphony, 1786, with their kaleidoscopic changes of affect and figure, exemplify this aspect of his personal style as illustrated in Ex. 6–18 and discussed below.

This introduction begins conventionally, with a standard French overture figure using the *coups d'archet*, the unisons of Parisian taste. Ordinarily, we might expect three strokes, regularly spaced, but here we have five, with a stretto effect, until a quarter-note pattern is established by the end of m. 2. This merges with the eighth-notes and rests of m. 3 which continue the arpeggio figure implied by the *coups*, upward to an F♯. Thus, despite the abrupt contrast in style between mm. 2 and 3, elements of melody, rhythm, and harmony maintain a connection. When the F♯ of m. 4 is reached as a routine continuation and apex,

Ex. 6-18. *Motive connection.* Mozart, *Prague* Symphony, K. 504, 1786, introduction.

French overture; *coups d'archet*
exordium (introduction)

the harmony makes an abrupt change, and the new figure is counterstated twice
in descending thirds, making a new and contrasting motive. The upbeat to m. 7
would ordinarily be taken as a cadential figure, but in m. 7 this becomes a long
appoggiatura to the leading tone, thereby changing the meaning of the D; the

dominant in m. 7 is resolved deceptively in m. 8 to the dominant of E minor, using a figure which is parallel to that of m. 7, except for the *last two notes*; these notes skip a third, an interval picked up by the figure in m. 9; meanwhile a hint of imitation in a second voice is introduced to give more substance to the momentary sing-song of m. 9; this second voice introduces a dotted rhythm that lends a bit of piquancy to the give-and-take.

Taken individually, the dozen or more figures here would hardly seem to be compatible. But Mozart has managed to provide links by taking *some feature of a preceding motive as a means for connecting the discourse to the next motive*, so that the transition is made smoothly and organically. This connection, as well as the aptness and elegant shapes of the individual figures, represents felicity of invention. These qualities in Mozart's music were singled out in the review of his *Marriage of Figaro* that appeared in the London *Examiner* of July 12, 1812:

> The subject is taken, with little alteration, from Beaumarchais' celebrated comedy of "La Folle Journée", and its quick succession of incident gives full scope to the fancy, which teemed with delightful combinations of sound, and sprung from subject to subject with inexhaustible freshness, vigour, and originality. Every air, and almost every close, has strong character of novelty, and seems carefully to shun resemblance to other authors; for even when the passages seem to lead to something we have heard before, a dexterous trun or an unexpected change redeems them from all charge of plagiarism. This attempt at constant novelty would be dangerous in unskilful hands, and might repress merit, or draw it into passages original only for their extravagance.

Felicity of invention and connection, of unbroken rhetorical trajectory, was felt by Rousseau to be the distinguishing mark of genius. He describes it in his *Dictionnaire*, in the entry on "*Prima intenzione*," 1768:

> Technical word in Italian which has no correspondence in French. A work of *Prima intenzione* is formed in the spirit of the composer, all at once, and complete with all its parts. These works are those rare strokes of genius in which the ideas are so closely connected that they make a single idea and one cannot be conceived without the other. They are comparable to those long but eloquent Ciceronian periods in which the sense, suspended throughout their entire duration, is determined only at the last word, having been formed thus by just a single idea in the mind of the author. . . . The first without the last makes no sense. . . . Such kinds of exercise of the understanding, which can hardly be explained even by analysis, are prodigies for the reason . . . their effect is always proportional to the mental effort they have cost, and in music, the compositions of *prima intenzione* are the only ones which can cause ecstasies, ravishments, bursts of spirit which transport the hearers outside of themselves; one feels them, one senses them immediately, connoisseurs never fail to recognize them. . . . After a work of *prima intenzione*, all other music is without effect.[20]

Here Rousseau has touched upon the relationship between rhetoric and expression: the composer of genius will guide his music according to the laws of rhetoric, whether consciously or by habit; his declamation, propelled by the force of his idea, will build toward the sublime, and the eloquence will reach its peak at the end of the period.

NOTES

1. Deutsch, *Mozart*, p. 531.
2. Rousseau, *Dictionnaire*, p. 275.
3. Daube, *Melodie*, II, p. 1.
4. Koch, *Lexikon*, p. 941.
5. Ibid., p. 747
6. Kirnberger, *Kunst*, I, p. 81; Marpurg, *Kritische Briefe*, II, p. 13; Spiess, *Tractatus*, p. 161; Christmann, *Elementarbuch*, p. 244; Koch, *Lexikon*, pp. 597, 1451-1459. This distinction corresponds to the "stylus gravis" and "stylus luxurians" referred to by Bukofzer, *Music in the Baroque Era*, p. 383.
7. Quantz, *Versuch*, p. 118.
8. Ibid., p. 77.
9. See Putnam Aldrich, "Ornamentation," in Apel, *Harvard Dictionary*, pp. 629-633, for a survey of the practice of ornamentation.
10. Jones, *Treatise*, p. 53.
11. Tartini, *Traité des agrémens*, 1771.
12. Mattheson, *Capellmeister*, p. 122.
13. Avison, *Essay*, p. 36.
14. Koch, *Versuch*, III, p. 253ff.
15. See the present author's article "Ars Combinatoria," in Landon & Chapman (eds.) *Studies in Eighteenth-Century Music*, p. 343ff.
16. Kirnberger, *Polonoisen- und Menuettencomponist*, p. 5f.
17. Riepel, *Grundregeln*, table of contents.
18. Marpurg, *Historisch-kritische Beyträge*, III, pt. 1, p. 167ff.
19. *AMZ*, 1812, p. 42.
20. Rousseau, *Dictionnaire*, pp. 385, 386.

7 Texture: Basic Premises

Texture denotes the relationship of the component voices in a composition. It involves (1) the *number* of voices heard, (2) the *action* assigned to them, and (3) the effects of *sonority* created. Two aspects of classic texture are covered in this chapter: the two-part framework and counterpoint.

THE TWO-PART FRAMEWORK

Polarity of Treble and Bass

Classic texture maintained a tradition that was established in the early baroque style, circa 1600—*the polarity of the treble and bass*. The treble carried the leading melodic line, supported by a bass that set the harmony and provided rhythmic punctuation; middle voices completed the texture with chord tones.

Much classic music was written in two voices; composition manuals give attention to melody-bass texture, first to train the student in simple and figured counterpoint, eventually as a refinement in duet composition, when full chords were reduced to two voices.[1]

Two-part texture characterized much keyboard music, as in Ex. 7-1. Dances and simple vocal music often appeared in two-part settings. Many full-voiced compositions—quartets, concertos, symphonies—were published in reductions for duet performance by musical amateurs.[2]

Ex. 7-1. *Two-part keyboard texture.* Haydn, Sonata in E♭ major, H.V. XVI, No. 49, 1789-1790, finale.

Reinforcement of the Two-Part Framework

Many fuller textures represent amplification or reinforcement of the basic two-part framework. The minimum reinforcement occurs when a third voice moves parallel to either bass or melody. Ex. 7-2 doubles the melody in thirds, a typically ingratiating Italian device. More complex and varied distributions of the two outer voices and their amplification will be seen in examples given in Chs. 8 and 9. Much of this reinforcement is given to middle voices, and represents increased richness of sonority rather than a more involved counterpoint.

Ex. 7-2. *Reinforcement of melody in thirds.* Guglielmi, *Le Pazzie d'Orlando*, 1771[?], "Son le tenere faville dell'amor" ("These are the tender sparks of love").

COUNTERPOINT

Species Counterpoint

Recent studies have documented the importance of contrapuntal techniques, embodying the learned style in classic music.[3] The learned style—fugue, canon, free and invertible counterpoint, and free imitation—represented a strong link between classic music and its predecessors.

In the middle and late 18th century, the point of departure for instruction in the learned style was the *alla breve*, in which notes of various values were placed against a *cantus firmus* in whole- or half-notes. Johann Joseph Fux codified this technique in his *Gradus ad Parnassum*, 1725. Fux explained the *stile antico* as he saw it, presumably the style of Palestrina, covering strict control of dissonance, part-writing, and melodic behavior of notes of all values. The cornerstone of the Fuxian system was *species counterpoint*; the five species dealt respectively with whole-notes, half-notes, quarter-notes, suspensions, and mixed values against a *cantus firmus*.[4]

Every well-trained musician had his tour of contrapuntal duty as a student. Haydn worked directly with the *Gradus*; Mozart's instructions to Attwood show his reliance upon this discipline; Beethoven had solid instruction from Albrechtsberger along these lines.

Species counterpoint is an artificial system. Its codifications lead to a rigidity of procedure quite different from the flexible flow of Renaissance polyphony; its oversimplified view of the church modes overlooks the structural and expressive subtleties of 16th-century theory and practice. Paradoxically, its greatest value for classic music was to provide a firm textural underpinning for *galant* music, far removed from the lean and rigorous terms of the *stile antico*. Classic style retained some features of the Fuxian system, while making some profound modifications. The following features were retained:

1. A *cantus firmus* in long notes used as a structural melody
2. Species counterpoint against a *cantus firmus*
3. Two-part writing as a basic texture

4. Relatively short periods or phrases, comparable in length to the exercises of Fux

5. Slow and regular changes of chord, one or two per measure

6. Extensive use of fourth species counterpoint

Modifications of Fuxian procedure included the following:

1. The major-minor system of harmony replaced the church modes. Fux retained the interval and chord structure of the modal system, using cadential action only to close a phrase. Classic music saturated its counterpoint with cadential formulas and reinforced the key with secondary dominants. Ex. 7-3a is a typical two-part first species counterpoint by Fux. Exs. 7-3b and 7-3c are from Koch's *Versuch*, 1782, the first diatonic, the second chromatic; both use cadential formulas exclusively; their "modern" flavor contrasts strikingly with the austere "antique" manner of the Fux example, which contains but one cadential formula and carefully avoids the tritone. Koch completely ignores the *stile antico*. His examples all have a cadential-periodic thrust. On the other hand, Kirnberger, with his retrospective view, is still concerned with the ancient modal system and its presence in the music of J. S. Bach.[5]

2. Ecclesiastical melodies were eliminated as *cantus firmi*, except for chorale tunes and a few liturgical melodies of Catholic origin. In their place, structural melodies that sketch cadential formulas, sequences, and conjunct lines were used.

3. The melodic declamation of the *stile antico*, flowing and continuous, was set aside in favor of figured melodies, punctuated and symmetrical.

4. The careful mixing of harmonic intervals in the Fuxian system, to provide variety, often gave way in classic counterpoint to chains of similar intervals, thirds or sixths. Tritones, always the *diaboli* in the *stile antico*, were prominent among the useful intervals in classic counterpoint, as in Ex. 7-3c.

Ex. 7-3.   *Two-part first species counterpoint.*

a. Fux, *Gradus ad Parnassum*, 1725, ch. 1.

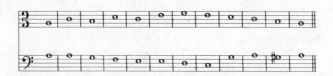

b. *Diatonic*, Koch, *Versuch*, I, 1782, p. 282.

c. *Chromatic*, Koch, *Versuch*, I, 1782, p. 298.

Alla breve was referred to in Ch. 2 as a topic in classic music. Some further examples of *alla breve* melodies serving as *cantus firmi* are:

First species, note against note

Beethoven, Sonata in C minor, Op. 13, circa 1798, finale, m. 80 et seq.

Haydn, Quartet in C minor, Op. 17, No. 4, 1771, first movement, mm. 70-85

Third species, four or more notes against one

Haydn, Symphony No. 40 in F major, 1763, entire finale

Mozart, Quintet in D major, K. 593, 1790, first movement, mm. 81-84, 206-211

Fourth species, suspensions

Haydn, Symphony No. 95 in C minor, 1793, m. 33 et seq.

Beethoven, Quartet in E♭ major, Op. 74, 1809, third movement, mm. 96-103

Figured Counterpoint

Figured counterpoint was synonymous with musical composition itself in the prevailing free style. To show the relationship of figured counterpoint to *alla breve* counterpoint — comparable to the relationship of figured and simple melody — Exs. 7-4 and 7-5 reduce passages in galant style. These reductions reverse the processes of composition — elaboration, variation, paraphrase — to expose some of the underlying structural configurations.

In Ex. 7-4 the floridity and variety of ornamentation typical of C. P. E. Bach's keyboard music decorate a bourrée rhythm; the reduction makes this clear and points up the sequence that provides an initial symmetry for the period. Both the topic and the structure are disguised by the irregularity of the figured melody.

Ex. 7-4. *Reduction to first and second species counterpoint.* C.P.E. Bach, *Kenner und Liebhaber*, series I, 1779, Sonata No. 3 in B minor, 1st movt.

a. Figured melodic lines

Breitkopf

Ex. 7-4, cont'd.

b. Structural lines

In Ex. 7-5 the figures ornament a simple three-voice counterpoint. Perhaps Mozart began with this framework, elaborating the bass with *mordents, tiratas,* and *groppi.* Having devised the figured melody, he may have decided to isolate it as the opening unison theme of the overture. Later, upon its return, it would assume its original role—that of a florid lower voice in a species counterpoint. This effervescent melody, free as it seems, is still subject to the law of the strict style, to the rule of old Grandpa Fux. (See also Beethoven, Quartet in C major, Op. 59, No. 3, 1806, finale.)

Ex. 7-5. Mozart, *The Marriage of Figaro,* K. 492, 1785-1786, overture.

Philharmonia

reduction of mm. 156-164

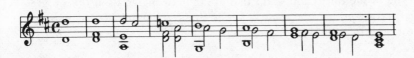

Descending Sixth Chords

Classic counterpoint, as demonstrated above, deals principally with cadential formulas. Apart from cadential formulas, we often find harmonic progression by descending sixth chords. Like the sequence by descending fifths, this was a highly useful pattern, appearing many times in 18th-century music, from Alessandro Scarlatti to Beethoven. Basically, it is an amplification of a descending conjunct melodic line, capable of sustaining a high degree of ornamentation and ideal for incorporating elaborated suspensions. It could be fitted into a period at any point preceding the cadence, and thanks to its thrust, it built cadential drive. Its fixed structural lines and its length (two to five or more measures) suggest that it was an even more obvious prefabricated stereotype than cadences themselves.

C. P. E. Bach used descending sixth-chords in his "Einfall einen doppelten Contrapunct von sechs Tacten zu machen ohne die Regeln devon zu wissen," ("A Scheme for Writing Six Measures of Double Counterpoint without Having to Know the Rules Thereof"), 1757.[6] He adapted the method of the dice games to distribute the melodic material. He invented nine different figures for each measure of the treble and bass, then placed the notes in tables according to a code which the player himself had to decipher. Each figure of each measure can serve either as bass or treble to any of the other figures; some trillion or more variants are available. Ex. 7-6 gives the first measure of the scheme, a sample counterpoint taken from Bach's figures, and the two-part species counterpoint upon which the scheme must have been based, not set down by Bach himself. All the figures, when reduced to their structural lines, converge precisely upon this species counterpoint. In this scheme the alpha and omega of 18th-century music are joined; the mindless toss of the dice is linked to the strict style, setting forth the wonder of the *Ars Combinatoria*.

Bach's ingenuity in the "Einfall" was involved in exploring the possibilities of figuration within the narrow confines of a six-measure simple counterpoint. Ingenuity of another sort was applied by Mozart in carrying a descending line of thirds and sixths throughout a 12-measure period, in the Duo for Violin and Viola in G major, K. 423, first movement, mm. 112–123 (see Ex. 7-7). The period begins innocently enough, as a singing melody with a quasi-Alberti accompaniment. But very soon its real structural purpose is revealed—to build the theme upon a long line of descending thirds and sixths. Starting with the B of the violin, the descent covers more than four octaves (with necessary transpositions) until the C that fixes subdominant-function harmony is reached; at this point there is a broad gesture of hemiolia on the half-note level, a powerful braking effect to the accumulating stretto of the preceding four measures. Texture and harmony contribute thrust and tension to this remarkable passage. The melody gradually becomes entangled with the accompanying eighth-notes; the two instruments alternate as upper and lower voices; changes of register, inversions, and a rich color of secondary dominants provide a subtle yet kaleidoscopic illumination of the thirds and sixths that are the raw materials of this progression. This is truly *prima intenzione*, a period that has but one idea, carried forward inexorably to its final peroration.

Ex. 7-6. *"A Scheme for Writing Six Measures of Double Counterpoint ...,"*
C.P.E. Bach, 1757.

a. Measures 1 & 2 of treble and bass.

b. Sample counterpoint.

c. Species counterpoint; basis for scheme [ed.].

Ex. 7-7. *First species counterpoint in descending thirds and sixths.* Mozart, Duo for Violin and Viola in G major, K. 423, 1783, 1st movt.

a. Figured melodic lines

Edwards

b. Structural lines

While classic music maintained the tradition of treble-bass polarity, it changed the emphasis to give the melody more responsibility as the governing voice in the texture. This difference in emphasis was reflected in music theory. Some theorists saw the advantages, especially for amateurs and dilettantes, of dealing with the melodic stereotypes that had become so familiar.[7] On May 14, 1778, Mozart wrote to his father that one of his pupils "filled in quite a good bass" to a minuet melody he had provided.[8] As was pointed out in Ch. 6, this shift of focus on melody arose from the ability of classic melody to delineate a greater proportion of the musical content of a passage while the previously very active continuo bass receded to a modest role of punctuation and chord support in a context of relatively slow rate of chord change. The focus on melody also opened the way to dispersal of melodic activity among the component voices in a texture, to a freer and more lively give-and-take. How this was done is the subject of the next three chapters.

NOTES

1. Koch, *Versuch*, II, p. 257ff; Daube, *Dilettant*, p. 15ff; Jones, *Treatise*, ch. 8; Momigny, *Cours complet*, passim.
2. In Hoboken, *Haydn: Werkverzeichnis*, I, most of Haydn's later symphonies are listed as having been published in various arrangements — keyboard alone or with flute, violin, violoncello — as well as in orchestral parts and later in full score.
3. See Kirkendale, *Fuge und Fugato*; W. A. Mozart, *Neue Ausgabe sämtlicher Werke*, series 10:30, pt. I, "Attwood-Studien," prepared by Erich Hertzmann, Cecil B. Oldman, Daniel Heartz, and Alfred Mann, Bärenreiter, Kassel, 1965.
4. Other works oriented similarly are Martini, *Saggio*; Kirnberger, *Kunst*; Marpurg, *Handbuch*; Albrechtsberger, *Gründliche Anweisung*. Koch, *Versuch*, I, also applies this technique (see p. 111 of the present work).
5. Kirnberger, *Kunst*, II, pt. 1, pp. 41-67.
6. Marpurg, *Historisch-kritische Beyträge*, III, pt. 1, p. 167ff.
7. Treatises principally oriented to figured bass are Heinichen, *General-bass*; Gasparini, *L'armonico*; Paisiello, *Regole;* Jones, *Treatise*; C. P. E. Bach, *Versuch*; Mattheson, *Exemplarische Organisten-Probe* (as well as his two thorough-bass treatises). Treatises principally oriented to melody are Daube, *Melodie*; Langlé, *Traité de la basse*; Riepel, *Anfangsgründe, Grundregeln*; Reicha, *Mélodie*; Koch, *Versuch*, III.
8. Anderson, *The Letters of Mozart*, p. 538.

8 Texture: Chamber Music

Classic textures have strong mimetic values. Individual voices or parts in an ensemble can move with or against each other much as actors or dancers do on the stage. Their musical figures are like gestures, taking on bold relief in the free and varied interplay of classic part-writing. The typical sound of classic instrumental music—transparent, with neat and uncluttered layouts and luminous, balanced sonorities—promotes this "little theater" in each of the textures described below.

CHAMBER MUSIC

Chamber music, throughout the 18th century, signified music performed in a salon or private chamber or in the concert room of a noble establishment. According to this definition, most genres of classic instrumental music could be subsumed under the title *chamber music*—sonatas, concertos, symphonies. The number of players was not prescribed. A concerto for an evening's entertainment could have one or more players to a part, according to its style.[1]

Chamber music had its own stylistic features (see Ch. 1), but church, chamber, and theater music borrowed heavily from each other. A symphony played as an overture to an opera would be a theater symphony, but if it opened a chamber concert it was a chamber symphony. A sonata could do double duty as a church or chamber sonata.

Toward the end of the century a sharper distinction was drawn between lightly scored chamber music—one to a part—and orchestral music. The term *chamber style* was coined to designate this genre,[2] a distinction that holds to the present day.

Chamber music includes solos, duos, trios, quartets, and larger genres with one to a part. The term *sonata* was often applied to these genres; critical and theoretical comments on the sonata cover the chamber style generally. The sonata is an elite genre, says Sulzer, 1771–1774, ideal for the expression of the feelings:

> Instrumental music has no better form in which to depict the sentiments without words than the sonata. . . . The composer is able to express sadness, lamentation, pain, gentleness, pleasure, and cheerfulness in a monologue of tones; . . . or simply to depict vigorous, stormy, contrasting, or light and flowing qualities of feeling.[3]

Koch, 1802, describes the sonata as "the most thoroughly-worked-out category of instrumental music."[4]

Chamber music scoring involves a wide range of options, given the basic framework of melody and bass. Brook's index to the *Breitkopf Catalogue*,

1762-1787, lists violin, viola, violoncello, flute, cembalo, guitar, lute, horn, bassoon, clarinet, mandolin, fortepiano, organ, etc., in hundreds of different combinations.

An aspect of classic chamber music scoring retained from earlier music was the distinction between *obbligato* voices—those essential to the texture—and *ad libitum* voices—those that were optional and could be omitted. This distinction applied principally to keyboard music, which will be discussed later in this chapter. Another *ad libitum* aspect was the interchangeability of instrumentation, whereby, in some works, the treble part could be performed by a violin, flute, or oboe and the bass by a violoncello, contrabass, or bassoon, in addition to other substitutions. The textural parameters for the following survey are (1) the *roles* played by the component voices—principal line, doubling or reinforcement, counterfigures, accompaniment, and bass; (2) *sonority effects* created by various combinations of instruments.

CHAMBER MUSIC WITHOUT KEYBOARD

Solo

Music for a single instrument—violin, flute—was used principally for pedagogical purposes in the later 18th century. String instruments lend themselves to unaccompanied solo music, since they can create, across the strings, the impression of several levels through the process of *Brechung*[5]—arpeggiation as well as changes of register to imply two or more voices in alternation—a procedure constantly used in baroque instrumental music (e.g., J. S. Bach's solo sonatas and partitas).

Ex. 8-1 illustrates this multilevel action, adapted to an Italianate galant style. In addition to the changes of register, there are changes of figure, as if a solo actor were portraying several roles. An alto voice begins, then is answered in m. 3 in the same singing style by the soprano. The *Brechung* in mm. 5-6, a brilliant bit of duet between alto and tenor, is answered in m. 7 by a touch of the *stile legato* as a duet between soprano and alto.

Ex. 8-1. *Solo texture.* Cambini, *Préludes, points d'orgues, airs varies, pour l'étude du violon..., n.d.*

VIOLINO SOLO

L'art de moduler sur le Violon avec l'emploi de tous les coups d'archet
pour servir de guide aux amateurs.

Duet

The instrumental duet is one of the most striking phenomena of the late 18th and early 19th centuries. Its repertory grew enormously during this period, especially after 1790. The *Breitkopf Catalogue*, 1762–1787, lists about 450 duets for violins and 300 for flutes, but an even greater number were written in later decades, particularly for violins. No doubt the popularity of the violin and flute as dilettante instruments encouraged this trend, but the essential features of the classic style were even more significant for the growth of this genre. The ability of a two-part texture to sketch the entire action of a piece, sometimes to provide a true bass, at other times to imply the bass by clearly defined, slowly moving cadential harmonies, enabled two voices to constitute a complete ensemble.

Duets were efficient teaching pieces, allowing mutual participation by master and pupil. They are also ideal *closet* pieces for the amusement of amateurs on every level of competence. Most of the string duets of the late 18th century were written by composers of the French violin school — Viotti, Rode, Kreutzer, Pleyel, and others. Mozart wrote only two, the Duos for Violin and Viola, K, 423, 424, 1783, which are masterpieces ranking with the very best of his chamber music. Haydn composed a half-dozen modest works; C. P. E. Bach just three.

Duets for instruments were classified as (1) compositions for a treble instrument with bass accompaniment, and (2) compositions for two melody instruments. The term *duet* was also applied to vocal compositions for two voices with accompaniment (see Ch. 10).

Melody-Bass Duets.   These cover two types of scoring:

1. A melody instrument with continuo accompaniment represented by the bass line. These are sonatas for solo and keyboard.

2. A melody instrument accompanied by violoncello, possibly viola or bassoon.

These two categories overlapped; a melody-bass duet could be performed either by two solo instruments or by solo and keyboard in many instances. Witthauer, in his 1791 revision of Löhlein's *Clavier-Schule*, includes six sonatas for treble and bass, with recommendations for realization of the continuo. In the foreword he says, "If one should perform these six sonatas with only violin and violoncello, hopefully they also will be pleasing."[6] Daube, 1773, comments similarly concerning trios, with an even stronger recommendation to use violoncell instead of clavier for better balance of sound.[7] Ex. 8-2 illustrates a duet texture that prescribes violin and violoncello. First the violoncello has a continuo-type figure; later it reverses roles with the violin, and in the last two measures quoted it proceeds with the violin in the typical parallel sixths of duet texture.

Ex. 8-2. *Duet for melody and bass.* Joseph Schmidt, Duet in C major, n.d., 1st movt.

Duets for Two Melody Instruments.   This genre achieved great popularity during the classic era, and the violin duet in particular flourished well into the 19th century.

Koch makes a distinction among earlier duets which are truly polyphonic and those newer compositions, which, in his words, are "almost entirely homophonic, and which are only to be differentiated from the solo by the fact that the two voices alternate in playing the melody, and that the accompaniment has more figuration than otherwise."[8] Sharing melody and accompaniment between phrases and periods is a hallmark of the French style of the turn of the century; it is present in the duets of Viotti, Pleyel, Cambini, and others, and points the way to the broadly blocked phrase and period structure of early romantic music.

To illustrate highly imaginative treatment of duet scoring, excerpts from a duet by Sébastian Demar are offered in Ex. 8-3. Demar was a contemporary of Viotti and director of the Conservatory in Orléans. This work, totally unknown and its composer forgotten, shows a felicity of invention and a skill of workmanship equal to those of the masters of the classic style, and demonstrates that there is still much of value to be discovered in the classic repertory.

Ex. 8-3. *Duet textures.* Demar, Duet for Two Violins in C major, Op. 3, No. 3 (from edition of Jean Böhme, Hamburg, n.d.).

a. *Parallel thirds.* Parallel thirds and sixths provide the fullest and sweetest sounds for two similar instruments. Koch recommends that these intervals be used, especially on accented beats, in two-part writing (*Lexikon*, p. 1773). Demar makes sparing use of this device, the overworking of which can quickly become cloying (see Ex. 7-2). Mozart solved the problem of maintaining a long line of thirds and sixths by ingenious modification of textural nuances (see Ex. 7-7).

b. *Brilliant figuration.* This important feature of late 18th-century violin duets is exemplified here by a brilliant tirata followed by arpeggios in dotted march rhythm. The octaves here act as a concerto-like tutti to set off solo sections that precede and follow.

c. *Singing style.* Note the varied figures in the accompaniment—*alla zoppa* rhythm as a countergesture to the steady 8th-notes of the melody, then parallel tenths, finally a touch of the Alberti bass .

d. *Fuller texture.* The three-part scoring here combines the suspensions of the *stile legato* in the first violin with march rhythms in the second in a tightly woven texture characterized by dense harmonic action.

Trio

The term *trio* was applied to (1) compositions for three instruments; (2) compositions for keyboard and another instrument providing a three-part texture; (3) the trio-sonata, a composition for two solo instruments accompanied by keyboard and a bass instrument; (4) the second of the pair of minuets often included in multimovement works—frequently written for three voices. In addition, the term *terzetto* was used to refer to vocal trios with accompaniment and to keyboard works in which violin and violoncello were *obbligato*.

String trios formed the bulk of the trio repertory—two violins and viola or violoncello; violin, viola, and violoncello. Yet the most celebrated collection of string trios in the classic era are the 126 trios for baryton (an instrument of the viola da gamba family, supplied with sympathetic strings), viola, and bass composed by Haydn during his service with the Esterhàzy family.

The trio that included a violoncello could supply what was only indicated in violin duets—a true bass, fuller texture, complete harmony. Daube, 1773, felt that this genre encompassed the essentials of good part-writing:

> This topic [three-part writing] is one of the most important in all composition. He who knows well how to combine three voices will find it a simple matter to work with many voices. The essentials of harmony depend upon three-part writing.[9]

Among the many hundreds of trios written in the classic era, the finest is Mozart's E♭ major Divertimento, K. 563, 1788. The scope of this work extends far beyond the entertainment usually provided by the divertimento, especially in the broadly scaled first movement and the profoundly pathetic Adagio. The textures of this work touch upon the buoyancy and transparency of the string duet and the fullness of the string quartet. The lightness of the three-voice setting is exploited thoroughly by Mozart in a brilliant and richly varied play of figures. Ex. 8-4a shows a typical trio scoring, with two voices in parallel motion playing an attractive melody over a trommel-bass, the viola set below the violoncello to allow the latter to support the violin melody in a resonant range. A bold contrast interrupts this pattern as the three voices each take up a different style—singing, brilliant, and true bass. Ex. 8-4b combines *stile legato* and florid melody in a four-part texture. Ex. 8-4c illustrates tightly spaced three-part imitation, while Ex. 8-4d reduces the texture to two parts, a melody and simple accompaniment.

Ex. 8-4.   *Trio textures.* Mozart, Divertimento in E♭ major, K. 563, 1788.

a. *Typical trio scoring.* 1st movt.

b. *Four-part writing.* 1st movt.

c. *Three-part imitation.* 1st movt.

d. *Melody and bass.* 4th movt.

Eulenburg No. 70

Wind instruments often figured in trio settings, the flute in particular sometimes being indicated as an alternative to the violin. As a rule, however, wind chamber music involved a larger ensemble (see p. 130f).

Quartet

For classic music the string quartet was a favorite genre. Koch, 1802, provides a contemporary view of the quartet:

> *Quatuor.* This instrumental composition for four instruments, which has been such a favorite for many years, is a special category of sonata, and in the strict sense, consists of four concerting instruments, none of which can claim exclusively the role of a leading voice [*Hauptstimme*]. If this is to be accomplished without confusion and without overloading the melodic material, the quartet, in the strict sense, must be composed as a fugue, or entirely in the strict style. In the modern quartets the free style is generally used; the four voices alternate in taking the lead; of these, now one, now another will provide the kind of bass which is usual in galant compositions. While one voice takes the leading melody, the two others [aside from the voice serving as a bass] must continue with complementary melodic material that will reinforce the expression without beclouding the leading melody. Therefore, it is easy to see that the working out of such a composition requires a composer who lacks nothing of genius or of the broadest knowledge of harmony.
>
> Furthermore, the quartet, in the last forty years, represents that category of sonata which has been most thoroughly cultivated, among which, without doubt, the masterworks of Haydn have contributed most. Among all

the pieces in this genre presently known to us, Mozart's four-voiced sonatas (apart from their aesthetic beauty) represent best the concept of a composition with four obbligato principal voices.[10]

Circumstances favorable to the rise of the quartet in the later 18th century included:

1. The diminishing role of the continuo in chamber music. In baroque music, the keyboard continuo was the center of the ensemble, governing harmony, rhythm, and sonority. As periodic structure became clarified, harmony grew simpler, with fewer and more regular changes; rhythmic symmetry enabled performers to maintain precision in tempo without the help of the continuo, while the melodic material assigned to leading voices was better projected with a minimum of support, due to its popular style. The sense of the music could be communicated without the support of a continuo.

2. Increasing activity among amateurs in chamber music and larger numbers of performers. The study of string instruments grew steadily, creating demand for music to meet the needs of this market.

3. The blend and balance of four string instruments, regarded at this time as an optimum texture, encompassing the lively play of solo instruments as well as the full harmony and richness of sound of a larger ensemble. Refinements in the construction of the instruments themselves contributed to the favored position of the string quartet.

In the duet and trio the problem was to create an impression of fullness and self-sufficiency with few parts. In the quartet and in larger ensembles, the material had to be arranged to give all voices a share in the action. One of the most remarkable features of the fully evolved classic string quartet is the imaginative distribution of important melodic material, a procedure that adds depth to the textural perspective and promotes the broad discursiveness which characterizes the masterworks of this genre.

As the string quartet matured in the 1760s and 1770s, this greater sophistication of part-writing is clearly visible. The early works of Haydn have a rather stiff patchwork of textures; his later works are marvels of ingenious part-writing. This is also true of Mozart. Boccherini, on the other hand, had a special flair for texture in all his chamber music.

While the quartets of Haydn and Mozart were much admired and performed, it was the Parisian composers—Viotti, Cambini, d'Alayrac, Gaveaux, St. Georges, and dozens of others—that produced the greatest number of quartets, writing for a lively market and contributing immensely to the popularity of this genre. Concern with texture was a striking feature of Parisian quartets, frequently designated as *quatuors concertants*. The term *concertant* also appears on the title pages of many *duos, trios, quatuors,* and *quintuors*. For chamber music, this term would mean:

1.   One instrument to a part
2.   All voices *obbligato*
3.   All voices sharing the principal melodic material
4.   Some passages in brilliant style[11]

Ex. 8-5 illustrates texture in a Parisian *quatuor concertant*. In the nine measures there are six different textural layouts, and more than 15 different figures. While the main line of discourse is taken by the first violin, the lower voices enliven the texture in a busy but orderly fashion, adding effervescence and flavor to the simple harmony and regular scansion. Within its expressive range, limited to an ingratiating interplay of the singing and brilliant styles, this work, as well as many others of its genre, achieves a fine balance of sound and motion which was utterly pleasing to its fashionable listeners.

Ex. 8-5.   *Concertant texture.* Cambini, Quartet No. 2, from *Twelve New Quartets,* 1788, 1st movt.

From Janet Levy, *The Quatuor Concertant in Paris* ..., unpublished dissertation, Stanford University, 1971. Copyright by the author and used by kind permission of the author and by courtesy of the Stanford University Libraries.

Most classic composers, at one time or another, wrote string quartets. Haydn, Mozart, Beethoven, Boccherini, Viotti, Pleyel, Cambini, and Albrechtsberger were specialists in this genre, as well as other composers mentioned by Momigny, 1806:

> The quartets of Haydn and Mozart are the admiration and delight of connoisseurs. Those of Pleyel, less profound but full of a natural quality and grace, appeal to the charm of sensitive and delicate souls. One cannot mention those of Boccherini without recalling a thousand pleasant feelings, and everyone has played with pleasure, in their time, those of Stamitz, [Carl], Davaux, and Cambini. In our day, we are happy to hear those of Kreutzer, which possess genuine beauties.[12]

Ex. 8-5 illustrates a decorative treatment of texture, each pattern neatly juxtaposed with its neighbors. The melody-accompaniment texture of Ex. 5-8, with its percussive rhythms, epitomizes the direct, single-minded thrust that carries throughout most of the movement. Ex. 5-6 illustrates texturally the furious give-and-take and the irregular scansion of the polonaise rhythm that governs this finale. Ex. 3-13 shows a typical broadly singing style, notable for the role of the texture in maintaining motion beyond the cadence point. The ultimate achievement in this aspect of quartet texture—broadly spun-out singing style—appears in the first movement of Beethoven's F major Quartet, Op. 59, No. 1, discussed in Ch. 24, and in the slow movements of his last quartets.

When a wind instrument—flute, oboe, clarinet—was included in the quartet, the piece was treated much in the manner of a solo wind concerto, as in Mozart's F major Quartet for Oboe and Strings, K. 370, 1781, and in his flute quartets. According to the writer of an article on "Quartettmusik" in *AMZ*, chamber music with winds was inferior to the string quartet, since it did not permit the free play of texture so prized in the latter, and consisted mostly of a series of solos taken in turn.[13]

The finale of Mozart's D major Quartet, K. 285, 1777, illustrates a typical texture for quartet with wind instrument. The flute begins the lively contredanse as a solo, to be answered at m. 9 by a tutti on the same tune. Such clear blocking out, typical of this genre, is infrequent in the string quartets of the classic masters.

Quintet

In his article on "Quintuor," Koch, 1802, refers the reader to "Quatuor" for specific commentary, considering these genres to have much in common. Yet the addition of a fifth string instrument—viola or violoncello—creates an added dimension, introducing the following two factors:

1. *Sonority*. The fifth voice, a second viola or violoncello, adds to the richness and fullness of chords, strengthens accents, and permits frequent doublings.

2. *Part-writing*. There is expanded textural play due to the great number of combinations, including the ability of the ensemble to separate into two tiny orchestras.

Mozart's and Boccherini's quintets are the most important in the classic repertory. Boccherini wrote 126, principally for two violins, viola, and two violoncellos, with the first violin and first violoncello serving as leaders in their respective
registers. Boccherini favored a sound in which slowly moving cadential harmony
was enlivened by sparkling figures, creating a "glitter," a rippling yet static effect. He must have learned this technique from his Italian predecessors, especially Vivaldi, whose concertos abound in such effects, as in "La Primavera" from
Le Stagione, circa 1725. Ex. 8-6 illustrates this procedure.

Ex. 8-6. *Quintet texture.* Boccherini, Quintet in E major, Op. 11, No. 5,
1771, 2nd movt.

Copyright 1941 by G. Ricordi & Co., Milan. Used by kind permission of the publisher.

The quintets of Mozart, K. 515, 516, 593, and 614, are the finest classic
achievements in this genre. Texture plays a significant role in the rich expressive
and rhetorical content of these works. The opening Allegros of each first movement contain, in their first measures, typical Mozartean manipulations of rhetorical elements.

Without prior knowledge, a listener might take the opening of the C major
Quintet, K. 515, 1787, as a string quartet; only at m. 16 is the integrity of the
quintet asserted, when all five instruments join on a wildly dissonant chord, a
quadruple appoggiatura over F in sharp contrast to the preceding tonics and
dominants. The beginning of the G minor Quintet, K. 516, 1787, is a trio for
two violins and viola, but the answering phrase opens the tenor and bass registers
to establish the quintet scoring; only at m. 18 does the full ensemble come together, again upon a striking change of harmonic quality. The blocked-out texture of mm. 1–17 frames the operatic style—a broadly singing melody in a pathetic vein.

In the Quintets in D major, K. 593, 1790, and Eb major, K. 614, 1791, the full
ensemble is introduced rather quickly in the opening Allegros, with contrasts of
solo and tutti. The neatly trimmed structure of the first movement of the Eb
Quintet is epitomized by the formal opposition of solo and tutti in mm. 1–4.

However, in the D major Quintet, the texture is crazy-quilt, in line with the *opera buffa* style of the piece. Ex. 8-7 outlines the changes in scoring that occur in mm. 1–8. (See also p. 387f.)

Ex. 8-7. *Changes in number of voices.* Mozart, Quintet in D major, K. 593, 1790, 1st movt.

Measures	1		2	5		4		5	6	7		8
Topics	fanfare			alla zoppa				brilliant		alternating		chords
Voices	5 2		2 6 5	6 5 6		5 4 4 10 8			8 1 8 3 6 3			6 3

Mozart used a decorative treatment, similar to that of Boccherini, in the second movement of the Eb major Quintet (Ex. 8-8), but instead of dispersing the action, the ornaments add a sparkle around the suave gavotte tune.

Ex. 8-8. *Decorative texture.* Mozart, Quintet in Eb major, K. 614, 1791, 2nd movt.

Edwards

A wind instrument gives the quintet the quality of a concerto. Mozart did not try to assimilate the sound of the horn to the strings in his Eb major Horn Quintet, K. 407, 1782, but highlighted their contrasting timbres. The instruments merge only at important cadential points. The Clarinet Quintet, K. 581, 1789, treats clarinet and first violin as soloists but also blends the clarinet with the ensemble effectively, thanks to the compatible tone qualities of clarinet and strings. Ex. 2-21 quotes from this work.

Larger Ensembles

Wind instruments generally figured in larger ensembles. While no standard scoring existed, the convention was to use flutes, oboes, horns, clarinets, bassoons, occasionally trumpets in pairs. Whatever the combination, the wind sound imparted an outdoor flavor — military, rustic, ceremonial — to the texture. Some of Haydn's early partitas use pairs of oboes, horns, and bassoons; Mozart's Serenade in E♭ major, K. 375, was scored for clarinets, horns, and bassoon, and Mozart himself later rescored it to include oboes.

Toward the end of the 18th century, wind instruments came into great prominence. This relatively new trend was noted in the following comment in *AMZ*, 1799:

> No advantage of the newer music over the old is more striking at first glance than the manifold and brilliant use of wind instruments. While older composers used these instruments singly and sparingly, only to reinforce the strings, the newer masters use them in so many different ways that it would be too laborious to list them. . . . This advantage arises in part from the fact that almost all wind instruments have achieved an inner perfection, for example, the improved flute, bassoon, the horns and trumpets with changeable crooks, etc. . . . How seldom do we hear an aria without an accompaniment of a company of horns, oboes, flutes, and bassoons! Certainly, one becomes so accustomed to this musical luxury provided by the otherwise charming, truly heavenly tones of the wind instruments that a kind of surfeiting takes place. . . . Wind instrument tones approach most closely that most divine of all instruments, the human voice. . . . They touch the feelings much more quickly and surely than do those of the strings. . . . [14]

Classic instrumental music took full advantage of the special qualities of the winds — clear, crisp, penetrating, yet capable of handling a beautiful *cantilena*, excellent in parallel thirds and sixths, in octaves, and horn fifths. With strings they add richness and a clear edge to the sound; alone they create a layered texture, giving a tutti the effect of a colorfully banded spectrum. Ex. 8-9 contains many typical wind effects — fanfare, unison, two-part writing doubled, parallel thirds, horn fifths, colorful give-and-take.

Ex. 8-9. *Wind texture.* Haydn, *Feldpartie* in C, ca. 1765.

Ex. 8-9, cont'd.

Wind chamber music was composed principally for light entertainment. Mozart's early divertimenti consist mainly of short dances, marches, and arias. But his Serenades in B♭ major, K. 361, 1781, in E♭ major, K. 375, 1782, and in C minor, K. 388, 1782, are important works comparable to his string chamber music. The C minor Serenade was rewritten as a string quintet, K. 406, 1787, but this arrangement still betrays the wind style and does not have the idiomatic string treatment of the other string quintets.

The *first movements* of these serenades carry the greatest musical content. K. 361 retains much of the divertimento flavor with a pleasing variety of short, well-turned melodic ideas, bold contrasts, and many passages in parallel thirds. K. 388 has the character of a fantasia, or perhaps an operatic scene, with its noble pathetic manner. K. 375 has the grandest scale of all, with striking affinity to the first movement of the *Symphonie Concertante* in E♭ major, K. 364, 1779. Its opening in high ceremonial style, the frequent use of *stile legato*, its broad melodic sweep, the variety of texture with relatively little use of parallel thirds, such details as the drawn-out cadential drive in the first period, mm. 13–25 (note the texture of this passage), and its considerable length, 238 measures of deliberate allegro maestoso—all contribute to the scope of this movement. Ex. 8-10 quotes the first period showing the topics—ceremonial march, *stile legato*—and the opening of the second period with its alternation of fanfare and brilliant styles.

Ex. 8-10. Mozart, Serenade in E♭ major, K. 375, 1782, 1st movt.

stile legato

Ex. 8-10, cont'd.

fanfare

brilliant
(fourth
measure)

brilliant

Kalmus

CHAMBER MUSIC WITH KEYBOARD

Although the harpsichord and clavichord were still in use in the late 18th century, the principal keyboard instrument in classic music was the *fortepiano*. Schubart, 1785, called it an "excellent" instrument; Koch said that it was the favorite of the keyboard player. The keyboard was used as (1) solo, (2) continuo, accompaniment, (3) principal ensemble instrument, or (4) *obbligato* partner in the ensemble.

Solo

The newly evolved fortepiano of the later 18th century was a popular house instrument; it could serve as a surrogate for the large ensembles of the opera house, church, and concert hall. An amateur could recreate scenes from the theater, battles, dances, arias, processions, Turkish and rustic effects. Dent refers to this use of the keyboard:

> What the Germans were aiming at in their harpsichord sonatas [the same could apply to piano sonatas] was the reproduction for domestic consumption of those wonderful Italian arias which every Italian could hear in the theatre as often as he liked, but which only rarely came the way of the music lover north of the Alps.[15]

In the first movements of Mozart's keyboard sonatas, we can hear the following styles:

Concerto: K. 279, 309, 457

Wind serenade, K. 281, 282, 330, 332, 333, 576

Italian *opera sinfonia*: K. 284, 311

Turkish music: K. 310

As a self-contained ensemble, a classic keyboard instrument could range through solo, duet, trio texture to the point that it became a full seven- or eight-part tutti. Nevertheless, the natural "grain" ran to two parts, simple or reinforced, a typical layout for the relatively uncomplicated teaching and entertainment pieces of this era.

The most characteristic feature of classic keyboard texture is the *Alberti bass*, presumably invented by Domenico Alberti about 1735–1740. Its broken chord figures, rarely exceeding an octave, provided a facile way to achieve full harmony, establish rhythmic punctuation, and give a modest yet firm support to a singing melody. Newman considers the Alberti bass a critical factor in the evolution of the classic keyboard style.[16] Its efficiency and ease of performance bespeak the growth of amateur music-making with the newly popular fortepiano. This figuration was also called the *Harfen-bass* (harp-bass).[17] (See Ex. 3-4.)

Another popular accompaniment figure, even simpler than the Alberti bass, is the *murky*, a bass in broken octaves. More than once we read disparaging comments about the dullness and "cheapness" of this figuration, yet in Ex. 8-11 the murky bass aptly suits the topic, a rustic, somewhat "flat-footed" contredanse.

Ex. 8-11.   *Murky bass.* Koch, *Lexikon*, p. 985.

While the Alberti and murky basses and similar figures are typical of much classic keyboard texture, they by no means constitute the principal textures in many works. Ex. 8-12 illustrates keyboard textures that suggest various genres. Ex. 8-12a is in dialogue, as if performed by winds in a playful contredanse finale to a divertimento. Ex. 8-12b is a grand peroration to the most broadly scaled and fantastic first movement that Mozart wrote for keyboard, and it imitates the final flourishes of a concerto movement. Ex. 8-12c is an *alla breve* in strict style, with the flavor of a Turkish march, and could easily be imagined for orchestra with tremolo support by the bass strings or timpani.

Ex. 8-12. *Keyboard textures.*

a. *Dialogue texture, two and three parts.* Haydn, Sonata in Bb major, H.V. XVI, No. 41, 1784, finale.

From Haydn, *Sämtliche Klaviersonaten* (Christa Landon, ed.). Copyright 1964 by Universal Edition A.G. Wien. Used by kind permission of the publisher.

b. *Elaborate figuration.* Mozart, Sonata in F major, K. 533, 1788, 1st movt.

From Mozart, *Sonatas and Fantasias for the Piano* (Nathan Broder, ed.). Copyright 1956, 1960 by Theodore Presser Company, Bryn Mawr. Used by kind permission of the publisher.

c. *Bound or strict style in four voices.* Mozart, Sonata in A minor, K. 310, 1778, 1st movt.

From Mozart, *Sonatas and Fantasias for the Piano* (Nathan Broder, ed.). Copyright 1956, 1960 by Theodore Presser Company, Bryn Mawr. Used by kind permission of the publisher.

Four-hand keyboard music, at one or two keyboards, adds a dimension to the texture but does not alter the basic premises of the keyboard genre. In the four-hand sonatas of J. C. Bach and Mozart, doubling marks out the component lines more heavily, there is more give-and-take, a decided *concertante* aspect in statement and response, and occasional very full sonorities. Layouts include (1) the master-pupil relationship in teaching pieces, in which the master plays an Alberti-type bass and the pupil takes the singing treble; (2) chamber-style dialogue; (3) some imitation of full orchestral sound with doubling of outer voices. The spirit of chamber music comes alive in four-hand sonatas, but like two-hand works they are also surrogates for the grander ensembles of classic music. Mozart's D major Sonata, K. 448, 1781, is in the manner of an Italian *sinfonia*; his F major Sonata for four hands at one keyboard, K. 497, 1786, is a great symphonic piece, on the scale of the *Prague* Symphony.

Continuo; Accompaniment

In baroque music, ensemble pieces normally specified a *continuo*, played by a keyboard instrument, with the bass line reinforced by some string or wind instrument. The keyboard, generally a harpsichord, was the "authority figure" in the ensemble, leading the quick and often irregular changes of chord, completing the rather thin sonority, and controlling the steady compact rhythm. The continuo performer also had to be something of a composer himself, to introduce melodic figures where apt, to ornament the bass. Manuals of continuo instruction such as Mattheson's *Grosse General-Bass-Schule*, 1731, and Heinichen's *Der General-Bass in der Composition*, 1728, require a high degree of musicianship for the realization of their very elaborate basses for arias, sonata, and concerto movements.

Late 18th-century continuo practice called for simpler realizations, as a rule. Unobtrusive supporting harmony, with some doubling of the melody and occasional bass elaboration, constituted the conventional procedure. Türk's *Kurze Anweisung zum General-Bassspielen*, 1787, the leading continuo manual of its time, is rigorous in its rules for part-writing but gives exercises in straightforward chord progressions with very little elaboration.

The replacement of the harpsichord by the fortepiano as the favorite keyboard instrument had some effect upon continuo practice. Koch says, 1802:

> In a concert hall, and in lightly-scored works, the penetrating tone of this instrument [harpsichord] is too shrill for passages that should be performed with light tone and fine nuance, and the sound is too choppy, partly because the performer must strike the chords with the right hand and partly because the instrument is incapable of any modification of tone quality . . . because of this drawback, in music in the present taste which is scored more lightly than music of previous times, the weaker but softer fortepiano has taken the place of the harpsichord. . . .[18]

These comments imply a thinner texture and a more active participation by the fortepiano in the give-and-take of melodic material, stylistic features that reduce the need for a continuo or eliminate it entirely.

Still, the continuo remained a factor in classic performance. It was thoroughly explained in composition manuals, such as Kirnberger's *Kunst*, 1771–1779, Paisiello's *Regole*, 1782, and Türk's *Anweisung*, 1787; in Witthauer's revision of Löhlein's *Clavier-Schule*, 1791, part II consists principally of six sonatas for violin and bass (unfigured) with detailed recommendations for the realization of the bass (see p. 120). The continuo was mandatory in church music and simple recitative. It was often used in full-voiced compositions. It disappeared in the new style of chamber music, yet was available, and may well have been used at times to substitute for missing parts or to reinforce the bass.

Keyboard as Principal Instrument

The keyboard as a *principal* instrument had much the same purpose as in solo texture — to create a complete ensemble.[19] Works in this genre were published as *sonatas* for cembalo or clavier with violin, flute, etc., *ad libitum*, or as *trios* specified for cembalo *obbligato* with another instrument. The added instrument played sustained tones, doubled melodic lines, reinforced accompanying figures, proceeded in parallel thirds and sixths to leading voices, but took little or no independent material; hence it could be omitted in performance, but the availability of an *ad libitum* part opened a new market area for publishers of keyboard sonatas.

Ex. 8-13 demonstrates a minimum *ad libitum* part, here provided by the composer (but in many other works added by another composer, as Burney did for some Haydn sonatas). The violin moves in thirds and sixths or simply holds a pedal tone. The texture is typical of J. C. Bach's style—full of ingratiating melodic content, neatly turned, with little room for complicated and sophisticated *obbligato* texture.

Ex. 8-13. *Ad libitum texture.* J. C. Bach, Sonata in B♭ major, Op. 10, No. 1, 177[?], 1st movt.

In the sonata excerpted in Ex. 8-14, Boccherini added a dimension of color and action by inserting some well-turned violin figures to supplement the self-sufficient keyboard texture.

Ex. 8-14. Boccherini, Sonata for Cembalo and Violin obbligato, Op. 5, No. 4, 1768, 1st movt. (violin and cembalo issued separately).

Ex. 8-14, cont'd.

[Cembalo]

Keyboard as Obbligato Partner in the Ensemble

In *obbligato* chamber music, the keyboard retains its preeminent role. Works are often designated as trios or quartets for cembalo with accompanying instruments; occasionally, the term *violin obbligato* or *violoncello obbligato* appears on a title page. Mozart began some 59 of 67 movements in his keyboard chamber music with solo or leading piano, establishing this instrument as the principal frame of reference. In the Beethoven piano-violin sonatas, 24 of the 33 movements begin similarly.

No clear line can be drawn between substantial decoration and true *obbligato* texture. In Exs. 8-14 and 8-15, the melodic material of the violin might be omitted. In Ex. 8-15, the structural progression is a fourth species counterpoint with the bass brilliantly elaborated. The violin figure is interpolated, yet this dance-like figure adds a new dimension through its striking contrast to the strict style of the keyboard.

Ex. 8-15. *Obbligato cembalo and violin texture.* Mozart, Sonata in A major, K. 526, 1787, finale.

a. Figured melodic lines

From Mozart, *Sonaten für Klavier und Violine* (Arthur Schnabel and Carl Flesch, eds.). Copyright 1912, 1940 by C.F. Peters Corporation, New York, London, Frankfurt. Used by kind permission of the publisher.

b. Structural lines

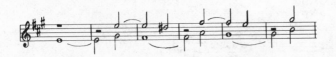

The usual roles for the cembalo in accompanied chamber music were tutti and solo. In Ex. 8-16 the clavier plays a different part, as if to furnish a flute and a second bassoon to the principal winds.

Ex. 8-16. *Piano in complementary role.* Mozart, Quintet for Clavier and Winds (Oboe, Clarinet, Horn, Bassoon) in E♭ major, K. 452, 1784, 1st movt.

Edwards

Texture was taught principally in terms of correct voice-leading, proper realization of the harmony, and assignment of material to various parts. Comments on tone color and sonority are very scarce. One of the few works to deal with texture extensively, Daube's *Dilettant*, 1773, says the following about sonority:

It is certain that harmony has many effects. A chord that has wide intervals creates an entirely different impression than a chord in close position . . . a chord sounds best in the middle range. Its effect is good on the organ, *Flügel*, or *Klavier*, even better when played by two violins and violoncello. Played by wind instruments of similar and different classes, with or without string instruments, again the effect is quite different . . . two oboes sound better in thirds, flutes in sixths . . . a complete chord, assisted by horns, has a magnificent sound. . . . When the violins are muted, and the winds blow softly, a doubled chord sounds delicate. When the oboe plays an octave above the violin, this unusual setting creates an excellent effect. The truth is: the tone quality of each instrument contributes much to the expression of the affects.[20]

Daube's comments are consistent with modern ideas of scoring, by tone color, not by clef exclusively; his ideas reflect the newer and more precise view of scoring of the late 18th century.

Chamber music ranked below church and theater music in the 18th century both in importance and dignity. Yet it served as a clearinghouse for texture and topic. It provided something for everybody—simple duets and trios for beginners, brilliant works for virtuosi. More important, in drawing upon material from church, theater, and concert hall, it could treat this material flexibly and speculatively, enjoying a freedom of rhetoric and structure not present in the protocol of church and theater. This speculative trend achieved its apex in the mature works of Haydn and Mozart, and above all in the later quartets of Beethoven, but the music never lost touch with topic; indeed, it is in classic chamber music that the kaleidoscopic variety of the classic style is most vividly manifested.

Classic chamber music was published in sets of parts; hence it remains inaccessible for study in score except for the works of Haydn, Mozart, Beethoven, as well as items from Boccherini, the Bach sons, and a few others. But recent research has produced modern editions acquainting us with a wealth of brilliant, finely drawn, ingratiating music by Viotti, Cambini, d'Alayrac, St. Georges, Dittersdorf, Karl Stamitz, and many others. As this enormous corpus of music becomes more visible, we can more surely assess the role of the chamber style in classic music—to assimilate material from other genres and deliver it to the rapidly growing musical public of the late 18th century in neat and manageable packages.

NOTES

1. Quantz, *Versuch*, p. 295.
2. Koch, *Lexikon*, p. 1454.
3. Sulzer, *Allgemeine Theorie*, p. 1094.
4. Koch, *Lexikon*, p. 1417.
5. This term was generally applied to arpeggios (Türk, *Klavierschule*, p. 249f.), but can be extended to cover the string procedure described here.
6. Löhlein, *Löhleins Clavier-Schule*, rev. Witthauer, II, preface.
7. Daube, *Dilettant*, p. 89.
8. Koch, *Lexikon*, p. 502. Jones, *Treatise*, p. 43, also speaks to this point: "the moderns; who are apt to throw their Air into a single part; one taking it while another has laid it down; while all the rest are servile accompaniments; and the Base little more than a divided drone."
9. Daube, *Dilettant*, p. 40.
10. Koch, *Lexikon*, pp. 1209-1210.
11. See Levy, *Quatuor Concertant*, for a detailed study of this genre.
12. Momigny, *Cours complet*, pp. 693-694.

13. *AMZ*, 1810, p. 513ff.
14. Ibid., 1799, pp. 193-194.
15. Dent, "Italian Opera in the Eighteenth Century," *SIMG*, XIV, 1912-1913, p. 509.
16. See Newman, *Sonata in the Classic Era*, p. 180ff., for a discussion of this technique.
17. Koch, *Lexikon*, p. 722; Türk, *Klavierschule*, p. 326.
18. Koch, *Lexikon*, pp. 587-588.
19. See Newman, *Sonata in the Classic Era*, p. 48ff.
20. Daube, *Dilettant*, pp. 4-6.

9 Texture: Orchestral Music

Orchestral music represented the most spectacular manifestation of a new trend in the later 18th century—the increasing importance of instrumental music. This was noted in critical comment in *AMZ*: "Instrumental music increasingly freed itself from vocal music . . . ."[1] In 1796 John Marsh spoke of "the revolution in instrumental music."[2] Toward the end of the century we find greater attention given to scoring in theoretical treatises.[3]

Originally, the symphony, the most important orchestral genre, served to open or close theatrical or church performances. While it fulfilled much the same purpose in late 18th-century concerts, its scope increased and the comments of critics are evidence of its rise to a position of great dignity.[4]

The sample program given below includes three symphonies. While these serve to frame the "star" attractions of the concert—the concertos, arias, and virtuoso chamber-style works—the amount of time and attention given to pure orchestral music bespeaks an importance that it lacked formerly.

HANOVER-SQUARE

WEDNESDAY, MARCH THE 26TH, 1783

First Act.

Overture—HAYDN.
Song, Superbo di me stesso—Signor BARTOLINI.
Concerto, Violin—Mr. SALOMON.
Concerto, Harpsichord—Master CRAMER.
Song, Idol mio serena i rai—CANTELO.
Concerto Grosso, for Two Violins, and Two Violoncellos—
by Messrs. CRAMER, PIELTAIN, CERVETTO. and DUPORT;
composed by Mr. GRAFF

Second Act.
Sinfonie, for Two Orchestras—BACH.
The favorite Trio for Flute, Hautboy, and Violoncello—
by MESSRS. WEISS, FISCHER, and DUPORT; composed by PLA.
Song, So che fedele—Miss CANTELO.
Concerto, Violoncello—Mr. DUPORT.
Sinfonie—STAMITZ.

The Doors to be opened at SEVEN, to begin at EIGHT
o'Clock precisely.

THE CLASSIC ORCHESTRAL STYLE

The fully evolved classic orchestral style arose out of the confluence of theater and chamber music. From the theater came the size of the orchestra and its fullness of sound. Chamber music provided the basic texture — the polarity of melody and bass and the preeminence of the strings. These two aspects are inferred in the following remarks by Koch, 1793:

> In the first *allegro* of a symphony, the melodic material, for reasons given above, is not so completely rounded as in those compositions in which one main voice performs . . . rather, this material must distinguish itself through inner strength and emphasis, and the feeling must carry all before it, rather than be presented in minutely detailed fashion. In the first *allegro* of such a composition there generally prevails a somewhat exalted feeling which is projected with a certain intensity; consequently most of the half- and full-cadences do not arrive at a point of rest . . . but by telescoping measures, these caesuras are passed over, so that the melody flows forward. So that the caesuras can be disguised in such a piece, the auxiliary voices, second violin, or bass, take over motifs from the first violin, when the first violin moves on to new motifs; or the auxiliary voices imitate each other while the first violin acts as a filler; this is because, in the symphony, the auxiliary voices fail to appear to best advantage when, for example, the second violin only fills out the harmony, or always plays in unison with the first violin, and the bass takes only the bare groundtones of the chords.[6]

Koch also quotes from Sulzer's *Allgemeine Theorie*, 1771-1774:

> The symphony is especially dedicated to the expression of the grand, the solemn, and the exalted. Its object is to prepare the listener for an important musical event, or in a chamber concert, to offer the full splendor of the orchestra. If it is to realize these aims sufficiently, and become an integral part of the opera or church music to follow, then it must, in addition to the expression of the grand and solemn, contain something of the expressive quality of the succeeding music, and distinguish stylistically between theater and church manner, according to the occasion.
>
> The chamber symphony, which constitutes a self-sufficient entity, without reference to any following music, achieves its aims only by means of a full-toned, brilliant, and fiery manner. The *allegros* of the best chamber symphonies contain grand and bold ideas, free handling of compositional techniques, apparent irregularity in the melody and harmony, strongly-marked rhythms of various sorts, powerful bass melodies and unisons, concerting middle voices, free imitations, often a theme handled fugally, sudden transitions and shifts from one key to another, which are the more striking the weaker the connection is, bold shadings of *forte* and *piano*, and particularly the *crescendo*, which has the greatest effect when used with a rising and climaxing melody.[7]

The "exalted" feeling in the symphony comes from the *opera seria* and church music; the interplay of voices is taken from *concertante* chamber music. These two aspects appear constantly in classic symphonies. The opening of Mozart's *Jupiter* Symphony sets them in juxtaposition, maintaining their alternation throughout, with the grand, exalted vein dominating.

Strings constituted the four principal voices in a classic orchestral score. Kollmann, 1799, refers to the four principal instruments as "the first Violin, the second Violin, the Viola or Tenor, and the Violoncello or Bass."[8] The same distinction is made in Koch, 1802,[9] and Momigny, 1806.[10] Various recommendations are made for adding winds to the strings. Momigny, in his analysis of Haydn's Symphony No. 103 in Eb major, 1796, says:

> . . . one sees that the general plan is established by these instruments, [strings] and the wind instruments, when they are not assigned a leading part, only serve to reinforce the plan with a clearer or more decisive color. As solo instruments, they will then take, momentarily, the place of the first violin, at the unison or octave above. The bass is reinforced by the bassoon.
>
> Oboes also reinforce the first and second violins, at the unison, the octave below or above, according to the register of the violin parts. Often the first oboe doubles the second violin at the unison and the second oboe doubles the first violin at the octave below, but with simplified figures.
>
> Clarinets play an octave below the oboe or double the viola and second violin in a simpler figure. The horns reinforce the most important notes of the bass or the intermediate parts.[11]

Kollmann, 1799, provides considerable detail in his description of scoring.[12] Marsh, in his *Hints to Young Composers*, 1800, is still more specific, as he explains carefully the scoring in each measure of two short pieces for full orchestra used as examples.[13]

Marsh's purpose was to provide the young composer with a full score. He says, concerning the symphonies of Haydn:

> And this ingenious contrivance [of Haydn's technique of composition] would be much more apparent were his grand symphonies published in score. . . . On account of the great length of the modern instrumental compositions, and the multiplicity of their parts and accompaniments, such a publication, especially of the symphonies, would be too expensive for general use.[14]

Publication of full scores rarely took place until about 1800–1810. The first editions of Haydn's symphonies appeared in 1806 and later. Symphonies were made accessible to the general public in chamber music arrangements. Haydn's Symphony No. 104 in D major, 1796, was published in arrangements for string quartet, clavier trio, four-hand clavier, two-hand clavier, and an ensemble of flute, string quartet, and clavier. The only orchestral scores customarily published were those included in the full scores of French operas (see Ch. 21).

Although the continuo no longer figured in classic orchestral scores, keyboard instruments, fortepiano or harpsichord, were available. Marsh says, 1800:

> In noticing the several instruments, used in a modern orchestra, I ought not wholly to omit the Piano Forte . . . .[15]

Koch, 1802, includes a reference to the use of the harpsichord in heavily scored operatic music.[16] Its purpose would be to reinforce the full sound and assist in maintaining rhythmic precision. Notices of Haydn's performances in London, 1794–1795, say that the composer will direct from the Piano Forte; Landon's edition of the Symphony No. 98 in B♭ major, 1792, includes the cembalo part which Haydn played, along with a solo violin, as a brief cadenza toward the end of the finale.[17]

Classic orchestration modified baroque scoring by clefs, in which the four main voices deployed according to register. Winds accompanied strings, eventually becoming *obbligato* as they were assigned independent material. *Contrasts of color* were thus introduced, matching the *contrasts of topic* in classic rhetoric. The strings were sometimes released from their traditional function as main voices, and they began to take part in the *play of color* that became one of the chief appeals of 19th-century orchestral music, as for example in the "fairy" music of Mendelssohn's *A Midsummer Night's Dream*, 1826.

TEXTURES

Strings

The string textures illustrated below have much in common with chamber music, with light, relatively high tessitura and individualization of parts. The difference lies in the greater weight of tone given to each part by multiple performers, thus establishing the orchestral presence.

Two Strings.   In Mozart's Symphony No. 41, K. 551, 1788, mm. 1–4 of the finale, the first violin plays an *alla breve* melody, the second violin an Alberti-bass figure; these disperse the three-part first species counterpoint by *Brechung*. In Haydn's *Oxford* Symphony, 1788, opening of the finale, the contredanse melody of the first violin is accompanied by a rustic murky bass.

Ex. 9-1.   Haydn, Symphony No. 95 in C minor, 1791, 1st movt.

123

Eulenburg No. 480

Three Strings.   In Ex. 9-1 Haydn pairs the violins against a counterline in the viola in a *stile legato* passage whose lightness and complexity embodies a pure chamber style. Ex. 9-2 pairs the lower voices in thirds against an effervescent gigue tune that has a typical *buffa* flavor. Two treble strings and continuo (bass) constitute the minimum mid-century orchestral scoring, as in Ex. 7-2. Johann Stamitz's *Orchestertrio* in C major, Op. 1, No. 1, circa 1750, represents this texture; the viola generally doubles the bass line, while winds might reinforce the treble.

Ex. 9-2.   Mozart, Symphony No. 34 in C major, K. 338, 1780, finale.

Broude Bros.

Four Strings.   Four strings constitute a standard classic texture. In Ex. 9-3, note the profile Haydn gives to the lower strings by rhythmic figures and parallel third reinforcement. Mozart ingeniously modifies the traditional trio-sonata texture—two violins and bass—beginning at m. 145 in the first movement of his *Prague* Symphony. The violins are paired in fourth species counterpoint; the viola takes an *alla breve* ascending line, while the bass strings ornament this lower line with octave leaps *alla zoppa*, a galant touch in a strict-style progression that builds eventually to a powerful climax in an unbroken contrapuntal thrust.

Ex. 9-3.   *Four-part string texture.* Haydn, Symphony No. 101 in D major, 1794, 1st movt.

Eulenburg No. 439

Five Strings.   Ex. 9-4 gives separate lines to each of the lower strings; the contrabass has the only true bass part; the compact upper voices intensify the agitato style with its off-beat accents. The opening measures of Mozart's Symphony

No. 40 in G minor, K. 550, 1788, are scored as a string quintet with two violas, but the mass of the strings (many to each part) and the doubling of outer voices convey a velvety orchestral quality to the lyric pathetic melody, quite different from the lighter texture of his G minor Quintet, K. 516, 1787.

Ex. 9-4. *Five-part string texture.* Beethoven, *Egmont,* Op. 84, 1810, overture.

Philharmonia

Strings and Winds

The incorporation of winds into the orchestra can be traced in the *Breitkopf Catalogue,* 1762–1787. In 1762 many symphonies for four voices (strings) are listed, with others calling for oboes and horns as well. In 1787 we find only a few symphonies, all calling for three or more pairs of winds.

Oboes and horns might support strings with full tonic and dominant harmony. Flutes were interchangeable with oboes but the latter were preferred for their more penetrating tone, a support for the military or ceremonial style of many first movements.[18] Bassoons normally reinforced the lower strings.

Marsh, 1800, credits winds with a basic role in the new style, referring to the "mixture of wind and string instruments, introduced into the modern symphony";[19] Burney, 1789,[20] and Schubart, 1785,[21] also make this point.

The growth of the wind component opened new areas of tone color. Ex. 9-5 illustrates a striking early use of winds as solo instruments, in which the familiar parallel thirds in the treble accompanied by a *Trommel-bass* are given a fresh aspect by the wind dialogue. The entire passage is a delightful play of color as the winds trade short singing and fanfare figures in a texture that floats on the dominant pedal point.

Ex. 9-5. *Solo winds with string accompaniment.* J.C. Bach, *Lucio Silla,* 1776, overture, 1st movt.

Peters Edition 10452

The color of winds puts an edge on the contrapuntal play in Mozart's overture to *The Magic Flute,* 1791. Throughout most of the overture, the winds double strings or take solos, but in mm. 145-153 Mozart creates a kaleidoscope of textures by more than a dozen quick changes of scoring, intensifying the counterpoint with contrasts of color involving winds.

Winds Alone

Winds had strong associations with military topics—marches and fanfares. Exs. 9-6 and 9-7 are marches, the former with a parodistic flavor, as if the winds were imitating a barrel organ or music box, the latter with a Turkish color, furnished with piccolo, triangle, cymbals, and bass drum.

Ex. 9-6. *Wind scoring.* Haydn, Symphony No. 100 in G major, 1794, 1st movt.

Peters Edition 5654

Ex. 9-7. *Wind scoring.* Beethoven, Symphony No. 9 in D minor, Op. 125, 1822-1824, finale.

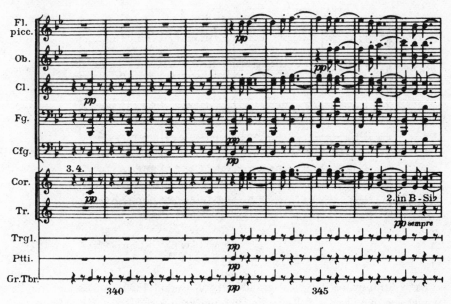

Philharmonia

All the textures illustrated above are based upon chamber music principles; yet for the listener, the awareness of many combinations and doublings establishes the presence of the orchestra with its broader dimensions of sound and space.

The Orchestral Tutti

Koch was surely referring to the orchestral tutti when he spoke of the "inner strength and emphasis" that must "carry all before it" (p. 145 above). The figures that distinguish the orchestral tutti from the chamber style — full wind chords sustained, string tremolos and related effects, powerful chords — can develop powerful thrust to intensify periodic drive; often melodic profile and interplay are reduced to a minimum in a "grand" orchestral tutti.

But a tutti was not necessarily overpowering; in most 18th-century music, it served principally to establish a clear perspective between solo and ensemble, either by contrasted material or by fuller scoring of a chamber music texture. Such sharp demarcations are typical in classic symphonies. Ex. 9-8 illustrates a minimum standard tutti for classic music; the three-part chamber music texture, layered in parallel thirds and *Trommel-bass*, is reinforced by oboe, horn, and viola doublings. At m. 9 the violins and viola, as a concertino, will restate the opening material in a true chamber music texture.

Ex. 9-8. *Minimum tutti, amplified chamber music scoring.* Boccherini, Symphony in B♭ major, Op. 22, No. 1, 1775, 1st movt.

Grähl's Orchester-Serie 8

Ex. 9-9 illustrates a typical grand tutti of around 1800. Winds and middle strings are deployed in full chords for sonority and rhythmic reinforcement of the treble-bass polarity. The Storm and Stress style here exemplifies an orchestral idiom cultivated by Gluck, which became prevalent at this time. The block-like sonorities are matched by the perfect symmetry of the four-measure phrases.

Ex. 9-9. *Grand tutti.* Cherubini, *Medea*, 1797, overture.

The tutti in Ex. 9-10 is an agitated mêlée lacking a salient melodic line but urged on by the measured tremolo of the strings, the sting of the sforzando and the bite of the appoggiaturas, doubly forceful in their low placement—an idiomatic orchestral tutti that must have created great excitement at its first performance in London.

Ex. 9-10. *Tutti.* Haydn, Symphony No. 102 in B♭ major, 1794, 1st movt.

Trombones, traditional in church music to double voices, also were heard in ceremonial brass music and upon solemn occasions, as in the Handel commemoration of 1784; Mozart used them in *The Magic Flute*, 1791, to signify the serious aspects of this opera. Marsh says that they were the most powerful instruments of the orchestra.[22] Possibly for this reason, they could not be assimilated into the chamber-style symphony and the elegant accompaniments in opera. Ex. 9-11 shows an early classic use of trombones, substituting for horns as the "core" of sound; in this case, their heavier, less mellow tone befits the mood of tragedy with which the opera *Alceste* begins.

Ex. 9-11.   *Tutti with trombones.* Gluck, *Alceste,* 1763, overture.

From Christoph Willbald Gluck, *Collected Works,* series I, vol. 7, *Alceste* (Paris version, 1763). Published under the auspices of the Institut für Musikforschung, Berlin, with the cooperation of the city of Hannover by Bärenreiter-Verlag, Kassel, Basel, Tours, London. Rudolf Gerber, ed. Used with kind permission of the publisher.

The tutti establishes a strong presence in Beethoven's orchestral music; its vigor, often violent, distinguishes this aspect of Beethoven's style from that of Haydn and Mozart. Yet only 3 of the 37 movements in the symphonies—the finales of the Fifth and Seventh and the first movement of the Eighth—set the tutti as a norm of texture, and *f* as the ruling dynamic level. The opening of the finale of the Fifth represents a maximum tutti, lacking only the second pair of horns. The brass chorale dominates the massive chordal texture, except for the *concitato* of the violas; the ceremonial affect provides scope for the trombones at the center of the sound, while the piccolo and contrabassoon expand the outer pitch limits.

The finale of the Seventh is unique in its treatment of tutti. Almost two-thirds of its 466 measures, 498 if repeats are taken, are set with full orchestra, generally on an *f* level, in a melody-accompaniment texture supporting the wild contredanse theme. Here, at mm. 428 and 444 *fff* is required to provide an apex that stands above the generally high level of intensity. Much the same purpose is served by the *fff* at m. 349 of the first movement of Beethoven's Eighth Symphony. Curiously, this movement ends *pp*, as an odd counterstatement to what went before, a quirk matched by other surprises in this symphony.

Beethoven often did not maintain the nice sense of balance that characterizes the tuttis of Haydn and Mozart. An extreme imbalance, to express the frantic "victory symphony" in the coda of the overture to *Egmont* Op. 84, 1810, has the entire orchestra shrieking the horn-fifths fanfare on all levels, except for the viola *concitato*—a fantastic distortion of a familiar 18th-century three-part texture.

The chamber music quality that is retained in classic symphonies may be linked with the tone qualities of instruments and the size of orchestras. Instruments generally had softer, less brilliant tone qualities than they have today and were less able to blend with each other to create an impressive mass of sound. On the other hand, their lightness enabled them to maintain a clear, layered texture, a transparency in which individual characteristics were even more sharply defined than at present. Orchestras ranged in size from 20 to about 40 players; in 1783 the largest orchestra, that of Dresden, had about 40. When we read about the brilliance and excitement created by an orchestra, we must remember that this effect was in contrast to the very light sound of chamber music, and was not comparable to the fullness and force of today's ensembles.

As orchestras grew in size around the turn of the century, the sharp demarcation between tutti and solo was sometimes modified to a gradual blend, in which a passage would increase both in dynamics and richness of sound to a climax. Many sections of Beethoven's music are built along such lines, as the beginning of the Allegro of his *Leonore* Overture No. 3, Op. 72a, 1806.

The later symphonies of Haydn and Mozart and the symphonies of Beethoven constitute the most familiar classic repertory. But many lesser-known works have striking features and great appeal. The orchestra symphonies of C. P. E. Bach are saturated with the fantasia elements characteristic of his keyboard music. His younger brother, Johann Christian, writes in an Italianate style full of ingratiating melodies, nicely turned contrasts, and effective wind solos. Johann Stamitz's symphonies feature a powerful orchestral tutti sound, novel in the 1750s but eventually standardized in the mature classic style. Christian Cannabich's Symphony in Bb major is full of delightful melodic ideas and expert play of texture. Boccherini's vivacious style, his scintillating play of texture and deft turn of phrase, marks his symphonic music, as in the Symphonies in F major, Op. 35, No. 4, 1782, and in D minor, *La Casa del Diavolo*, 1771. Cherubini's grand manner, his precise, clear scoring, and his impeccable counterpoint impressed Beethoven strongly; the *Medea* overture, 1797, (see Ex. 9-9) creates a stormy, pulsating effect that later would be embodied in Beethoven's overtures to *Coriolanus*, 1807, and *Egmont*, 1810.

Modern scholarship has generally regarded the Mannheim school as the decisive factor in establishing the classic orchestral style. Recently, the important role of Giovanni Battista Sammartini, 1700 or 1701-1775, in this area has been recognized.[23] Sammartini's symphonies display a more imaginative treatment of texture, rhythmic play, and development of melodic material than do the *sinfonias* of his mid-18th-century contemporaries.

NOTES

1. *AMZ*, 1801, p. 324. See also pp. 330, 368.
2. Marsh, quoted in Cudworth, "An Essay by John Marsh," *ML*, XXXVI, 1955, p. 156.
3. Marsh, *Hints*; Momigny, *Cours complet*; Kollmann, *Composition*; Galeazzi, *Elementi*; Schubart, *Ideen*; Daube, *Melodie*.
4. See Landon, *Symphonies of Haydn*, for critical comments on Haydn's symphonies; see also p. 145 of the present work.
5. Cramer, *Magazin*, 1783, p. 549.
6. Koch, *Versuch*, III, pp. 384ff.; reprinted from *MQ*, XLII, No. 4, October 1956, p. 452 by permission.
7. Koch, *Lexikon*, pp. 1386-1387.
8. Kollmann, *Composition*, p. 12.
9. Koch, *Lexikon*, p. 747.
10. Momigny, *Cours complet*, p. 585.
11. Ibid., pp. 585-586.
12. Kollmann, *Composition*, p. 12.
13. Marsh, *Hints*, p. 1ff.
14. Ibid., pp. 1-2.
15. Ibid., p. 9.
16. Koch, *Lexikon*, p. 587.
17. Joseph Haydn, *Critical Edition of the Complete Symphonies*, H. C. Robbins Landon ed., 12 vols., Universal Edition, Vienna, 1965-1968.
18. Koch, *Lexikon*, p. 1081.
19. Marsh, *Hints*, p. 1.
20. Burney, *History*, p. 865.
21. Schubart, *Ideen*, p. 44ff.
22. Marsh, *Hints*, p. 11.
23. Jenkins, Newell and Churgin, Bathia, *Thematic Catalogue of the Works of Giovanni Battista Sammartini*. Harvard University Press, Cambridge, Massachusetts and London, England, 1976.

10 Texture: Vocal Music

Classic vocal music had a rich and extensive repertory. It was performed more often and by greater numbers of people than pure instrumental music. Every degree of dignity was represented, from simple unaccompanied songs to elaborate and impressive operas and masses. About half of Mozart's works include voices; Haydn's vocal music, although not fully catalogued, clearly constitutes a major part of his oeuvre, including masses, oratorios, cantatas, operas, and songs. Indeed, vocal music in classic times retained the superior position it had enjoyed in the earlier 18th century.

MUSIC FOR VOICES ALONE

Solo Songs

Song was the most universal genre of vocal music in the 18th century. Koch speaks of the *Lied* as "the one product of music and poetry whose content today appeals to every class of people and every individual."[1] Songs involved every level of sophistication, from simple folk songs and popular airs to imitations of Italian and French operatic pieces. Their expressive content was sentimental, didactic, narrative, satiric, comic, even heroic; all regions of Europe had their own song literature, which often furnished melodic material for larger works. The musical and poetic material of these songs can be traced as far back as the 16th century and earlier.

Most 18th-century songs were furnished with accompaniments, but some unaccompanied melodies appear in collections of popular and traditional tunes.[2] Ex. 10-1, a French tune of the type called *brunette, vaudeville,* or *ariette,* represents the kind of melodies used in the French popular theater of the earlier 18th century, later imitated in the *opéra comique.* The collection from which this example was taken did not furnish accompaniments for the tune, but a clavier, lute, or guitar may have supplied simple chordal backgrounds at the option of the performer. The principal interest of this song is in its text—sentimental, with a touch of pathos, the syllables themselves melodious and flowing. The music, a simple line, principally conjunct, adds profile to the declamation without imposing a distinctive shape of its own; this relationship between music and text is typically French. Although the period structure is well defined in six-measure phrases and in repetitions, the lack of strong cadential punctuation promotes a flow that reduces the sharpness of the periodic profile, a feature of French songs and dances criticized by Chastellux, 1765 (see p. 35).

Ex. 10-1. From *Recueil de romances historiques, tendres et burlesques,* 1767, vol. I, pp. 118-119.

"At the edge of a fountain,
Thyrsis, burning with love,
Thus spoke of his pain
To the distant echoes:
Vanished happiness,

Which cannot return,
Torment of my thoughts:
Vanished happiness,
Oh, that in losing thee,
I had lost the memory as well!"

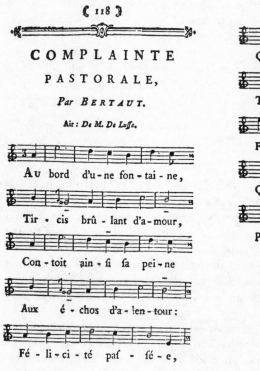

Ex. 10-2 is taken from an English collection, again without accompaniment for the tune. This ballad is a war song. Its principal interest is in the story it tells and in its sharply profiled march tune, strongly articulated into three four-measure phrases by authentic cadences. Music and text have a less comfortable fit than in Ex. 10-1; scansion and delivery do not have a smooth flow. A rhythmic accompaniment could well be imagined to complete the effect intended by this song.

Ex. 10-2. Ritson, *Songs*, vol. III, 1813, pp. 308-309.

The unaccompanied song represents a simple and direct appeal to the feelings, a gentle framing and coloring of its poetry.

Ensemble Music for Voices Alone

Among 18th-century musical genres choral music was ranked highest. As church music, it represented the word of God. Texturally, it created the most intense and moving impact. Sulzer, 1771–1774, says:

> When we observe one or two persons moved by a feeling, we can contemplate this somewhat calmly; however, when an entire mass of people is moved by this feeling, one is irresistibly carried away by joy, fear, or terror.[3]
>
> The simplest song . . . can have the greatest effect when sung by a large group.[4]

The purest medium of ensemble vocal music is the *a cappella* chorus. Ex. 10-3 illustrates this texture in the traditional *stile antico*. The section contains (1) a passage in the *stile famigliare*, note-against-note counterpoint set syllabically in an *alla breve* style; (2) two-part canons, representing the *learned* style, alternating between the upper and lower voices, syllabic except for one melismatic figure.

In mm. 1–6 observe the simplicity of harmony often associated with the *stile antico*; triads alone are used; the only tritone heard is that which makes the cadence, and it is prepared by a suspension; the bass takes the 2–1 progression of the ecclesiastical *tenor* cadence. The canonic section could have been written during the time of Josquin Després, in respect to both its harmony and its neat fit of short figures. Note especially the progression in mm. 1–2, from G to E minor to D minor chords, very likely a deliberate archaism, effective in the setting for unaccompanied voices.

Ex. 10-3. *Stile antico in four-part a cappella texture.* Galuppi, Mass in C major, "Credo."

"I believe in the Holy Ghost, who, together with the Father and Son, is worshipped and glorified, who spoke through the prophets. And in one holy Catholic and Apostolic church."

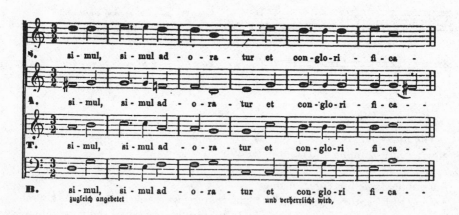

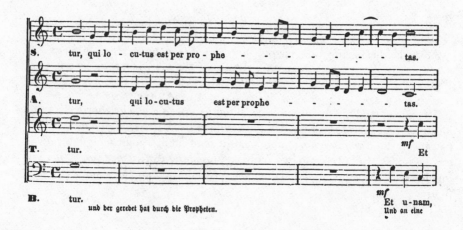

From *Sammlung ausgezeichneter Compositionen für die Kirche*, Stefan Lück, ed., Trier, 1859. According to the editor, the original meter was *alla breve;* MGG states that no dates appear on the many manuscripts of Galuppi's sacred music.

The Italians made great use of the *stile antico* in their church music, since this style was part of their national tradition. Very little of this music has been published, but vast quantities still exist in manuscript in Italian libraries and churches. Koch, 1802, makes the following comment regarding this type of music:

Many Catholic churches possess very valuable collections of such pieces by old and new composers, in which the reverence and solemnity of the church style is retained, unmixed with the theater and chamber styles.[5]

A letter printed in Cramer's *Magazin*, 1783, described the marvelous effect created by Allegri's *Miserere* as sung in Rome by four members of the papal choir, three *castrati* and a tenor; its simple *alla breve* style, sung a cappella, with pure intonation, delicacy, pianissimo, in a very high register moved all who heard it.[6]

The *canon* touched both ends of the expressive spectrum — the severely religious and the bawdy secular. Canon as a genre is discussed in Ch. 15; here a part of a canonic two-part song is given as an example of unaccompanied vocal texture. Many vocal canons, *catches*, (English secular canons), and *rounds* make a play with their texts to create humorous effects, sometimes indecent. Ex. 10-4 has an amusing conceit, the idea of artful weaving, as its figures move back and forth. The melody itself is in the style of a contredanse. Note the symmetrical period structure, the repetition of the period, customary in dances, and the possibility of performing this canon as a melody and accompaniment, the bass taking the first eighth-note of each beat. The style of this piece is similar to that of many tunes that Hiller and other late 18th-century German composers used in songs intended for social singing. Songs of this type were often included in the *Singspiele*, the German comic operas. In this excerpt the original German scans as a quatrain, each line set in iambic tetrameter; lines 1 and 3 rhyme ("ich" and "mich"), and so do lines 2 and 4 ("finde" and "Bewinde"); the scansion and the rhyme create the sing-song effect so prevalent in popular songs.

Ex. 10-4.   *Two-part canon.* Hiller, "Kunstvolle Weberin" ("Artful weaver-woman"), from Christmann, *Elementarbuch*, 1782, examples, pp. 59-60.

"Artful weaver-woman whom I find here so busily at work:"

MUSIC FOR VOICES AND INSTRUMENTS

Accompanied Solo Songs and Arias

This category includes a wide range of genres, from simple songs to elaborate operatic arias. Solo vocal music was often published in two lines—the solo and a bass, which would usually involve a continuo; in simpler pieces the bass could be played by a single instrument.

Ex. 10-5 illustrates the minimum accompaniment texture to a vocal melody. This simple tune, with its syllabic setting livened by a touch of ornamentation here and there, speaks in the manner of the sentimental French song (like the tune in Ex. 10-1) of the 18th century. Vaudevilles and other genres of the French popular theater interspersed such songs; their subject matter might be sentimental, satiric, comic—whatever provided light entertainment (see Ch. 20). Ex. 10-5 has one or two special touches: (1) the five-measure first phrase answered by a six-measure second phrase gives an odd motion to the phrase rhythm; (2) the rise to E in the second phrase creates a rhetorical emphasis that gives a sharper focus to the entire period.

Ex. 10-5. *Vocal melody with bass accompaniment.* Rousseau, *Le Devin du Village,* 1752, "Quand on sait bien aimer."

"When one knows how to love well, how charming is life."

Ex. 10-6 is taken from a collection of songs compiled and arranged by Domenico Corri, a prominent figure in the London music business around the turn of the century. Corri's arrangement of this song, adapted from the finale of Monsigny's opera *Le Déserteur,* 1769, is actually a *parody* of the original; it is somewhat longer as a result of phrases being repeated and added, and the melodic lines are changed in many details. There is a simple realization of the continuo, with two treble parts instead of the standard three: Corri's instructions indicate that at this late date, 1795, continuo accompaniment was still part of current practice in secular music.

Ex. 10-6. *Voice part and bass with continuo realization.* Domenico Corri, ca. 1795, adapted from Monsigny, *Le Déserteur,* finale.

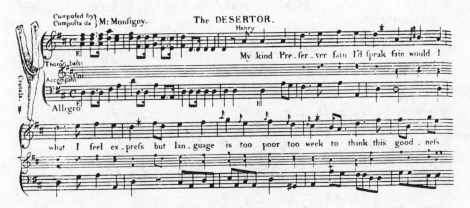

Note: The stars indicate strokes on the crotola (cymbals).

Ex. 10-7 is set for keyboard, with an idiomatic Alberti-bass accompaniment for the melody. The voice doubles the melody, but the piece could just as well be performed as an instrumental contredanse. The first two collections of Haydn's *Lieder*, 1781 and 1784, were published in the same type of setting—two staves, with the keyboard doubling the voice. Ex. 10-8 is from *Schillers lyrische Gedichte*, 1810, a collection by Johann Friedrich Reichardt, one of the leading song writers of the time. Again we have a popular and sentimental notion, with a pretty little sing-song tune. Songs of this type found their way into many collections for home use, were reprinted many times, and are still part of the repertory of present-day German *Gesellschaft* (social) singing. Reichardt's treble doubles the voice, except for a few details, but the piano part provides a full harmony that acts as a solid background of sonority for the voice. The texture represents the fullest type of support found in classic song literature. The musette style in the first two measures, the sing-song alternation of basic functional harmonies, and the rather high placement of the piano part act principally for resonance.

Ex. 10-7. *Vocal melody with keyboard setting.* Christmann, *Elementarbuch,* 1782, "Es war einmal" ("Once upon a time"), examples, p. 27.

"Once upon a time there was a little bird, pit!"

Ex. 10-8. Reichardt, *Schillers lyrische Gedichte, 1810,* "An den Frühling" ("To spring").

"Welcome lovely youth! Nature's delight. With your little basket of flowers, welcome to the field!"

Song composition called for great sensitivity and taste. In the article "Lied" in Sulzer's *Allgemeine Theorie*, 1771-1774, a number of points essential to good song writing are made. These include the proper choice of key, reflecting the differences in scale in the mean-tone tuning system; the ability of the melody to stand alone, without the bass (harmony); a familiarity with the various dance melodies of all nations; proper scansion of the poetry; and proper choice of intervals for the expression of each turn of the poetry.[7]

Textures in operatic solos range from a song-like doubling of the voice by instruments to marked separation of the orchestra from the soloist's line. Ex. 10-9, a soprano aria, employs a favorite Italian texture for both church and opera—the voice reinforced by violins playing in thirds and sixths. (See Ex. 7-2; see also Ex. 8-4a for an instrumental use of this texture.) The style borrows from the sarabande, with the *fioritura* typical of the Italian galant in both voice and instruments. The composer, Lambert Kraus, was a priest in the German Benedictine cloister at Metten, and director of its chorus.

Ex. 10-9.   *Voice doubled by violins in thirds and sixths.* Kraus, *Lytaniae Lauretanae VII*, 1764, "Salus infirmorum" ("Health to the infirm").

Doubling the voice with instruments gave the voice the support it often needed; it also reinforced the melody to make it more salient. *Multiple* doubling of the voice line characterized the *unison* aria of Italian comic opera and late 18th-century *opéra comique*. These arias were sung by the bass voice; the eccentric scoring added a faintly ludicrous touch to the comic affects in such arias, as in Ex. 10-10, from Pergolesi's *La Serva Padrona*, 1733. The bass voice in unison with the orchestra, if set in the high style *alla breve*, can stir affects of gravity, anger, and terror, as in the music of the Commandant in the opening scene and the "supper" scene of *Don Giovanni* (see Ch. 22).

Ex. 10-10.   *Unison bass aria.* Pergolesi, *La Serva Padrona*, 1733, "Aspettare" ("To wait").

"To wait and no one comes, in bed and not to sleep, to be kind without thanks."

Copyright 1941 by G. Ricordi & Co., Milan. Used by kind permission of the publisher.

In Ex. 10-11 the scoring departs from literal doubling to introduce characteristic figures in the orchestra as a foil to the vocal line. The topic in the text is the "whirlwind." Jommelli invented a figure in the strings to suggest the motion of turbulence; note that the first note of each measure in the first violins doubles the tone being sung. The separation of voice and strings is striking in the aria "La vendetta" from Act I of Mozart's *The Marriage of Figaro*, K. 492, 1785–1786. Here, as in so many other arias of Mozart, the orchestra assumes the principal action while the voice declaims in a simple narrative style to explain the dramatic sense of the scene.

Measures 1–4 signal to the audience that this is a basso unison aria; all participants play a unison variously decorated in the strings and winds. But in m. 5 a change of topic ensues, along with a change in texture. Bartolo's rage is reflected in the agitated orchestral action, while his firm intention for revenge is made clear by his slow trochaic rhythm. His relish in contemplating his revenge is expressed by a crescendo. Later, when he sings "what confusion I shall create," his music remains steady on a pedal point A, while all around him the orchestra is

twisting and turning back and forth between tonic and dominant harmonies, repeatedly touching upon the "false" note D♯; this texture is a vivid picture of Bartolo's intended machinations.

Ex. 10-11.   *Independence of voice and accompaniment.* Jommelli, *Fetonte,*
1768, Act I, "Fugan qual turbine" ("They flee the hurricane").

Denkmäler Deutscher Tonkunst

Melodrama

Texturally, the maximum musical separation of voice and accompaniment is
found in the recitative, examples of which are found in Ch. 18. But a still further
separation, in which the voice no longer sings, occurred in the 18th-century
melodrama.

In opera, poetry and music proceed together, reinforcing each other; in
melodrama, they alternate, as though they were commenting upon each other.
According to Heinrich Gottlieb Schmieder, quoted in Koch's *Lexikon,* the
melodrama does not depict action, but touches upon the affects set in motion by
the action.[8] Thus the music of a melodrama will be highly charged, with strong
impact, but without rhetorical extension, much in the manner of the recitative
obligé (see p. 316). Both the actor and the audience stand at a distance from the
music.

The most famous work in this genre was Georg Benda's *Ariadne auf Naxos,*
1775. This work was composed almost entirely in the style of the recitative
obligé, with some small set pieces interspersed. Ex. 10-12 illustrates Benda's procedure. Beethoven staged the entrance of Leonora and Rocco into the dungeon
in Act II of *Fidelio* as a melodrama, taking advantage of its "broken" rhetoric to
create an atmosphere of suspense.

Rhetorically, one of the strongest effects of melodrama setting is that of
parenthesis, in which poetry and music are constantly interrupting each other;
the end of a poetic or musical line will connect to its next entry, so that both

Ex. 10-12. Georg Benda, *Ariadne auf Naxos*, 1775, Theseus speaking, "Dieux! ils s'approchent" ("Gods! they come closer").

poetry and music could be performed continuously by themselves. But the mutual interruptions can engage the viewer's attention even more compellingly than in continuous discourse.

Vocal Duets, Trios

Textural options in vocal ensembles—duets, trios, as well as larger groups—added a *concertante* element lacking in solo vocal music.[9] Rousseau's remarks, 1768, concerning duets reflect his bias for Italian vocal music:

1. The importance of duets in *dialogue*, in which the two voices alternate phrases. (This is actually a distribution of solo material, as in "Là ci darem" from Act I of *Don Giovanni*, 1787, but the dialogue layout reflects the dramatic situation.)

2. The importance of *equal* voices (generally treble) in serious opera, to promote the *unity of affect*, as well as to provide a fuller harmony by means of thirds and sixths. Rousseau claims that this is one of the principal advantages attached to the *castrato* tradition, in which all duets would be performed by equal or closely matched voices. (The duet "Suis un époux" from Act III of Gluck's *Orfeo*, 1762, represents this type of vocal setting.)

3. The effect of unequal voices, as in the *buffa* duet for a *male* and *female* voice. The difference in range and tone quality sharpens the separation of affects characteristic of comic opera. Rousseau cites the famous duet "Lo conosco" from Pergolesi's *La Serva Padrona*, 1733, as an example of this texture.[10]

Koch, 1802, distinguishes among duets with a dramatic dialogue involving two characters and those dedicated to the expression of a single sentiment. The former would have a free interchange between the voices as well as a merging from time to time (the Gluck duet cited above would represent this type). The latter represents an extension of the solo song or aria; here both voices proceed in the same melodic vein, doubling the melody with a steady stream of thirds and sixths. Koch recommends this texture for cantatas and other church music.[11] This texture was chosen by Mozart in "Là ci darem" to close the duet; the separation of voices at the beginning reflects the opposing feelings of Giovanni and Zerlina; the parallel thirds and sixths which they sing as they go off together bespeak sweet agreement.

When three or more voices are engaged in the ensemble, the texture is comparable to that of instrumental chamber music. Dialogue and doubling become part of a fuller and more complete ensemble in which the give-and-take of the voices is the principal line of action. One of the most exquisite examples of such an ensemble is the trio in the finale of Act I of *Don Giovanni*, "Protegga il giusto cielo." Here Mozart has borrowed the texture and sonority of the wind serenade, treating the two sopranos—Anna and Elvira—as upper winds, while Ottavio, the tenor, sings the lowermost part. These three form a solo trio group against the tutti of the orchestral winds. The adagio tempo, written in *alla breve* for *dignity*, not *pace*, and the luminous sounds of the voices and winds project the sublimity of this moment of prayer.

Choral Music with Instruments

Classic choral music, with or without accompaniment, represents the strongest link that the classic style had with the past. In both the Catholic and Protestant churches, the tradition of the strict style was maintained; for the Catholic church, it was the use of the *alla breve* style; for the Protestant church, it was the *chorale*. Ex. 10-3 illustrates the *stile antico* in an unaccompanied texture; Exs. 10-14, 10-16, and 10-17, discussed below, typify the accompanied texture. Galant and sentimental qualities, as well as "modern" textures, were often intermingled with the conservative styles.

Chorale. The chorale, a central feature of German church and domestic music since the time of Luther, had become highly figured and elaborated in many early 18th-century settings. Johann Adam Hiller undertook a reform of the Protestant hymn repertory in his capacity as cantor of the great St. Thomas Church in Leipzig in the 1790s. Hiller wished to return the chorale to its declamatory style, one that would deliver the sacred message clearly and simply. His settings for four-part chorus with continuo represented a drastic simplification, an interpretation of the strict style that eliminated any touch of 18th-century artifices, learned or galant. The first period of Hiller's setting of "Werde munter mein Gemüthe" ("Be cheerful my soul") is given as Ex. 10-13a. Compare this simple note-against-note setting with the elaborate treatment given the same melody by J. S. Bach in the *St. Matthew Passion* (Ex. 10-13b), with the lower voices running in counterlines to the melody and the distribution of eighth- and quarter-notes tracing a complex pattern of cross rhythms. The same melody, rather neutral in its constant stepwise motion, serves two very different affects. Hiller's setting is a simple statement of feeling. Bach's, on the other hand, is an elaborate comment upon the chorale tune.

Ex. 10-13.   *Chorale style with accompaniment.*

a. Hiller, "Werde munter mein Gemüthe" ("Be cheerful my soul"), 181[?].

b. J.S. Bach, *St. Matthew Passion*, 1728-1829, "Bin ich gleich von dir gewichen."

("I have fallen from Thee, but I return.")

Eulenburg No. 2654

The learned aspect of traditional choral writing is shown in the excerpt from the *Miserere* that Mozart wrote while studying with Padre Martini in Bologna in 1770 (Ex. 10-14). This is a fragment of motet writing, *alla breve*, with points of imitation. The only notable features of this passage are those "modernisms" that would not appear in Renaissance music—chords marked $\frac{7}{3\sharp}$, $\frac{4\sharp}{2}$, and $\frac{6}{4}$, and the rhythmic "kink" caused by the eighth-notes in m. 9.

Ex. 10-14.   Mozart, *Miserere*, K. 85, 1770, opening section, "Miserere mei, Deus."

"Have mercy on me, Lord, according to thy great mercy."

Edwards

Accompanied Part-Singing. *Part-singing* had been an important aspect of German musical life for centuries. This tradition was exemplified in classic times by the collection of short songs and poems from which Ex. 10-15 is taken. The instrumental accompaniment is *ad libitum*, and the mood is typically sentimental in its celebration of the beauty of spring.

Concerted Choral Music.   Instruments could accompany the chorus in various ways: (1) literal doubling of voices, (2) chordal accompaniment, (3) separate lines of action for each section. In Exs. 10-13b and 10-14, the organ supports the voices with a chordal continuo, while the instruments double the voices. In Ex. 10-15, there is also literal doubling. The examples to follow demonstrate different degrees of instrumental autonomy, that is, concerted treatment.

Ex. 10-15. Reichardt, *Lieder geselliger Freude*, 1796-1797, "Mailied" ("Song of May"), poem by Goethe.

"Wie herrlich leuchtet mir die Natur! Wie glänzt die Sonne! Wie lacht die Flur!" ("How splendidly nature shines on me! How the sun glitters! How the meadow laughs!")

Classic church music that employed the *alla breve* style retained the traditional scoring for such passages, *to double the voice at pitch*. This is the "scoring by clefs" recommended by Praetorius (1619)[12] in which soprano, alto, tenor, and bass are doubled by instruments of corresponding range. The effect is a mixed sound that reinforces the melodic lines; precise effects of sonority play little or no part in such a texture, although the effect is unquestionably bold and brilliant. Ex. 10-16, from the Mass in C minor by Mozart, illustrates such a setting. Trumpets and timpani reinforce the harmony and anchor the rhythm by sounding tonic or dominant at the beginning of each measure.

We have seen, in Chs. 6 and 7, how 18th-century composers introduced galant elements into the strict style by melodic elaborations. A subtle yet deadly undermining of the *alla breve* appears in the "Et vitam venturi" from the "Credo" of Mozart's Mass in C major, K. 167, 1773. While the voices declaim traditionally, the violins play galant figures that might well have been taken from a comic aria or a sonata (see Ex. 10-17). For the 18th-century listener, this provided a touch of entertainment to lighten the gravity of the mood of worship.

Ex. 10-16. *Alla breve style with voices doubled by instruments.* Mozart, Mass in C minor, K. 427, 1782-1783, "Credo."

From Mozart, *Missa C moll* (H.C. Robbins Landon, ed.). Copyright 1956 by Edition Eulenburg. Used by kind permission of the publisher.

Galant elements figured prominently in 18th-century church music, especially in the classic era, as Einstein discusses at length in his biography *Mozart*.[13] The presence of these elements was deplored by some critics, as in Sulzer, 1771-1774 (see also p. 26):

Here we remark especially that short phrases or sections accommodate themselves better to light and frivolous feelings, and, in certain circumstances, to impetuous, violent passion; longer phrases [accommodate them-

Ex. 10-17. *Galant elements in alla breve choral texture.* Mozart, Mass in C major, K. 167, 1773, "Credo," "Et vitam venturi."

("And the life of the world to come.")

Edwards

selves] to serious feelings. All that is pathetic, serious, thoughtful, and devotional requires long phrases which are merged one into another; . . . the cheerful as well as the furious [require] very short phrases, more clearly separated from one another. It is a very serious error when the composer allows himself to be seduced by the applause that unpracticed and inexperienced listeners give to the pleasant so-called *galant* pieces, and thereby introduces small, chopped-up, dainty music instead of beautiful music into serious works and even into church music.[14]

Galant elements included topics, figuration, and texture; they appeared frequently in the music of Bach and Handel (see the "Et resurrexit" from Bach's Mass in B minor, 1733, in the style of a polonaise). The music is raised to a serious level of expression by the thrust and firmness with which the ruling affect is maintained and explored.

Mozart's *Coronation* Mass, K. 317, 1779, has many galant elements. Ex. 10-18, set to an incisive march rhythm, conveys a firm, even exuberant affirmation of belief. The voices act as an inner pedal point to the principal melodic material in the orchestra; some attention is given to doubling the figures of the violins, especially when four voices open out into full harmony in m. 3 and the following measures. The entire passage has a buoyant quality, thanks to the brilliant figuration and the transparent texture.

Ex. 10-18. Mozart, *Coronation* Mass, K. 317, 1778, "Credo" (voices scored as inner pedal point to principal melodic action in orchestra).

"I believe in one God, the Father Almighty, maker of heaven and earth."

Ex. 10-19 is set as a bourrée-contredanse, in a singing style befitting the blessing of the "Benedictus." The principal melody is given to oboes in parallel thirds, in the vein of the wind serenade. The voices piece out a dialogue-type texture from the melody and the harmony, while the violins double the oboes an octave lower; the second violin lightens the rhythm by a simple Alberti-type bass. The horns bind the active texture with their sustained C.

Ex. 10-20 is a minuet in the brilliant court manner. After the ornamental figures in the violins in mm. 1-2 the voices join the orchestra to create a tutti effect.

Ex. 10-21, from the "Credo," the most serious passage in the Mass, takes up the *ombra* style, in the manner of a recitative *obligé* (see Ch. 18); the orchestra and voices have completely independent figures, which they alternate in a responsorial arrangement.

Ex. 10-19.   Mozart, *Coronation* Mass, K. 317, 1779, "Benedictus" (bourrée-contredanse).

"Blessed is he, who comes in the name of the Lord."

Philharmonia

Ex. 10-20. Mozart, *Coronation* Mass, K. 317, 1779, "Osanna in excelsis" ("Hosanna in the highest") (minuet in court manner with military flavor).

Ex. 10-21. Mozart, *Coronation* Mass, K. 317, 1779, "Credo," "Et incarnatus est." (Fantasia-*ombra;* compare to introduction to *Prague* Symphony).

"And was incarnate by the Holy Ghost of the Virgin Mary, and was made man."

Ex. 10-22, from the Requiem Mass in C minor by Cherubini, quotes part of the "Dies irae." The massive effect, the syllabic setting of the voices, the sharply defined yet restrained contrast of orchestra and voices, the full scoring for brass—all contribute to the severe manner that recalls the earlier *alla breve* style.

Ex. 10-22.   Cherubini, *Requiem* Mass in C minor, 1815, "Dies irae," "Tuba mirum."

"The trumpet sending its sound through the sepulchers of all lands shall gather all before the throne."

From Cherubini, *Requiem, C minor* (Rudolf Luck, ed.). Copyright 1964 by C.F. Peters Corporation. Used by kind permission of the publisher.

Beethoven's *Missa Solemnis*, Op. 123, 1821, the broadest in scope of all classic choral works, exhibits his characteristic modifications of 18th-century procedure in scoring. Generally, he retains the traditional doubling of voices by instruments but assigns more of this function to the winds and brass than did Haydn and Mozart. In some parts of the score, the violins are conspicuously silent, as in sections of the "Et vitam venturi" from the "Credo," an *alla breve* fugue; the voices are heavily doubled in winds, brass, and bass. The role of the organ as a continuo in this work has remained a mystery to the present day, since no autograph of the organ part has yet been found. However, in some passages the fullness of the wind choir would seem to be a replacement for the organ sound, as in the *Preambulum* to the "Benedictus."

In the "Dona nobis pacem," the final section of the work, the winds have a dialogue with each other against the sustained tones of the horns and voices. Here Beethoven achieves some of the most luminous sonorities in all his music.

The spectrum of classic vocal textures, ranging from unaccompanied solo to concerted choral-orchestral scorings, has a much larger potential for varying sonorities than pure instrumental music; these sonorities reinforce the greater expressive power and focus provided by voices and text. Opera offers the most open field for the realization of this potential, as we shall see in Ch. 22, where Mozart's *Don Giovanni* is discussed.

NOTES

1. Koch, *Lexikon*, p. 903.
2. See *Recueil de romances*; *Vriendenzangen*.
3. Sulzer, *Allgemeine Theorie*, p. 202.
4. Ibid., p. 203.
5. Koch, *Lexikon*, p. 969.
6. Cramer, *Magazin*, 1783, pp. 157, 158.
7. Sulzer, *Allgemeine Theorie*, p. 719.
8. Koch, *Lexikon*, pp. 945, 946.
9. Galeazzi, *Elementi*, II, p. 278.
10. Rousseau, *Dictionnaire*, p. 179ff.
11. Koch, *Lexikon*, p. 499.
12. Praetorius, *Syntagma*, III, p. 152.
13. Einstein, *Mozart*, ch. 4.
14. Sulzer, *Allgemeine Theorie*; reprinted from *MQ*, XLII, No. 4, 1956, p. 440, by permission.

11 Performance

Classic concern with expression has been documented in this book, and expressive values have been kept in focus in the analyses undertaken. From the notation we have clear indications of expressive stances through specific signs for key, meter, melodic shape, and texture. Yet the finishing touches which put the polish on expression by means of nuances are largely lacking in the notation of classic music. Apart from general tempo marks and a few phrasing signs, we have little to signify *how* the music was interpreted. This chapter investigates aspects of performance not specified in the notation in order to suggest some guidelines for present-day performers.

NOTATION

The notation of the 18th century resembles that of later eras, yet it rests in part upon an older tradition—a close partnership between composer and performer. After the composer had written his score, he expected the performer to complete the composition with respect to tempo, dynamics, sonority, nuance, and ornamentation, with a tasteful regard for the expressive qualities of the piece. Evidence exists that this tradition was still alive in classic times despite important changes in the composer-performer relationship toward the end of the century. When a keyboard performer addressed himself to a continuo part, he added substantially to the music; when a soloist performed a melody, he might add ornamental notes as taste dictated; all performers had to judge the length and strength of notes they played; *agréments* could be read in several ways. In time, however, the approach to performance became more rigid, due in part to the widening gap between composer and performer. Many expressive indications appear in printed scores by the time of Beethoven, possibly to achieve a more faithful performance or as a rein against willful distortion.

Paradoxically, the repertory most widely performed today—the easier keyboard music of J. S. Bach, Haydn, Mozart, and Beethoven—contains *few* instructions for performance. Later editions have tried to compensate for this lack, but often impose their own conventions upon the music. Exs. 11-1 and 11-2 present two versions of an excerpt from Mozart's C major Sonata, K. 330, 1778, to illustrate a typical editorial emendation. This piece is in the style of a contredanse; its texture strongly suggests a wind serenade played by two oboes and bassoon. Ex. 11-1, based on the autograph, allows the performer to shape the reading to imitate the crisp, bright style of the winds. The second version obliterates this *topical nuance* by adding an *overlay of legato* in the bass; the continuous legato also erases the contrast of manner between mm. 4 and 5, a contrast defined by the change from root-position cadential action to descending conjunct bass action.

Ex. 11-1.   Mozart, Sonata in C major, K. 330, 1778, finale, according to the autograph.

From Mozart, *Sonatas and Fantasias for the Piano* (Nathan Broder, ed.). Copyright 1956-1960 by Theodore Presser Company, Bryn Mawr. Used by kind permission of the publisher.

Ex. 11-2.   Mozart, Sonata in C major, K. 330, 1778, finale, Novello edition, 188[?].

Musical notation suffered from countless errors and inconsistencies, both in manuscript copies and in published music. Rousseau's long article on "Copiste" in his *Dictionnaire*, 1768, mentions many requirements faced by the copyist as he transcribes the composer's notation. These include a thorough knowledge of harmony and a familiarity with the composer's style in addition to the usual strictures concerning clarity and accuracy. Music copying was an important source of employment in the 18th century; most of the items in the *Breitkopf Catalogue*, 1762-1787, were obtainable only through handwritten copies. Amateurs also built their own libraries in part by copying music. The possibilities of error in these transcriptions were very great, to say nothing of willful mutilations and arbitrary modification. Recent research has focused on correcting inaccurate notation; the new editions of the works of Haydn and Mozart give a clearer picture of the performance practice of that time.

Lacking clear instructions in the scores, present-day performers can turn to 18th-century treatises to obtain clues about tempo, dynamics, articulation, and ornamentation.

TEMPO

Tempo was determined in two ways:

1. *Descriptively*: adagio, largo, andante, allegro, presto, etc., and modifications of these — allegretto, prestissimo, etc.

2. *Mechanically*: a watch, pendulum, clockwork, or pulse

Ralph Kirkpatrick has summarized 18th-century views of tempo in an article in *PAMS*, 1938.[1]

The *descriptive* reflected the performance practice of the time more faithfully, since it was based on a set of expressive conventions. Tempo indicated the ruling sentiment, as Koch's comments, 1802, indicate:

Largo, actually signifies broad or expanded; this term indicates the most familiar slow tempo, which accommodates itself only to those sentiments which should be expressed with solemn slowness. With respect to performance, the comments given in the article on Adagio must even more carefully be observed in the Largo. . . .[2]

Adagio, moderately slow . . . calls for a particularly finely-drawn performance, partly becasue the slow tempo emphasizes every turn which does not correspond to the ruling sentiment, and partly because the music will become boring and unpleasant if the tempo is not maintained with sufficient momentum . . . the Adagio must be performed with very fine nuances and a very noticeable blending of the tones. . . .[3]

Andante, moving, walking. This term indicates a pace midway between fast and slow. When this term is not used for characteristic pieces, such as processions, marches, etc., then it applies to pieces in which the sentiments of calmness, quiet, and contentment are embodied. Here the tones should neither drag nor blend into each other much as in the Adagio, nor be as accentuated and separated as in the Allegro. . . .[4]

Allegro, quick. . . . moderately quick tempo. . . . The performance of an allegro calls for a firm [*männlichen*] tone quality, a simple and clear delivery, the notes themselves in this tempo being connected only when expressly indicated or when a prominent cantabile section appears; otherwise, the tones are generally separated rather decisively . . . without prejudice to the value of the so-called accented notes. . . .[5]

Presto, rapid, quick . . . the quickest category of tempo . . . in purely instrumental music the presto calls for a fleeting and light, yet straightforward delivery; in the opera, on the other hand, where this tempo is used for sentiments of the greatest intensity, more vigor must be expressed in the sharper accentuation of the tones, and the clarity of the performance must not thereby suffer.[6]

Türk, 1789, gives 4 main speeds — very fast, moderately fast, moderately slow, and very slow — and lists many modifications within these categories.[7] Scheibe, 1773, recommends that the composer specify the amount of time for a movement; an allegro assai movement might take five minutes and three seconds when both reprises are repeated.[8]

Between the years 1807 and 1822 William Crotch, professor of music at Oxford University, published three volumes of *Specimens of Various Styles of Music*. In the preface of each volume he specifies a tempo for each piece, basing his figures upon the period of oscillation required by a pendulum whose cord could be varied in length to obtain different speeds. In vol. III he quotes music of C. P. E. Bach, J. C. Bach, Pleyel, Haydn, Mozart, Schobert, Boccherini, Gluck and others. Some of his tempo suggestions are presented in Example 11-3.

Ex. 11-3.   Tempos suggested by Crotch in *Specimens*, vol. III, p. vi, 1807-1822.

(The numbers represent modern metronome marks, corresponding to the oscillations of Crotch's pendulum.)

C. P. E. Bach, Fantasia in C major (*Kenner und Lièbhaber*, vol. 6)	♩ = 124 (presto) ♪ = 96 (andante) ♪ = 78 (larghetto)
J. C. Bach, Concerto in E♭ major, Op. 9, No. 2	♩ = 88 (allegro) ♪ = 112 (andante) ♩ = 130 (menuetto)
Gluck, overture to *Iphigenia in Aulis*	♩ = 116
Boccherini, Quintet, Op. 12, No. 3	♩ = 78 (andante)
Clementi, Sonata, Op. 11	♩ = 84 (larghetto con espressione)
Mozart: "Recordare" from *Requiem* Mass	♪ = 124 (andante)
"Benedictus" from *Requiem* Mass	♪ = 76 (andante)
Overture to *The Marriage of Figaro*	♩ = 124 (presto)
Haydn, Quartet in C major, Op. 76, No. 3	♩ = 88 (allegro moderato) ♪ = 112 (poco adagio)

The moderate tempo for the overture to *Figaro* permits the subtle detail work to be heard—part-writing, suspensions, and sudden changes of topic. Crotch's tempo corresponds to Mozart's view, quoted in *AMZ*, 1798, that "where fire is lacking in the music, speed cannot add anything."[9] Complaints about tempo generally referred to excessive speed:

Still another major error, that betrays so clearly the lack of knowledge as well as taste in music, is the abominable rushing in each and every piece, which I have heard in the performances under Herr Pitterlin's direction. I noticed this most evidently in a concert given last December in Leipzig by the organist Müller, where the orchestra went completely to pieces because of this constant rushing. . . . A symphony of [Mozart] was taken so quickly that the second violinist, a fine player, could not play eight eighth-notes in a row, but in almost every measure had to drop one or two notes.[10]

Writing to his father, Mozart praised Aloysia Weber's reading of his "difficult" sonatas, in which she played slowly but did not miss a note.[11]

The taste of musical audiences around the turn of the century—brilliant show pieces such as concertos and grand fantasias, and quickly moving *opera buffa*—must have encouraged rapid tempos. Concert pieces, whose principal material consisted of flashy runs, arpeggios, and other passage work, could capture an audience only when played at blinding speed. The other extreme, an exaggerated largo in pathetic or sentimental passages, could also be very effective, considering the richer and more powerful tone of the improved piano, about 1800.

Irregularities of pace also drew the fire of critics. Koch, in his *Journal*, 1795, complains that many soloists neglect a steady tempo, as a matter of fashion (*Modegeschmack*).[12] Much earlier, Pier Francisco Tosi, 1723, levels the same criticism:

because, even among the Professors of the first Rank there are few, but what are almost insensibly deceived into an Irregularity, or hastening of Time, and often of both; which though in the beginning is hardly perceptible, yet in the Progress of the *Air* becomes more and more so, and at last the Variation, and the Error is discovered. . . .[13]

Also:

The Presumption of some Singers is not to be borne with, who expect that an whole *Orchestre* should stop in the midst of a well-regulated Movement, to wait for their ill-grounded caprices, learned by heart, carried from one Theatre to another, and perhaps stolen from some applauded female Singer, who had better luck than skill. . . .[14]

The slight quickening or holding back of the strict tempo was regarded as an important *expressive nuance*, to be used when appropriate and only by the most accomplished performers. Again from Tosi, 1723:

Whoever does not know how to steal the Time in Singing, knows not how to Compose, nor to Accompany himself, and is destitute of the best Taste and greatest Knowledge. . . . The stealing of Time, in the *Pathetick*, is an honourable Theft in one that sings better than others, provided he makes a Restitution with Ingenuity . . . when the Bass goes an exactly regular Pace, the other Part retards or anticipates in a singular manner, for the Sake of Expression, but after That returns to its exactness, to be guided by the Bass. Experience and Taste must teach it. A mechanical Method of going on with the Bass will easily distinguish the Merit of the other Manner.[15]

(Tosi's remarks concerning the regularity of the bass and the rubato of the melody in a pathetic or adagio style find an echo in Mozart's letter to his father, October 23, 1777.)[16]

Türk, 1789, justifies modifications of tempo as follows:

> Even when a composer specifies the sentiment as well as he is able, for the entire piece and for individual passages and the performer applies all the techniques discussed in the preceding sections of this chapter, still there remain special situations in which the expression can be heightened by *extraordinary* means. Among these I include especially (1) performance without measure [*ad libitum*], (2) quickening and holding back, (3) the so-called *tempo rubato*. These are three means which can have great effect when employed *seldom and at the proper time*.
>
> Passages marked *Recitativo*, as well as free fantasias, cadenzas, fermatas, etc., must be played more according to one's feeling than according to regular meter. Here and there we find such passages in sonatas, concertos, etc., as for example in the Andante of the first sonata dedicated to the King of Prussia by C. P. E. Bach. Such places would have a poor effect if the exact note values were to be observed. The most important notes thus should be played slowly and stronger, the lesser notes quickly and lighter, as though a sensitive singer were singing or a good orator were declaiming.
>
> Places where quickening or holding back of the tempo may be used are difficult to specify. . . . These should be restricted to solo performance or when those who accompany are very careful.
>
> The most powerful passages in pieces whose character expresses vigor, anger, fury, madness, etc. can be somewhat hurried (*accelerando*). Also some ideas that are repeated louder (generally higher) can be somewhat quickened. When a gentle sentiment is interrupted by a lively passage, the latter may be played a bit faster. Also, an unexpectedly vigorous idea may be so played.
>
> Unusually sweet, languishing, sad passages . . . can be made much more effective by an increasing retard of the tempo. . . . Toward the end of a piece, where *diminuendo, diluendo, smorzando*, etc. are indicated, one may hold back the tempo slightly. . . .[17]

Tempo rubato, in the 18th century, signified specific disturbances of the normal *quantitas intrinseca*—syncopations, anticipations, and retardations. The *modern* sense of the term, referring to slight variations in note lengths, is described by Koch, 1802:

> This term [*tempo rubato*] also refers to the procedure in which a solo singer or the performer of a concerto changes two adjacent notes of the melody so that a disturbance seems to take place within the measure, but immediately resumes the proper meter with the following notes. It is impossible to give an example of this manner of performance in notation, and it should be allowed only to virtuosos to be used very seldom.[18]

Earlier 18th-century music used a limited number of tempo signs, relying on *text* and *topic* to provide clues for a proper tempo. As the gap between composer and performer widened, some composers qualified the simple terms with expressive indications. Türk, 1789, lists 78 modifications of basic tempos, all of which point to an expressive stance; some of his terms are *affettuoso, agitato, giocoso, lagrimoso, mesto, patetico, con tenerezza, con spirito*.[19] Beethoven frequently made use of qualifying terms; the second movement of the F major Quartet, Op. 18 No. 1, 1800, is to be played *adagio affettuoso ed appassionato*. On the other hand, Mozart used the standard terms *allegro, allegretto, andante,* and *allegro* for the four movements of his C major Quintet, K. 515, 1787. C. P. E. Bach, the master of the sensibility style, was rarely more specific.

DYNAMICS

Dynamics in the classic era ranged from *pianissimo* to *fortissimo*. *Forte* and *piano* (*f, p*) were most frequently used; many movements contain only these two. This usage reflects the clearly articulated rhetoric of classic music—the sharp delineation among figures and phrases—and it represents the continuance of the earlier tradition of *terraced* dynamics. Ex. 3-4 illustrates the opposition of *piano* and *forte*. Other dynamic signs appeared occasionally to indicate nuances or to highlight some important point of declamation; they included *ff, pp, mf, rf, pp, crescendo,* and *diminuendo*. Beethoven used *fff* in the final measures of his *Leonore* Overture No. 3, Op. 72a, 1806, to carry the music to a higher point of climax than reached by the *ff*s indicated earlier in the piece; he used *ppp* just before the final cadence in the finale of his F major Quartet, Op. 59, No. 1, 1806, as a foil for the *ff* which ends the movement.

The absence of detailed dynamic signs in classic music placed the responsibility upon the performer. Türk addresses himself to this problem. Ex. 11-4 shows his citation of some familiar melodic figures, indicating which notes should receive greater dynamic emphasis. (Emphasis for Türk also involves length and articulation, which will be discussed later in this chapter.) Stresses in Ex. 11-4 involve (a) dissonances, (b) suspensions, (c) syncopations, (d) chromatic tones, (e) and (f) salient melodic tones.

Ex. 11-4.   *Emphasis of individual tones.* Türk, *Klavierschule*, 1789, p. 30.

Crescendo, decrescendo, their appositives, and their signs—< and >—appeared with increasing frequency in musical scores toward the end of the century, but these nuances were present in musical performance much earlier.[20] Many media of performance were capable of a gradual increase or decrease of sound. These nuances applied either to a *single* tone or a *group* of tones.

Upon a *single* tone, this nuance imitated the *messa di voce* in singing, in which a swell and drop of force was applied to a given sustained tone. It has an extraordinary effect at the beginning of Haydn's Symphony No. 102 in Bb major, 1794, where the entire orchestra performs a *messa di voce* in unison.

Classic music used *crescendo* and *decrescendo* with a *group* of tones to reinforce rhetorical action, especially in approaching cadences, as in Exs. 11-5 and 11-6.

Ex. 11-5. *Crescendo to a cadence.* Mozart, Sonata in A minor, K. 310, 1778, finale.

From Mozart, *Sonatas and Fantasias for the Piano* (Nathan Broder, ed.). Copyright 1956, 1960 by Theodore Presser Company, Bryn Mawr. Used by kind permission of the publisher.

Ex. 11-6. *Decrescendo to a cadence.* Mozart, Sonata in G major, K. 283, 1774, 2nd movt.

From Mozart, *Sonatas and Fantasias for the Piano* (Nathan Broder, ed.). Copyright 1956, 1960 by Theodore Presser Company, Bryn Mawr. Used by kind permission of the publisher.

The crescendo followed by a sudden *p* also appears, especially in the music of Beethoven, as in mm. 54–55 of the third movement of his B♭ major Quartet, Op. 130, 1826. In his C major Quintet, K. 515, 1787, (Ex. 5-10), Mozart employs the sudden *p* after a crescendo in a *contresense*; the *p* has a fuller texture and heavier style than the preceding crescendo. In the restatement of this passage immediately following, the crescendo is carried to an *f*; these dynamics here create a statement-counterstatement relationship that gives profile to the structure. The crescendo to a *p* can have much the same effect as a delayed cadence — to defer a strong point of arrival or to pass over it completely.

The *orchestral crescendo* had a unique expressive effect. "From rustling tones to thunderstorm" was Schubart's characterization, 1785.[21] Mannheim's orchestral crescendo intrigued Burney, 1776–1789, who was always receptive to new and fashionable things.[22]

According to Harding,[23] the crescendo was used by Jommelli at Stuttgart, and then by the Mannheim orchestra under Stamitz, where it became internationally famous through spectacular performances of this effect. Each of the seven symphonies of Stamitz edited in a modern edition by Hugo Riemann[24] contains a number of crescendo passages, many of them intended apparently to create pure excitement. The *Sinfonia à "8,"* in D major, n. d., begins its first crescendo after eight measures of rather undistinguished material, while the crescendo itself uses neutral scale passages. As a novelty, this was undoubtedly striking.

An especially extensive use of the crescendo appears in the Symphony in D major, Op. 3, No. 6, ca. 1756, by Gossec, reproduced in Brook, *La symphonie française*,[25] in which, of the 110 measures comprising the first movement approximately one-half are involved in crescendos and the *fortes* to which they lead. Gossec's symphony is very much in the vein of the Mannheim works of this genre and period.

Actually, the orchestral crescendo came into its own in the early 19th century, when larger orchestras, more powerful instruments, and a grander style of declamation were evolved. Beethoven, in the *Eroica* Symphony, 1803, and the *Leonore* Overture No. 3, 1806, gave this effect a sense of consequence within a large design.

The spectacular orchestral crescendo apparently did not impress Haydn and Mozart; their crisp rhetoric, well-chiseled ideas, and clean-cut opposition of *piano* and *forte* leave little room for the grand crescendo. However, it appears occasionally with telling effect, as in the final measures of the overture to *The Marriage of Figaro*, where all the ingredients of the orchestral crescendo are laid out — bustling figures in the violins, gradual addition of instruments, sustained tones, increasingly full harmony, rise in pitch, to be capped by the final reinforcement with the trumpets and timpani.

Composers and editors were quite inconsistent in the extent to which they provided marks of expression and dynamics in scores. A single mark, *p* or *f*, may cover an entire piece or extended section; at times, no dynamic indications whatsoever are provided. The first movement of Mozart's C major Sonata, K. 545, 1788, contains just six dynamic marks; on the other hand, Ex. 11-7, from the C minor Sonata, K. 457, 1784, provides an expressive nuance for each figure.

Ex. 11-7. *Dynamic markings.* Mozart, Sonata in C minor, K. 457, 1784, Adagio.

From Mozart, *Sonatas and Fantasias for the Piano* (Nathan Broder, ed.). Copyright 1956, 1960 by Theodore Presser Company, Bryn Mawr. Used by kind permission of the publisher.

ARTICULATION

Articulation signifies the degree of separation between notes and figures in performance; it also refers to degrees of emphasis. Instructions for articulation in performance stressed *clarity* above all (*Deutlichkeit*); this is understandable, considering the subtle shadings and juxtapositions we have observed.

Treatises gave much attention to articulation; the fullest and most sensitive discussion was in Türk's *Klavierschule*, 1789, where ch. VI deals with clarity in performance. Türk's views agreed generally with those of his predecessors—Quantz, Leopold Mozart, and Johann A. P. Schulz.[26] They are valid for the keyboard music of Haydn and Mozart, less so for Beethoven. In his "Erinnerungen aus meinem Leben," Carl Czerny refers to the differences in the styles of piano playing between the time of Mozart (*detached*) and his own time (*legato*).[27]

Melodies around the turn of the century began to acquire a more continuous and broader sweep, calling for a legato style of performance. This shift represents a fundamental change in declamation; Haydn and Mozart were linked to the older tradition, Beethoven to the newer style. To clarify this distinction, often not recognized in performances of classic music, the following material explains 18th-century views; they are represented best by Türk, 1789, whose coverage of this topic is comprehensive. His remarks apply to keyboard music, but they run parallel to those found in treatises on vocal performance—Hiller, Marpurg, Mancini. Indeed, many of Türk's recommendations appear to be influenced by vocal declamation. *Clarity*, according to Türk, depends on:

1. Mechanically proper delivery
2. Emphasis
3. Proper connection and separation of musical periods[28]

Mechanical Clarity

Mechanical clarity is achieved when each tone of the most rapid passage in a piece is heard distinctly separated from the other tones. Tones without specific *staccato* or *slur* signs are played somewhat shorter than their indicated duration, followed by a slight *rest* which completes the note length (see Ex. 11-8). These recommendations corroborate those of C. P. E. Bach, 1753-1762, Quantz, 1752, and Leopold Mozart, 1756, and apply to notes of half-note value or less. While there is some difference of opinion concerning the exact degree of detachment (Türk feels that C. P. E. Bach exaggerates when he recommends cutting the note at half its value),[29] all evidence points to some degree of *détaché* as a norm for performance. *Détaché* must have been overdone at times, in view of the comment in Sulzer, 1771-1774, that "light" and "even" performance had gained the upper hand and that no difference in performance was being made between a church solo and an opera aria.[30] The prevailing galant taste of that time is indicated in this comment.

Ex. 11-8. *Modifications of note length.* Türk, *Klavierschule*, 1789, p. 356.

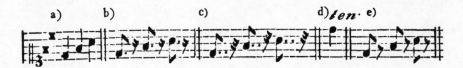

Emphasis

Détaché promoted the management of *emphasis*—*quantitas intrinseca*, accent, and *tempo rubato*. Türk gives recommendations for dynamic differences to emphasize the "good" notes in a measure (Ex. 11-9). Emphasis was also achieved by playing "good" notes slightly longer than "bad," as Koch, 1802, recommends:

> The manner in which accent is expressed can be better felt than described; strictly speaking, it arises partly from an increased strength of a tone, partly from a certain stress of length, in which it appears that the accented tone is held an instant longer than its prescribed length.[31]

Rousseau, Hiller, Koch, and Christmann distinguish between

> *Grammatical* accent, the normal stress that occurs at the beginning of a measure or other metric group
>
> *Oratorical* accent, a stress given to an important melodic note, whether or not it falls upon the normal grammatical accent
>
> *Pathetic* accent, an especially intense oratorical accent, often upon a salient dissonant melodic tone[32]

In Ex. 11-4 above the notes checked all take oratorical or pathetic accentuation. Those in group (a) coincide with the normal grammatical accent. Those in groups (b) to (f) create special accents upon normally weak parts of the measure.

Ex. 11-9.   *Emphasis by means of dynamic differences.* Türk, *Klavierschule,* 1789, p. 335.

Connection

Emphasis also assists in the proper *connection and separation of phrases and periods,* according to Türk:

> Every tone that begins a period must have a still stronger accent than that of the *usual* "good" note. To be sure, such tones that begin a section should be accented more or less according to the extent of the section to follow; that is after an authentic cadence, the beginning tone must be more strongly marked than after a half cadence or after a simple pause.[33]

Türk then gives a brief example (Ex. 11-10).

Ex. 11-10.   *Hierarchy of accents.* Türk, *Klavierschule,* 1789, p. 336.

Note: The crosses represent degrees of accent; the circle represents an unaccented tone that begins a phrase.

The phrase and period accents marked by Türk apply to the complementary relationships that govern simple dance music and music based on dance rhythms, and should come into play whenever a phrase embodies dance-like topics.

Türk's view of accent, typical in the 18th century, is *trochaic*, placing the accent at the beginning of a group. This differs from 19th-century ideas, represented by Riemann, which interpret opening measures or figures as upbeats—i.e., an *iambic* meter.[34]

Legato—which became a norm for *declamation* in the 19th century—represented a *nuance* in the 18th. It was indicated by slurs or by the term *legato,* when it applied to the entire piece. Most of Türk's examples of legato cover two, three, or four tones; *not one* of his examples carries the legato over the bar line. *This principle should guide the performer in the music of Haydn and Mozart.* Even the most extended roulades should be articulated often enough to maintain the clarity of declamation and crispness of rhythm.

Türk distinguishes two basic types of declamation, "heavy" and "light," between which there are many gradations. His comments are so much to the point that they are given here *in extenso*.

The *heavy* or *light* performance adds profoundly to the expression of the ruling sentiment . . . it is not possible to determine in each case the degree of lightness or heaviness. The effect depends on the ways in which *staccato, connection* [*Tragen, appoggiato, portamento di voce*], *slurring* and *sustaining* [*Schleifen*] are properly used. First we shall describe these means and then discuss their application.[35]

Türk then provides clear explanations with examples. *Staccato*, he says, can be indicated by a stroke or a dot; although they have the same meaning, some musicians take the stroke to indicate a shorter staccato than the dot.[36] *Tragen* is indicated by a series of dots connected by a slur; in the examples of slurring, the groups are short, four notes or less, except for one group of eight eighth-notes; this again points to a style that rests upon a detached delivery.[37]

In a *heavy* performance each tone must be firmly produced and held to its full length. *Light* refers to a performance in which each tone is produced less firmly and the finger leaves the keyboard a bit sooner than the prescribed length of the note. To avoid misunderstanding I must remark here that *heavy* and *light* refer more to the sustaining or separating of notes than to loud and soft. In certain cases, for example, in an *allegro vivo, scherzando, vivace con allegrezza*, etc., the delivery must be rather light (short), but more or less strong; on the other hand, a piece with pathetic character, for example, an *adagio mesto, con afflizzione*, etc., to be slurred and therefore somewhat heavy, should not be played loud. But in most cases, *heavy* and *strong* go together.

Whether the delivery is heavy or light must be determined by (1) the character or mood of the piece, (2) the indicated tempo, (3) the meter, (4) the categories of notes [lengths], (5) the way the piece progresses. In addition, we must consider the local color (*Nationalgeschmack*), the composer's personal style, and the instrument for which the piece is written.

Compositions of an elevated, serious, ceremonial, pathetic, etc., character must be *heavy*, full and powerful, strongly accented, etc. In this category we place pieces that are marked *grave, pomposo, patetico, maestoso, sostenuto*, etc. A *somewhat lighter* performance and distinctly gentler style are called for in pieces that are pleasant, soft, agreeable, etc., such as those marked *compiacevole, con dolcezza, glissato, lusingando, Pastorale, piacevole*, etc. Cheerful, playful, joyful feelings indicated by *Allegro scherzando, burlesco, giocoso, con allegrezza, risvegliato*, etc. must be *entirely light* in their delivery; on the other hand, sorrowful and similar affects call for *slurring* and *sustaining* of tones. This latter type of composition carries such indications as: *con afflizzione, con amarezza, lagrimoso, languido, mesto*, etc. . . .[38]

Meter has a marked effect upon light or heavy delivery. . . . The greater the meter, the heavier the delivery. . . . Thus a measure of $^3/_2$ (a) is much heavier than a measure of $^3/_4$ (b) or $^3/_8$ (c) [see Ex. 11-11]. Graun wished to modify a quicker pace for example (d) and specified a heavy style by means of the meter.

Ex. 11-11. *Heavy and light style in performance.* Türk, *Klavierschule,* 1789, p. 360.

In examples (a) and (d) all tones must be emphatically produced and fully sustained. In (b) and (e) the performance is somewhat lighter, in (c) and (f) very light. Also, if adagio is prescribed for (c) and (f) a good performer will play them somewhat lighter than if the meter were *Allabreve,* as in (a) and (d). Otherwise, it follows . . . that $^2/_8$, $^4/_8$, $^3/_{16}$ and $^6/_{16}$ call for the lightest manner.[39]

Various note values call for a more or less heavy style, regardless of the meter. When for example a piece has mainly long notes, whole and half notes, it requires a heavier style than when many eighths and sixteenths, etc., are commingled. Dotted notes require a particularly special treatment. It is the custom to sustain dotted notes longer than their indicated value and to play the following short notes more quickly, as for example [see Ex. 11-12]:

Ex. 11-12. *Performance of dotted notes.* Türk, *Klavierschule,* 1789, p. 361.

The execution indicated in (b) above is selected when the style of the piece is serious, ceremonial, elevated; this is the case not only in the *Grave* itself, but also in overtures or pieces marked *sostenuto* in which cases the dotted notes are heavy, i.e., to be held longer. To express cheerful, joyous sentiments, the style must be somewhat lighter, as in (c). The style of (d) is used particularly in violent or bold expression or when the piece is marked *staccato*. The keys are attacked strongly and the fingers raised sooner than in cases where a ceremonial quality is called for. In pleasantly singing melodies, as in (e), the dotted note is also held over a bit — although not so decidedly — thus it is performed more softly (less accented). Especially in such cases the short notes following the dotted note must be played lightly and slurred. In the case of a second voice being present, as in (f), one retains the prescribed division, thus [see Ex. 11-13]:

Ex. 11-13. *Performance of dotted notes.* Türk, *Klavierschule*, 1789, p. 362.

Here and there in contrapuntal passages, the dotted note is [written only] in one voice, and the short notes are played in both voices in the same manner, so as to be consistent. For example [see Ex. 11-14]:

Ex. 11-14. *Resolution of dotted rhythms.* Türk, *Klavierschule*, 1789, p. 362.

In addition, the short pauses, which substitute for the dots, are often lengthened in lively pieces as in (b), below [see Ex. 11-15]:

Ex. 11-15. *Lengthening of rests.* Türk, *Klavierschule*, 1789, p. 363.

Figures in which the first note is short and the second dotted are slurred without exception and performed generally in a caressing manner. Although the first (short) tone is accented, it should receive a very light emphasis.

One should not rush the first note, especially in a slow tempo, because this can easily degrade the melody into a saucy manner . . . .

A piece composed according to the *Italian* taste is generally performed in a moderate style (between heavy and light) although there are many exceptions. *French* music requires a lighter style. On the other hand, *German* music calls for a heavier, more powerful style, as a rule.

. . . Heavy or light style should correspond not only to the general manner of the piece but to each section thereof. In a cheerful piece that takes a light touch, there still may be more exalted passages that need a heavier style . . . .[40]

In a legato, Türk says, the first note of the passage should receive a slight accent even when it begins on a weak beat.[41]

ORNAMENTATION

Melodic ornaments added by the performer were confined to solo music or to the leading voice in an ensemble. Beyond conventional prescribed signs, the performer might add figures of his own, following a tradition of improvised ornamentation reaching back to medieval times.

Treatises give full and explicit instructions on the performance of melodic ornaments (*Manieren, agréments*).[42] Yet no full agreement existed concerning notation or performance of these figures. For example, the appoggiatura in m. 2 of the first movement of Mozart's A minor Sonata, K. 310, 1778, is written to be played short, since it is one-quarter the length of the principal note; yet the written-out figure in m. 10 that restates this pattern makes it a long appoggiatura. The context would appear to call for the long ornament in both places. On the other hand the biting "Turkish" nuances in mm. 1 and 9 suggest short appoggiaturas struck almost together with their main notes.

Melodic ornaments written in signs or small notes were *Spielmanieren* (performance ornaments); written out, they were *Setzmanieren* (composition ornaments). Use of *Spielmanieren* declined from the lavish distribution of ornamental signs that fill the sonatas, rondos, and fantasias of C. P. E. Bach. Figures were absorbed into the notation and melody. Had the theme of the finale of Mozart's D major Sonata, K. 576, 1789, been composed some decades earlier, it might have been notated as in Ex. 11-16.

Ex. 11-16. *Ornaments in context.* Mozart, Sonata in D major, K. 576, 1789, finale.

Allegretto

The ornaments in mm. 1, 3, 5, and 6 are *Nachschläge* (following notes); those in mm. 2 and 4 are appoggiaturas. (See Ex. 11-18 for the actual notation.)

The two most important melodic ornaments were the *trill* and the *appoggiatura*; both took a number of different forms. The trill could be short or long, begin on the upper or lower note, and carry an additional ornamental turn either at its beginning or at its end. The appoggiatura was either short or long, dissonant or consonant. According to Koch, in his *Journal*, 1795, the appoggiatura was indicated in small notes to distinguish it as a special nuance; otherwise, it was notated in the normal manner. When the appoggiatura was played as a long note, it assumed the role of the "good" note in *quantitas intrinseca*. It received somewhat greater emphasis than the note of resolution. This process was called *Abzug* (abatement) and was marked for attention by many theorists,[43] since it was an important expressive nuance. The same could apply to appoggiaturas in normal notation.

One convention observed consistently in 18th-century opera was the addition of an appoggiatura at the end of a line in a recitative when the phrase closed upon a weak syllable. The music was notated as two notes of the same pitch; the singer took the appoggiatura upon the first tone, as an expressive nuance.[44]

Improvised ornamentation no longer occupied the central position it had enjoyed in baroque and mid-century music; in fact, it was openly frowned upon. But the tradition did not disappear entirely in the classic era. Koch concludes his article on "Manieren," 1802:

> However, if one must ornament, one must be careful not to misrepresent the sense of the melody and to avoid harmonic errors.[45]

Improvised ornamentation might be tastefully added in a slow movement, a simple continuo part, a cadenza or fermata, or where a literal repetition took place.[46] Instructions for improvised ornamentation were given in a number of later 18th-century treatises.[47] The decline of the practice, as signaled by the fully written-out ornamentation of most classic music, seems to be an effort to preserve melodic elegance against its deterioration in the hands of unskilled amateurs and charlatans. Judging from the ornamentation illustrated in many treatises (see note 42), additions could become extremely florid (see Ex. 20-3). To illustrate what might be added upon the repetition of a passage, an excerpt from the C major Sonata, K. 330, 1778, by Mozart is quoted in Ex. 11-17; the ornamentation consists of an arpeggio in m. 1 and an anticipation in m. 3. Such elaborations exemplify the views of Quantz[48] and Türk[49] that repetitions of a passage may be ornamented. (See also p. 337f.)

Ex. 11-17.   Mozart, Sonata in C major, K. 330, 1778, 2nd movt.

a. As written.

Ex. 11-17, cont'd.

b. Possible ornamentation upon repetition.

Applying the information on performance covered in this chapter, some recommendations can be made concerning details of performance in a typical classic movement, the finale of Mozart's D major Sonata, K. 576, 1789 (Ex. 11-18). It is in the quick and lively style of the contredanse, like many classic finales. The tempo designation is *allegretto*. Whenever Mozart uses allegretto in his piano sonatas, the measure clearly is divided into four beats, regardless of the 2/4 or 4/4 signature. Here, a moderate tempo in which the eighth-note beat is clearly projected is indicated. The theme itself has nuances that call for a clear and light declamation. Unlike that of most contredanses, the accompaniment does not accentuate the strong beat. The melody does double duty: it serves as a tune and also to provide the accent normally taken by the bass. The first eight measures embody a symmetrical period, which would normally be enclosed by reprise signs (see Chs. 12 and 14). On its restatement, the theme is recomposed and the running bass provides an accent at the beginning of each measure. In Ex. 11-18 note the regular hierarchy of phrase accents (shown by Türk's signs), broken in mm. 13-16; m. 15 does not take on its normal intermediate stress; rather, it should be played even lighter than the preceding measure to emphasize the very strong accent of m. 16.

Ex. 11-18. *Texture and performance.* Mozart, Sonata in D major, K. 576, 1789, finale.

From Mozart, *Sonatas and Fantasias for the Piano* (Nathan Broder, ed.). Copyright 1956, 1960 by Theodore Presser Company, Bryn Mawr. Used by kind permission of the publisher.

Some of the subtleties of texture, harmony, and change of topic in this movement require a moderate tempo for clear declamation; they are quoted in Ex. 11-19.

Ex. 11-19.   Mozart, Sonata in D major, K. 576, 1789, finale.

a. Ornamental suspensions.

b. Learned style—imitation; note also the harmonic ambiguities created by the appoggiatura figures.

Ex. 11-19, cont'd.

c. Rapidly shifting chromatic harmonies.

From Mozart, *Sonatas and Fantasias for the Piano* (Nathan Broder, ed.). Copyright 1956, 1960 by Theodore Presser Company, Bryn Mawr. Used by kind permission of the publisher.

In his *Dictionnaire* on "Expression," Rousseau, 1768, says:

> One thing that the composer must not overlook is that the more searching the harmony, the less rapid the tempo, so that the mind has the time to grasp the progression of dissonances and the rapid changes in the modulation; it is only the ultimate peak of the passions that permits the rapidity of tempo combined with the tightness of harmony.[50]

Rousseau's recommendations would apply specifically to the passages in Ex. 11-18. The *Nachschlag* in m. 1 and the appoggiatura in m. 2 appear many times, literally or altered. A clear and easy declamation in a moderate tempo is necessary to articulate these changes. More than half the duration of this movement incorporates triplet 16ths in a wide variety of patterns. This rich tracery requires a moderate tempo, clear articulation, and lightness of sound. With the softer tone of the early piano, *p* and *f* are principally foils for each other; *forte* should be taken at a moderate level of strength.

This piece shows Mozart in a speculative, searching vein, much absorbed with the learned style notwithstanding the ruling topic of the contredanse. A moderate tempo not only permits the turns and twists of the texture to emerge but also allows for the imperceptible modifications of tempos that can articulate and set off each of the many changes of treatment in the discourse.

The foregoing discussion of classic performance practice has centered upon keyboard music for several reasons: (1) the keyboard had the largest repertory in the late 18th century; (2) very likely more persons played the keyboard than other instruments; (3) the keyboard constituted a complete ensemble, often acting as a substitute for other groups; (4) the most comprehensive manual for late 18th-century performance practice was Türk's *Klavierschule*, 1789. Yet, paradoxically, among the various performing media extant at that time, keyboard instruments had more difficulty in achieving expressive nuances than the voice, string instruments, and winds; in these latter, subtle and minute variations of breath or bow could give expressive shadings to tones already sounding, a resource not available to the fortepiano and harpsichord, and only to a limited extent available to the clavichord. However, apart from this circumstance, Türk's recommendations regarding tempo, articulation, accent, and dynamics are valid generally for the music of his time.

Performance manuals of the later 18th century were concerned with clarifying the composer's intentions. Therefore they were much less concerned with virtuosity than the treatises of a later age. For example: the early editions of Löhlein's *Clavier-Schule*, 1765 through 1782, deal with some aspects of continuo realization and composition as well as the basic technique of keyboard performance; a later edition, edited by Müller, 1804, discards virtually all of the stylistic and performance material in favor of hundreds of exercises designed to develop digital velocity.

One view pervades all discussions of performance: attention to detail is the secret of expressive declamation. The fine points made by Türk have their counterpart in many other treatises. This suggests that each performance of a work might be subtly different from others in detail, but with taste, judgment, and skill each performance could be persuasive and faithful to the expressive qualities written into the piece.

NOTES

1. Kirkpatrick, in *PAMS*, 1938, p. 30ff.
2. Koch, *Lexikon*, p. 890.
3. Ibid., pp. 62–65.
4. Ibid., pp. 142–143.
5. Ibid., pp. 130–131.
6. Ibid., p. 1169.
7. Türk, *Klavierschule*, p. 110.
8. Johann A. Scheibe, quoted in Kirkpatrick, op. cit.
9. *AMZ*, 1798, p. 462.
10. Anonymous comment in ibid.
11. Anderson, *The Letters of Mozart*, p. 460.
12. Koch, *Journal*, p. 112ff.
13. Tosi, *Florid Song*, p. 99.
14. Ibid., p. 100.
15. Ibid., p. 156; see also Quantz, *Versuch*, pp. 254, 260.
16. Anderson, *The Letters of Mozart*, p. 340.
17. Türk, *Klavierschule*, pp. 370–371.
18. Koch, *Lexikon*, pp. 1502–1503.
19. Türk, *Klavierschule*, pp. 114–116, 359.
20. See Boyden on "Dynamics" in *Davison Essays*, p. 185ff.
21. Schubart, *Ideen*, p. 364.
22. Burney, *History*, p. 945.
23. Harding, *Origins of Musical Time*, p. 102.
24. *Mannheim Symphonists*, Hugo Riemann ed., 2 vols., Broude Bros., New York, n.d.

25. In vol. III, p. 19ff.
26. Quantz, *Versuch*; L. Mozart, *Versuch*; Schulz, in Sulzer, *Allgemeine Theorie*.
27. Czerny, *Vortrag*, Badura-Skoda ed., p. 11.
28. Türk, *Klavierschule*, p. 334.
29. Ibid., p. 356.
30. Sulzer, *Allgemeine Theorie*, p. 1253.
31. Koch, *Lexikon*, p. 50.
32. Rousseau, *Dictionnaire*, p. 2ff.; Hiller, *Musikalisch-zierlichen Gesange*, p. 27f.; Koch, *Lexikon*, pp. 50–53; Christmann, *Elementarbuch*, p. 207.
33. Türk, *Klavierschule*, p. 336.
34. Hugo Riemann, *System der Musikalischen Rhythmik und Metrik*, Breitkopf and Härtel 1903, Leipzig, p. 198.
35. Türk, *Klavierschule*, p. 353.
36. Ibid.
37. Ibid., p. 354.
38. Ibid., pp. 358–359.
39. Ibid., pp. 360–361.
40. Ibid., pp. 361–364.
41. Ibid., p. 355.
42. Koch, *Journal, Lexikon*; L. Mozart, *Versuch*; Tartini, *Traité des agrémens*; Quantz, *Versuch*; Martini, *Melopée*; Hiller, *Musikalisch-zierlichen Gesange*; Wolf, *Unterricht*; etc. See also Putnam Aldrich on "Ornamentation," in Apel, *Harvard Dictionary*.
43. Koch, *Lexikon*, p. 47; Türk, *Klavierschule*, p. 218.
44. Hiller, *Musikalisch-zierlichen Gesange*, p. 102.
45. Koch, *Lexikon*, p. 929.
46. Hiller, *Musikalisch-zierlichen Gesange*, p. 96.
47. Tartini, *Traité des agrémens*; Zuccari, *Method of Playing an Adagio*; Wolf, *Unterricht*.
48. Quantz, *Versuch*, pp. 120, 141, 172, passim.
49. Türk, *Klavierschule*, p. 323ff.
50. Rousseau, *Dictionnaire*, pp. 210–211.

Conclusion to Part II

The following analysis of the first reprise of the menuetto from Haydn's Symphony No. 101 in D major, the *Clock*, 1794, incorporates the criteria of expression and rhetoric discussed in the preceding chapters. Ex. 1 gives the structural line of the melody; Ex. 2 quotes the full score.

1. *Expression*. A brilliant, high-style piece, with an air of triumph or high ceremony.

2. *Topic*. A court minuet, rather stately in manner, with a hint of the military in the prominence of the horn fifths in the brass and the strokes of the timpani; singing style in contrast to the brilliant, m. 5.

3. *Periodicity*. A long first period; the first phrase is eight measures long, comprising two contrasted ideas; the second phrase is twelve measures long, with an internal four-measure extension beginning at m. 13, leading to a firm cadence in the dominant, m. 20. The second period is eight measures long and acts as a cadential reinforcement of the dominant by means of four authentic cadences.

4. *Harmony*. With the exception of two incidental chromatic tones, G♯ in m. 7 and A♯ in m. 24, all harmony consists of simple cadential formulas in tonic or dominant keys. This straightforward, simple harmony, involving tonic and dominant mostly, contributes to the brilliance of the piece. The only authentic cadences appear in the dominant; the tonic is firmly established, but moves forward toward the dominant without an authentic cadence. The dominant is approached with great intensity and force by means of six cadential formulas, and is then confirmed with strong authentic cadences. In this way, a powerful harmonic periodicity is generated.

5. *Rhythm*. A completely symmetrical beginning, both with respect to measure groups and with respect to chord changes. At m. 11, a three-measure group breaks the symmetry, underscoring the shift to the dominant. Measures 14–20 might be scanned as 4 + 3, or 4 + 2 + 1. The final period introduces an imbroglio to intensify the cadential action while the melody scans as 3 + 3 + 2 + 1 to complicate the rhythmic displacement. The final measures reestablish rhythmic symmetry.

6. *Melody*. The structural melodic line comprises two ascending scales, each followed by a balancing descent, as sketched in Ex. 1. Note the leveling off of the structural melody once the key of A is reached, and the centering of the line around the note A; this action contributes to the effect of periodicity, of arrival. A minuet pattern is superimposed (see Ex. 2), mostly in quarter-notes, with relatively little elaboration, so that the structural melody shines forth clearly behind the figuration. The contrasting cantabile phrase at m. 5 of the score (Ex. 2) ornaments its structural melody in the same manner, but introduces an octave upbeat, mm. 4–5 of the score, as an elegant gesture. As the music moves toward the

dominant, the heightened harmonic and rhythmic activity is reinforced by a more elaborate brilliant-style melody, only to be pulled up short at m. 20 by the most intense action in the section — imbroglio, cadences, and simple, terse melodic figures.

Ex. 1.   Haydn, Symphony No. 101 in D major, the *Clock*, 1794, menuetto, structural line of the melody.

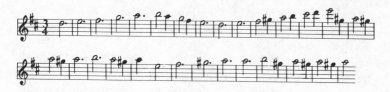

7.   *Texture.* The brilliance of a military orchestral tutti, with winds and brass doubling the strings in fanfare style; sharp contrast, as in the tutti-solo of a concerto, with strings in a parallel third passage in the singing style. A basic two-voice texture, reinforced with thirds, sixths, for the most part. The outer voices carry the important melodic material, the strings representing the focus of textural action. This minuet could be (and was) reduced for home performance by clavier or a few instruments.

8.   *Performance.* The stately style calls for a moderate tempo, with marked *détaché*, a full but not overloud sound in the *forte*. In the *piano* section, the upbeats should be lightly stressed to lend a piquant nuance, and the first two notes of mm. 5 and 6 should be rather short, to set off the sliding legato of m. 7. The high E in 14 is an oratorical accent and should be the target of the passage preceding it; being stressed it will help to define the triple scansion of mm. 11-13; this is also the first point at which the structural melody interrupts its stepwise motion. The counterrhythms in mm. 20-25 should be emphasized by marked stresses upon the attack, followed by a decided drop in intensity (*détaché*) to allow the rhythmic counterpoint to emerge.

To conclude, the following quotation from Koch is cited, in which he indicates some of the connections between expression and rhetoric, 1802:

As we turn our attention briefly to the means by which the *materials* of music, or the way in which musical tones may be connected to express a wide variety of feelings, then this variety of expression is based especially upon slow or quick tempo . . . or upon the use of the high or low range of a voice or instrument; [it lies] in the emphasis on stepwise or disjunct melody; in the smooth or separate connection of tones; in the use of easy, flowing intervals, or intervals that are difficult to perform; in the greater or lesser use of accent, on the strong or weak parts of measures; in the use of similar or different figures; in the greater or lesser sense of rhythmic definition; in the connection of more natural or more strange, more consonant or more dissonant chords, etc. Thus, for example, the expression of *sorrowful* feelings calls for a slow tempo, lower, rather than higher tones which are connected rather

Ex. 2.   Haydn, Symphony No. 101 in D major, the *Clock*, 1794, menuetto.

Ex. 2, cont'd.

19

Peters Edition 5623

than separate, heavy and severe melodic continuity, many dissonances in the harmony and their heavy accentuation in the performance, and somewhat less emphasized rhythm, etc. — The expression of *joyous* feelings, on the other hand, is signalled by a lively motion, higher instead of lower notes, separate instead of connected notes that leap rather than proceed stepwise; the rhythm is easy to grasp and should avoid unevenness; it is however not to be heavily marked; tones call for moderate accentuation, and this type of affect should avoid difficult melodic intervals and excessive use of dissonance. — The expression of the *exalted* calls for a rather slow pace, a strongly marked rhythm, separate rather than connected tones; it is well expressed with long notes and large leaps, although they should be consonant, a full harmony without being overloaded with dissonances, and extremely strong accentuation; thereby one uses, in pieces of this character, dotted notes in a moderate tempo . . . .[1]

In Part II, the basic criteria for each aspect of rhetoric have been defined and a range of options illustrated — ways in which the various parts of classic musical discourse could be put together to establish *coherence* and to promote *eloquence. These techniques and their expressive potential represent the heart of the classic style.* A clear understanding of the criteria and the techniques is essential to gain a perspective of classic form.

NOTE

1. Koch, *Lexikon*, pp. 896–897; see also Quantz, *Versuch*, p. 108.

III Form

C lassic forms are based upon a small number of plans, simple, flexible, accessible to student, dilettante, and professional composer alike. These plans represent, in form, the counterparts of the structural lines in melody and texture.

The degree of sophistication and originality applied in working out a form ranged from frank paraphrase in the teaching of composition to unique adaptations of standard layouts.

Simple formulas could be managed easily; putting together little dances was a popular pastime, judging from the following "prescription" quoted from a review in Johann Adam Hiller's *Nachrichten*, 1766:

Recipe for composing dances:
1. Take any tonic chord you prefer. . . .
2. Place after it the chord of the fifth. . . .
3. Repeat the tonic chord.
4. Do this at least four times, so that you will have the entire harmony of the dance before you.
5. See now that the melody agrees with your harmony, divide it in the middle; set the repeat sign in the middle and at the end, and so your dance is finished. Notice that if all the phrases agree well with the basic harmony, you will have the option of putting the first second and the second first.[1]

Musical dice games reflect the same dilettante spirit. Also, a beginner could follow the recommendations of Kirnberger, Crotch, Portmann, Galeazzi, or Czerny to select a model, retaining the harmonic and rhythmic schemes and paraphrasing melodic figures. J. S. Bach himself, as well as Mozart, made use of this procedure.[2] Paraphrase was used for teaching but may have enabled a hard-pressed composer to deliver a piece on short notice.

For the serious composer, three stages in the planning of a movement are specified by Spiess, 1746, Sulzer, 1771-1774, and Koch, 1787, 1802:

1. *Anlage*: plan, in which the principal melodic ideas, the ruling expression, and the structural voices, i.e., melody and bass, are sketched

2. *Ausführung*: amplification, in which the main periods are laid out, the modulations are set, and the working out of the material and its restatements are fixed

3. *Ausarbeitung*: polishing, in which the highlights and the details of voice-leading, scoring, melodic ornamentation, and nuance are fitted to the piece[3]

Whatever form was being used, it had to embody an overall unity comprising:

1. *A ruling affection or topic*, represented by the opening melodic idea or principal theme

2. *A ruling key*, established at the beginning and confirmed at the end

3. *Clearly defined rhythmic order*, represented by carefully planned scansion and cadential hierarchy

Classic forms have been a chief point of interest for scholars during the past century. These forms have impressed with their ability to embody rhetorical coherence on a broad scale and to incorporate a powerfully persuasive eloquence. One of the difficulties in analyzing these forms has been the tendency to measure each example against a prototype or "ideal" plan, a tendency that leads to a rigid view of classic forms. In this book, the opposite view is taken; classic forms are interpreted as countless options within a few working schemes, the schemes themselves arising from the idiomatic rhetoric of classic music. Each composer could work within the familiar and accepted framework and modify to express his unique personal message.

NOTES

1. Hiller, *Nachrichten*, I, p. 132f.
2. See p. 356; see also the Mozart piano concertos K. 39 in B♭ major, K. 40 in D major and K. 41 in G major, all 1767, which are reworkings of sonata movements by other composers.
3. Spiess, *Tractatus*, pp. 133-135; Sulzer, *Allgemeine Theorie*, p. 94ff.; Koch, *Versuch*, II, p. 52ff., and *Lexikon*, p. 146.

12 Small Two-Reprise Forms

When we look at classic forms according to harmonic plan, we find a remarkable consistency of procedure. By far the greater majority of movements, large and small, carry out a *two-phase* action, first moving away from the tonic to make a decisive cadence somewhere in the middle of the movement, then returning to the tonic to make an even more decisive final close.

The origin of this plan reaches back into the dances of medieval, Renaissance, and baroque music. These dances were most often laid out in two well-defined sections, each of which could be repeated: A A B B. The repetition of a section was termed a *reprise*; eventually, the section thus repeated was called a reprise. Hence a piece modeled upon this pattern can be described as a *two-reprise* form.[1] This designation will be used in the following discussion of classic form.

For classic music, the *two-reprise* form was a generic plan, furnishing a basic pattern for works on every scale, from dances to symphonies. In its simplest version, it consisted of two sections, each a period in length, and each enclosed by repeat signs. A two-reprise form could be expanded by means of extensions and period groups to the length of a symphonic movement without modification of its original contour.

Harmony defined the form by locating the principal points of reference. This harmonic layout is designated by the following formulas:

I–I, X–I when the middle cadence is in the tonic

I–V, X–I when the middle cadence is *in* or *on* the dominant

In both cases X, chosen at option by the composer, represents the approach to the final close in the tonic.

MINIMAL FORMS

Koch describes the simplest complete piece as 16 measures in length, with two reprises and four melodic members of equal length. His first example is quoted in Ex. 12-1.

Koch, 1793, explains the example as follows:

This short piece possesses the most perfect unity. It contains four melodic sections, with but one principal idea, modified in various ways. This idea comprises the first four measures, which first appear as a tonic phrase [cadence on the tonic but not final], and which are immediately repeated, modified to make a closing phrase [authentic cadence]. In Part II the domi-

209

Ex. 12-1. *Small two-reprise form.* Koch, *Versuch,* III, 1793, pp. 58-59—Haydn, Divertimento in G major, H.V. II, No. 1, before 1766.

nant phrase, repeated to make a closing phrase, differs only melodically from the preceding phrases, but actually is the same, presented differently, only by contrary motion and a passing modulation, so that more variety will be introduced.

One can see here that a single phrase is sufficient as melodic material for a small piece when the composer knows how to incorporate different turns and connections so that the unity of the piece, however, will include the necessary variety.[2]

Unity is expressed by the key, the symmetry of the four phrases, and the single melodic idea, while variety is provided by cadences on different tones. According to Riepel, 1755, and Koch, 1787, *adjacent cadences should not pause upon the same melodic tone.*[3]

The form of this minuet is I-I, X-I. Still, the presence of the dominant in reprise II creates a V-I polarity. When reprise I *closes* on V, the dominant, with either an authentic or a half cadence, a *decisive* harmonic polarity is created. Reprise II *must* then reverse this action, as in Ex. 12-2.

Ex. 12-2. *Two-reprise form with middle cadence on dominant.* Koch, *Versuch,* III, 1793, pp. 82-84.

Note the recall of mm. 1-2 in mm. 13-14, and the rhyme of mm. 7-8 in mm. 15-16.

When the middle cadence rests upon V (half cadence), a continuation is still required harmonically, as in the Tempo di menuetto of Haydn's Sonata in A major, H.V. XVI, No. 30, 1774-1776.

MELODIC MATERIAL

Melodic material in small two-reprise forms can be arranged in many ways. Ex.
12-1 illustrates the use of a *single* figure throughout. Ex. 12-3, from Löhlein,
demonstrates the opposite: *not one figure is restated*. Löhlein's explanation deals
exclusively with harmony and punctuation. He offers this piece as a model for
small-scale composition, but points out that all the components of a large piece
are present here in miniature.

Ex. 12-3. *Variety of figures in small two-reprise form*. Löhlein, *Clavier-
Schule*, Vol. 2, 1781, pp. 181-182.

Melodic restatement serves to highlight significant points in the second reprise. The return to I is announced by the *recall* of the opening melodic idea.
The melodic figures of the middle cadence in V can be transposed to I to close
the second reprise. This creates a melodic end-*rhyme*. *Such rhymes are optional
in small forms but are prescriptive in larger forms.* Ex. 12-2 recalls the opening
measures at mm. 13-14, and rhymes the last two measures of each reprise. Ex.
12-4 does not recall the opening material but rhymes the final four measures. As
in poetry, end-rhyme in the two-reprise form creates a strong effect of closure.

Ex. 12-4. *Melodic rhyme in two-reprise forms.* Koch, *Versuch*, III, 1793, pp. 85-86.

THE X SECTION

The X section, whose function is to open the way to the final confirmation of the tonic in reprise II, may traverse a number of harmonic paths. Riepel, 1755, uses his own colorful terms for three options that were standard in 18th-century music:

Monte — a rise, signifying a sequential progression that rises. In C major this would proceed from F to G.

Ponte — a bridge, signifying a progression that remains on the dominant.

Fonte — a well or source, to which a descent must be made; this signifies a sequential progression. In Ex. 12-5 there is a descent from D minor to C major at the beginning of reprise II; *Monte* and *Ponte* are also illustrated.

Reprise II of the menuetto of Mozart's *Eine kleine Nachtmusik*, K. 525, 1787, opens with a *Fonte*; reprise II of the trio begins with a *Ponte*.

Ex. 12-5. *Monte, Ponte, Fonte as options for second reprise.* Riepel, *Grundregeln,* 1755, pp. 44-47.

Reprise I.

Reprise II.

Monte

Ponte

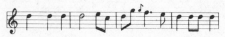

Fonte

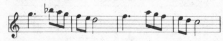

EXTENDED FORMS

The polarity of classic harmony (see Ch. 4) provides opportunities for extension of two-reprise forms, especially when reprise I closes in V. The rise to the dominant can create considerable thrust, to furnish scope for several periods and for periodic extensions (see Ch. 3). The minuet of Mozart's Quartet in G major, K. 387, 1782, illustrates such expansion.

In this movement, the first two measures could well begin an eight-measure period. But symmetry is shattered by the off-beat punctuation in the accompaniment, followed by hemiolias that alternate *piano* and *forte* in duple rhythm. Phrase groupings become irregular. This imbalance is answered, starting in m. 21, with a series of tuneful four-measure phrases, more waltz-like than minuet. Frequent changes in texture reinforce this expansive and eccentric treatment of the two-reprise form. Thus this minuet moves from instability to stability as part of its grand plan.

The stages of action in this minuet are each much longer than those of the minimal 16-measure form. All three options for the X section, *Monte, Ponte,* and *Fonte,* are incorporated. In harmonic contour, this two-reprise form resembles the 16-measure type; in extent, it approaches the dimensions of large-scale classic forms, exemplifying the speculative treatment of a dance topic.

When a two-reprise form becomes extended, reprise II is longer than reprise I, often considerably so. The principal reason is harmonic. As keys appear in the I–V (or III in minor), X–I plan, each succeeding key requires greater length and emphasis. Reprise I starts with a fresh sound, the tonic, and this requires but a phrase or short period to establish the key. The dominant, which replaces I, needs more time to erase the first impression and to confirm itself with emphasis at the end of reprise I. Reprise II begins a phase of harmonic digression, in turn to erase the impression of the dominant and then to prepare for the return to the tonic. The final part of reprise II confirms I. Türk, in *Klavierschule*, 1789, recommends the following proportions:

I	V	X (*Nebentöne—related keys*)	I	
ca. 15	25	20-30	30	= ca. 100 measures[4]

In Mozart's minuet discussed above, the proportions designated by Türk are embodied as follows: I holds for 12 measures; from that point, V is the target, making its cadence 28 measures later; reprise II, with I as its final objective, is 53 measures long. Ex. 12-6 sketches the form.

Ex. 12-6. *Sketch of form.* Mozart, Quartet in G major, K. 387, 1782, minuet.

reprise I			reprise II				I	
I		V	X					
1-12	13-20	21-40	41	50	54	62	63-73	74-93
G major	shift to	D major	D major-	E minor-	D major-	D major	G major	G major
	D major						varied	rhyme,
			Monte	*Fonte*	*Ponte*		recall of	closing
							opening	material
							material	

The discrepancy in length between reprises may be so little as to be hardly noticeable—four measures in the theme of the finale of Haydn's D major Sonata, H.V. XVI, No. 37, circa 1779-1780. Or it may be so great as to distort the form enormously. Beethoven, in his scherzos, sometimes sets up a quick movement to V in reprise I and an immediate cadence to end the reprise. In reprise II, both the X section and the tonic return are vastly extended. The third movement of the *Eroica* Symphony has 14 measures in reprise I and 138 in reprise II. The entire scherzo, from the beginning, is focused toward the final confirmation of the home key, achieved with an emphatic and extended peroration. This issue is dramatized by the headlong momentum, some irregular scansions, and the uncertainty with which Beethoven first announces the home key, E♭, treating it as IV of B♭.

TWO-PART VERSUS THREE-PART DIVISION

Since the melodic recall and rhyme in reprise II generally restate fully the material of reprise I, the melodic plan of a two-reprise form has a three-part layout:

reprise I	reprise II	
A	B (X)	A

For this reason, these forms have often been designated as *three-part, ternary,* or *rounded binary.* A B A melodic layouts occur in all types of music, but the three-part melodic layout in classic forms rests upon a two-part harmonic-rhythmic structure; the interaction between these two levels of structure provides both firmness and vitality.

The two-reprise form furnishes a structural plan for a great many smaller forms in classic music. Dances, marches, songs, shorter arias, rondo themes, variation themes, as well as sections within larger works — all of these display the typical contour of the small two-reprise form. Despite their small scope and immediate appeal, many small two-reprise pieces have subtleties of structure and texture that exhibit the greatest skills of the masters. The minuet, especially, was the classic composer's workshop; in this compact yet flexible plan he could introduce many delicious details of composition and striking mannerisms, play with the learned style, recall pastoral moments — all these and much more without the added burden of an extended form.

Dances and rhymed poetry had used a two-phase arrangement of movement and text since medieval times; the music that accompanied dances and poetry mirrored this pairing. The principle is still used today in popular music. But the apogee in the life history of the two-reprise form occurred in the 18th century, when it became a generic plan for both small- and large-scale structure.

NOTES

1. The term *two-reprise* is applied here in preference to *binary* or *bipartite* since it reflects more accurately the cadential punctuation and the historical context of this plan. References to two-reprise form include Koch, *Lexikon*, p. 345, where it is said that a coda may be added after the two reprises of an allegro movement; Momigny, *Cours complet*, pp. 695-696: "*Reprise*, the 1st or 2nd part of a piece which is divided into two equal or unequal portions"; and Walther, *Lexikon*, where dances are described as consisting of two reprises; they are described similarly in Christmann, *Elementarbuch*.
2. Koch, *Versuch* III, pp. 59-60.
3. Riepel, *Grundregeln*, p. 44; Koch, *Versuch*, II, p. 390.
4. Türk, *Klavierschule*, pp. 62-63.

13 Sonata Form

The chief structural plan in classic music was the extended two-reprise form. This form came into prominence after 1750 through the confluence of many style trends; it is the structural basis of most first movements, of overtures, and of many slow movements and finales; elements of this form are present in many arias. Today, it is known as *sonata form*.

During the past century sonata form has received more critical and historical attention than any other form in the history of western music. Its sudden rise to prominence in the mid-18th century without a clear prehistory and its universal application in the classic era as well as later have fascinated musicologists. Aesthetically, its breadth, its ability to encompass a great richness of content, and its finely balanced proportions are objects of wonder. Analytically, it is a complex and rich object for investigation.

Most analysis of sonata form has taken its thematic content to be the principal parameter; this has been explained as being constituted from two principal themes which are presented, developed, and restated; this results in a *three-part* form. Classic theorists, on the other hand, explained the form of a long movement as a harmonic plan, with two large phases of action, resulting in a *two-part* form. In this chapter these two views are evaluated.

THE HARMONIC PLAN; THE KEY-AREA FORM

Classic theorists described the form of a long movement as a *tour of keys*. The following, from Kollmann, 1799, summarizes the scheme, also described in Koch, 1787 and 1793,[1] Portmann, 1789,[2] Löhlein, 1781,[3] Momigny, 1806,[4] Galeazzi, 1796,[5] and Reicha, 1813:[6]

> In its outline a long movement is generally divided into two sections. The first, when the piece is in major, ends in the fifth of the scale, and the second in the key; but when the piece is in minor, the first section generally ends in the third of the scale and the second in the key. . . . Each section may be divided into two subsections, which in the whole makes four subsections.
>
> The first subsection must contain the setting out from the key to its fifth in major, or third in minor, and it may end with the chord of the key or its fifth, but the latter is better. The second subsection comprehends a first sort of elaboration, consisting of a more natural modulation than that of the third subsection; it may be confined to the third, or fifth, of the key, or also touch upon some related or even non-related keys if only no formal digression is made to any key other than the said fifth in major and third in minor. The third subsection comprehends a second sort of elaboration, consisting of digressions to all those keys and modes which shall be introduced

besides that of the fifth (or third); and being the place for those abrupt modulations or enharmonic changes which the piece admits or requires. The fourth subsection contains the return to the key, with a third sort of elaboration, similar to that of the first section.

The above is the plan of modulation, which is to be found attended to in most sonatas, symphonies, and concertos. . . . But it may be varied almost to the infinite. For the different sections and subsections may be of any reasonable variety of length and the said sorts of modulation and elaboration may be diversified without end.[7]

The two sections in Kollmann's outline correspond to the reprises of a two-reprise form; the harmonic scheme is I–V (III), X–I for both the small and large versions of this generic pattern. The surest way to achieve mastery of the larger form was to develop skill in handling the smaller, according to the leading classic theorists.[8] This plan is here designated as the *key-area form*, to reflect its harmonic layout. It represents periodicity on the broadest level; each part becomes a macroperiod as it carries its harmonic drive to the closes in V and I. A tabulation of classic sonata form movements, whatever their scope and style, will show the I–V (III), X–I plan to be a structural common denominator.

DISTRIBUTION OF MELODIC MATERIAL

In the thematic view of sonata form, the principal elements are the "first" and "second" themes, presented in the exposition, worked over in the development, and restated in the recapitulation. The first theme is held to be "masculine" in character, the second "feminine," and their opposition creates the conflict that gives sonata form its scope. While many sonata forms have two salient themes, often contrasted in style, many others contain but one main theme, and still others contain three, four, or more. If bithematism were taken as a norm, hundreds of exceptions would have to be acknowledged, reducing the validity of this view.

The actual role of thematic material in form, as viewed in the classic era, is expressed by Koch, 1802:

As the theme or principal idea in an oration specifies the actual content and must contain the material for the development of primary and secondary thoughts, so must music hold to a single sentiment through the possible modifications of a principal idea, and as an orator passes from the main thought by means of rhetorical figures to accessory ideas, contrasts, analyses, etc., all of which reinforce the main thought—so must the composer be guided in his treatment of his main idea, working out the harmonies, modulations, repetitions, etc. in such relationships, that he constantly maintains novelty and increase of interest; and so that the episodes and accessory ideas that are especially necessary in composition do not disturb the prevailing sentiment and hence damage the unity of the whole.[9]

This view retains something of the baroque idea of a ruling idea or affection. A movement with many themes, such as the first movement of Mozart's *Prague* Symphony, 1786, or the first movement of Beethoven's *Eroica* Symphony, 1803, is unified by contrasting its main theme against intervening material and by well-timed recall of the main theme. With Haydn, who preferred to evolve most of his melodic material from a single main idea placed in different rhetorical arrangements, unity was no problem, but variety became the challenge, as in the finale of his F major Quartet, Op. 77, No. 2, 1799. In the same monothematic vein, Mozart wrote the finales of his F major Quartet, K. 590, 1790, and Eb major Quintet, K. 614, 1791, following Haydn's lead.

Melodic contrast was indeed an essential aspect of classic melodic rhetoric, but it took place principally at short range, with rapid changes of affect and topic among figures and motives. *Long-range* melodic contrast, between salient themes in the tonic and dominant sections, was frequently incorporated; this helped to stabilize the principal harmonic areas of the form. The opening theme represented the home key. To secure the effect of the second key, a clearly defined symmetrical period, a tune with a striking melodic profile, could be introduced at some point. This generally took place when V was established, as in the first movement of Mozart's Eb major Quintet, 1791. On the other hand, such a tune might appear somewhere in the middle of the dominant section, as in the first movement of Mozart's *Prague* Symphony, 1786; or, as often with Haydn, at the end of part I. (See the first movement of his Symphony No. 103 in Eb major, 1795.) But the salient dominant theme need not stand in contrast to the opening; Haydn typically uses the same theme for both keys, setting each off by local contrasts of material and texture. (See his Symphony No. 104 in D major, 1795, first movement and finale.)

While the two-part I–V (III), X–I plan was the ultimate control in sonata form, it did not provide guidelines for the detailed working out of a movement. Sonata forms, as well as other forms, written by the thousands in the classic era, must have been put together partly by paraphrase and parody, even by the great masters. Conventions of harmonic progression and melodic distribution, centering upon the most effective formulas, became common property and, eventually, part of the theory of form. This is clearly seen in the last decade or so of the 18th century, when theorists could provide, in addition to the harmonic plan, some recommendations for the distribution of melodic material and its differentiation.

Koch, 1793, refers to a "cantabler Satz" (singing theme) when the dominant is reached after a vigorous passage.[10] Galeazzi, 1796, specifies a "passo caratteristico" (characteristic passage) in the dominant.[11] Vogler, 1778, says that a symphony generally has two main ideas, one stronger, the other gentler.[12] Kollmann, 1799, analyzes his Symphony where he employs two subjects for the movement, one vigorous, the other cantabile, but places them in juxtaposition throughout the form.[13] The contrast between the brilliant-vigorous and the gentle-cantabile, probably a continuation of the tutti-solo relationship of baroque music, permeates classic rhetoric on every scale of magnitude, but the long-range thematic contrast, an essential feature of 19th-century sonata form, begins to crystallize only toward the end of the classic era. For classic music, local contrast has a more powerful effect, contributing to the thrust of periodicity. Nowhere is the play of local contrast more brilliantly managed than in the Allegro of the first movement of Mozart's *Prague* Symphony, 1786 (see pp. 27–28).

Classifications of melodic material were given by Momigny, 1806:

A. Principal periods
   1. Periods of *début* (opening)
   2. Periods of verve (vigorous action)
   3. Melodic periods
   4. Brilliant passages
   5. Subsidiary periods
B. Subsidiary periods
   1. Intermediary periods (episodes)
   2. Complementary periods (rounding off a main period)
   3. Connecting periods (liaison between main periods)[14]

Periods of *début* open a piece; periods of *verve* end a grand reprise; *melodic* periods are not precisely located but occur somewhere in the middle of a reprise.

Galeazzi, 1796, gives a precise formula for the *order* of melodic material, including a "motivo" (theme) in the home key; "uscitá" (exit), shift to the second key, "passo caratteristico" in the second key, and a cadence in the second key.[15] He does not specify the styles to be used, although he requires that the "passo caratteristico" be expressive and gentle in almost all kinds of compositions for the sake of greater beauty. Galeazzi's example is 64 measures long, comparable to an extended minuet; his formula is remarkable for the precision with which it differentiates the rhetorical functions of melodic material in the form.

According to Koch, part I presents the "plan" of the form, "the principal melodic members in their original order"; part II rests upon this plan, drawing material *first* optionally, and later, to *end* the movement, in more or less the "original order."[16] The implication of this melodic arrangement and the options available are discussed below (pp. 228 and 229).

TWO-PART VERSUS THREE-PART DIVISION

The *two-part* division of sonata form arises from its harmonic contour, represented by a movement away from the tonic and then an answering return to it. The *three-part* division rests upon thematic layout — *exposition*, *development*, and *recapitulation* of themes. The two-part harmonic division recognizes the *dynamic* aspect of the form, since it focuses upon harmonic periodicity; the three-part melodic division is *static*, concerned with identifying and placing themes. Moreover, it does not account for the unique rhetorical elements of the classic style that enabled sonata form to attain its breadth and organic unity.

Classic theorists all describe the form as bipartite.[17] Nevertheless, the separation of part II into two major sections was recognized. Koch, 1793, divides part II into two "Hauptperioden";[18] Momigny, 1806, while retaining a basic two-part division, compares the form of a movement to an architectural configuration of a dome and two wings.[19] The three-part division, as well as the probable first use of the term *sonata form*, was sponsored by Adolph Bernhard Marx, 1841–1851;[20] his views were decisive in establishing the thematic view of sonata form. The two-part versus three-part controversy continued through the 19th century. Lobe, 1858,[21] and Tovey in the present century represent the former, while the majority of theorists have adopted the latter.

In summary, the two plans are outlined in Ex. 13-1; note that the two-part plan emphasizes the *close* of major sections, while the three-part plan emphasizes *opening* statements.

Ex. 13-1.   *Two- and three-part plans of sonata form.*

Two-part	Three-part
Part I	*Exposition*
Home key; key area I	
1. *Establishment*	Main theme
2. Optional close	
Shift to second key	
Second key; key area II	
1. Establishment	Subsidiary theme
2. *Close*	
Part II	*Development*
Harmonic exploration X	Development of themes
Point of furthest remove	
Return to home key	*Recapitulation*: themes restated
Close in home key	

To place these two plans in perspective, we can say that the harmonic plan establishes a two-phase *basis* into which the *three-phase thematic superstructure* is interlocked.

PART I: THE EXPOSITION; I–V

Part I carries the harmony forward in an *unbroken* line of action from the opening in I to the close in V. This represents a rise in intensity of feeling, expressed by Vogler, 1778:

> When the passion must rise then the progression must move a fifth upward, not downward, for example, C, G, D, A. . . .[22]
>
> As the rise and fall of the passions express themselves, so does the declamation wax and wane. Therefore, one cannot end the first part in G major [Vogler is discussing an aria in D major] since the declamation must be carried forward with greater energy. . . .[23]

Whatever the close in V may represent — heightened intensity of feeling in an aria, the limit of the outward movement in a dance pattern, or the summing up of the opposing argument in a chamber music or symphony movement — it is a crisis in the structural cycle, and a lodestone for all action in part I.

Key Area I

The function of *key area I* — to establish the home key as a central point of reference — is carried out immediately, as a rule, in the opening measures. Once this has been done, key area I may take various shapes, as a complete or incomplete unit, brief or extended, with or without internal harmonic digressions. Some options are:

1. *Closure; authentic cadence*
    Mozart, E♭ major Quintet, K. 614, 1791, first movement
    Haydn, Symphonies No. 102, B♭ major, 1794, and No. 103, E♭ major, 1795, first movements
    Beethoven, G major Quartet, Op. 18, No. 2, 1800, first movement

2. *Open end; no final cadence*
    Haydn, *Oxford* Symphony, 1788, first movement
    Mozart, D major Quintet, K. 593, 1790, first movement
    Beethoven, F minor Quartet, Op. 95, 1810, first movement

3. *Digressions within key area I*
    Mozart, C major Quintet, K. 515, 1787, first movement
    Beethoven, *Eroica* Symphony, 1803, first movement

4. *Deferred establishment of home key*
    Beethoven, C major Quartet, Op. 59, No. 3, 1806, first and last movements

A single period to announce the principal melodic idea is adequate for the first key area, as in the first movements of Mozart's E♭ major Quintet, and Beethoven's Quartet, Op. 18, No. 4, 1800. But the option to expand is available. The opening theme in the first movement of Beethoven's *Eroica* Symphony undergoes intensive development. The first key area of Mozart's F major Sonata, K. 332, 1778, presents successively three contrasted ideas — the singing style, the learned style, and a hunting fanfare.

With regard to topic, key area I may draw upon one or more ideas from the rich thesaurus of materials available. The symphony being an opening piece, the march is often chosen, as in Mozart's *Jupiter* Symphony, 1788, and J. C. Bach's overture to *Lucio Silla*, 1776. Other topics used include:

Hunt, Mozart, E♭ major Quintet, K. 614, 1791, first movement

Polonaise, Haydn, *Oxford* Symphony, 1788, first movement

Passepied, Haydn, Symphony No. 103, 1795, first movement

Waltz, Beethoven, *Eroica* Symphony, 1803, first movement

Recitative obligé, Beethoven, F minor Quartet, Op. 95, 1810, first movement

Singing style, Mozart, Eb major Symphony, K. 543, 1788, first movement

Alla breve, Haydn, C major Quartet, Op. 74, No. 1, 1793, first movement

Brilliant style, Mozart, F major Quartet, K. 590, 1790, finale

Contredanse, Mozart, Eb major Symphony, K. 543, 1788, finale

A similar freedom of choice in melodic style is available in other sections of the form.

Shift to Second Key

Once the tonic is established, the exposition enters the harmonic orbit of the second key; I then becomes a *point of departure*, initiating a series of increasingly firm gestures pointing to the eventual confirmation of the second key at the end of part I. This *transition* may be marked off by a cadence, or the music may move gradually into the second key without strong punctuation.

Some standard patterns of harmonic shift from the tonic to the dominant or relative major keys are diagrammed below. The second key, representing a rise in harmonic thrust, is pictured higher than the harmony representing the tonic key.

1. *Equivocal approach to V.*

$$
\begin{array}{l}
\qquad\qquad \text{I (in key of V)} \\
\qquad\qquad \uparrow \\
\text{I:} \qquad \text{I} \longrightarrow \text{V} \\
\text{(major)}
\end{array}
$$

Key area I ends on a half cadence; V is then treated as a *key*: Mozart, overture to *Don Giovanni*, 1787; Haydn, C major Sonata, H.V. XVI, No. 35, before 1780, second movement.

2. *Circle of fifths, involving tonicized degrees.*

$$
\begin{array}{llll}
\text{II} \longrightarrow \text{V} \longrightarrow \text{I (in V)} & & \text{V} \longrightarrow \text{I (in V)} \\
\uparrow & & \uparrow \\
\text{I:} \quad \text{I} \longrightarrow \text{VI} & \quad or \quad \text{I} \longrightarrow \text{II} \\
\text{(major)} & & \text{(major)}
\end{array}
$$

These provide strong leverage toward V. The first is a common formula, initiated by a smooth sideslip from I to VI: Mozart, Eb major Quintet, K. 614, 1791, first and last movements; Haydn, *Oxford* Symphony, 1788, first movement. The second formula involves a peremptory shift from I to major II; II may be given considerable importance, including some melodic autonomy: Mozart, C major Quintet, 1787, first movement; Beethoven, Quartet in F major, Op. 59, No. 1, 1806, first movement.

3. *Interchange of mode.*

$$\text{IV}^{3\flat} \longrightarrow \text{V} \longrightarrow \text{I (in key of V)}$$
$$\text{I:} \quad \text{I} \longrightarrow \text{I}^{3\flat} \uparrow$$
(major)

Interchange of mode undermines the tonic, opening the way to V. Often a parallel melodic arrangement is used, where a major phrase is restated in minor: Beethoven, Symphony No. 2 in D major, Op. 36, 1802, first movement.

When the home key is minor, the shift to III corrects the chromatic alteration of the leading tone, resolving the harmony into its pure diatonic state. Clarification characterizes the opposition of keys here, rather than the increased tension of the I–V shift: Haydn, D minor Quartet, Op. 76, No. 2, 1797, first movement; Mozart, C minor Sonata, K. 457, 1784, first and last movements. In Mozart's A minor Sonata, K. 310, 1778, the first movement incorporates some formulas from the I–V transitions:

$$\text{dominant extension}$$
$$\text{IV} \longrightarrow \text{II} \longrightarrow (\text{V} \longrightarrow \text{I} \longrightarrow \text{II} \longrightarrow \text{V} \longrightarrow \text{I}^{3\flat} \longrightarrow \text{V}) \longrightarrow \text{I (in III)}$$
$$\text{I:} \quad \text{I} \longrightarrow \text{VI} \uparrow \qquad\qquad\qquad\qquad\qquad\qquad\qquad\qquad \text{(major)}$$
(minor)

These basic patterns are often linked. Beethoven, in the finale of his G major Quartet, Op. 18, No. 2, 1800, surprises the hearer by starting upon the simplest path — the equivocal cadence — and then reaching for the most powerful effect — interchange of mode as follows:

$$\text{I}^{3\flat} \longrightarrow \text{VI}^{\flat} \longrightarrow \text{V of V} \longrightarrow \text{V} \longrightarrow \text{I (in V)}$$
$$\text{I:} \quad \text{I} \longrightarrow \text{V} \uparrow$$
(major)

Melodic options for the transition include (1) new material, Mozart, F major Sonata, K. 332, 1778, first movement; (2) the opening theme, Beethoven, Symphony No. 2, 1802, first movement; (3) contrasting brilliant-style material, Mozart, C major Sonata, K. 545, 1788; or (4) a combination of these, Mozart, E♭ major Quintet, K. 614, 1791, first movement.

Key Area II

The second and larger part of the first *Hauptperiode*, says Koch, 1793, is devoted to the dominant.[24] This greater length may incorporate a variety of melodic material, harmonic digressions, and a firm melodic statement to emphasize closure. The placement of the salient theme has been discussed above (p. 219); the other striking feature is the breadth of the *effect of arrival* at the end of key area II. Haydn dramatizes this phase by introducing here the chief melodic contrast in his expositions. Mozart will sometimes recall the opening material, as in the first movement of his C major Quartet, K. 465, 1785. In the first movement of his E♭ major Divertimento, K. 563, 1788, he begins the closing action at m. 43, spinning out the action in a chain of 15 cadential formulas to reach the final period at m. 73. Texture, melodic momentum, and light cadential action join to build this broad drive, also used in many opera arias to carry the intensity of the affect to a climax.

Delay in establishing the second key at the beginning of key area II can dramatize its final confirmation at the end of the exposition. Beethoven begins key area II of the first movement of his Quartet in A major, Op. 18, No. 5, 1800, in the minor mode of the dominant, thereby highlighting the subsequent assertive effect of the major. Mozart slips almost unnoticed into the second key in the first movement of his Quintet in G minor, K. 516, 1787, and makes no cadence in this key until the closing section; strikingly, he introduces the most important contrasting idea in the home key, G minor, immediately following the first key area. In both of these examples the confirmation of the second key has a bold triumphant ring.

Despite its importance, the dominant cadence remains a "way station" in the key scheme. Hence a full close *or* a continuation is available. The exposition in the first movement of Haydn's *Oxford* Symphony, 1788, makes a full close; the first movement of Mozart's C major Quintet, K. 515, 1787, spins out the final phrase of the exposition, adding the seventh to V so that either repetition of the exposition or continuation to the development becomes mandatory.

PART II: DEVELOPMENT, RECAPITULATION, CODA

Development; X Section

The principal object of the development, or X section, is to *regain* the tonic. The highest priority is thus assigned to the progression that leads the harmony to I, whatever may precede it. Two links are available:

1. Dominant harmony
2. VI, or V of VI

The first creates a strong drive to the tonic; the second represents a sudden shift; both involve a *change of harmonic intention* — from a centrifugal motion (away from I) to a centripetal motion (toward I).

This change of direction is a critical point in the form and may be handled in various ways. In arias that use the key-area plan, the tonic may reenter directly following reprise I, as in "Ah, che mi dice mai" from Act I of Mozart's *Don Giovanni*, 1787, A few measures of dominant following part I may suffice in slow movements, as in the second movement of Beethoven's F minor Sonata, Op. 2, No. 1, 1795. In broadly scaled movements, the change of direction represents a *point of furthest remove*, dividing the development into two phases of action:

1. *Continuation* of the outward movement from I initiated at the end of key area I
2. *Reversal* of direction to create an expectation for returning to the tonic

The development thus may have *two* successive harmonic targets: (1) the *point of furthest remove*, generally a cadence on a *modal* degree—III, VI, or V of VI; (2) the *tonic*.

Continuation. Taking V as the point of departure at the end of the exposition, the harmony may move immediately away from V or remain for some time in that key. The latter reflects earlier practice, in which part II recalls the principal theme in V; the former is a newer technique, cultivated in the later classic era. Rarely, however, does the dominant remain to become the link to the returning tonic. The harmonic momentum of the exposition offers the opportunity to create an even broader trajectory and a more dramatic return to I than a simple dominant extension can provide. Harmonic momentum continues further in an outward direction, reaching the point of furthest remove by a series of patterns involving tonicized degrees related in some way to I; these patterns may be sequences by rising or falling fifths, rising or falling bass lines, or various combinations of these; deceptive cadences also figure in these patterns.

Point of Furthest Remove. The use of the third or sixth degree as a turning point stems from church modal practice. A cadence on either of these degrees in Ionian, Lydian, or Mixolydian (major) modes may be followed immediately by a triad on the first degree. When the third is raised to major in such cadences, the harmonic juxtaposition is striking. This progression, which we designate as V of III-I, is described by Gasparini, 1708:

> At times the composition makes a kind of cadence that closes on a tone with a major third, then continues, changing the tone to the third below, and begins in a special manner, in which the note is not a sixth, but a fifth. This is used in vocal compositions, ecclesiastical as well as secular, chamber, and theater works; and it is used to terminate an interrogative period or one that is exclamatory, and then one proceeds to the next; ordinarily, this kind of cadence is used in the serious style or the recitative.[25] (See Ex. 13-2.)

This progression was widely used as a structural fulcrum to link sections within a movement—Haydn, Symphony No. 103, 1795, finale, mm. 263-264—and to link movements—Bach, Brandenburg Concerto No. 3, 1721, the interpolation between the first and second movements.

Ex. 13-2. *Bass dropping a third.* Gasparini, *L'armonico*, 1708, p. 23.

The point of furthest remove received varying degrees of emphasis. It passes virtually unnoticed, imbedded in a set of sequences, in the first movement of Mozart's C major Sonata, K. 279, 1774, m. 45. It is approached with great ceremony in the first movement of Haydn's *Surprise* Symphony, 1792, m. 149. It is the climax of the development, an *area* of furthest remove that introduces a striking new theme, in the first movement of Beethoven's *Eroica* Symphony, 1803, m. 284. Its placement is optional, at *any* point within the development, as seen in the outlines of Ex. 13-3 below. While the point of furthest remove itself was an *option* in the development, most sonata forms took advantage of the leverage it provided to give an additional thrust to the harmony.

    Return to the Tonic.   As explained above, the simplest means to regain the tonic was to remain on the dominant after part I, as in the first movement of Mozart's G major Sonata, K. 283, 1774. When the harmony takes a wider trajectory, the dominant can become a point of arrival, to level out the action in approaching the tonic. The strongest approach to V from the point of furthest remove is via the circle of fifths, as in the first movement of Mozart's D major Sonata, K. 576, 1789. A quick shift from VI to I was frequently employed in earlier forms (see Sammartini, D major Symphony, HAM 283, 1740, and Monn, D major Symphony, HAM 295, 1740).

    Ex. 13-3 sketches the harmonic plans of several development sections. Note the long trajectories following the point of furthest remove in Exs. 13-3a and 13- 3b; note the extension of the point of furthest remove in Ex. 13-3c by the sideslipping of the harmony (m. 167), so that the extreme point and the tonic are connected by a deceptive cadence, and note the great breadth of the development in Ex. 13-3d, calling for an *area* of furthest remove.

Ex. 13-3.   *Sketches of development sections* (keys italicized).

a. Mozart, Quintet in C major, K. 515, 1787, 1st movt.
    Rising conjunct bass: E F F♯ G G♯ *a*, mm. 152–169
                                                    C♯
    Point of furthest remove: E (V of *a*), m. 170
    Descending circle of fifths: *a d g c f* B♭ E♭ A♭ D G, mm. 170–192
    Dominant approach: V alternating with minor I, mm. 193–204

b. Beethoven, Quartet in F major, Op. 18, No. 1, 1800, 1st movt.
    Point of furthest remove: A (V of *d*), m. 115
    Descending circle of fifths: *d g c f*, mm. 129–150
    Minor I region: *b♭ G♭ f D♭*, mm. 150–166
    Dominant approach: mm. 167–178

c. Haydn, Symphony No. 104 in D major, the *London*, 1795, finale.
    Descending circle of fifths: *A D G*, mm. 118–127
    Ascending circle of fifths: *e b F♯*, mm. 128–165
    Point of furthest remove (?): F♯ (V of *b*), m. 165
    Descending circle of fifths: G♯ *c♯ F♯ b e*, mm. 167–180
    Descending bass: e d c♯, mm. 180–192
    Recapitulation; deceptive cadence: c♯ *D*, m. 193

d. Beethoven, Symphony No. 3 in E♭ major, Op. 55, 1803, 1st movt.
    Pedal point and cadence: G (V of *C*) *C*, mm. 156–177
    Rising bass: *c c♯ d*, mm. 178–186

Ex. 13-3, cont'd.

Descending circle of fifths: d g c f bb Eb Ab, mm. 186-220
Pedal point and cadence: Eb (V of Ab) Ab, mm. 220-232
Sideslip: Ab f, mm. 220-236
Ascending circle of fifths: f c g d, mm. 236-247
Falling bass and cadential drive: d C B A$\sharp$ A G A B, mm. 248-283
Area of furthest remove: e a, mm. 284-299
Approach to dominant: C c Eb eb, mm. 300-337
Dominant approach expanded by rising bass: Bb C Db D Eb Cb C D·
   Eb Bb, mm. 338-398

The end of the development probably carries the greatest burden of suspense
in the sonata form as it stages the return to the tonic. No classic movement accomplishes this with the dramatic force that Beethoven generated in the first
movement of the *Eroica* as he first circled V, then reduced it to the merest whis-
per to allow the horn to signal the opening theme four measures before the tonic
is regained. At the other end of the spectrum, the drones that characterize the finale of Haydn's *London* Symphony, 1795, allow the tonic to creep in impercepti-
bly upon pedal points a half step apart.

Melodic Material in the Development Section.   The thematic view holds that,
to maintain unity, no *new* material is to be introduced following the exposition;
the development is dedicated to an intensive working over of the main themes,
rearrangement of motives, etc., creating a heightened sense of melodic action.

This view is also implied in the harmonic plan. For Koch, 1793, part I establishes the plan of the form — the melodic material in its original order.[26] Reicha,
1814, discussing "la grande coupe binaire," (the great binary division) says that
"in general, Part II is built and developed from the ideas of Part I."[27] But wide
latitude exists in actual practice. Some typical procedures:

1.   Part II begins with opening theme in V, reflecting an earlier 18th-century
    practice: J. C. Bach, G major Sonata, Op. 17, No. 4, HAM 303, after
    1770, first movement; Mozart, Bb major Sonata, K. 333, 1778, first move-
    ment.

2.   Part II is a modified review of exposition material: Beethoven, C minor
    Quartet, Op. 18, No. 4, 1800, first movement; Mozart, C major Quintet,
    K. 515, 1787, first movement.

3.   New material is introduced: Mozart, Bb major Quartet, K. 458, 1784,
    first movement; F major Sonata, K. 332, 1778, first movement; Bee-
    thoven, Symphony No. 2, Op. 36, 1802, first movement, and C major
    Quartet, Op. 59, No. 3, 1806, finale.

4.   Part I material is freely rearranged: Mozart, *Jupiter* Symphony, K. 551,
    1788, first movement; Beethoven, *Eroica* Symphony, 1803, first move-
    ment.

5. There is little or no reference to part I material: Mozart, *Symphonie Concertante*, K. 364, 1779, first movement, and C major Sonata, K. 330, 1778, first movement; Beethoven, F minor Sonata, Op. 2, No. 1, 1795, finale.

The basic function of melodic material in the development — to articulate the underlying harmonic action — can thus be served by (1) *review* of exposition material; (2) *discursive treatment* of exposition material; (3) *contrast* of melodic material. This last item has some parallels with the *da capo* aria, a point discussed below (p. 232). Conceivably a sonata movement might constantly introduce new material until the tonic is regained at the recapitulation, as in 5 above.

The Recapitulation

The *recapitulation* — the second section of part II, according to Koch, 1793,[28] or Kollmann's, 1799, "fourth subsection"[29] — "begins with the opening theme or another important melodic figure. . . . the second half of Part I, that is, the melodic material heard originally in the dominant, is heard in the tonic and the allegro closes."[30]

The recapitulation thus secures the unity of the form by a broad and final confirmation of the tonic and by *recall* and *rhyme* of the melodic material of part I. Here the restatement of melodic material becomes *essential* — to embody the regained tonic and to reinterpret the second half of part I in the home key. Quantz, 1752, says that "choice and beautiful progressions at the end of the first part" should be "so arranged that, in a transposition, they may conclude the second part also."[31]

While a strong return to the tonic at the *beginning* of the recapitulation has dramatic force, it is not essential to the harmonic unity of the form, since the end of part II provides the confirmation. A play on the idea of return, both harmonically and melodically, can be made without prejudice to the overall plan. Haydn's "false recapitulations" are well known — e.g., his D major Quartet, Op. 64, No. 5, 1790, first movement. The actual point of recapitulation in the first movement of Beethoven's F major Quartet, Op. 59, No. 1, 1806, cannot be fixed (see Ch. 24). In the second movement of the same quartet, he begins the review of the exposition material (at m. 239) in a distant key, G♭ major, but ends the period at m. 265, in the home key, B♭ major.

Ordinarily, melodic material retains the order it had in the exposition. But Haydn's listeners had to be on the alert for permutations of the original order, a procedure which raised the level of rhetorical interest beyond a routine review and rhyme of the exposition. The recapitulation of the first movement of his *Oxford* Symphony, 1788, thoroughly rearranges the half-dozen salient motives of the exposition, retaining only the opening and closing themes approximately in their original positions.

Frequently, some element of development is used to give the final tonic some freshness. Thus the shift to the second key in the exposition may become a harmonic digression in the recapitulation. A striking example occurs in the first movement of Beethoven's Quartet in F major, Op. 59, No. 1, 1806, where the harmony suddenly drops to D♭ major, then passes through B♭ minor on its way to the final establishment of F major.

Following the protocol of earlier 18th-century two-reprise forms, many classic sonata forms called for repetition of each reprise, e.g., Mozart, E♭ major Quintet, K. 614, 1791, first movement. In his greatest sonata-form composition, the first movement of the *Eroica* Symphony, Beethoven specified a repeat of part I, a procedure almost always observed in classic sonata forms. For a listener attuned to the subtleties of the melodic rhetoric and the deft play of harmony and texture, one hearing was insufficient. Hiller, 1770, expressed this view:

> . . . the pleasure of music depends on the charm which the ear senses when it grasps the harmony and the unity of the musical expression, where a composer, following no other rules than those of his imagination, will consistently create a brief and compact theme and make certain that it is heard four times. We must not ascribe this simply to the custom of playing each reprise of an *allegro* or *andante* twice. The first time a reprise is played, the listener enjoys making the acquaintance with the material; the second time, he already knows it and relishes it. Since the second part of a symphony movement is little else than the imitation of the first, so the listener has the further pleasure to rediscover the melody he has already heard and to follow it through other modulations . . . one of the greatest pleasures in music is to hear a fine theme handled with all possible relationships and modifications. . . .[32]

The Coda

Often, the rhyme in the recapitulation carries enough weight to "lock up" the form tidily; the final cadence of part II becomes the final cadence of the movement, as in the Mozart G major Quartet, K. 387, 1782, first movement. At other times, a stronger effect of closure is needed to arrest the momentum generated throughout the movement. This is accomplished by a *coda*. It may consist of a few emphatic chords or cadential gestures, but it can also be extended to make final arrival a critical issue. This is done in the following sequence of events:

1. A harmonic digression (optional)
2. A firm return to the tonic, generally with the opening theme
3. A set of emphatic cadential gestures

These events review those of part II in compressed form—development, recapitulation, and closure.

Beethoven consistently shifted the responsibility for final arrival to the coda, present in most of his sonata-form movements. In the first movement of the *Eroica* Symphony, the coda is 134 measures long, almost one-fifth of the entire movement. The coda of the first movement of his Symphony No. 8, Op. 93, 1812, occupies 72 of the 373 measures in the movement. Its principal events are:

1. Digression: Db major, Eb minor, F minor, 301–322 (note rising tonics)
2. Return: F major, mm. 323–350
3. Cadential gestures: mm. 351–373

Codas are not second developments, as they are often called, but extended areas of arrival; their opening digressions create a harmonic "whiplash" that prepares the final tonic with increased force, a supreme effect of periodicity.

Definitions of the term *coda* reflect the growing importance of this section. Koch, 1802, describes the coda as "a more complete closing section, following the second reprise of an allegro"[33]; this corresponds to the type of coda Mozart added at the end of the first movement of his C major Quartet, K. 465, 1785, a period 20 measures long. Reicha, 1813, is clearly referring to the codas in Beethoven's music, which by this time was being performed widely, when he says that the coda "that finishes a large piece is comparable to an oratorical peroration."[34]

HISTORICAL PERSPECTIVE

The life history of sonata form reaches far back into the 18th century. Some of the formative elements were:

1. *The two-reprise dance form*, traceable to medieval antiquity
2. *The I–V (III), X–I harmonic scheme*, established as a standard plan by the beginning of the 18th century
3. *Clarification of periodic structure by articulations and symmetries*, principally in early 18th-century Italian music
4. *Melodic recall and rhyme in two-reprise forms*
5. *Local contrasts in melodic material, texture, and declamation*, present in the early 18th-century concerto and in comic opera ensembles
6. *An improvisatory style of composition in the fantasia* (see Ch. 18) involving harmonic digressions and a free treatment of melody and rhythm as well as texture
7. *The modal cadence*, as a point of harmonic leverage to connect sections, used from Renaissance times through the 18th century

From the historical perspective, several important aspects of *mid-century form* should be noted:

1. The "Scarlatti" sonata form
2. The *da capo* aria form
3. The influence of fantasia procedures upon sonata form

The "Scarlatti" Sonata Form

In this earlier form symmetry is even more palpable than in the later sonata form, as Ex. 13-4 shows. Mozart used this form, typical of the Scarlatti sonatas and *eccercizi*, in many of his earlier works, and harked back to it in the finale of his G major Quartet, K. 387, 1782. The neatness and balance of the form constituted its principal advantages, but it did not provide for the kind of staging that made the return to the home key and the opening theme a dramatic event in classic sonata form.

Ex. 13-4. *"Scarlatti" sonata form.*

Melodic material	A	B	A	B
Key		I	V	V (X)	I

The Da Capo Aria Form

The *da capo* aria form will be discussed in Ch. 16; its relevance here lies in the fact that the form calls for a full return to the opening material, often following a modal cadence on VI or V of VI. A comment by Burney, 1789, suggests some mutual influence between the aria and the sonata—elements of the aria parallel some critical points in the sonata:

> The operas of this master [J. C. Bach] are the first in which the *da capo* disappeared, and which, about this time, began generally to be discontinued; the second part being incorporated into the first, to which, after modulating into the fifth of the key, the singer generally returns.[35]

Extrapolating from Burney's remark, we can suggest these points:

1. The cadence in the sixth or its dominant that often ends the middle part of the *da capo* aria corresponds in placement and function to the point of furthest remove in the sonata form.

2. The full recall of the exposition corresponds to the *da capo* of the aria; this is especially significant because of the dramatic return of the opening theme in both forms.

3. The first part of the aria, instead of carrying through a full I–V, X–I plan, consists, in Bach's modification, of only the first half of this scheme; the X represents the contrasting middle section, while the final I is a full review of part I.

4. The X section of the classic sonata form may well have achieved its final definition by the incorporation of elements of part II of the *da capo* aria—the contrast of affective quality, the more distant harmonies, the fulcrum of the modal cadence. Conversely, the aria may have gained a more succinct and dynamic quality by compressing its events into a I–V, X–I plan taken from instrumental music.

The Guglielmi aria presented in Ex. 16-3, exemplifies the form described by Burney. In instrumental music, a clear example of the *da capo* influence is seen in the overture to Mozart's *Abduction from the Seraglio*, K. 384, 1781–1782, where the X section, set in the tonic minor in a slower tempo than the exposition and recapitulation, quotes from an aria in the opera. The introduction of new material into the X section of a sonata form was an option exercised more often than we might suspect; perhaps this was a glance at part II of the *da capo* aria.

There is no direct line of evolution from the Scarlatti-type sonata to the full-return type, since examples of the latter were composed by Sammartini, Conti, J. S. Bach, and C. P. E. Bach early in the 18th century. On the other hand, there is no question that the two types represent their respective periods. Furthermore, the symmetrical Scarlatti type has a kinship to French two-reprise dances; the *da capo* type, with its dramatic staging of the return of the opening theme, has a kinship to Italian opera. It is suggested here that the final synthesis that established the classic sonata form with its characteristic schedule of events included some elements of the *da capo* aria.

Fantasia Elements

Löhlein, in his *Clavier-Schule*, 1779, 1781, analyzes a two-reprise movement. This constitutes one of the earliest analyses of a sonata form in music theory. He calls his piece an "arioso," but it is a typical tempo di menuetto. The significant point in Löhlein's comments appears in the first sentence: "When one wishes to compose out of free fantasy. . . ."[36] Fantasia as a genre is discussed below (Ch. 18), but the hint given by Löhlein suggests that the speculative treatment of *topical* material, especially dances, in sonata forms represents the element of fantasia. In sonata form, dance and fantasia complement each other; periods begin as dances but often move to the fantasia by means of digressions and extensions, to return to the dance at the beginning of the next period. This coordination had a long history; it was present in the music of J. S. Bach, Handel, Telemann, and their contemporaries, whose allemandes, sarabandes, minuets, and gigues were often saturated with fantasia elements. Indeed, we can visualize the discursive sonata style of classic music as a play between two poles, (1) rigorously regular dance patterns and (2) totally free fantasia. These are worked together so deftly that neither controls the other. The dance shapes the rhythmic scansion and the cadences to create the contour of the form, while the fantasia thrusts against rhythmic and harmonic controls with harmonic digressions and melodic elaborations to impart warmth and expressive color to the style.

ANALYSES

Chs. 23 and 24 provide analyses of three sonata forms. The following outlines list some distinctive features of a number of movements, elements that have decisive influence upon structure.

Haydn, Quartet in C major, Op. 74, No. 1, 1793, first movement

Monothematic form, typical of Haydn.[37] *Alla breve* motive at beginning of each key area and in closing sections, extensively worked over in X.

Brilliant intervening material.

Recapitulation *thoroughly recomposed*; only 27 measures from exposition re-called or rhymed.

C. P. E. Bach, Kenner und Liebhaber, series IV, 1783, Sonata in E minor, first movement

Opening and closing sections of exposition provide "profile" material in *bourrée* and *gavotte* rhythms, respectively.

Unstable harmony following key area I, stabilized only at end of exposition.

Many *short figures*, counterstated once or twice.

Development a *modified exposition*.

Haydn, Quartet in D major, Op. 76, No. 5, 1797, second movement

Celebrated Largo—*two themes*, both slow march rhythm, both heard in keys areas I and II.

Coloristic exploitation of quartet sonority; thematic statements in F♯ major, C♯ major, E major, E minor, G major, F♯ minor, and F♯ major, all delineated luminously by the arpeggiated opening theme and rich chordal texture.

Beethoven, Quartet in F minor, Op. 95, 1810, first movement

Juxtaposition of key area I in *recitative obligé style* (see Ch. 16) and key area II in *aria style*.

Strong emphasis on *flat side*—G♭, D♭, mm. 6, 24—with striking *half-step shifts*, mm. 38, 48, recalling opening figure in key area II.

Short, abrupt transitions, highlighting the supercharged operatic effect.

Mozart, Quintet in C major, K. 515, 1787, first movement

Most broadly scaled movement in Mozart's chamber music.

Key area I (see pp. 57, 79).

Transition, a *plateau* on D major, mm. 69–77, recalling opening theme.

Key area II, prominence of *musette* topic.

X section (see pp. 80 and 227).

Recapitulation: *telescoping* of key area I events with *modified harmonic plan*, rhyme of key area II events with extended *written-out cadenza*, mm. 322–352, *literal* end-rhyme.

Beethoven: Quartet in B♭ major, Op. 130, 1825, first movement

Interlocking key-area forms; the material of the introduction, if laid together in a series as it recurs throughout the movement, makes a small *two-reprise form* in the style of an *aria*, as illustrated in Ex. 13-5.

Ex. 13-5.   Beethoven, Quartet in B♭ major, Op. 130, 1825, 1st movt.

Note. Tempo changes from m. 218 to m. 222 are as follows: m. 218, allegro; m. 219, adagio ma non troppo; m. 220, allegro; m. 221, adagio ma non troppo; m. 222, allegro.

The sudden shifts of tempo and expression in this movement set up a climate of surprise, embodied in a rather episodic structure. Thus the unexpected twist just before the second key area is consistent with the general stance of this movement. After some 11 measures of great flourish and bustle that lead us to expect the dominant, F, the music overshoots the dominant of F at the end of a chromatic scale by one half-step, landing us on D♭, the dominant of the second key, G♭ major, as shown in Ex. 13-6, m. 53.

Ex. 13-6.   Beethoven, Quartet in B♭ major, Op. 130, 1825, 1st movt.

The second key, G♭ major, is "soft" and "dark" in relation to the home key, B♭ major. Beethoven here used a key related to the tonic by interchange of mode instead of proceeding to the usual dominant for the second key area. This striking and sudden key contrast reinforces the abrupt change in style from the stop-and-start, often bustling activity of the first key area and the transition to the smoothly spun-out motion of the second key area. Both in key and style, the second key area represents a *drop* in intensity instead of the usual *lift* we find in key area forms. The entire movement is a collage of unassimilated sections, including a hurdy-gurdy episode that serves for X. The *adagio* and the *allegro* twice in this movement find points of common action: (1) the hurdy-gurdy section picks up the cadence figure of the adagio and quickens it so that it becomes a rhythmic ostinato that accompanies a rather simple melody; (2) in the coda this cadence figure is again taken up into the allegro to lead to the final area of harmonic arrival.

Beethoven, Eroica Symphony, Op. 55, 1803, first movement. This movement achieves a high-water mark in the history of sonata form. It is much longer than any first movement that had previously been written. Throughout its great length of 691 measures it builds out the key-area plan of sonata form to a broader and more powerful embodiment of key than had ever been heard before. Two factors are decisive in this process: (1) the simple triadic shape of the theme, which gives a clear and firm sense of key whenever it appears, (2) Beethoven's choice of 3/4 meter; this meter is susceptible to rhythmic shifts— mm. 25, 45, 66, 84, 99, 110, 119, 240, etc.—that help build the powerful drives that characterize its many extended periods. Typically, Beethoven begins a period on a low level of intensity—mm. 3, 15, 37, 45, 57, 83, 178, 236, 338— and increases the tension as the period moves toward its cadence. Although this movement has many melodic members, including a new theme in the development, almost half of its 691 measures involve some aspect of the opening theme —statement, continuation, variation, etc. (see above, p. 218, on the role of the principal theme).

The breadth of the movement opens new *areas* of arrival—the area of furthest remove (see p. 225 above) and the final statement of the opening theme in the coda, mm. 631–662, where it achieves the symmetry—a balancing counterstatement—which it did not have throughout the movement. Ex. 13-7 illustrates this point; the first three statements digress after the first waltz-like phrase. Beethoven maintained this procedure consistently until the final symmetrical version is reached, mm. 631–662, given in the fourth staff. When the theme thus appears symmetrically, it acts to stabilize both itself and the key, a grand confirmation unequaled in any other sonata form, fulfilling the great harmonic plan and reaffirming basic elements of the style—the dance, symmetry, and the alternation of tonic and dominant.

Ex. 13-7. *Treatment of opening theme.* Beethoven, *Eroica* Symphony, Op. 55, 1803, 1st movt.

The analysis in Ex. 13-8 of the first movement of Mozart's Quintet in E♭ major, K. 614, 1791, incorporates some of the criteria for sonata form discussed in this chapter, including stylistic features and periodic structure. The names given to various periods follows the plan of Momigny, 1806 (see p. 220).

Ex. 13-8. *Analysis of a sonata-form movement.* Mozart, Quintet in E♭ major, K. 614, 1791, 1st movt.

Ex. 13-8, cont'd.

sensibility

extension by
deceptive cadence

period 2, *verve;* extension by sprung scansion

learned style

indication of dominant key

extension by reciprocation

dominant extension
brilliant style

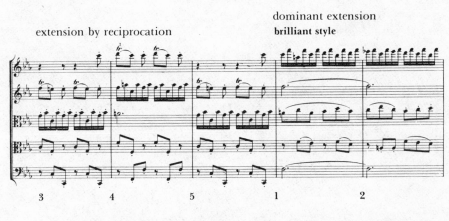

key area II (dominant)
period 3, *melodieuse, passo caracteristico,* symmetrical
singing style

40

Ex. 13-8, cont'd.

period 4, *verve,* symmetrical

gigue

period 5, *verve,* peroration leading to final
cadence in dominant

gigue   learned

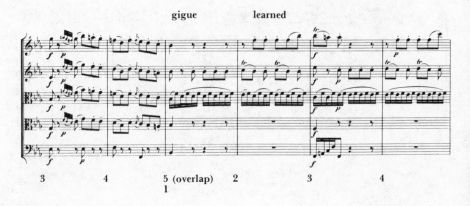

extension by digression to II of dominant   **brilliant**

grand cadence of first reprise

fanfare

period 6, *conjunctionelle* (connecting)

sensibility   80

Ex. 13-8, cont'd.

development: X section
period 7, covering entire development section

sensibility

period 8, recapitulation

Ex. 13-8, cont'd.

coda; recapitulation ends with
inconclusive cadence, setting stage
for brilliant-style peroration

Edwards

For the casual listener, the verve and clarity of this movement are a sheer delight, the quintessence of the 18th-century galant style. For the connoisseur, this movement is an ultimate refinement of 18th-century chamber music composition with its kaleidoscopic play of texture, spun-out periods, and deft manipulation of figures.

Mozart was clearly beholden to Haydn in his treatment of the opening figure, a hunt gigue built with driving repeated notes and crisp trills. This figure dominates the movement, cast at various times into the hunt, the learned, the singing, the brilliant, and the sensibility styles. It begins every period in the exposition, recapitulation, and coda and is prominent in the development. The concentration on the opening figure stages the introduction of a striking new theme in the development, contrasting the opening theme in all its principal features—wide leaps, irregular rhythms, Storm and Stress style, solo with *concitato* accompaniment. The dramatic, even explosive entry of this new theme adds a dimension of depth to the expressive range of the movement, sharpening the profile of the galant style by contrast.

Texturally, the quintet scoring exploits the division into upper and lower groups and into solo-tutti oppositions. The opening has a paradoxical relationship in texture, since the two violas represent a solo group, yet their *forte* in a rather vigorous style is that of a tutti, while the answering phrase, for the entire ensemble, has the character of a soloistic opposition, with its light figures, and sustained *piano* support. Throughout the entire movement, no texture holds for more than four or five measures, the effect being a scintillating, ever-changing play with marked mimetic color.

The impression of symmetry is strong throughout the movement. The ingratiating beginning, with its neat opposition of galant figures on tonic and dominant harmonies, prepares the listener for a pleasant tour, and the broadly flowing *passo caratteristico* reinforces this impression by balancing two singing eight-measure phrases. Most phrases can be scanned as four-measure groups, with much less irregularity than in other works of Mozart—for example, the first movement of the Quintet in C major, K. 515, 1787. Yet, except for the first two periods in the dominant key area, each period in this movement undergoes some extension, mostly for reinforcement of cadential action. This well-defined periodicity with a specific role assigned to each period in the exposition—statement, shift to dominant, singing, reinforcement, and peroration—results in a very clear layout that matches the "textbook" plan for sonata form, except for the new material in the development. Such structural clarity provides a background for tremendous effects of climax, greater than in any other chamber work of Mozart. In each case the brilliant style, taken from the divertimento, spearheads the rise to a peak of intensity. These phases of action take place at the following points:

1. Measure 35, during the shift to the second key.

2. Measures 70–75, the peroration of the second key area.

3. Measure 90 et seq., where the new theme breaks in.

4. Measure 161, corresponding to m. 35.

5. Measures 196–201, corresponding to mm. 90–95. (These last two climactic points have less force than their corresponding points in the exposition due to the lower pitch necessary in the transposition to the tonic.)

6. Measure 215 et seq. The coda fulfills the need for a final grand climax, the most powerful in the movement, a furious outburst with melodic lines moving at striking tangents to each other. Perhaps the most striking gesture is the entry of the violoncello on the bass of a V_2^4 chord, a densely dissonant effect, intensified by the short appoggiaturas.

Viewed as a harmonic plan, organized by periods and colored by rich thematic content, classic sonata form has something of the character of a forensic exercise, a rhetorical discourse that reflects in its own way the spirit of 18th-century philosophy. The opposing keys are the premises to be argued; their respective positions are set in the exposition, and their forces are represented by their respective thematic material. The victory of the tonic, a foregone conclusion, is signaled by the incorporation of the melodic content of the second key into the tonic at the end of the movement. The analogy with the enlightened absolutism of the 18th century is very attractive; in each case, authority enforces its hierarchical supremacy, incorporating opposing elements into their proper place in the scheme as a resolution of conflict. The logic by which the dominant asserts itself is overcome by the greater logic that calls for the unity of the tonic.

Above all, sonata form became an important structural vehicle when elements from many sources—dance, theater, fantasia, the learned style, the singing style, the concerto—were coordinated on a grand scale by the genius of a handful of composers. The chief difference between the two-reprise dance forms and classic sonata form is not the order of keys or structural events, but the richer expressive and rhetorical content that expands the form to its broad dimensions.

NOTES

1. Koch, *Versuch*, II, p. 223, and III, pp. 301ff., 341ff.
2. Portmann, *Lehrbuch*, p. 50.
3. Löhlein, *Clavier-Schule*, p. 182ff.
4. Momigny, *Cours complet*, p. 332.
5. Galeazzi, *Elementi*, II, p. 253ff.
6. Reicha, *Mélodie*, p. 46ff.
7. Kollmann, *Composition*, p. 5.
8. Riepel, *Anfangsgründe*, p. 1, says that the working of a minuet is no different from that of a symphony. See Ch. 6 of the present work on Koch's techniques for expanding a short reprise.
9. Koch, *Lexikon*, p. 746.
10. Koch, *Versuch*, III, pp. 364, 385.
11. Galeazzi, *Elementi*, II, p. 253. See Churgin, "Francesco Galeazzi's Description (1796) of Sonata Form," *JAMS*, 1968, for a full discussion of Galeazzi's description of sonata form.
12. Vogler, *Kuhrpfälzische Tonschule*, II, p. 62.
13. Kollmann, *Composition*, preface.
14. Momigny, *Cours complet*, pp. 397, 398.

15. Galeazzi, *Elementi*, p. 251ff.

16. Koch, *Versuch*, III, p. 304ff.

17. See passages cited in notes 1 to 7 above.

18. Koch, *Versuch*, III, p. 307.

19. Momigny, *Cours complet*, p. 397.

20. Marx, *Komposition*, III, p. 282.

21. Lobe, *Komposition*, I, p. 315; also Czerny, *Practical Composition*, I, p. 33; Tovey, *Musical Articles*, p. 209.

22. Vogler, *Kuhrpfälzische Tonschule*, II, p. 195.

23. Ibid., p. 196.

24. Koch, *Versuch*, III, p. 306.

25. Gasparini, *L'armonico*, p. 23.

26. Koch, *Versuch*, III, pp. 304, 305.

27. Reicha, *Mélodie*, p. 48.

28. Koch, *Versuch*, III, p. 311.

29. Kollmann, *Composition*, p. 5.

30. Koch, *Versuch*, III, p. 311.

31. Quantz, *Versuch*, p. 296.

32. Hiller, *Nachrichten*, IV, p. 83.

33. Koch, *Lexikon*, p. 345.

34. Reicha, *Mélodie*, p. 31.

35. Burney, *History*, p. 866.

36. Löhlein, *Clavier-Schule*, p. 182.

37. Framery & Guingené, *Encyclopédie*, II, p. 409, says, on Haydn's Symphony No. 104 in D major, 1796, "It is well to observe that this repetition of the first motive spares him from having to create a new melodic phrase, which is ordinarily placed after the effervescent and tumultuous period that leads to the repose of the dominant."

14 Couplet Forms

When a listener wanted pleasing tunes, he would find them in the songs, dances, rondos, and variations that were produced in vast quantities in the late 18th century. These were written either for teaching or for entertainment, and provided a major part of the musical fare of that time. Unlike sonata form, extended and discursive, these forms were put together by joining or *coupling* symmetrical periods or small two-reprise forms.

The coupling in a *song* is *strophic* because the melody is repeated to different stanzas of the text; in *dances* the coupling *pairs* two-reprise forms in an A B A layout; the *rondo* couples the principal *melody* with *episodes*; *variations* couple *a number of short pieces* based upon the principal theme. Specifically, the term *couplet* refers to the episodes in a rondo,[1] but here it is extended to include forms in which short, complete sections are joined.

PAIRED DANCES; THREE-PART FORM

Dance movements in classic instrumental music are arranged as a *pair* of contrasted dances in minuet time, laid out as an A B A rondeau (see p. 249). The contrast consistently is that of *style*, and often there is contrast of *key* as well. A typical contrast is a brilliant, active minuet followed by a quieter second minuet — a trio in pastoral vein using musette figures. This arrangement is represented by the minuet of Mozart's *Haffner* Symphony, K. 385, 1782, where the bold arpeggios of the minuet theme are answered by the gentle stepwise motion of the trio theme.

The *trio* acquired its name from the orchestral practice of Lully, in which a trio of wind instruments alternated as a solo group against the full orchestra. Haydn, Mozart, and Beethoven typically score their trios more lightly, often highlighting the winds. Curiously, both Koch and Türk define the trio as a *three-voice* piece in contrast to the minuet with its *two-voice* texture.[2] This distinction probably refers to minuets played by a small ensemble for social dancing, but it also applies to some keyboard music, as in the minuet of the D major Sonata of Haydn, H.V. XVI, No. 14, 1767. It is also reflected in the bold polarity of outer voices in the minuet of Mozart's *Haffner* Symphony, K. 385, 1782, where the effect of two-part writing is clear, as against the three-part texture of the trio, with its paired treble voices against a musette-like bass.

The *Marcia funèbre* of Beethoven's *Eroica* Symphony begins conventionally, pairing small two-reprise forms. Ordinarily, a *da capo* of the first march would round off the form neatly; in view of the slow and deliberate pace, this simple A B A scheme might have been sufficiently long to match the scope of the other movements. The march returns after the trio, only to break into a gigantic fugato that reaches a climax in mm. 150–158 equal to that of the point of furthest remove in the first movement. This climax consists of almost total suspension of action, following an immense buildup—as though it were "the eye of the hurricane." The "storm" explodes anew, subsiding to the full *da capo* of the march, followed by a coda that breaks the figures of the march into fragments, an ultimate tragic statement. Measures 111–178 thus stand as a huge parenthesis in this version of the paired-dance form.

Three-part forms organize some slow movements, again suggesting the influence of the *da capo* aria. The slow movements of Haydn's G major Trio, H.V. XV, No. 25, 1795, Mozart's C major Sonata, K. 330, 1778, and Beethoven's E♭ major Sonata, Op. 7, 1796, represent this type. Beethoven contrasted a florid adagio with a brisk contredanse in the second movement of his G major Quartet, Op. 18, No. 2, 1800; the extremes of expression here have a parodistic flavor.

RONDO

Two versions of this term were extant in the 18th century. *Rondeau*, from the French, was used exclusively in the early and middle 18th century, and continued in use less frequently in classic music. *Rondo*, from the Italian, became the standard term in classic times to cover all versions of this form. The prescription for a rondeau was explicit, as in Walther, 1732:

> *Rondeau* (French) signifies a circle; derives from *round* and is a melody set in 3/4 or even meter; its first section is so arranged that it can make a cadence. The other *reprises*, of which there are three or four, must be composed so as to fit well with the first section. The number of measures in a *rondeau* is not fixed, but the first part must be neither too long or too short; since, if it is too long, the frequent repetitions will annoy the ear, and if it is too short, its period will not be clearly noticed. Eight measures is a good length; but they must be worked out so attractively that they can be heard five or six times. This first section is the actual *rondeau* . . . the other reprises or sections are not repeated.[3]

Couplets and refrains in a rondo could vary in number. A rondeau with one couplet, a standard French form in the earlier 18th century, resembled a two-reprise form in which reprise I ended in the tonic. After the X section reprise I could be repeated verbatim, making an A B A melodic form, identical to that of a small rondeau with a *da capo* sign at the end of the couplet to indicate the repetition of the refrain. Koch, 1793, gives a detailed analysis of an aria in *"rondo* form" (Koch's term) from Georg Benda's *Walder*, 1777, describing the refrain and the three intervening couplets. He says:

> The first period, or the so-called Rondo-theme, is composed of a single independent melodic phrase, which is first carried out to a cadence on the fifth, and upon its immediate repetition is modified to make a cadence upon the tonic.[4]

The immediate repetition of the first phrase secures the "tunefulness" essential in a rondo theme. This sharp definition of melodic character, in turn, provides an excellent foil for clearly contrasted melodic episodes. Ex. 14-1 quotes Benda's refrain.

Ex. 14-1. *Rondo refrain.* Koch, *Versuch*, III, 1793, pp. 250-251, from Benda, *Walder*, 1777, "Selbst die glücklichsten der Ehen" ("Even the happiest of marriages").

The form of this rondo is:

introduction (10)	A (10)	B (8)	A (10)	C (8)	A (10)	D (8)	A (10)
A major	A major	to E major	A major	B minor	A major	A minor	A major

All the material in the refrain and the couplets is based on one topic, a graceful slow gavotte, although there is some modest contrast between sections. This piece exemplifies the earlier 18th-century French type of rondeau, a form suited for vocal music set to poetry with refrains.

Gluck employed the same formal arrangement in the lament of Orpheus, "I have lost my Euridice," from *Orfeo*, 1762, Act III (see Ex. 2-20). His phrase structure is less symmetrical than in the standard rondeau, and the flow of the piece, set in slow bourrée time, is interrupted by an arioso (see Ch. 18) that serves as a second episode.

Portmann, 1789, discusses the rondo, and the remarkable aspect of his instruction is his treatment of a basic theme, a simple progression in the strict style, illustrated in Ex. 6-3. The elaborations in this example provide *all* the melodic material for a rondo—refrain, couplet, transitional material. The rondo itself has some discursive sections—extension, pedal points, reinforced cadences—that show the influence of sonata procedure.

Rondos used as finales of concertos, symphonies, and quartets often display a more integrated structure than those of a typical couplet rondo. Apart from the discursiveness that carries the music from one stable section to another, the sections themselves take on the character of sonata-form key areas with complex thematic plans; there is often a rhyme of the first episode in the latter part of the form, corresponding to the return of the material in key area II in the sonata. When these elements of sonata form appear in a rondo, the form is designated in present-day analysis as *sonata rondo*. Mozart often suppressed the third refrain to create an A B A C B A form. This takes place in the finale of his Piano Concerto in A major, K. 488, 1786. This exuberant movement has a wealth of melodic material. Its refrain theme begins with a striking angular figure which acts as a bold foil to the episodic material with which it is contrasted. Apart from the refrain, a vivacious contredanse tune, we hear themes in singing style, brilliant style, *empfindsamer* style, another contredanse, this time in gavotte rhythm, and fanfares. As a closing theme for the episodes and for the movement itself, Mozart threw in a saucy bit of hurdy-gurdy music, running shamelessly up and down the scale.

One of the most brilliant examples of the 18th-century sonata rondo is the finale of Haydn's Symphony No. 103 in E♭ major, 1796. The entire movement is built upon two motives, a hunting fanfare and a contredanse tune, which make good counterpoint with each other (see Ex. 14-2).

Ex. 14-2. *Sonata rondo theme.* Haydn, Symphony No. 103 in E♭ major, 1796, finale.

The *only* feature that identifies this movement as a rondo is the *return of the opening material* in the home key at m. 158. This separates the following X section from the preceding broad cadence in V, thus breaking the harmonic trajectory of the key-area form and eliminating the issue of the return to I. The X then becomes an *episode*, not a counterstatement to the dominant key. This rondo, like many others in the classic style, includes a *rhyme* of the dominant material; thus we have an incorporation of large-scale key-area procedure. The two motives are combined into different rhetorical constructions in an incredibly resourceful manner.[5] The opening refrain, equivalent in scope and structure to a key area I, has a rondo-like alternation:

A	episode	A	episode	A
mm. 5-12	mm. 13-44	mm. 45-52	mm. 53-72	m. 73 et seq.

The form of this movement is delineated by key relationships in the following manner:

Section	A	B	A	C	A	B	coda
Key	I	V	I	(X)	I	I	I
Measure	1	91	158	182	264	300	351

These Mozart and Haydn examples show flexibility in the disposition of melodic material in a large scale classic form. Mozart typically introduces new material while Haydn deftly juggles one or two short and sturdy figures.

Outlines of rondo forms are given below, illustrating the widely divergent patterns to which the rondo principle could accommodate.

Haydn, Sonata in D major, H.V. XVI, No. 37, before 1780

A	B	A	C	A
D major	D minor	D major	G major	D major

The rondeau pattern, coupling refrains and episodes in small two-reprise forms; lively contredanse style.

Beethoven, Quartet in E♭ major, Op. 74, 1809, second movement

A	B	transition	A	C	transition	A	coda	
A♭ major	A♭ minor		A♭ major	D♭ major		A♭ major	A♭ minor	A♭ major

Also a rondeau pattern, modified by transitions and half cadences to end episodes. Each statement of refrain an octave higher than the preceding, also more elaborately ornamented, creating a progression among refrains; aria style in sentimental-pathetic vein.

Beethoven, C major Sonata, Op. 53, 1804, finale

A	B	transition	A	C	(X)	A	coda
C major	A minor		C major	C minor		C major	

Simple contredanse theme, stated three times in first two refrains, twice in third. Coda an extended fantasia on theme.

C. P. E. Bach, Kenner und Liebhaber, series V, 1785, Rondo I

A	B	A	C		A	D			A	coda
G	D	G	a f♯ b		G	b c b (X) a F (X) E (X) g♯ a b			G	

Monothematic rondo, typical of C. P. E. Bach (see Ex. 14-3); episodes in contrasting keys, figuration, rhetorical arrangements. Adaptability of theme to manipulation because of (1) shifting stresses of polonaise rhythms, (2) descending bass line, trimmable to various lengths.

Ex. 14-3.   C.P.E. Bach, *Kenner und Liebhaber*, series V, 1785, Rondo I.

Breitkopf

Mozart, Quintet in G minor, K. 516, 1787, finale

Interlocking couplet rondo and sonata forms.

Rondo layout: each section a small two-reprise form	Key-area layout
A. Refrain, G major, mm. 1-20	Key area I, G major, mm. 1-42
B. Couplet I, G major, mm. 21-42	Shift to second key, D major, mm. 43-50
	Key area II, mm. 51-100
A. Refrain, G major, mm. 109-129 (not complete)	
C. Couplet II, C major, mm. 139-154	
	X, mm. 155-178
	Rhyme of key area II, mm. 179-235
A. Refrain, G major, mm. 253-262 (shortened)	Coda, mm. 236-308

Several rhythmic details play important roles in generating the momentum and breadth of this movement. The theme, set as a Ländler with a typical off-beat waltz accompaniment, appears to begin on the strong part of the measure, but it is shifted one-half measure. This shift is retained until the beginning of key area II, when the downbeat is powerfully asserted, giving a firm periodic anchorage to the first 100 measures of the piece. Within the theme, the figure groups are oddly set — three, then four. Ordinarily, the first figure would be stated twice or four times as:

Ex. 14-4 quotes the opening phrase. The refrain and couplets of this rondo provide the tunefulness of the simpler rondeau forms to contrast with the breadth and discursiveness of the second key area, the X section, and the coda.

Ex. 14-4. Mozart, Quintet in G minor, K. 516, 1787, finale.

Edwards

Beethoven, Symphony No. 8 in F major, Op. 93, 1812, finale. A totally unique combination of rondo and sonata; each section is a major phase of action of a sonata form. Note that the events following m. 266 represent the typical structure of an extended coda.

A. Exposition, mm. 1–90, key relationship F major to A♭ major, then C major

B. First development, mm. 91–160

A. First recapitulation, mm. 161–266, F major to D♭ major, then F major

C. Second development, mm. 267–354

A. Second recapitulation, mm. 355–437, F major to F major
    Coda, cadential section, mm. 438–502

Two features are critical for the form:

1. *Sudden half-step shifts.* The sudden *fortissimo* C♯, m. 17, following a *pianissimo* C is an unassimiliated interruption of F major harmony, and is followed by an abrupt continuation of F major. This gesture is restated literally, m. 178; then, beginning at m. 372, it is made three times and the harmony is resolved tangentially to distant keys—D♭ major, C♯ minor, F♯ minor. None of these resolutions are satisfactory answers to the question raised by the chromatic half-step shift.

2. *Deceptive approach to second key.* The half step, C–C♯, is transposed to G–A♭ to open the second key area, m. 48. This false beginning is eventually corrected to C, the dominant. In the first recapitulation, this progression is transposed upward by a fourth, C–D♭, again a false relation, m. 224. The final resolution of the key relationship is accomplished by a second recapitulation in which the theme previously introduced in A♭ and D♭ is finally settled in F major, m. 408.

Beethoven's manipulation of the half-step progression exerts tremendous leverage in the form, tilting important sections away from their proper harmonic direction and requiring massive corrective measures. Expressively, the rondo-finale character is embodied in the feather-light contredanse tune of the first key area and its return, rondo-like, at the beginning of each development. The headlong momentum of this movement carries the form along a broad trajectory, and has much in common with Beethoven's scherzos (Symphonies No. 3 and No. 7).

Rondos were important in every stratum of 18th-century secular musical life — street music, comic and serious theater, the exquisite cosmopolitan salons of the great capitals — and as a vehicle for some of the most searching explorations into rhetoric and structure. Simple or complex, the base of the rondo remains popular; whatever may happen in the episodes, the refrain can easily be grasped and enjoyed by any listener, so that the form remains clear. This familiar aspect of the rondo is reflected in 18th-century music theory: the rondo, or rondeau, is one of the few forms for which prescriptions are given (see p. 249).

VARIATION

Many sets of variations were published in the later 18th century, as separate works or as movements of instrumental compositions. The appeal of this genre was twofold, namely: (1) the theme itself, generally very tuneful and often familiar through having been heard elsewhere — in opera, song, popular dance, and other works; (2) the embellishment, which added something fresh to the melody.

Variation required both skill and taste on the part of the composer. Reicha says, 1814:

It is very important that a composer know how to vary a melody well, and to vary it so that one can easily recognize the original ideas.[6]

Reicha appends samples of variations upon an eight-measure period; these are *division* variations, in which greater floridity of ornamentation is added.[7]

Variation as a *process* was widely discussed in 18th-century music, and practiced both by composers and performers wherever taste allowed. Variation as a *form* involves more than the incidental elaboration of a tone or phrase, as Momigny, 1806, points out:

The art of varying a theme and the talent of embroidering a canvas [adding ornamentation] are not one and the same thing. The first demands more of science, the other, more of taste.[8]

Embellishment is the variation of one or more musical propositions and variation is the embellishment of an entire melody, or at least of one of its reprises.

An entire melody may be embellished, but the pattern of the embellishment changes or may be varied in each phrase, while that of the variation should be carried out as long as the theme allows.[9]

Embellishment can be added in virtually any type of composition. Variation, which must retain recognizable features of the theme, makes use of simple forms — periods and two-reprise plans — to achieve this purpose. The location of melodic, harmonic, and rhythmic events in a small two-reprise form can easily be grasped by a listener, whatever elaborations or modifications may be incorporated upon the structural plan. Hence most 18th-century variations are composed as a set of short two-reprise pieces. Later, in the 19th century, free fantasia variations upon familiar tunes depart from this format.

The protocol for variations included the following methods:

1. *Division variations; increasingly smaller notes*. This is the original sense of variation since Renaissance times. Adlung, 1758, spells this out as follows: "variiren, that is, to make many smaller notes out of larger ones."[10] The variation set in Mozart's D major Sonata, K. 284, 1775, observes this protocol: the theme moves largely in 8th-notes; variation 1 takes up triplet 8ths; variation 2 mixes triplet 8ths and 16ths; variation 3 has running 16th-notes. Division variations create an immediate sense of excitement, an exhilaration for the listener because of the quickening pace.

2. *A minor couplet*, or major if the theme is in minor. Mozart, D major Sonata, K. 284, 1775, variation 7 of the finale.

3. *An Adagio* in the manner of an Italian vocal aria with elaborate ornamentation, as in variation 11 of the Mozart set cited above.

4. *A contrapuntal study*. Variation 9 of the Mozart set, or variation 1 in the third movement of Beethoven's A major Quartet, Op. 18, No. 5, 1800.

5. *A new tune*, based wholly or in part upon the underlying harmonic-rhythmic progression of the theme. Such a tune will have autonomy; it will not sound like a variation of a theme, and only its juxtaposition to the genuine variation couplets and its association with the theme will legitimate its position in the set. Thus Mozart, in the finale of the C minor Concerto, K. 491, 1786, among the nine variations, highlights Nos. 4 and 7, the first of these being a military march in A♭ with a new tune, and the second, also with new material, in C major, beginning as a kind of trio sonata for winds on a canzona-like figure. Both of these variations give the impression of episodes, so that the movement has a rondo-like form, A B A C A.

6. *A finale*, a return to the theme or its transformation into a quick piece — gigue or contredanse — or a fantasia upon the theme. The coda of the finale of Mozart's C minor Concerto, K. 491, 1786, is a contredanse in quick gigue time.

This list by no means covers all the resources for variation upon which classic composers drew, nor does the order given above indicate a strict protocol. Thus Beethoven, in the D major variations of his A major Quartet, Op. 18, No. 5, 1800, begins the set with a combination of procedures 4 and 5 above, introduces 1 (division variations) later, and incorporates no Adagio or *minore*, but gives us the sound of the minor mode in the coda, which is a fantasia upon the theme, contrasting the qualities of irregularity and the unexpected with the symmetries of the formal variations.

Beethoven's treatment of variation often reached epic proportions. The variations in the last quartets, Op. 127 and Op. 131, the *Diabelli* Variations, Op. 120, 1823, and the *Eroica* Variations, Op. 35, 1802, treat their themes speculatively, at times drastically modifying their character and even their internal structure. Traditional division variations appear in his *Harp* Quartet, Op. 74, 1809, finale, and in the second movement of the *Appassionata* Sonata, Op. 57, 1804. Some features give the *Appassionata* variations a distinctive aspect:

1. The theme itself is hardly a tune; it is a harmonic progression which sets a rare and magic mood thanks to the rich sound of the low register. Occasional fragments with melodic profile are heard first in the bass and later in the top voice.

2. Each succeeding couplet quickens the motion, in a higher tessitura. The lowest melodic tone in the movement, Ab, is heard at the very beginning; the highest melodic tone, Bb, two octaves and a seventh above middle C, is heard at the end of the last variation, just before the music returns to its original range; intervening melodic apices touch Bb above middle C, and Ab a seventh above the Bb.

Thus Beethoven has made use of *musical space* in establishing the contour of this second movement; we have the effect of a gigantic ascent with a steadily lightening texture, abruptly followed by a drop to the original range and style of the piece.

Two more Beethoven variation movements are sketched below. The first, from the C♯ minor Quartet, Op. 131, 1826, follows the plan of the traditional couplet variation. The second, from the *Eroica* Symphony, Op. 55, 1803, is a combination of several structural principles.

Beethoven, C♯ minor Quartet, Op. 131, 1826, Andante, ma non troppo e molto cantabile. Typical 16-measure variation theme—I–half cadence, X–I with rescored repeats. Very rich texture; hocket effect between violins; first measure of theme truncated, giving an odd initial 3/8 effect, becoming a syncopation in m. 2 (see Ex. 14-5). Changes of tempo for variations 2-6.

Variation 1. Only variation in which theme is clearly recognized; accomplishes in one couplet what usual division variations do in three or four—increasingly smaller divisions, from quarter-notes to 32nds; equivalent enrichment of texture.

Variation 2. Più mosso. In march style; new thematic material. Change in harmonic rhythm of theme; again increase in texture.

Variation 3. Andante moderato e lusinghiero. A contrapuntal study based on the stepwise progression in the theme, m. 1–2. Reprise II on another canonic subject, also based on stepwise melodic motion.

Variation 4. Adagio. Ornamentation in Italian aria style.

Variation 5. Allegretto. A sonority study, based upon the truncated-syncopated pattern of first measure of the theme, as modified at end of theme to introduce variation 1. See Ex. 14-5.

Variation 6. Adagio, ma non troppo e semplice. Again a striking contrast —
full chordal texture, emphatic regular rhythm, with action on every quarter-
note except the first of the measure (again the truncation). No formal close,
but a transition to return to theme, whose final statement is interrupted by key
shifts and parenthetical material. Variations 5 and 6 represent the purest
treatment of the string textures that form an important part of the expressive
quality of this movement. The two chords that end the movement echo the
truncated rhythm of the opening measure.

Ex. 14-5. *Rhythmic patterns.* Beethoven, Quartet in C# minor, Op. 131,
1826, variation movt.

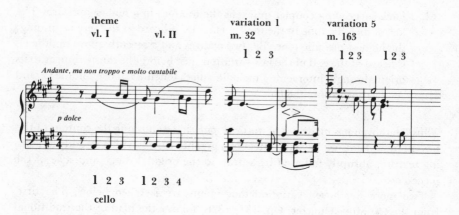

Beethoven, Symphony No. 3 in Eb major, the Eroica, Op. 55, finale. Variations arranged to form a *suite*; each section characterized by some familiar 18th-
century topic. Two themes, forming a treble and bass to each other. Key
scheme: Eb major; X comprising C minor, B minor, D major, G minor, C major,
C minor; final section Eb major. Alternation of bass (b) and treble (t) variations
in a rondo-like plan:

$$\text{b b b t b t b t } \overset{\text{b}}{\underset{\text{t}}{}} \text{ t t coda}$$

Introduction, mm. 1-11. Out of key, interrupting the Eb-to-Eb connection between third and fourth movements; a point of furthest remove, beginning on D
and leading to Eb. (See Ex. 14-6.)

Eb major variations
   1. Theme, rescored upon repetition of each eight-measure reprise, mm.
      12-40.
   2, 3. *Species counterpoint* against bass theme, mm. 45-75.
   4. Treble theme in style of *Lied*, with increasingly fuller accompaniment,
      mm. 76-107.

X variations

    5. *Fugato* on bass theme, C minor, mm. 117–174.

    6. *Contredanse* on treble theme, B minor to D major, mm. 175–210.

    7. *Turkish march* on bass theme, G minor, mm. 211–256.

    8. *Lied* on treble theme, C major then C minor, mm. 257–276.

E♭ major variations

    9. *Fugato*, first on bass theme, later incorporating treble theme, mm. 277–348.

    10. *Aria* in Italian style on treble theme with increasingly elaborate ornamentation, mm. 349–380.

    11. *Chorale* with treble theme in slow march style, mm. 381–395.

Coda

    Fantasia, first leading far afield harmonically to stage the final fanfares in E♭ major, mm. 395–473. These fanfares, in addition to closing the fourth movement, serve as a final triumphant affirmation of E♭ major for the entire symphony.

Ex. 14-6.   Beethoven, Symphony No. 3 in E♭ major, the *Eroica*, Op. 55, 1803, finale.

For the later 18th century and the early 19th century, the set of variations was a *stylish* piece. It created a bit of musical theater by dressing a tune in different ways to make a series of colorful tableaux, much as the model in a fashion show would appear in different costumes. With its tunefulness and its refreshing ways of elaborating the tune, the variation was a darling of musical audiences.

NOTES

    1. Türk, *Klavierschule*, p. 398; Koch, *Lexikon*, p. 397. Rousseau, *Dictionnaire*, p. 136, applies the term to each of a set of variations.

    2. Türk, *Klavierschule*, p. 395; Koch, *Lexikon*, p. 950.

    3. Walther, *Lexikon*, pp. 531–532.

    4. Koch, *Versuch*, III, p. 249.

    5. See the present author's *Music: The Listener's Art*, 2nd ed., 1966, pp. 229–230, for illustrations of these motivic arrangements.

    6. Reicha, *Mélodie*, p. 86.

    7. Ibid., plates, pp. 58–60.

    8. Momigny, *Cours complet*, p. 607.

    9. Ibid., p. 614.

    10. Adlung, *Anleitung*, p. 736.

15 Forms of the Learned Style

Classic composers were less concerned with the learned style than their predecessors. Still, they gave it considerable scope in canons, fugatos, formal fugues, and in textures that added substance to galant topics.

TYPES OF SUBJECT

Since Renaissance times, subjects for contrapuntal imitation had represented two general types, reflecting *church*, or strict, and *galant*, or free, styles:

1. *Ricercar*, in *alla breve* style — the instrumental counterpart of the sacred motet, maintaining the declamation of plainsong
2. *Canzona*, from the 16th-century French chanson, with subjects based on poetic modes and dance figures

Subjects in classic fugatos and fugues were drawn from a wide range of topics, much as they were in the earlier 18th century. The following list demonstrates the range of style and structure:

1. *Alla breve* — motet, ricercar, *stile legato*
   Mozart, G major Quartet, K. 387, 1782, finale
   Beethoven, A♭ major Sonata, Op. 110, 1821, finale
   Haydn, F minor Quartet, Op. 20, No. 5, 1772, finale
2. *Dance-derived subjects* — canzona
   Beethoven, C minor Quartet, Op. 18, No. 4, 1800, second movement — waltz
   Haydn, C major Quartet, Op. 20, No. 2, 1772, finale — gigue
   Beethoven, A major Sonata, Op. 101, 1816, finale — bourrée
   Mozart, E♭ major Quintet, K. 614, 1791, finale — contredanse

CANON

Classic rhetoric lent itself easily to the brevity and neat trim of *canon*. Parallel thirds and sixths and the conjunct voice-leading of cadential formulas — deftly elaborated and often arranged in give-and-take texture — enabled composers to spin out the strict imitation in alternations of I, IV, and V harmonies. Ex. 15-1 illustrates a canon based upon parallel thirds and sixths; the full score and the structural line are given. Parallel motion supports the canonic procedure in the menuetto of Mozart's D major Quintet, K. 593, 1790, and the menuetto of Haydn's D minor Quartet, Op. 76, No. 2, 1797.

Ex. 15-1. *Canon based upon parallel motion.* Mozart, Quintet in C minor, K. 406, 1787, menuetto.

a. Figured melodic line

Eulenburg No. 37

b. Structural line

Classic canons touched opposite poles of the stylistic spectrum. Mozart's *Alleluia*, K. 553, 1788, is in *stile antico*, an *alla breve* piece using species counterpoint. Most canons, however, capture the spirit of the round, a social genre, using galant figures and sometimes bawdy texts. Haydn, Mozart, Cherubini, and Beethoven wrote many canons. As it appears in classic music, the canon has much in common with classic use of fugato—a short, well-turned contrapuntal exposition that is not required to extend itself on the grand scale of the fugue (see Ex. 10-8).

FUGATO

A section of a composition set imitatively was designated as *fugato*. Fugato was distinguished from true *fugue* by Türk, 1789:

> The *fugue* is a two-, three-, four-, or more-voiced composition in which the principal idea (theme, subject, leader, *dux*) is set forth first only in one voice, then in turn by the others in the tonic key or in others, with minor alterations. The theme also appears during the piece very often in one voice or another.[1]
>
> *Sections in fugato* [*fugirte Sätze*] signify particular places of imitation that frequently appear in duets, trios, etc.[2]

Koch, 1802, refers to "fugirte Motette, Chorale"[3] as distinguished from compositions in which fugal procedure is maintained regularly and thoroughly during the entire piece.

Classic rhetoric absorbs fugato much more readily than it does fugue. Fugato becomes a *topic*, a formal bow in the direction of the learned style, eventually yielding its contrapuntal play to the demands of a strong periodic cadence. The harmonic *polarity* of classic forms does not accommodate the searching treatment of contrapuntal imitation characteristic of the circular or solar harmonic schemes of baroque fugues.

Fugatos appeared in classic forms at various points. Some of these are:

1. *Opening of key area I*
   Mozart, G major Quartet, K. 387, 1782, No. finale
   Beethoven, C minor Quartet, Op. 18, No. 4, 1800, second movement

2. *Shift to second key*
   Haydn, Symphony No. 95 in C minor, 1791, finale

3. *Key area II*
   Mozart, G major Quartet, K. 387, 1782, finale

4. *X, . . . development*
   Haydn, A major Quartet, Op. 55, No. 1, 1790, finale
   Beethoven, F major Quartet, Op. 59, No. 1, 1806, first movement (see Ch. 24)

5. *Coda*
   Mozart, *Jupiter* Symphony, K. 551, 1788, finale
   Beethoven, F minor Quartet, Op. 95, 1809, finale

6. *Refrain of rondo*
   Haydn, Symphony No. 101 in D major, 1794, finale, final refrain

7. *Episode in rondo*
   Mozart, Divertimento in E♭ major, K. 563, 1788, finale

8. *Variation*
   Haydn, E♭ major Quartet, Op. 76, No. 6, 1797, finale
   Beethoven, *Eroica* Symphony, Op. 55, 1803, finale

The order of entries generally observes the tonic-dominant plan of the formal fugue, especially when opening a movement as a *narratio*; see 1 above. Imitations at the octave can build a sense of climax or of *peroratio*, as in 5 above. Entries through the circle of fifths perform a harmonic *confutatio*, as in the X section of the finale of Mozart's E♭ major Divertimento, K. 563, 1788. The formality and salience of a fugal exposition in a classic work raise its rhetorical effect to a higher level of emphasis than that of its neighboring sections. One of the most impressive uses of fugato for climax occurs in the finale of Beethoven's C major Quartet, Op. 59, No. 3, 1806. The *andamento* theme relies on sheer momentum, rather than contour, for its effect. As voices enter, this momentum gathers force until, at the fourth entry, part-writing is reduced to two voices, both doubled, sacrificing counterpoint for sonority. Finally, all sense of fugue is erased as the powerful cadence in C major is hammered out. The fugato in the finale of Mozart's G major Quartet, K. 387, 1782, gives way to a series of galant flourishes; in the second movement of Beethoven's C minor Quartet, Op. 18,

No. 4, 1800, the counterpoint levels out to become an accompanied Ländler melody.

FUGUE

Fugue, the chief genre of the learned style, was considered the ultimate stage of a composer's training and the finest test of his skill. Important treatises— Marpurg, 1753-1754, Daube, 1773, Martini, 1775, Albrechtsberger, 1790, Sabbatini, 1802, Vogler, 1811—dealt exhaustively with fugue; early anthologies of music—Crotch, 1806, Clementi, 180[?]—include many fugues.

Honored as it was, the fugue suffered a decline in the late 18th century. Koch's comments, 1795, testify to this trend,[4] and Marsh, 1800, speaks of "the want of fugue . . . in modern pieces."[5] While this may be ascribed partly to the taste for less serious and complex music at this time, it also reflects changing criteria in more serious speculative compositions. Classic composers, while trained in thorough bass and imitation, did not have the opportunity to practice fugue composition as intensively as their predecessors, and thereby to acquire the fluency and sureness of syntax that stems from constant usage. The symmetries and punctuations of classic rhetoric inhibit the steady rhythmic flow essential to a convincing fugal discourse, and, as mentioned above, the polarity of tonic and dominant does not provide room for a series of expositions in closely related keys, necessary to give a fugue its scope and unity.

Among classic composers, Haydn had perhaps the greatest fluency in fugal composition. He applied his remarkable talent for elaborating a simple progression with crisp, short, and lively motives to fugal texture, juggling figures in a brisk and often witty manner. In the finale of his A major Quartet, Op. 20, No. 6, 1772, he draws two subjects from a descending line of parallel thirds—a leaping canzona figure and an *alla breve* subject with suspensions, their contrasted topics disguising the fact that they are variants of the *same* structural line (see Ex. 15-2). Haydn worked out this fugue with intensive development of the subject, including a number of strettos; this treatment represents the truly "learned" approach in the grand tradition of fugue. On the other hand, the fugue that serves as the finale of the C major Quartet, Op. 20, No. 2, 1772, has a more relaxed rhetoric. There are four subjects, carefully introduced at widely spaced points for maximum clarity and lightness, qualities which typify the entire movement. In the first 37 measures, four-part harmony is used sparingly, despite the presence of several subjects; indeed, the texture appears much more responsorial than contrapuntal as voices hand their figures back and forth. No more than 12 entries appear in the 162 measures, but the episodic material draws heavily upon the motives of the subjects. Irregular rhythmic scansion is maintained throughout most of the fugue, but the climax asserts a four-square regularity along with the fullest texture in the piece. If the A major fugue represents a firm traditional treatment, the C major fugue has an ease of declamation with a true classic ring. Haydn's instrumental fugues fit well with the spirit of *galanterie* that pervades his music. His light, often minimal counterpoint serves his playful ideas to perfection.

Ex. 15-2. *Fugue subjects.* Haydn, Quartet in A major, Op. 20, No. 6, 1772, finale.

a.

Boosey and Hawkes

Reduction.

Mozart, on the other hand, seems to move out of character in his instrumental fugues—C minor, K. 426, 1783, later scored for strings as Adagio and Fugue, K. 546, 1788; Prelude and Fugue in C major, K. 394, 1782, Fantasia and Fugue in F minor, K. 608, 1791. In each of these works his typically elegant declamation becomes turgid and thick; a sense of effort pervades these works, as if Mozart felt his contrapuntal obligations heavily. For him, fugato was a happier medium; after a set of entries he moves on to other material, giving free rein to his inimitable skill in mixing and coordinating various topics. Nowhere does this mixture occur more felicitously than in the finale of his G major Quartet, K. 387, 1782; here, fugatos are constantly pulled short, giving way to galant figures, only to break out anew into imitation. The final *coup de grâce* comes in the last measures, where a tight stretto on the *alla breve* subject relaxes into a graceful cadence.

Fugue and fugato were cultivated in the chamber music of middle- and late 18th-century Austrian and Italian composers, as Kirkendale points out.[6] Johann George Albrechtsberger, best known as Beethoven's counterpoint teacher, was one of the most industrious workers in this field. He wrote more than 200 instrumental fugues, far more than any of his contemporaries. These fugues show competence, both in part-writing and in layout, but little imagination. They are filled with sequences; two-measure groupings prevail;[7] melodic contours lack distinction, and the style bespeaks its habitat—the studio of the composition professor. It lacks any of the characteristic flavor of string writing that gives life even to the most learned passages in Haydn and Mozart.

The fugal finale of Boccherini's D minor Quintet, Op. 13, No. 4, 1772, has much in common with Haydn's finale to Op. 20, No. 2 (see p. 263). The subject itself is a variant of the *pathetic* type (see p. 268), quite different from Haydn's passepied-gigue, but the treatment is much the same. Although Boccherini's

fugue is 136 measures long, the last entries are at m. 74 in F major and m. 106 in
G minor. Motives from the principal subject are constantly in view, as with
Haydn, but there is no full-dress final exposition in the tonic.

Salieri's *Scherzi istrumentali* have their special way of dealing lightly with
what he calls the *stile fugato*. The symmetrical subjects of these four pieces all
have strong cadences, so that a statement of a subject stands as a short period. At
the beginning of each piece entries are linked without episodes, giving the impression of regular period structure, a type of rhetoric far removed from the discursive irregularities of the baroque fugue. The final measures of each *Scherzo*
are galant cadential flourishes, with no trace of learned style. In the fugues of
Haydn, Boccherini, and Salieri, fugal procedure is not an end in itself, but a device used to organize a galant play of motive and texture. However thin the fugal
treatment may be, the skill in part-writing is superb, which contributes to the
bizarrerie of Salieri's *Scherzi*. These light contrapuntal works fulfill their objective admirably — to be pleasant diversions.

Fugal composition was an option in instrumental music. In church music,
competence in fugue was a requirement because traditionally certain sections
were treated fugally — the "Et vitam venturi" and the "Cum sancto spiritu" of the
Mass, as well as parts of the *Te Deum* and litany. However, the degree of contrapuntal rigor could vary greatly, as well as the style and the amount of concern
with the subject.

Haydn, in the "In gloria" of his *St. Cecilia* Mass, circa 1773, composed an extended fugue of 93 measures, maintaining a tight grip on the subject with unre-
lenting contrapuntal activity and constant use of the *stile legato*; this is a choral
concertato in the ancient tradition. The subject itself is an *andamento*, with a
faithful countersubject, dropped only at the end, when the subject is treated in
stretto. This movement, one of Haydn's most conservative, recalls the manner of
Bach and Handel. The "In gloria" of the *Lord Nelson* Mass, 1798, receives similar treatment, with 18 entries, including strettos, in the 40 measures of the
fugue. Key schemes for these fugues reflect baroque tradition, exploring the
closely related keys, making a decisive gesture toward VI (point of furthest remove), and returning to end with a broadly scaled section in the home key. Ex.
15-3 quotes the subjects and countersubjects of both fugues, with structural lines
sketched below; the elaborate figuration, especially in the countersubjects, in
the alto voice has a strong flavor of baroque style.

Ex. 15-3. *Subjects and countersubjects in the "In gloria" fugues.*

a. Haydn, *St. Cecilia* Mass, ca. 1773.

Ex. 15-3, cont'd.

b. Haydn, *Lord Nelson* Mass, 1798.

Mozart's early Masses make the formal bow to *alla breve* fugue in the "Cum Sanctu Spiritu" and "Et vitam venturi" sections; these include the Masses in C major, K. 66, 1769, C minor, K. 139, 1768, C major, K. 167, 1773, C major, K. 220, 1775, C major, K. 257, 1776, and C major, K. 262, 1776. The short Masses contain no fugal sections. This is true also of the *Coronation* Mass, K. 317, 1779, one of Mozart's most ingratiating church works (see Ch. 10). The great fugue, "Kyrie," in the *Requiem* Mass, K. 626, 1791, is worked out with two subjects in ornamented *alla breve* style, using the traditional formulas for entries and episodes. There are two striking divergences from the normal harmonic orbit of a strict fugue—the entries in C minor and F minor, m. 23 and 31. Following the latter entry, the harmony moves in one quick thrust back to D minor, the home key, m. 36. These descents into the distant flat areas deepen the pathetic affect of this serious fugue, while the wrench back to D minor shows a violence that exceeds the usual expressive range in fugues. Harmonically, this fugue has something in common with the "supper" scene in *Don Giovanni*, where the distant key, B♭ minor, underscores a climactic moment (see Ch. 22).

If the fugues discussed above represent traditional treatment, the "Et vitam venturi" from Haydn's so-called *Paukenmesse* (*Timpani* Mass), 1796, touches the other end of the spectrum with its saturation of late 18th-century stylistic features. The piece is laid out in key-area form, with solo passages forming the typical end-rhyme for the two reprises. The only full set of entries occurs at the beginning, although motives from the subject are used consistently. Throughout the fugue there are nine authentic cadences, as well as clearly defined lesser cadences; these cadential gestures are inconsistent with traditional fugal style but idiomatic to classic music. Ex. 15-4 quotes the subject and countersubject, and a choral tutti preceding a solo section. Note the repetition in the subject and the regular rhythm, which establish a sing-song effect that will color the entire fugue. Despite the differences in melodic detail, both subject and countersubject have similar rhythmic patterns, lacking a countertime effect. This will be expanded to the full choral texture, so that many passages emerge in *familiar* style, as in Ex. 15-4b. The rich chromatic passage quoted introduces a touch of color inconsistent with the harmonic climate of traditional fugues, especially the augmented $^6_3$ to cadential $^6_4$ progression.

Ex. 15-4. *Subject and countersubject.* Haydn, *Paukenmesse*, 1796.

a. "Et vitam venturi" ("And in the life to come").

b. Choral tutti.

BEETHOVEN'S TREATMENT OF FUGUE

Beethoven addressed himself to fugue late in his career, from 1815 to 1826. By this time the spirit of the 18th-century fugue had dissipated; its inner mechanism had come to a halt although the parts remained in place. Haydn and Mozart's fugues retained something of the quality of the baroque fugue, thanks both to the central position this genre enjoyed during their early years and to their considerable involvement with church music. In dealing with fugue, Beethoven could not look to current or recent practice, but only to the techniques of the past. Therefore his fugues have a strong retrospective stamp.

This orientation is seen in the overture *The Consecration of the House*, Op. 124, 1822, where the flavor of Handel is strong; in the fugue of the A♭ major Sonata, Op. 110, 1821, whose subject would have delighted Fux and other 18th-century pedagogues; in the final section of the *Heiliger Dankgesang* in the A minor Quartet, Op. 132, 1825, a fugato that imitates the motet style of the Renaissance; and in the finale of the *Hammerklavier* Sonata, Op. 106, 1818–1819, which recalls the variation canzona.

The fugue from the C♯ minor Quartet, Op. 131, 1826, and the *Grosse Fuge*, Op. 133, 1825, illustrate two different approaches to fugue in Beethoven. The first develops the conjunct motion of its subject to spin out an unbroken flow; the second relentlessly explores the possibilities of its two subjects in a highly articulated episodic structure.

Quartet in C♯ Minor, Op. 131, 1826, First Movement

This piece is *topically* a motet without text for strings, a reincarnation of the imitative ricercar of the Renaissance. Steady half- and quarter-note movement, sweetness and richness of sound, whether in two-, three-, or four-part writing, duet sections à la Josquin, Phrygian color of the lowered second degree — all these hark back to the grave manner of the 16th-century motet. The subject itself is a variant of the *pathetic*[8] type, but subtly permuted in the order of tones; the leading tone precedes the tonic, and thus invites an answer in the fifth *below*, instead of in the dominant (see Ex. 15-5). This single circumstance sets the *harmonic* direction for the entire quartet, a deep descent into subdominant regions followed by a rise to the fifth above just before the finale (see Ch. 19). As Kerman points out,[9] the sixth degree in the subject must be answered by the lowered second degree in the response, introducing this note as an integral harmonic element. We hear the lowered second degree again in the dominant harmony of mm. 113 and 115; this gives the final cadence the effect of a drawn-out half cadence. When the C♯ major chord proceeds deceptively into the next movement, D major comes to center stage.

Melodically, the conjunct lines create an unbroken flow reminiscent of the motets of Lassus and Palestrina; this melodic motion also contributes to the unique structure of the piece, since it enables the melody to ascend deliberately in a wave-like contour to a climactic point, high A, m. 64. Such melodic apices are frequently used by J. S. Bach to create a macromelodic dimension separate from other aspects of structure. This Beethoven fugue contains only *two* full sets of entries, beginning at mm. 1 and 93, but, proper to ricercar procedure, there are diminutions, augmentations, stretto, and use of material from the subject in the episodes.

Rhythmic scansion brings some striking contrasts to light. Basically, two- and four-measure groups control the articulation, with some groupings by three, either in individual voices or for the entire ensemble. This fundamentally regular scansion, without strong punctuation, contributes a sing-song element to the steady flow of the piece. But the subject itself has a built-in rhythmic ambiguity. As the first violin enters by itself, with no ictus for rhythmic orientation, we can read each of the longer notes in turn as a strong beat. The B♯ is strong in relation to the preceding short G♯; the C♯ is strong in relation to B♯ as a tonic to a leading tone; the A is strong both by length and emphasis, but contradicts its accent harmonically. This equivocation of rhetorical emphasis pervades the entire fugue, and indeed, continues through the variation movement. Ex. 15-5b illustrates these various readings.

Ex. 15-5.   Beethoven, Quartet in C♯ minor, Op. 131, 1826, 1st movt.

a. Initial entries.

Philharmonia

b. Some variants in order of tones in a pathetic subject.

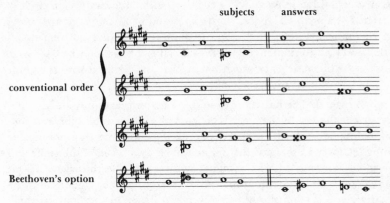

c. Implied alternate scansions in subject.

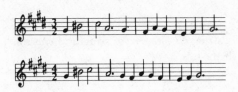

Grosse Fuge in B♭ Major, Op. 133, 1825

The underlying structural principle of the *Grosse Fuge* is a *variation canzona*. Of the 12 expositions in the work, 11 are rhythmically different from each other; only the final exposition in the G♭ major fugue, a single entry, retains the style of the opening exposition. A synopsis of the sections follows, with some comments bearing upon criteria used in this study:

> *Introduction.* A table of contents, *in reverse*, of the principal sections, beginning on G and moving down the circle of Fifths to B♭; mm. 1–25.

> *Fugue I.* A powerful, unrelenting march rhythm and the only fully worked-out fugue in the piece; variation canzona procedure represented by modifications (16ths, syncopations, triplets) of the original march and *alla breve* rhythmic patterns of the subjects; five expositions; mm. 25–158.

> *Fugue II.* A minimal fugue, in G♭ major, in lyric style, steady 16th-notes against quarter-notes; the contrapuntal element also minimal, as the 16ths take on the quality of an accompaniment to the arioso of the quarter-note subject; two expositions, initial for four entries, final for one; mm. 159–232.

> *Gigue.* A short two-reprise form, twice stated, in B♭ major; a *premature* return to B♭ major; mm. 233–269.

Fugatos. Based on rhythm of the gigue (6/8); section begins and ends in A♭ major; first exposition in A♭ major; second exposition moves through circle of fifths from F major to G♭ major; third exposition in E♭ major; fourth in A♭ major; rhythmically and melodically the basic themes undergo tremendous distortion and transformation; mm. 273-492. (It is this section which seems to foreshadow the thematic transformations of Liszt and Richard Strauss and the serialism of Schoenberg and his school.)

Fantasia on themes. The harmonic drop to A♭ major is carefully and deliberately reversed; the rest of the piece is concerned with reestablishing and confirming B♭ major on a scale proportionate to the enormous trajectory of the preceding sections; B♭ major is first reestablished by a recall of the gigue and an enormous spinning out of the gigue rhythm; then Beethoven recalls his table of contents, this time in proper order (march, arioso, gigue), all in B♭ major; the gigue rhythm slowly takes over and drives to the final cadence, which is in a galant manner adapted to the heavy textures and angular melodic contours that characterize so much of this work; mm. 492-741.

The key-area plan of this piece is its strongest element of structural control. Without the usual melodic recall and rhyme it is

$$I\text{-}VI♭, \quad (I)\,X\text{-}I$$

This is also the plan of the first movement of the Quartet in B♭ major, Op. 130, 1825-1826, for which the *Grosse Fuge* was orginally intended as a finale. Lacking a rhyme, the final section relies entirely upon harmony for the confirming periodic gesture. Six times the music moves toward a cadence in B♭ major, only to be thwarted. When the expectation is almost too much to bear, B♭ major is finally confirmed. In this light, the "premature" return to B♭ major at the gigue might be considered the first feint toward the home key, to be rudely thrust aside by the fugato section; or the fugato section could be taken as an enormous harmonic parenthesis, enclosed by the two statements of the gigue. In any case, the gigue, by virtue both of its key and its rhythm, would appear to be the ruling idea from m. 233 onward.

Further legitimation of the gigue as the prevailing topic of the *Grosse Fuge* arises from its original position as a finale in a quartet laid out along the lines of a baroque suite of dances and arias. March, aria, and finally gigue, as the principal topics of Op. 133, fit in with the styles of the five preceding movements of Op. 130.

Beethoven's fugal writing shows the same speculative approach, the same sense of struggle, that characterizes much of his music. His fugues do not have the powerful confident thrust of Bach's or the easy deftness of Haydn's. In solving problems of declamation and form, he created some unique works of art, fugal in their arrangement but unlike any other works of their kind.

NOTES

1. Türk, *Klavierschule*, p. 396.
2. Ibid., p. 397.
3. Koch, *Lexikon*, p. 1453.
4. Koch, *Journal*, p. 95ff.
5. Marsh, *Hints*, p. 1.
6. Kirkendale, *Fuge und Fugato*, p. 16.
7. Anton Reicha, in his *Fugue phrasée*, before 1826, deliberately punctuated with full cadences preceding each new exposition, in the effort to adapt the newer concepts of periodicity to the traditional procedures of fugue.
8. Kirkendale, *Fuge und Fugato*, uses this term, p. 137, to designate a subject in relatively long notes where the diminished seventh appears in alternation with the minor tonic triad. The order of notes is optional, but the affect is pathetic. The subjects of the "Kyrie" of Mozart's *Requiem*, K. 626, 1791, his Fugue in C minor, K. 426, 1783, Beethoven's *Grosse Fuge* Op. 133, 1825, Handel's "And with His Stripes" from the *Messiah*, 1742, Haydn's F minor Quartet, Op. 20, No. 5, 1772, finale, and many others draw upon this model.
9. Kerman, *The Beethoven Quartets*, p. 296.

16 Aria

The *aria* in the 18th century drew together many stylistic and structural elements. Through its text-music relationship it provided sharp definition of rhetoric and affect. It covered a wide range of textures—solo, chamber music, orchestral tutti—and offered opportunities for striking effects of scoring. It was the heart of 18th-century opera, the most important genre of the time, and it was a featured item in concerts. It offered scope for the beauty and brilliance of the great virtuoso singers who were the most famous performers of their age. In addition, the aria furnished a model for countless instrumental works.

FORMS OF THE ARIA

Full Da Capo Aria (Grand Da Capo)

The most important form of the aria was the *full*, or *grand*, *da capo*. Koch, 1802, provides a detailed description:

> *Aria* . . . signifies in the broadest sense of the word not only poetry written for a musical setting in which a particular sentiment is expressed, but also the melody to which this poetry is set; therefore this term is used in poesy as well as in music. Since the expression of a sentiment in poetry as well as in music may be set in different forms, more or less extended or limited, the custom is to classify the various types of aria by different names (out of this variety arises the *Lied*, ode, the rondo, the romance, the aria, the ariette or cavatina . . . etc.), and we understand by the term aria in the narrow sense a selection from a vocal work in which one person expresses a sentiment amply, or to the fullest outpouring of the heart, according to the requirements of the textual content.
>
> The poetry in such an aria heretofore comprised two sections, the first of which gave the general expression of the sentiment, the second a particular aspect of the sentiment. The musical setting has had, until the last quarter of the past century, a fixed form, from which no deviations were made. It consists, according to Sulzer's[1] description, of the following plan:
>
> "First, the instruments play an introduction, called the *ritornello*, in which the main expressive quality of the aria is briefly presented; then the voice enters and sings the first part of the aria without a great deal of expansion [*Ausdehnung*]; it then repeats the phrases and develops them [Koch's footnote: "The modulation then turns to the dominant, or when the piece is in minor, to the relative major, in which this first period closes."], then the voice rests for some measures for the singer to take fresh breath. Meanwhile, the instruments play a short interlude in which the gist of the principal affect is repeated; following this, the singer begins again, working over the text of the first part, taking up the essential elements of the ruling sentiment, and concludes the melody of the first part [Koch: "and in the principal key, in which the following ritornello will also close"]; the instruments, however, continue

in order to emphasize the sentiment, and finally close the first part of the aria. The second part is sung without the repetitions and working over that took place in the first part, with the instruments here and there underlining the expression during the short pauses for the voice. When the singer has finished the instruments enter again with a ritornello, after which the first part is repeated. This is the usual form of present-day arias."

Koch then continues:

This form was the most suitable, and in the past, the most usual, when the poet incorporated the essence of the particular sentiment in the first part and only sketched a particular modification in the second part, which could lead directly back to the first part. Since the power of custom required that this form also be used in texts wherein the second part was better suited to expansion and working over than the first . . . and where the repetition of the entire first part would be unsuitable and boring . . . lately . . . this form has been altered so that the second part constitutes a separate period and only the first line of the first part is repeated. When a text of two sections requires no restatement of the first part, the aria nowadays is usually composed in two sections . . . . Generally, the first section is composed in a slow or moderate tempo, the second in a quick tempo.[2]

Koch's footnotes spell out the I–V, X–I form for part I. No comment is made regarding the harmony of part II, but it was customary to proceed to a related key. In major-mode arias, this would generally be VI, and part II would close on I or V of the relative minor.

To illustrate the full *da capo* aria in its late and most expanded scope, excerpts from an aria by Galuppi are quoted in Ex. 16-1; this aria appeared in a collection called the *Favourite Songs in the Opera Call'd L'Olimpiade*, published by Walsh in 1755. The version from which these numbers were drawn was a *pasticcio*, with text by Metastasio, including four arias by Galuppi, one by Pergolesi, and one by Minuti.

Ex. 16-1. *Full da capo aria.* Galuppi, *L'Olimpiade*, 1755, "Superbo di me stesso."

("Proudly I carry that dear name, openly as in my heart. The Greeks will then say that we are as one, in thought, in feeling, and finally, in our gods.") Part I sets the first sentence, part II, m. 93, the second.

Ex. 16-1, cont'd.

(15)

In part I, Allegro, the opening ritornello sets the martial style and reviews the principal material of the solo—vigorous opening, pathetic middle phrase (see m. 32), and brilliant cadential section (see m. 35). The solo opens in martial style, followed by a lyric phrase on "come" (note sprung rhythm in m. 21; a flourish on "portando," mm. 26–31; a pathetic nuance on "caro nome," mm. 32–33; and a firm cadential gesture to close on V, mm. 38–39). Upon the return to I these events are reviewed with much incidental variation, melodically, and a fermata for the mandatory cadenza, preceding the final ritornello.

Part II, Andante, involves a gentler affect; it begins in C major (IV) and ends in E minor (VI); and is set in slow minuet time. The lack of harmonic focus and the brevity of the section—17 measures—create the effect of an interlude, a foil for the principal part of the aria, a function served by most middle parts of full *da capo* arias.

Galuppi's aria is a polished, attractive, and impressive representative of the Italian operatic style of the mid-century. The same can be said of many other representatives of this genre, including those of Hasse, the most famous "Italian" composer of his time; his *Arminio*, 1745, consists principally of elaborate *da capo* arias.

Earlier *da capo* arias were clearly modeled on dances and songs. The *da capo* layout antedates the aria, because it was used in some genres of vocal and instrumental music in the Renaissance. When the two-reprise I–V, X–I plan was coordinated with the arrangements borrowed from paired dances in the operas of Scarlatti and his contemporaries, the full *da capo* was established. Scarlatti's "E ben far" ("And thus to do like the bee") from *Il Trionfo d'Honore*, 1718, parallels the A B A plan of paired dances, except that part II does not carry out the two-reprise dance pattern. Its brevity keeps the tripartite structure within reasonable bounds and provides a closer fit with the text, virtues often lost in the extended *da capo* arias of mid-century. The clarity and precision of the design, the happy turn of figure, the strong cadential reinforcements—these are marks of Scarlatti's style, which prompted Burney to remark, that "I find part of his property among the stolen goods of all the best composers of the first forty or fifty years of the present century."[3] The greater our acquaintance with the music of Alessandro Scarlatti, most of which is still unavailable, the clearer it seems that he, more than any other composer, deserves credit for codifying the Italian musical idiom of the 18th century through his felicitous shaping of musical figure and structure.

The full *da capo* was used in other media of performance. Bukofzer points to J. S. Bach's use of this form in the "Et resurrexit" of Bach's B minor Mass, 1733, and in the first movement of his E major Violin Concerto, 1720.[4] Mozart's early arias employ this form (see "Fra cento affanni," ["Among one hundred afflictions"], K. 88, 1770). After 1770–1775 the full *da capo* was no longer in fashion, but its influence upon classic composers was strong in their early years, and its principal feature—the restatement of part I—was retained in modified form throughout the classic era.

Compressed Da Capo Aria

The full *da capo* aria was a symmetrical, closed form. Its monumental static aspect, secured by the cadence in I at the end of both parts I and II, was proper for the symbolic expression of grand passions in the manner of a brilliant tableau. But the sense for a freer dramatic flow, arising from changing concepts of theater, brought about modifications of the form. Chief among these was the integration of key-area elements with the *da capo*, resulting in a *compressed* form, referred to by Koch, 1802 (see p. 273 above), and Burney, 1789 (see p. 232 above). Ex. 16-2 shows the differences between the full and the compressed forms.

Ex. 16-2. *Da capo aria, full and compressed.*

Full	I	II	I (*da capo*)
Key	I– V; V (X)I	X	I– V; V (X)I
Thematic order	A B A B	C	A B A B
Compressed			
Key	I V	X	I	I
Thematic order	A B	C	A	B

The scheme of the compressed *da capo* aria is identical to that of sonata form. Its advantages are that (1) it allows part I to open out freely on the rise to the dominant; (2) it incorporates the X section in the action of the harmonic trajectory; (3) it closes the form, and the expression of the ruling sentiment, only at one place, the final cadence, allowing the dramatic action to proceed more fluently by eliminating the static effect created by a full three-part A B A structure.

To illustrate the compressed *da capo* form, excerpts from an aria from Guglielmi's *Le Pazzie d'Orlando* are given in Ex. 16-3. This work was composed about 1771, a few years after the time referred to by Burney, 1789, when he credited J. C. Bach with evolving the form. The style, a quick gigue, suggests the quick trot of the text's "smart little coach." Some touches of parodistic pictorialism may be noted: "little nothing" ("petit rien"), "two trills," "sighing" ("sospirar"). The text has the macaronic multilingual mixture sometimes affected in elegant 18th-century prose. The translation of the entire text:

In Paris, perfumed, in a smart little coach, I used to go every morning to flirt with a hundred beauties, and sang an arietta in French style; with two trills and four bows, and some other little nothing I passed my time very well without sighing. The ladies in France who have a little malice used to call me "my caprice."

Ex. 16-3. *Compressed da capo aria.* Guglielmi, *Le Pazzie d'Orlando,* ca. 1771, "A Parigi."

a. First solo (preceded by 12 measures of ritornello).

b. Latter part of second key area; note repetition of text and cadences.

Ex. 16-3, cont'd.

c. X section, comparable to part II of *da capo* aria; note shift of key to dominant of VI.

When the middle section of a compressed *da capo* aria is set in a different style and tempo than that of part I, the traditional effect is retained — the contrast of two sentiments. Mozart borrowed this procedure for the overture to his *Abduction from the Seraglio*, K. 384, 1781–1782, touching upon two of the principal topics — Turkish music and Belmonte's aria "Hier denn soll ich dich sehen" ("Here then I shall see you"). (See also the discussion of the trio "Ah taci, ingiusto core" ["Be quiet, cruel heart"] from Act II of *Don Giovanni*, p. 408.) When the material retains the tempo and meter of part I, the resemblance to sonata form is very close, as in Ex. 16-3 above.

Key-Area Form without X or I–V, I

The key-area or sonata form of the aria without a middle, or X, section can be taken as a further compression of the *da capo* form. Here the melodic material of part I is recalled and rhymed as a recapitulation. "Ah, chi mi dice mai" ("Who can tell me") from Act I and "Il mio tesoro" ("My treasure") from Act II of *Don Giovanni*, 1787, as well as the finale of Act I of Gluck's *Orphée*, 1774, "Amour, viens rendre à mon âme" ("Oh love, restore to my soul"), use this form, which is suitable for the expression of a single affect or a unified group of ideas.

In slow movements of instrumental works, where the style of the aria was imitated, this form was also employed, as in the second movement of Beethoven's F minor Sonata, Op. 2, No. 1, 1795.

Rondo

The rondo form can accommodate any aria that has an especially appealing principal subject, set as a dance or song period. Benda's aria "Selbst die glücklichsten der Ehen" ("Even the happiest of marriages") (see Ex. 14-1) exemplifies this treatment, as does "J'ai perdu mon Euridice" ("I have lost my Euridice") from Act III of Gluck's *Orphée*, 1774 (see Ex. 2-20). The finale of Act I of Mozart's *Figaro*, 1785–1786, "Non piu andrai" ("You'll no longer strut"), is also an A B A C A rondo. Its principal tune is a delightful melodic invention, and probably one of those referred to by Mozart when he said that the people of Prague were dancing quadrilles and waltzes to the music from this opera.[5]

Cavatina

The term *cavatina* had several meanings in the 18th century. Generally, it referred to a short aria, with few embellishments; it also referred to a short, song-like section in a recitative.[6] Schubart, 1785, defines the cavatina as

> . . . a branch of the aria. It should have no coloratura. It is a simple artless expression of a single sentiment, and thus has but one section. The motive of the cavatina must be full of feeling, moving, easily understood, and light.[7]

The cavatina thus is specifically distinguished from the aria *da capo* by lacking both the second section and the *da capo*.

"Porgi amor" ("Give, oh love") from Act II of Mozart's *Marriage of Figaro*, 1785–1786, is designated as a cavatina in the score. It has a brief I–V, X–I harmonic plan without melodic recall or rhyme. Despite its brevity it has an intense poignancy created largely by the texture, with frequent string appoggiaturas and winds in parallel thirds. It thus fulfills Schubart's prescription for the cavatina. The cavatina in Graun's *Montezuma*, HAM 282, 1755, however, has a full key-area plan, with the "Scarlatti" arrangement of melodic material, including an extensive, somewhat modified rhyme in part II.

Composite Aria

The composite aria, described by Koch (see p. 273), consists of two or more contrasted sections, allowing scope for change of feeling and thus for some development of plot. Zerlina's two arias in *Don Giovanni*, 1787, "Batti, batti" ("Beat me, beat me") and "Vedrai, carino" ("Come, my dearest"), both shift from moderate tempo into quick 6/8 as she moves from persuasion to high spirits.

ARIA STYLES

Arias were characterized according to style and expression. The categories described below represented standard items in *opera seria*, distributed according to a well-established protocol, especially in mid-century operas. Christmann, 1782, says:

> Arias in opera are classified according to the respective character; an aria which is marked by difficult passages and impassioned melody is called an *aria di bravura* since it requires much boldness in its execution. If the voice has more declamation than flowing melody, and if the accompaniment is active and full, it is an *aria di strepito* [agitation], and an aria which contains many changes and digressions in the expression of various passions, and in which the tempo changes a number of times, is called an *aria d'espressione*.[8]

John Brown, in his *Letters*, 1789, gives a somewhat different list:

1. *Aria cantabile* (a flowing melody) — tenderness
2. *Aria di portamento* (long notes, alla breve) — dignity

3. *Aria di mezzo carattere* (midway between first two)—seriousness

4. *Aria parlante* (many quick notes set syllabically)—agitation

5. *Aria di bravura, aria d'agilitá* (virtuoso material, brilliance of execution) —no particular affection[9]

"Porgi amor" from Act II of Mozart's *Figaro* is an *aria cantabile*; "Amour, viens" from Act I of Gluck's *Orphée*, 1774, begins as an *aria di portamento* and becomes an *aria di bravura* when Orpheus breaks into an extended coloratura; "Il mio tesoro" from Act II of *Don Giovanni* has elements of the *aria d'espressione* as Ottavio's feelings are expressed in various styles—*cantabile, portamento, agilitá*.

TEXT-MUSIC RELATIONSHIPS

Text-music relationships in an aria involve (1) appropriate musical figures for the affection to be expressed, (2) correct grammatical and oratorical scansion, and (3) reconciliation of poetic and musical structures. The first two items have been discussed (Chs. 1 and 5); the third is the topic of this section.

Paradoxically, the full *da capo*, which had the greatest scope among aria types, used the briefest text. Galuppi's aria quoted in Ex. 16-1 contains more than 200 measures (including the improvised cadenza), its poetic text 57 syllables. On the other hand, the rondo of Benda quoted in Ex. 14-1 is 50 measures long and its text contains 92 syllables. In the latter type, poetry and music match closely, and the composer has only to avoid an improper stress. In the former, the music is the principal concern and the composer must distribute the text carefully and tastefully.

The conventional text of an Italian *opera seria* aria consisted of a single four-line stanza. Part I used the first two lines, part II the latter two. The accommodation of the text to the music called for much repetition, often carried to excess. This practice was deplored by Benedetto Marcello, circa 1720,[10] and Francesco Algarotti, 1756.[11] Still, the nature of the aria *requires* repetition of words. An aria text is not a dramatic vehicle, but the embodiment of a fixed affection that gains its power from the musical events, which require repetition of text to achieve clarity of sense and breadth of form. Galuppi's aria (Ex. 16-1) repeats the first phrase four times, the second and third phrases 14 times, and the final phrase 20 times. In "Ah, chi mi dice mai" ("Who can tell me") from Act I of *Don Giovanni*, the final phrase of the text is set 11 times. In both of these arias each repetition of the text has a different musical setting; skillfully handled, this process can maintain interest and build cumulatively to a peak of feeling. In neither of these arias does the final tonic section have a literal rhyme with the dominant section of part I. In Galuppi's aria only *one* measure repeats its corresponding figure. The gestures and the rhetorical continuity are restated, but the melodic material is thoroughly varied; the same is true of the Mozart aria in the final rhyme.

Another technique for fitting a brief text to a long musical statement was *coloratura*, an extended roulade upon a single syllable, as in mm. 26–31 of Ex. 16-1. Coloratura, as well as excessive repetition, was severely criticized in the

18th century. If repetition threatened to make nonsense of the poetic meaning, coloratura represented similar dangers for the music, especially if the syllable chosen for elaboration had no special expressive meaning. Properly used, coloratura could carry the affective level of an aria to a climax, as in the aria of the Queen of the Night, "Die hölle Rache" ("The hellish vengeance"), from Act II of Mozart's *The Magic Flute*, K. 620, 1791.

In the early 18th century, the function of the aria was to delineate formally an affective stance in a tightly bound form, while recitative carried the action forward. As the grand *da capo* disappeared in favor of simpler and more fluid forms, and as more duets, trios, and ensembles were incorporated into opera, the aria itself began to enter the flow of action, to develop character and attitude, and to furnish links in the plot. This trend is especially notable in the mature works of Gluck and Mozart.

Finally, the aria as an independent genre should be mentioned. As a vehicle for a virtuoso singer the aria, in its grander version, was a standard concert item in the later 18th century. Singers had their favorite arias and would at times substitute them for numbers originally written for an opera, often to the detriment of dramatic unity. Substitution also took place when composers wrote new arias for extant operas. All this bespeaks the aria as a musical commodity—useful, flexible, and adapted to many situations.

NOTES

1. Sulzer, *Allgemeine Theorie*, p. 77ff.
2. Koch, *Lexikon*, p. 159ff. See also *Versuch*, III, p. 240ff., and Hiller, *Musikalisch-zierlichen Gesange*, p. 95ff.
3. Burney, *History*, p. 629.
4. See Bukofzer, *Music in the Baroque Era*, p. 364.
5. Anderson, *The Letters of Mozart*, p. 903.
6. Rousseau, *Dictionnaire*, p. 77.
7. Schubart, *Ideen*, p. 358.
8. Christmann, *Elementarbuch*, p. 242.
9. Brown, *Letters*, pp. 34-36.
10. See the commentary on and translation of Marcello's *Il teatro* by Reinhard Pauly, *MQ*, April, July, 1948.
11. Quoted in Strunk, *Source Readings in Music History*, p. 669ff.

17 Concerto

The early 18th-century concerto evolved from the *canzona* of the early and middle baroque period, adapting the sectional layout available in the canzona to the alternation of tutti and solo, organizing the key scheme in a "solar" plan (see Ch. 4), and focusing the harmony by means of cadential formulas.

While retaining the tutti-solo relationship of the baroque concerto, the classic concerto absorbed important elements from the aria, as Koch, 1802, says:

> Inasmuch as instrumental music is, in general, an imitation of vocal music, so is the concerto an imitation of the solo song with full accompaniment, or in other words, an imitation of the aria.[1]

The opposition of soloist and ensemble, was, for Koch, 1793, a dramatic situation, linked to the theater:

> In short, I conceive the concerto to be somewhat similar to the ancient tragedies, in which the actor expresses his feelings not to the audience, but to the chorus, which, in turn, links itself intimately to the action, thus qualifying itself to take part in the expression of the feelings.[2]

Typically, baroque concertos open with vigorous, march-like patterns—idiomatic to instrumental performance. Classic concertos, especially the later piano concertos of Mozart, sometimes have a flavor of the aria, introducing the soloist with a lyric theme.

Aria and concerto share a distinctive *structural* feature as well—the *opening tutti* or *ritornello* that prepares the entry of the soloist. This section, which introduces some of the principal melodic material of the movement (see Ex. 17-1), must be centered upon the tonic; otherwise, it would introduce a structural harmonic issue—the rise to the dominant—which would detract from the effectiveness of the soloist's entry. Harmonic tension must yield to the dramatic confrontation of soloist and orchestra.

Early classic concertos—those of Schobert, J. C. Bach, the young Mozart—have short opening ritornellos, comparable to those of baroque concertos and full *da capo* arias. By the time Mozart wrote his concertos for Vienna in the 1780s, the first tutti had become a full-scale tour of most of the melodic material. It was comparable in length to a sonata exposition *without shift of key*, although passing modulations could be incorporated, as in Mozart's B♭ major Concerto, K. 595, 1795, and Beethoven's C minor Concerto, Op. 37, 1800. Despite its length, it remained an *introduction, not a first exposition*. Kollmann, 1799, describes the opening tutti:

The first Subsection is a *Tutti*, calculated to shew the grandeur of the piece, with the variety of instruments introduced in it; and to impress on the hearer the Key and Mode, the Subjects, and the Character of the Movement. It begins and remains therefore in the principal key; and no other than short touches upon other keys are proper in its modulation, which however may be as bold and rich, as the intended character of the piece permits. It should end rather with the half Cadence on the Fifth of the scale, than with a perfect Cadence on the Key Note, because the latter would be too much like a conclusion of the piece. And the whole of it ought to be like a *proposition* of what is to be more fully introduced in the rest of the Movement.[3]

Lacking the harmonic thrust to the dominant that begins soon in other key-area forms, the concerto compensates by offering immediate rewards—ingratiating melodic material, colorful scoring, a profusion of salient melodic members, and the brilliance of the soloist. This is especially true of Mozart's and Beethoven's concertos.

The basic form of the first movement, presented in Ex. 17-1, is identical to that of the compressed *da capo* aria (see Ch. 16). The grand tutti–solo alternation is generally interspersed with shorter responses between soloist and orchestra.

Ex. 17-1. *First movement, concerto form.*

tutti	solo	tutti	solo	tutti	solo	tutti
I	I-V	V	X-I	I	I	I

While the form and scope of the symphony and concerto were comparable, they served different program purposes. The symphony was an opening piece, as it was earlier for opera and ballet. Haydn's London symphonies, in the 1790s, were called overtures on some programs. The concerto, like the aria, was a star vehicle, occupying a central position on the program (see p. 144).

SOLO CONCERTOS (OTHER THAN KEYBOARD)

Classic concertos were written for a great variety of solo instruments—violin, viola, violoncello, contrabass, flute, oboe, clarinet, bassoon, horn, trumpet, harp, guitar, mandolin—and for curious instruments devised in the late 18th century, such as the five concertos for *lira organizata*—a combination of hurdy-gurdy and organ—which Haydn wrote for the King of Naples in 1786. But the violin concerto ranked first in importance. The violin alone could rival the voice in sweetness, power, and brilliance and exceed it in effective range—the qualities valued by 18th-century listeners. Momigny, 1806, says that the only good concertos are those for violin, and perhaps clavier.[4] Koch, 1802, says that the violin is the instrument most preferred to perform a solo part.[5]

The violin concerto reached its optimum stage in Paris, the musical capital of Europe. This took place when Viotti came to Paris in 1782, to perform, to compose, and to establish a school of violin playing whose traditions have been maintained without a break until the present day.

Viotti's concertos, of which there are 29, represent the epitome of late 18th-century violin style. Theirs is a bold and brilliant manner with many difficult yet felicitous violinistic figurations. Many of the first movements take up a march rhythm; the middle movements are highly elaborated romanzas, while the finales are cast in broadly scaled rondo form using rhythms of popular dances—polkas, polonaises, gigues, schottisches, etc. Viotti makes no effort to develop discursive structure; the image of a strikingly theatrical performance is clearly called forth by the literal repetitions that characterize his forms, especially re-playings of brilliant passage work that must have delighted and astounded his Paris audiences. Viotti is at his best in fashioning such passages; in all his violin music—duos, trios, quartets, and concertos—the figures are lined up with great intensity to thrust toward grand cadential points of arrival. He uses no tricks of violinism such as came into fashion in the 19th century; rather there is a purity and nobility about the line that calls for a clean-cut and eloquent declamation. The violin is always set out in high relief against a rather reticent accompaniment, and the music always sings, never struggles. The passage from his Concerto in G major, 1793, that is presented in Ex. 17-2 will serve to illustrate Viotti's style. This is the latter part of key area II in the first movement. At first there is considerable repetition, but the last 16 measures before the tutti constitute a magnificent drive to the final cadence of the exposition; the sense of accumulation developed here shows Viotti's command of periodic rhetoric.

Ex. 17-2.   Viotti, Concerto for Violin and Orchestra in G major, G. 93, 1793, 1st movt.

From Viotti, *Concerto No. XXIII in G major.* Copyright 1900, 1928 by G. Schirmer, Inc. Used by kind permission of the publisher.

Beethoven made extensive use of the Parisian violin technique in his D major Violin Concerto, Op. 61, 1806; the influence of the French violin school is also present in his string quartets and violin sonatas. Still, the roles assigned to violinistic figurations and *cantilenas* are different in Viotti and Beethoven. Viotti treats the violin as a true solo instrument, putting the accompaniment at a distance and giving it relatively little material of melodic importance. For him, the accompaniment is principally a support, a frame within which the violin is centered and highlighted. Beethoven in his D major Violin Concerto, often treats the violin as an elaborating heterophonic companion to the principal action, which is a discursive development of important melodic ideas in the orchestra. True, the violin stands out, but it leads less often than with Viotti; when it comes to the fore, it may be in a dialogue with the orchestra, or to spin out a gesture initiated by the orchestra, as in the opening cadenza of the concerto, where the violin picks up the dominant extension and continues some dozen measures to the authentic cadence. Throughout the first movement we can hear the orchestra behave as though it were playing a symphony much of the time, while the violin, with its figuration, binds phrases together and puts a brilliance of color as well as a sharp edge upon the rhetorical action. The only place where the violin truly sings in a melody which it introduces and in which the orchestra has no share comes at the section in G minor, just before the recapitulation, m. 331 and the following measures. Here the genuine Viotti-Parisian flavor is clear because the accompaniment simply supports the violin and has no major part in the discourse.

In Ex. 17-3, the violin plays the opening theme in decorated form, adding a tracery to a line in the winds that is itself quite self-sufficient. Ex. 17-4 shows the dialogue between the treble and bass strings — self-contained, albeit somewhat dull without the interlacing *fioritura* of the violin. In Ex. 17-5, the violin finally comes into its own as a singing instrument for the first time in the movement, at m. 331, playing the melody in which the orchestra has no part. Beethoven's violin style thus would seem to have evolved from an *ad libitum* voice within the orchestral texture; Viotti's violin style, on the other hand, represents the melody in a melody-bass sonata, and is therefore *obbligato*.

The scope of Beethoven's first movement is enormous. It is 535 measures in length. Viotti's run to about 250 measures. Oddly enough, *French concertos* have a broad opening *ritornello*, about 80 measures in length, but the rest of the movement, especially the X and return, runs *much shorter*. In both his 22nd and 23rd Concertos, 1793, Viotti reverses the order of material, bringing back some of the second-key-area themes before arriving at the tonic with the opening theme. The recapitulations are thus much shorter but achieve the effect of rounding off the form by a full-scale rhyme of the closing material, generally brilliant in style (see Ex. 17-2). Beethoven emulates the broadly gauged sweep of the French ritornello; he scales the remainder of the movement to comparable dimensions.

The boldest gesture in the Beethoven movement, one which provides a powerful lever toward expansion, is the deceptive cadence at m. 28 (see Ex. 3-10). In the opening ritornello this acts as a parenthesis; in both the solo exposition and the recapitulation it serves to bypass the confirming final cadence. Thus the only *grand* point of arrival in this huge movement appears at the end of the coda.

Ex. 17-3. *Violin as a heterophonic voice.* Beethoven, Concerto for Violin and Orchestra in D major, Op. 61, 1806, 1st movt.

Philharmonia

Ex. 17-4. *Violin as an ad libitum voice.* Beethoven, Concerto for Violin and Orchestra in D major, Op. 61, 1806, 1st movt.

Ex. 17-4, cont'd.

Philharmonia

Ex. 17-5. *Violin as an obbligato soloist.* Beethoven, Concerto for Violin and Orchestra in D major, Op. 61, 1806, 1st movt.

335

Philharmonia

Concertos for solo wind instruments bear even a closer resemblance to the aria than those for violin. Apart from the voice-like tone qualities of horn, flute, oboe, clarinet, bassoon, and even trumpet, concertos for these instruments generally have shorter movements, many aria-like passages, and the typical form of the compressed *da capo* aria, in which the X section is a modulating episode, introducing new and often contrasting material.

Haydn's E♭ major Trumpet Concerto, 1796, begins in the style of the *aria di portamento* and intersperses cantabile, brilliant, and military figures—all adapted to the tone quality and register of the keyed trumpet for which Haydn wrote this piece. Mozart's Bassoon Concerto in B♭ major, K. 191, 1774, capitalizes on the *buffa* possibilities of this instrument's agile basso character as it asks the soloist to make sudden wide leaps, stutter on rapid *parlando* passages, now sing, then revert to the mock-military style that governs the first movement. Mozart's Flute Concertos, G major, K. 313, and D major, K. 314, 1778, have affinities to the *aria d'agilitá*, while his Horn Concertos, K. 417 and 447 in E♭ major, 1783, and K. 495 in E♭ major, 1786, must necessarily emulate the *aria di cantabile*, due to the technical limitations of the instrument. The X sections of these latter works (first movements) bear the closest resemblance of all to the middle section of a compressed *da capo* aria—especially that of K. 495, which, in the second version, has a long pathetic song beginning in C minor.

Imaginative, warm, and sympathetic to the solo instrument as these concertos are, none of them approaches the stature of Mozart's A major Clarinet Concerto, K. 622, 1791. Together with the B♭ major Piano Concerto, K. 595, and the E♭ major Quintet, K. 614, also from 1791, this work represents the quintessence of the galant style, the final refinement and ultimate scope of its genre.

The theatrical flavor is especially marked in this work. The clarinet is truly a *buffa* character taking many roles—singing, dancing, coming to the fore, disappearing, mingling, changing roles quickly, a Figaro expressed in a pantomime of many melodic shapes.

The richness of content in this work, embodied in a wealth of short, beautifully turned, deftly connected figures, sometimes gathered into a marvelous tune, elsewhere strung out in a chain of kaleidoscopic effects, is matched by its breadth of form. In length the first movement is equal to those of the great piano concertos of Mozart — 359 measures — far longer than in any other wind concerto. Although the development retains something of the aria protocol in its emphasis on *cantilena*, it is a truly searching tour of the exposition material with an extended turn from F#, the point of furthest remove, and a surprising and grateful episode in the subdominant, m. 239. The variety and richness of content is epitomized in the first eight measures as each measure introduces a new rhythmic pattern.

The second movement is an Italian Adagio *en rondeau*, whose theme, in its luminous simplicity, calls for no ornamentation. The finale is a rondo of epic proportions.

CONCERTOS FOR SEVERAL SOLOISTS; SYMPHONIE CONCERTANTE

In the last third of the 18th century, the concerto with several soloists became a favorite concert item, and was designated as *symphonie concertante*. Koch, 1802, described this genre briefly:

> *Sinfonia concertata.* A symphony with various obbligato instruments, given not only individual phrases here and there, but at times heard performing entire periods, together or separately. The concert-symphony apparently differs from the concerto grosso in that the latter has more concerting instruments.[6]

In his study *La symphonie française*, Barry Brook characterizes this genre, whose principal locale was Paris, as an amalgamation of solo concerto, concerto grosso, divertimento, and symphony elements.[7] It might be added, in view of the parallel between aria and concerto, that operatic elements also figured in the *symphonie concertante*. Brook states that the simplest definition is "a symphonic work dating from the late eighteenth century for two or more solo instruments and orchestra."[8]

This last description, the most general, would then apply to all concertos for several solo instruments. Thus, Mozart's Concertos — for Three Pianos in F major, K. 242, 1776, for Flute and Harp in C major, K. 299, 1778, and for Two Pianos in Eb major, K. 365, 1779 — could also have been published as *symphonies concertantes*.

In most *symphonies concertantes*, the *divertimento* flavor is strong. Tunes and figures are ingratiating and plentiful; texture is light; rhythm is buoyant; sonorities are colorful and varied. Grand and pathetic accents, when present, are only touched upon. The works of Cambini, Boccherini, J. C. Bach, Haydn, and the many Parisian composers who wrote *symphonies concertantes* exemplify this preference for the qualities of the divertimento, with little of the discursiveness of the symphony.

Structurally, the *symphonie concertante* involves unique problems. Each instrument should have its turn with important solo material, and, as Koch, 1802, says, "for a passage of some considerable length, such as a period."[9] Double, triple, and even quadruple statements of the same material are essential aspects of the rhetoric of this genre. The form thus tends to be articulated clearly in large blocks, each with distinctive melodic material. Restatements of similar material taxed the composer's ingenuity. Contrasts in instrumental color, changes of key, and melodic variation were some of the resources available. Beethoven's Triple Concerto in C major, Op. 56, 1804–1805, seems somewhat forced in its threefold assignments of similar material.

The premier work of this genre, the *Symphonie Concertante* in E♭ major for Violin, Viola, and Orchestra, K. 364, 1779, of Mozart, has the qualities of the popular concerto for several instruments, but adds richness, depth of expression, and invention that raises it far above other works of this type.

The scoring of this work — two violins and two oboes in the treble register, two violas, two horns, violoncello, and bass in the middle and bass registers — provides a rich, low-centered sound, proper for the grandeur and depth of expression that distinguish its broadly scaled declamation. Since the sounds of the violin and viola are distinguishable but not in sharp contrast to each other, double statements can be set off against each other smoothly, without abrupt changes of sonority. The melodic material can then flow from one figure to another in a steady stream and be comfortably stated twice in the idiomatic manner of classic melodic rhetoric. As in Mozart's other concertos, there is a wealth of superb melodic material in the first movement of this piece.

The opening tutti has many distinctive melodic members, yet none of these have anything to do with the solo melodic material in the exposition. (The option of a new theme for the first solo entry was available in the early 18th century, as in J. S. Bach's Concerto for Two Violins in D minor, circa 1726. In Cramer's *Magazin*, 1783, three concertos of Vanhall are praised because "the ritornellos do not have the theme of the solo . . . and that is why they should please every listener."[10] When the opening tutti and solo themes are identical, the link with the aria is apparent; a new theme for the soloist recalls an option available in the concerto grosso procedure.) In Mozart's first movement, only one theme, beginning at m. 38, links the opening tutti with material within a solo section, m. 293. Tutti themes are counterstated only to frame the closing sections of the exposition, recapitulation, and return to the tonic, and not while the soloists are playing.

There are at least 18 distinctive melodic members in this movement, some sharply profiled melodies, others well-turned figurations. The style is a majestic march, more weighty than usually heard in *symphonies concertantes*; the oboes and horns lend a military-ceremonial quality with fanfares; these are alternated with lyric and brilliant episodes, but ever in a noble vein.

Mozart furnished the X section with its own melodies, as in the middle section of a compressed *da capo* aria. (Viotti also did this in his Concerto for Violin, No. 22 in A minor, 1793, first movement.)

The X section has some striking changes of pace, corresponding to phases of action in the form:

1. *A holding back*, reining in the headlong motion of the closing tutti in the dominant; this is embodied in an arioso (see Ch. 18), pathetic in vein, given in turn to violin and viola. The violin's passage is in G minor; the viola answers in C minor, the point of furthest remove.

2. *A hurrying forward*, worked out as a powerful stretto; the alternations of the 16th-note figures in the solo instruments close in from four beats, to two, finally to one; the harmony reinforces the stretto effect by quick shifts of tonal center.

3. *Balanced motion*, as the harmony settles on the dominant to prepare for the return to the tonic; the grouping here is in two-measure units.

This play of motion is so skillfully handled that there is hardly a more grateful moment in Mozart's music than the arrival at the dominant with its delightful fanfares and its effervescent solo figuration. Ex. 17-6 quotes the latter part of the stretto, Ex. 17-7 the opening measures of the dominant section.

Ex. 17-6. Mozart, *Symphonie concertante* for Violin, Viola, and Orchestra in E♭ major, K. 364, 1779, 1st movt., final measures of stretto in X section.

Eulenburg No. 3824

Ex. 17-7.   Mozart, *Symphonie concertante* for Violin, Viola, and Orchestra in E♭ major, K. 364, 1779, 1st movt., preparation for return to tonic.

Eulenburg No. 3824

THE KEYBOARD CONCERTO

The classic keyboard concerto, as represented by those of Mozart and Beethoven, achieved a magnificent synthesis of late 18th-century elements of style and structure. The opposition of two complete ensembles, the orchestra and the keyboard, was the decisive factor in this evolution. The term *clavier* (keyboard) was used to designate the soloist; for Mozart's later concertos and for Beethoven's this meant the fortepiano. For the Haydn Concerto in D major, discussed below, the keyboard instrument could be either a harpsichord or a fortepiano, as the early editions of this work specify. The mechanical improvements made in the fortepiano during the last third of the 18th century—greater effectiveness in pedaling, greater fullness and brilliance of tone, and, in some pianos, increased range—equipped this instrument to be a concert medium par excellence.

Three kinds of keyboard concerto were written by classic composers:

1. *Entertainment music*, with the piano used as a singing or decorative instrument in a neat give-and-take with the orchestra, as an expansion of the small ensemble

2. *Bravura pieces*, in which the piano completely overshadowed the orchestra in brilliance

3. *The counterpart of a dramatic scena*, where the material and the scoring has many sharply contrasted components

The Keyboard Concerto as Entertainment Music

Most keyboard concertos written for salon or chamber performance provided pleasant entertainment for the listener. The solo and tutti sections were neatly marked off, diverting the listener as each took up its proper material in a formal give-and-take reminiscent of the earlier 18th-century concerto. The piano could serve a double role—as *soloist* and as *continuo* in the tutti sections. Hence it was closely bound to the orchestra, a legitimate member of the ensemble. This category includes most keyboard concertos written before 1780.

Haydn's D major Concerto, 1784, maintains these relationships. The pianism is lively, but is kept tightly in rein by the orchestra and by the chamber music manner; the piano never takes flight on bold figurations of its own. Often it plays without orchestra, alternating phrases with the tutti in a formal conversation. Haydn provided a figured bass for the piano in the tutti sections. Ex. 17-8 illustrates some of these textures.

The Bravura Piano Concerto

The bravura concerto was an inevitable outcome of the mechanical improvements made in the construction of the fortepiano. The traveling virtuoso, a prominent figure in the musical scene of the late 18th and early 19th centuries, carried with him his own portmanteau of concertos, which were tailored to place him in the most brilliant and bold relief against his accompaniment. Actually, the technical difficulties in such works might not exceed those of the Mozart or Beethoven concertos; the works simply ornamented ordinary, albeit palatable themes, squared off against pure passage work, with much repetition, sing-song

Ex. 17-8. *Solo-orchestra relationships in piano concerto.* Haydn, Concerto for Clavier and Orchestra in D major, 1784, 1st movt.

a. Piano as continuo, End of tutti II.

b. Unaccompanied piano, melody and Trommel-bass accompaniment.

c. Conventional figured patterns activating three-part harmony with orchestral accompaniment.

alternation of figures and phrases, and *painfully obvious structural seams*. These works were immensely popular, and a leader in this trade was Daniel Steibelt. Ex. 17-9 gives an excerpt subtitled "L'orage" ("The Storm"), from his Concerto No. 3, illustrating the brilliant pianism that delighted audiences of this time.

Works of this caliber likely caused Koch, 1802, to make the following comment:

> Concerto performers who dedicate themselves to mechanical skill as their highest and only goal, are not content, as a rule, with the difficulties that are found in the current concertos for their instrument; rather, they go even further, to complete the degradation of their art. Each creates for himself a bundle of tricks [*angemessenes Hokuspokus*], and attempts, without the necessary knowledge of melody or harmony, to carry it off; confidently, he takes his music paper and quickly dashes off a half dozen solo parts, which an unhappy arranger [*Tonsetzer*] must patch up and provide with ritornellos and accompaniments. Now we have page after page of passages, each of which is more breakneck than the other; now the tempo quickens; now it slows down, so that the accompanist is often at a loss to know where he is in each measure. . . .[11]

Loesser quotes some devastating comments on Steibelt's music and his arrogant concert behavior, including refusal to rehearse with the orchestra.[12] To be sure, Steibelt himself was a competent craftsman in composition, but other virtuosi undoubtedly lacked "the necessary knowledge of melody or harmony" of which Koch speaks.

Ex. 17-9.   Steibelt, "L'orage" ("The Storm"), n.d.

The Piano Concerto as a Dramatic Scena

Mozart achieved two magnificent syntheses during the last decade of his life, in opera and in the piano concerto. These stem from a common source—his sense for theater. Here we touch upon some factors in Mozart's transformation of the piano concerto from an entertainment piece to the counterpart of a *dramatic scena*.

The factors in this transformation include the following:

1. *Mozart's orientation to opera,* which pervades all his work—sharply defined topics, aria, conflict among textural components, and the lift given by powerful reiterated cadential thrusts

2. *The keyboard as an imitator of larger ensembles*, a surrogate for the orchestra or the operatic ensemble, a role familiar to Mozart from his childhood

3. *The ability of the improved piano to match the orchestra as a sonorous body*

4. *The ability of the piano to incorporate a wide range of expressive nuances*—sustained tones, varied attacks, control of dynamics

5. *The new orchestral style*—greater prominence of winds, changing roles of the strings, promoting the rapid shifts of texture and *topic* characteristic of *buffa* rhetoric, although not necessarily comic in flavor

The role of the winds was especially significant in shaping the style of the later piano concertos. They join the strings to form a three-part ensemble with the piano, so that these works are virtually *symphonies concertantes*. Kollman recognized this aspect of Mozart's concertos in his article on accompaniment in *Composition*, 1799:

> §9. In all those three Movements, the *Solos* may be partly without accompaniment, and in other places with the accompaniment of any one, two, or more suitable instruments; and also with fewer or more accompaniments in one place than in another, according to the nature of the passage, and the purpose of the Composer.
>
> But the *accompaniments* of the Solos should be of the *concerting* kind, both among themselves, and with the Solo part (§1); though as accompaniments, they must not only remain less conspicuous than the principal part, but also be not so crowded as to overpower that part. Contrary to this principle are those modern Concertos, in which the Solo part has no apparent relation to the preceding and succeeding Tuttis; and the accompaniments take no other interest in the Solos, than now and then to form the harmony of them, like a kind of Thorough Bass.
>
> The best *specimens* of good modern Concertos for the Piano-Forte, are those by *Mozart*, in which every part of the accompaniments is interesting, without obscuring the principal part.[13]

The new role of the winds was initiated precisely at the opening of the Bb major Concerto, K. 450, 1784, where they begin with a jaunty little bourrée-march, as if to perform a divertimento. From this time, the winds become prominent in the concertos. For example, the first movement of the C minor Concerto, K. 491, 1786, assigns important material, sometimes solos, to the winds in at least 150 of the 523 measures.

As the winds became prominent, the focus of style in the concertos shifted from military-ceremonial to singing-style. From K. 450 on, only K. 451, 1784, K. 482, 1785, and K. 503, 1786, open in grand military style. The others begin with chamber music textures and aria-like themes.

Mozart retained the traditional protocol in his first movements — the grand tutti-solo alternations outlined in Ex. 17-1. But within these sections he deployed his concerting forces — strings and winds in the tutti; piano, strings, and winds in the solos — in an astonishing variety of combinations, rarely allowing a given texture to carry for more than six to eight measures, often less. Again and again, the counterstatement to a striking opening phrase will pick up a detail to use as a point of departure for an unexpected yet thoroughly logical continuation. Mozart's deft management of texture and topic enjoys broad scope in his piano concertos, thanks to the interplay of the three protagonist groups, piano, strings, and winds, and to the wealth of melodic material with which they discourse.

Solo I in the first movement of the C major Concerto, K. 467, 1785, encompassing the I–V exposition, embodies these procedures. The solo enters rather unobtrusively, with a modest figure that answers an expressive *cantilena* passage in the winds. It continues simply as a single strand in the texture, even to the point of furnishing a pedal to the principal theme in the strings. Only after 11 measures does it sing, again as a response to a statement in the orchestra, m. 84. Once it gets under way, it assumes its leading role, but often only as a glittering edge to the orchestra's purposeful harmonic line. Measures 107–127 constitute an extended parenthesis within the dominant key area, highlighted by a sudden turn to the pathetic style with a figure that resembles the opening theme of the G minor Symphony, K. 550, 1788 (perhaps its origin).

The opening figure of this concerto movement must have been a favorite of Mozart's, since it appears seven times during the course of the first tutti and solo. First heard as a galant mock-military march figure, it takes on important stature in later appearances in *stile legato* and in imitation. Throughout the entire movement, the vivid delineation of topics — military, signing, brilliant, pathetic, bucolic — suggests the range of characters and situations familiar to the opera-goer of Mozart's time, a dramatic scena. In this context, there is very little place for the bravura style, brilliance for its own sake. Some bravura passages appear in Mozart's C major Concerto, K. 503, 1786, and D major Concerto, K 537, 1788. There are none to speak of in the last concerto, the B♭ major, K. 595, 1791, in which the rhetoric has a wonderfully subtle flow.

Ex. 17-10 illustrates the typical Mozart technique of *interweaving* tutti and solo and the rhetorical subtleties which it delineates. First the piano and winds alternate solos, with overlapping entries, while the strings provide a minimal accompaniment. Then the winds take over the principal singing figure, in learned style, while the piano interlaces with brilliant figures. Finally the strings take part in the dialogue, with the winds, while the piano continues with its "curtain" of figuration. Within these general layouts, rapid incidental changes of texture succeed each other; some half-dozen figures are juggled among all three groups.

Ex. 17-10. Mozart, Concerto for Clavier and Orchestra in B♭ major, K. 595, 1791, 1st movt.

Ex. 17-10, cont'd.

Eulenburg No. 775

Mozart's letter to his father quoted at the beginning of Ch. 1 refers to a group of concertos intended both to please the less learned and to satisfy the connoisseur. Ex. 17-11 presents an excerpt from one of these works, in which we can see intermingled the popular and learned aspects of his art. The tempo di menuetto, the simple beginning of the tune, and the eight-measure phrase should have been familiar and pleasing to all listeners. On the other hand, the descending bass, the irregular rhythms in the accompaniment, the chromaticism, the hint of *stile legato*, and the twists and turns of the melody (mm. 5-7) are for the taste of connoisseurs. Perhaps this excerpt was one of the passages Mozart had in mind when he wrote to his father about pleasing all kinds of listeners.

Ex. 17-11.   Mozart, Concerto for Clavier and Orchestra in F major, K. 413, 1782-1783, 3rd movt.

Eulenburg No. 6067

Beethoven begins with the standard extended ritornello in his first three piano concertos. But in the last two, he gives the soloist an important statement at the outset; also, the soloist has a prominent role in the final cadence of each first movement, ordinarily assigned solely to the orchestra. The solo thus frames the standard concerto form, a bolder position than it usually took in the 18th-century concerto. The effectiveness of these gestures is due in part to the sonority of Beethoven's piano, enlarged from a five- to a six-octave range, with a more powerful tone and a new range to explore—the extremely high. These qualities are exploited in the opening solo statements. In the E♭ major Concerto, Op. 73, 1809, the four massive chords of the orchestra which introduce the first ritornello—I-IV-V-I—frame brilliant flourishes by the piano which exploit the ultrahigh registers that will continue to be heard throughout the piece.

In the G major Concerto, Op. 58, 1805-1806, the soloist announces the opening theme with a voicing rarely found in the 18th century—rich, full, a true *piano* sound. To match this striking effect, the orchestra responds with an entry upon a B major chord, far to the sharp side, a point of furthest remove in its own right, and then moves through the circle of fifths quickly past the tonic to IV, preparing a grateful and relaxed cadence to I. This progression is quoted in Ex. 17-12.

Ex. 17-12. *Solo opening.* Beethoven, Concerto for Piano and Orchestra in G major, Op. 58, 1805-1806, 1st movt.

Edwards

The initial rhetorical premises of the first movement of the G major Concerto include (1) a full texture supported by more continuous and sustained bass than was usual for this time, (2) a generally slow and regular harmonic rhythm, (3) the narrow range of the opening theme, its simple line animated by "sigh" figures. These features provide foils for striking contrasts throughout the movement. The full texture and slow harmonic rhythm set the stage for abrupt harmonic turns, such as:

1. The sudden turn to B major, m. 6.
2. The unexpected twist to A minor, m. 29, introducing a "Turkish" theme that moves quickly through E minor, C major, B minor, G major, and F♯ minor with exotic "Neapolitan" effects. This passage is reached following a half cadence that fails to resolve.

3. The wonderful Italian *cantilena*, m. 105, in B♭ major, the purest song in the movement, using interchange of mode to move from the tonic, G, to the dominant, D; also its counterpart in the recapitulation, m. 275, with a different melody.

4. The recall of the "Turkish" music, m. 134, this time arriving upon an authentic cadence in D minor; in retrospect, this places the A minor of the ritornello in an even stranger light.

5. The play upon the enharmonic reading of the chord E-B♭-D♭ as the music moves through the dominant harmonies of F major, D major, and B major, respectively, mm. 196–205, finally to resolve to B minor. This passage was paraphrased by Beethoven in the development section of his *Leonore* Overture No. 3, Op. 72a, 1806.

6. The most striking harmonic gesture in the movement, the extended approach to C♯ minor, the point of furthest remove, mm. 208–231, rhetorically the longest single statement in the entire movement. At the arrival in C♯ minor Beethoven introduces a new tune, as he did in the first movement of his *Eroica* Symphony and the finale of the C major Quartet, Op. 59, No. 3; all three of these movements incorporate a point of furthest remove that is more distant than the usual V of VI.

Melodically, the greatest contrast exists between the conjunct opening theme and the angular Turkish theme; this contrast is matched by the different harmonic treatment for each theme. The confrontation of "horizontal" and "vertical" gestures, both in the melody and harmony, thus represents one of the basic configurations in this movement, as it does in the first movement of the Quartet in F major, Op. 59, No. 1 (see Ch. 24).

Middle movements in classic concertos employed *standard* classic forms, in contrast to the *unique* combination of aria and sonata of first movements. Some typical examples are:

Rondo: Mozart, Concerto in D minor, K. 466, 1785, in the style of a *romanza*, a slow gavotte; Mozart, Concerto in C minor, K. 491, 1786, also a romanza

Variation: Mozart, Concerto in B♭ major, K. 456, 1784

Sonata form without X: Viotti, Concerto for Violin No. 22 in A minor, 1793, a florid Italian aria

Two-reprise: Beethoven, Concerto No. 5 in E♭ major, Op. 73, 1809, also a florid Italian aria, with some similarities in treatment to the Viotti No. 22

"Scarlatti" sonata: Mozart, *Symphonie Concertante* in E♭ major, K. 364, 1779, an aria in slow minuet time with Italianate ornamentation

The most striking plan for a classic middle movement is that of the Concerto No. 4 in G major, Op. 58, 1805–1806, of Beethoven. The style of the recitative *obligé* (see Ch. 18) is used, so that this movement has the aspect of an interlude or an introduction to the finale, creating an extremely sharp contrast between its pathetic mood and the brisk contredanse of the finale.

Concerto finales show their affinity to the divertimento and serenade, genres that often served the same purpose of entertainment as the concerto. Lively, ingratiating tunes—contredanses, gigues, minuets—were set in rondo and variation forms, so that these tunes could be heard often, either varied or following contrasting episodes. The theme of the finale of Mozart's Clarinet Concerto, K. 622, 1791, one of his most attractive and supple finale tunes, binds a complex rondo that has many digressions, a wealth of melodic material, and a continuous flow which erases most of the sharp points of demarcation that ordinarily articulate a rondo form. Perhaps to compensate for this discursive treatment, the refrain is heard three times in the final 106 measures of the movement.

The finale of Mozart's G major Concerto, K. 453, 1784, is a variation movement; the final section, in quicker tempo than the preceding variations, has the quality of a *buffa* finale, with its headlong pace, its sparkling figures, and its rapid give-and-take.

THE CADENZA

A standard feature of the classic concerto was the *cadenza*, also called *fermata, arbitrio,* and *point d'orgue.* Kollmann's comments, 1799, are:

> C. *The Fancy Cadence.*
>
> §10. When the perfect final Cadence which concludes a long section, is to be very formal, the Leading Chord on the Fifth of the final Bass note is not only suspended by a fourth and sixth before the fifth and third, but a Pause is also introduced over that suspension, and a long Shake in the resolution of it, after which, the Final Chord of that Cadence comes in with double satisfaction to the hearer.
>
> But as on the Harpsichord and the Piano-Forte, the sounds of the said suspension cease, before the intended termination of the pause, some Performers may have tried to continue them, by dividing repeatedly the notes of the supending chord by an harpeggio; either in their one position only, or in various positions over the whole instrument. This very proper flourish has degenerated into what is now called a Fancy Cadence; or that Fantasia, which the rage of musical fashion has introduced in the said mere suspension of a Leading Chord, and which very often is made so inconsistent with the character of the Concerto, as to *destroy* the good impression of it, instead of heightening it. . . .
>
> §11. . . . . Fancy Cadences *may* take place in all the three Movements of a Concerto; but as too much of a similar kind becomes disgusting, it is necessary, that if they *are* introduced in every movement, they should contain a sufficient variety of form and length, to produce that entertainment or admiration, which is expected from them.[14]

The cadenza has a compound function—(1) to set up the final area of arrival by means of an emphatic dominant gesture, (2) to allow the soloist some scope for the display of his technical skill and invention. In the course of drawing out the dominant, the harmony may introduce parentheses, digressions that serve as large-scale ornamentations of dominant harmony.

Mozart wrote cadenzas for many of his concertos, only a few of which are known. From these, we can see a consistent harmonic plan. Both ends of the cadenza are anchored on V; the intervening action connects these principally by stepwise bass movement. Ex. 17-13, from the A major Concerto, K. 488, 1786, exemplifies this procedure; the six measures of dominant pedal that open the cadenza and the 10 measures that close it are linked by a steady descent to D♯, followed by a tight turn to E. The material used is relatively unimportant — none of the leading themes appear — but it lends itself to the harmonic flow.

Beethoven's two cadenzas to the first movement of his Concerto No. 4 in G major, Op. 58, 1805-1806, go much further afield and have a more irregular trajectory than Mozart's. They both ignore the dominant fermata, beginning di-

Ex. 17-13. *Cadenza.* Mozart, Concerto for Clavier and Orchestra in A major, K. 488, 1786, 1st movt.

rectly upon the tonic, touch episodes in distant keys, and introduce enharmonic shifts, but eventually reach an extended dominant preparation for the tonic. The second cadenza moves quickly to A♭ major and includes changes of meter and tempo.

Ideally, a cadenza should be a peroration, consistent in style with the preceding material of the movement. It is vulnerable to the caprice of the soloist, who, lacking taste, can seriously impair the expressive unity of the movement by introducing incompatible material or by carrying on the cadenza too long. Beethoven himself missed the mark in his cadenza to Mozart's D minor Concerto, K. 466, 1785.

A cadenza may be introduced wherever dominant harmony can stage a dramatic approach to an important tonic point of arrival. The sense of periodicity is increased, using a break in the rhetorical continuity as the agent of escalation. One of the most effective places for a cadenza is just before the return to the refrain in a rondo or before the final statement of the original theme in a variation movement; the smooth, regular action which generally characterizes these forms is interrupted, to be resumed upon the reentrance of the theme. Mozart's *cadenza in tempo* in the rondo finale of his B♭ major Sonata, K. 333, 1778, illustrates this procedure. The cadenza as a peroration was often incorporated by J. S. Bach in his preludes, fugues, and concertos (see *The Well-tempered Clavier*, I, C minor, C♯ major Preludes, and the Brandenburg Concerto No. 5 in D major, 1722, first movement). Mozart broadened the scope even further in the spacious first movement of his C major Quintet, K. 515, 1787, by composing a cadenza-like parenthesis, mm. 320–352, before settling down in the final measures to complete the melodic rhyme of the recapitulation.

The classic concerto drew much from aria, divertimento, and symphony. Conversely, features of the concerto were constantly being absorbed in chamber and orchestral music. Classic quartets and quintets display the brilliant style prominently (Mozart, Quintet in E♭ major, K. 614, 1791). Tutti-solo alternations help to articulate the rhetoric of keyboard sonatas. The first movement of Mozart's Sonata in C minor, K. 457, 1784, is a concerto in miniature with a bold opening tutti and solo passages in both brilliant and singing styles.

NOTES

1. Koch, *Lexikon*, p. 351; see also Riepel, *Anfangsgründe*, p. 43.
2. Koch, *Versuch*, III, p. 332.
3. Kollmann, *Composition*, p. 14; see also Koch, *Versuch*, III, pp. 332–341.
4. Momigny, *Cours complet*, p. 674.
5. Koch, *Lexikon*, p. 1695.
6. Ibid., p. 1385.
7. Brook, *Symphonie française*, I, p. 244.
8. Ibid.
9. Koch, *Lexikon*, p. 1385.
10. Cramer, *Magazin*, p. 722.
11. Koch, *Lexikon*, p. 352.
12. Loesser, *Men, Women, and Pianos*, pp. 178, 179.
13. Kollmann, *Composition*, p. 15.
14. Ibid.

18 Fantasia; Introduction; Recitative

Fantasia, introduction, and *recitative* were distinguished from other 18th-century forms by their freedom from the usual prescriptions of key and section layout. They could move through any orbit of keys and juxtapose figures and textures freely; often they prepared the listener for a *set* piece.

FANTASIA

The term *fantasia* represents a class of composition variously called *fantasia, capriccio, boutade,* and, in the 17th century, *suonata* and *ricercata.* In the 18th century, several meanings were attached to *fantasia* and its related terms:

1. *Invention,* the ability of the composer to devise figures, progressions, textures, in the sense used by Löhlein, 1779 (see p. 233).

2. *Freedom of action.*

    a. *Improvisation,* as in Rousseau's description of "Fantaisie," 1768: "A piece of music that is composed as it is performed."[1] Rousseau distinguishes between "Caprice," which may have strange ideas but is composed at one's leisure, and "Fantaisie," which must be improvised.

    b. *Rhythmic and structural freedom.* No fixed number of measures, order of sections, fixed meters. This aspect of fantasia was described by C. P. E. Bach, 1753,[2] Türk, 1789,[3] and also Brossard, 1703: "A type of composition which has the effect of pure genius without the composer being subjected to a fixed number of measures or type of measure, using all kinds of modes. It is much like a *capriccio.* See capriccio, ricercata, suonata, etc."[4]

3. *Strangeness of effect.* Spiess, 1746, includes the following in his description of fantasia: "This is the freest musical style one can imagine . . . since all kinds of unusual passages, subtle ornaments, ingenious turns, and elaborations are used. . . ."[5] Exploratory harmonies contribute to this strangeness of effect. C. P. E. Bach, 1753, says a free fantasia consists of varied harmonic progressions which move through more keys than is customary in other pieces.[6]

4. *Figuration.* Koch refers to "many types of broken chords" in his description of fantasia in the *Lexikon,* 1802.[7]

Since the fantasia had no fixed plan, a number of examples are analyzed below to illustrate the range of structure and style.

Leopold Mozart, Little Music Book, *fantasias from Suites VIII, XIII, XX,*

308

XXII, 1762. Except for the fantasia from Suite XXII, these small pieces could well have dispensed with the title *Fantasia*. Those from Suites VIII, XIII, and XX take up a brisk gigue rhythm. The fantasia from Suite XIII is laid out in a small two-reprise form; that from VIII is similarly shaped but somewhat longer, while that from XX is so extended in its two reprises that it could qualify as the first movement of a clavier sonata. Their only claims to the title *Fantasia* lie in the presence of brisk, patterned figurations, principally along *murky* lines; some unevenness of phrase structure and quick give-and-take of melodic interest between treble and bass also contribute to the gentle oddness of affect. The fantasia from Suite XXII, on the other hand, leaves no question as to its fantasia character. It incorporates four alternations of tempo between presto and adagio; the prestos are quick allemandes; the adagios are set as ariosos. Structurally, the piece has two extended reprises; with 9 1/2 measures of end-rhyme in the second reprise, it embodies sonata procedure.

C. P. E. Bach, Kenner und Liebhaber, *1785, series V, Fantasia I in F major, and series VI, Fantasia II in C major.* These fantasias each have unique form. Fantasia I, series V, has a three-part form:

1. Wandering harmonies, unbarred
2. Barred arioso (see p. 317)
3. Wandering harmonies, unbarred

Ex. 18-1 illustrates the style of figuration and the manner in which Bach sketched the final harmonic progression as a simple figured bass.

Ex. 18-1. *Fantasia figuration and notation.* C.P.E. Bach, *Kenner und Liebhaber*, series V, 1785, Fantasia I.

Breitkopf

Fantasia II, series VI, has a rondo layout—A B A C A—in which A is a contredanse tune marked *presto di molto*, B a sarabande marked *andante*, and C an aria in slow march rhythm marked *larghetto sostenuto*. B and C are even more striking than usual as episodes, due to the drastic change in style. The A sections themselves can be organized as a monothematic rondo, with three returns to C major preceded by entries of the opening motive in various keys. The short phrases and frequent cesuras suggest the style of the capriccio (see below). This effect is enhanced by the frequent abrupt entries of the opening motive on the tonic of a new key without cadential preparation. It is set up by the tonic upbeat of the theme itself, entering after a rest. Ex. 18-2 illustrates this procedure.

Ex. 18-2.　C.P.E. Bach, *Kenner und Liebhaber*, series VI, 1785, Fantasia II.

a. Opening phrase (note upbeat on tonic triad).

b. Beginning of final *presto di molto* (note manner in which upbeat asserts new key without cadential preparation, a "capricious" turn).

Cramer's *Magazin*, 1783, praised Bach for such qualities:

> . . . boldness of modulation, digressions and returns, the inexhaustible passages and phrases, the variety of the individual figures, out of which the whole is put together . . . all these are great and important aspects of the art . . . for which a man such as Bach . . . merits no small part of the praise due him.[8]

Haydn, Capriccio, H.V. XVII, No. 1, 1765, and Fantasia, H.V. XVII, No. 4, 1789. Haydn's Capriccio exemplifies the later 18th-century idea of the form, described by Koch, 1802:

> *Capriccio, Caprice.* A composition in which the composer allows himself to be carried by the prevailing humor (whim) of his fancy, rather than by a governing plan, and in which he is not bound by the forms and modulations of ordinary compositions. The capriccio thus does not always have as its object the expression of a single, well-defined sentiment.

From this it must not be inferred that such a composition can take shape out of fragments snatched from anywhere, unconnected and without order. It is distinguished from ordinary pieces by its freer form, by its less fixed character, and by a looser connection of its ideas.[9]

This piece also retains some of the earlier notion of the capriccio as a free ricercar, an imitative elaboration of a theme without the restrictions of the fugue. Haydn's Capriccio has little imitation, but much elaboration of its theme, a folksong entitled "Acht Sauschneider müssen sein," in the spirit of the ricercar.

Both the Capriccio and the Fantasia are extended monothematic rondos, as outlined in Ex. 18-3.

Ex. 18-3.   Melodic and harmonic outlines of Haydn, Capriccio and Fantasia.

Capriccio

Sections	A	B			A	C		A	D		A		D
Key	G	D	a	e	C	G	C	F	G	G	Bb	G		g

Fantasia   key-area profile   key-area

Sections	A	B		A			C		A		
Key	C	G	(X)	C	(X)	F	(X)	C	(X)	C

The themes of these two works epitomize the treatment they will receive. The Capriccio has a minuet-like theme, with an odd phrase structure. Phrase I has five measures, the second being the added member; phrase II simply strums on the dominant, slowing to a complete halt. The only salient melodic profile occurs in the opening measure; hence Haydn is able to make many starts with the theme, in different styles and textures and continuations, capriciously. The theme is quoted in Ex. 18-4.

Ex. 18-4.   Haydn, Capriccio, H.V. XVII, No. 1, 1765, opening theme.

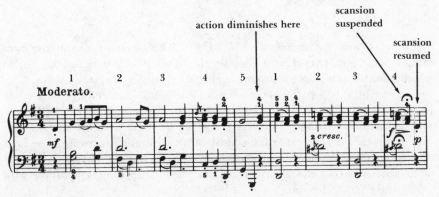

Ex. 18-4, cont'd.

Kalmus

In contrast to the theme of the Capriccio, the Fantasia's theme has an elegant design — a distinctive profile, balance of phrases, a typical closed rondo refrain in quick gigue time. Its periodicity is enhanced by the descending sixth chords in mm. 4–7, a powerful approach to the half cadence, restated to reach the authentic cadence in phrase II.

Phrase I of the theme is quoted in Ex. 18-5. This theme furnishes the motives for most of the material in this piece; the fantasia style is embodied in brilliant episodes of figuration. The harmonic orbit of the Fantasia is much wider than that of the Capriccio, touching at times C♯ major and B major. The sonata rhetoric is strongly projected by the key-area layout and the rhyme of the *hunt-style* closing theme.

Ex. 18-5.   Haydn, Fantasia, H.V. XVII, No. 4, 1789, opening theme.

Kalmus

Mozart, C minor Fantasia, K. 475, 1785.   This work is probably the most familiar representative of its genre. Its clear, beautifully designed layout, in which unstable and stable sections are alternated, is sketched in Ex. 18-6. Note the use of typical bass patterns in the unstable sections — descending and ascending bass lines, circles of fifths. The plan of keys — C minor, D major, X, B♭ major, X, C minor — circumscribes the home key by stable sections a whole step distant, an element of strangeness consistent with fantasia procedure. The final section, recalling the pathetic style of the opening, is stabilized by two broad cadential periods, using the same material to answer the opening explorations with a powerful effect of arrival.

Ex. 18-6.   *Sketch of bass line.* Mozart, Fantasia in C minor, K. 475, 1785.

The ability to improvise, to compose in the style of a fantasia, was considered to be a very special and precious talent in the 18th century, as C. P. E. Bach tells us at the beginning of his chapter on improvisation in the *Versuch*, 1753. It required a great command of harmony, unusual dexterity of performance, and the knack of inventing striking ideas and figures. Spiess's summary, written in 1746, is applicable generally to all periods in which the fantasia was current:

> From this [a foregoing description] we not only discover the main concepts of the style, but we must also say that those *fantasts*, for example, an organist, violinist, etc., that know how to provide their listeners with a pleasant diversion by extempore or improvised fantasias, capriccios, toccatas, ricercaten, bizarreries, boutades, etc. must have sharp wit, be well-practised virtuosi, with excellent ideas, rich and lavish in invention. Great praise![10]

The fantasia, with its ramifications, was a sign of the unique in classic music, embodying one aspect of the idea of genius that was taking hold in 18th-century thought. Fantasia, as a process, was far more important and pervasive at that time than is presently recognized; it was honored and admired as evidence of creative originality. Indeed, without the fantasia, the great forms of the classic style—the sonata, the concerto, and the sonata-rondo—could not have evolved. Fantasia makes its presence felt strongly in introductions, transitions, developments, cadenzas, and codas. Furthermore, we can sense the play of the fantasia process in unexpected, even eccentric turns of figure, texture, and harmony in the principal melodic materials of the masterworks of the classic style.

The fantasia, moreover, colored and placed a personal stamp upon the individual styles of classic composers, giving a fresh twist and new vitality to the familiar clichés of the 18th-century musical vocabulary. Each composer coordinated standard formula and fantasia in his own way. C. P. E. Bach saturated his music with close-grained, eccentric elaborations while maintaining a firm harmonic and rhythmic framework. Haydn manipulated a few figures in amazingly varied and witty ways. Mozart often veered from a straight line to spin out a fascinating line of discourse. Beethoven was the most eccentric of all, reaching high and low, far and wide, to saturate his language with fantasia elements so that even his opening statements would often pose problems of musical meaning. The audience in the classic era expected a composition to have some quality of fantasia to merge interest with clear formal orientation. Haydn was the most successful in reaching his audiences in this respect. Mozart and Beethoven were often quite puzzling.

THE INTRODUCTION

Introductory music was designated as *introduction, entrée, intrada, overture, sinfonia, Einleitung,* etc. The following is the entry for "Intrade" in Koch, 1802, similar to his description of "Introduction" itself:

> *Intrade.* A short section to serve as an introduction to a large composition scored for many parts. The Intrade generally contains a serious style in slow

tempo, in which the key is arbitrary (at the discretion of the composer). The short pieces in slow tempo with which most of our modern symphonies begin belong to this kind of introductory piece.[11]

Lully's overtures, modeled after Venetian operatic practice, established the slow introduction as a standard type of opening piece, as in his overture to *Alcidiane*, 1658. In classic music, the slow tempo of the French overture was retained, but not necessarily the typical dotted rhythms. Classic introductions represented the following styles:

1. *French overture*. Haydn, Symphony No. 104 in D major, 1795; Mozart, Eb major Symphony, K. 543, 1788.

2. *Sinfonia da chiesa*. A slow introduction for church sonatas and symphonies in strict style: Gluck, overture to *Iphigenia in Aulis*, 1774; Haydn, Symphony No. 103 in Eb major, 1795, in which plainsong is imitated, the first four notes suggesting the "Dies irae."

3. *Aria; slow dance*. Haydn, Symphony No. 94 in G major, 1791, in slow minuet time, and Symphony No. 97 in C major, 1792, aria-like. In this type of introduction, the two-reprise form was typical; the allegro entered at a strategic moment — the return to the tonic.

4. *Fantasia*. Mozart, C major Quartet, K. 465, 1785, a short section. Longer sections include Mozart, *Prague* Symphony, K. 504, 1786; Beethoven, Symphony No. 2, Op. 36, 1802, aria followed by fantasia, Symphony No. 4, Op. 60, 1806, in *ombra* style, and *Leonore* Overture No. 3, Op. 72a, 1806; Mozart, overture to *Don Giovanni*, 1787, in which the *ombra* style invokes hell instead of heaven, a reversal of the sense of a *da chiesa* introduction. Beethoven designated the middle section of the *Waldstein* Sonata, Op. 53, 1804, as *Introduzione*, as a preparation for the rondo to follow; a short aria-like section, mm. 10–17, is bracketed by fantasia sections.

The most impressive introduction in classic music opens Mozart's Symphony No. 38 in D major, the *Prague*, K. 504, 1786. This section comprises 36 measures of adagio 4/4 time. Mozart here has achieved an exquisite rhetorical balance between the two principal sections:

Part I, mm. 1–15	*Part II, mm. 16–36*
D major	D minor
Irregular rhythms	Regular rhythm
Changes of affect	Single affect (*ombra*)
Deceptive cadences	Drive to half cadence

Both the rhetorical instability of part I, centering around D major, and the regularity of part II, with the harmonic instability of the interchange of mode, contribute to the increase of tension that prepares the allegro, resolved only at the 7th measure of the allegro. The first part of this introduction is sketched in Ex. 6-18; the *ombra*-section bass line is given in Ex. 18-7

Ex. 18-7.   Mozart, Symphony No. 38 in D major, the *Prague,* K. 504, 1786, part II of introduction.

RECITATIVE

Koch, 1802, distinguishes "recitative" from "true song" in four ways:

> 1. It has no fixed and regular meter . . . (Germans and Italians notate it in four-four time . . . the French change meters, causing difficulties in comprehension and accompanying). . . .
> 2. It has no symmetrical melodic rhythm . . . the various points of punctuation are made without reference to balance of melodic phrases. . . .
> 3. It is syllabic, and has no melodic elaboration.
> 4. It has no main key . . . not only may it close in a key other than that in which it began, but it allows many freedoms in modulation that can be effective, but which are not part of formal song.[12]

Simple, Accompanied, Obligé

Three basic types of recitative were distinguished in the 18th century:

1. *Simple recitative.* This type is generally designated today as *secco* (dry) recitative. The voice is accompanied by a keyboard instrument with slow changes of chord. Ex. 22-1, from Mozart's *Don Giovanni* represents a kind of simple, or *secco,* recitative intensively cultivated in comic opera, in which the voice has a rapid-fire declamation covering a large section of text. Four/four time was prescribed for simple recitative, except for the French, who used changing meters (see Ch. 20).

2. *Accompanied recitative.* If Ex. 18-11 below were performed by string instruments in addition to keyboard, so that the harmonies would be held throughout their notated duration, the procedure would be designated as *accompanied recitative.* A much greater power of expression is achieved by the sustained chords, compared to the matter-of-fact punctuations provided by the usual harpsichord accompaniment in simple recitative.

3. *Obligatory recitative or recitative obligé.* In this style both the voice and the accompanying instruments take part in the melodic action, alternating figures that often stand in sharp contrast to each other; the melodic material may momentarily take on a sharper musical profile than the prose-like settings of simple or accompanied recitative (see Ex. 22-2).

Arioso

A combination of recitative with measured song, designated as *arioso*, was occasionally used for moments of high dramatic content. Arioso is described by Koch, 1802:

> When the content of the recitative rises toward the lyric, when a short section represents tenderness, melancholy, solemn devotion, etc.; then the composer alternates usual recitative with formal song, and sets such passages supported by the bass alone or with the accompaniment of other instruments—such a passage is called an *arioso* in the strict sense.[13]

Arioso was similar to what the French termed *recitatif mesuré*, which included sections with a regular, song-like delivery, according to Rousseau, 1768.[14] Gluck depicted Orphée's overwhelming grief at the loss of Euridice and his vow to follow her in a scene which incorporates a short arioso passage within a simple recitative (see Ex. 18-8).

Ex. 18-8.   Gluck, *Orphée*, 1774, Act III, Scene 1.

No. 44 Recitative

Ex. 18-8, cont'd.

44522

Recitative was sometimes introduced into instrumental music. The second movement of Beethoven's G major Concerto, Op. 58, 1805–1806, is a recitative *obligé*, as is the introduction to Mozart's D major Quintet, K. 593, 1790. Concerning the use of the recitative style in instrumental music, Türk says, 1789:

> Here and there in sonatas, concerti, etc., one finds passages in this style. . . . These will have a poor effect if they are played with metric exactness. The more important notes must be played more slowly and strongly, the less important more quickly and lightly, much as a sensitive singer would sing the notes, or a fine speaker declaim them.[15]

Türk refers to the passage presented in Ex. 18-9.

Ex. 18-9. *Instrumental recitative.* C.P.E. Bach, *Prussian* Sonata No. 1, 1742, 2nd movt.

Nagel

Harmonic Plan

The recitative was free from the usual controls of classic form. Yet it had certain restrictions: it had to observe the conventions of proper declamation, and, free as the harmony might be, chord connection had to be smooth and the progression had to link set numbers. Ex. 18-10 gives the bass line of the accompaniment to the recitative that precedes Leporello's "catalogue" aria in *Don Giovanni*, Act I. The chords themselves maintain a smooth connection by means of standard cadential formulas; note the frequency of first inversions, a device that promotes continuity rather than strong punctuation.

Ex. 18-10. *Harmonic sketch of simple recitative.* Mozart, *Don Giovanni*, K. 527, 1787, Act I, "Chi è là?" ("Who is there?").

The mood of the preceding number "Ah, chi mi dice mai" is broken by an abrupt shift in harmony from E♭ major to a first-inversion chord of C major. From this point the harmony hovers around D major and its related keys, shifting around in the manner of a prelude or fantasia to build a strong expectation for D major itself, the key of the "catalogue" aria. The recitative itself is the longest in the opera, 60 measures of rapid-fire declamation, full of subtle touches of humor.

Just as fantasia and improvisation were regarded as skills that distinguished the fine composer, so was recitative considered a special art, subtle and imaginative when successful.

Declamation

Recitative was as concerned with declamation as with harmonic progression. Rules for declamation cover two main aspects:

1. *Scansion*, i.e., the *quantitative* aspect. This draws upon poetic systems of codifying metric feet, and is applicable both to vocal and instrumental music. (See p. 71f)

2. *Emphasis*, i.e., the *qualitative* aspect. This deals with *expressive or oratorical accent*, an explicit nuance in vocal music, but also implied in instrumental music that imitates vocal styles. (See Ch. 11.)

The differences between these two aspects of declamation are described by Mattheson, 1739 (see Ex. 18-11). Mattheson gives two settings of the same text, explaining that the first setting merely scans the words properly, while the second evokes the quality of feeling suggested by the text.

Ex. 18-11. *Declamation: scansion and expressive nuance.* Mattheson, *Capellmeister*, 1739, p. 343.

"In sad solitude I always lament my beloved, who does not hear me, and in my great pain there remains but one gleam of hope."

a. *Scansion.*

Mattheson comments: "This section has some doubtful details; still, hardly ten beginners could do so well. Concerning the content, namely the imitation [of the feelings], it seems hardly to have been at all considered; *Grief, loneliness, pain*, and the *gleam of hope* are all expressed *similarly*. Therefore, I prefer the following original, which provides the recitative its best effect through striking turns of phrase."

b. *Expressive nuance.*

e nella doglia mia ne pur mi retta un balen di Speranza.

"*Sad, alone, pain,* and *gleam* are the important words; the first two are imitated through sad and lonely monotony; the third with a dissonant figure...the last expressed through an unexpected leap."

For Mattheson, *word-painting* makes the difference between a barely adequate setting and one which has expressive force. Precepts for setting recitative did not change materially throughout the 18th century; Mattheson's recommendations of 1739 could well apply to classic music. In 1802 we find a similar view of declamation presented by Koch:

Declamation is the vivid expression of specific ideas and feelings by means of intonation. The human being, possessing a highly-developed speech, can express, through intonation, ideas in their proper degree of clarity, and feelings in their proper degree of intensity. Through declamation only do words achieve their true meaning and weight; without this they are only dead syllables . . . it is the function of declamation to give life to words.

Although tones have a different relationship to each other in music than they have in speech, nevertheless it is necessary in music that words be treated in a manner similar to speech declamation, according to their grammatical and oratorical accents, their pauses and continuations, their rise or fall in pitch, so that the expression of ideas and feelings can be vivid and appropriate. Therefore, the knowledge of declamation is necessary for any composer who will deal with vocal music.[16]

NOTES

1. Rousseau, *Dictionnaire*, p. 215.
2. Bach, *Versuch*, ch. 7.
3. Türk, *Klavierschule*, pp. 395, 396.
4. Brossard, *Dictionnaire*, article on "Fantaisie."
5. Spiess, *Tractatus*, pp. 162-163.
6. Bach, *Versuch*, ch. 7.
7. Koch, *Lexikon*, p. 555.
8. Cramer, *Magazin*, p. 1251.
9. Koch, *Lexikon*, pp. 305-306; see also Rousseau, *Dictionnaire*, p. 74, and Momigny, *Cours complet*, p. 671.
10. Spiess, *Tractatus*, p. 163.
11. Koch, *Lexikon*, p. 817; see also Türk, *Klavierschule*, p. 392.
12. Koch, *Lexikon*, pp. 1231-1232.
13. Ibid., p. 164.
14. Rousseau, *Dictionnaire*, p. 404.
15. Türk, *Klavierschule*, pp. 370-371.
16. Koch, *Lexikon*, pp. 412-413.

19 Multimovement Cycles; Composite Forms

Unity, essential in the form of an individual movement, is also an important factor in an entire work consisting of two, three, or four movements. In classic music, the two most significant factors promoting unity among the movements of a sonata, symphony, concerto, etc., are *compatibility of affect* and *unity of key*.

COMPATIBILITY OF AFFECT

Compatibility of affect among movements may be regarded as an extension of the typical mixtures of topics and affects found in most classic movements, with the added contrast factor of different tempos. The types and styles described in Ch. 2 are distributed according to a wide range of options.

For opening movements, some sort of march tempo is often used, occasionally preceded by a slow introduction (see Ch. 18). Dances, such as minuet, bourrée, occasionally gigue, are also used. Haydn begins his Quartet in D major, Op. 76, No. 5, 1797, in a nontypical fashion, as a leisurely set of variations in a siciliano style, as Mozart begins the Sonata in A major, K. 331, 1778. Opening movements present the greatest challenge to the listener, as a rule, when they are cast in a broad-scale sonata form.

Contrast of affect among movements is essential, but it does not tend toward the extreme except in a few instances, as in Haydn's Sonata in D major, H.V. XVI, No. 37, before 1780, where a short yet deeply pathetic slow movement in sarabande rhythm separates a brisk opening march-like movement and a sprightly contredanse finale. Slow middle movements very often adopt the style of the aria or slower dance, in key-area layout with or without development, variation, or rondo form. A quick dance middle movement is almost invariably set as a minuet of some sort — high style, Ländler, pathetic, military, musette, etc.

Final movements are frankly entertainment music, with gigue or contredanse styles preferred. The only grand finale before Beethoven is that of Mozart's *Jupiter* Symphony, K. 551, 1788, which coordinates the learned *alla breve* manner with the military style.

Contrasts of style and tempo between movements are sufficiently clear and fresh to engage the listener and still maintain a mutual compatibility, an arrangement recommended in Sulzer's *Allgemeine Theorie*, 1771–1774, yet sometimes disregarded:

> The Andante or Largo between the first and last Allegros . . . is often pleasant, pathetic, or sad in expression; but it must conform to the style worthy of the symphony, and not, as it appears fashionable, be composed of trifles . . . that might be appropriate in a sinfonia to a comic operetta.[1]

Compatibility of style made it possible for composers to substitute movements (Mozart did so for his *Paris* Symphony, K. 297, 1778) and exchange arias in operas, and for *pasticcios* to be arranged. The *Ars Combinatoria* principle (see Ch. 6), which was based upon the interchangeability of melodic figures, was applied to entire movements by composers throughout the 18th century.

UNITY OF KEY

Unity of key among movements is confirmed by setting opening and closing movements in the same key. Middle movements generally have close relationships with the ruling key — I, V, IV, VII, III, tonic major or minor. Remoter relationships — III♯, III♭, VI♭, etc. — are occasionally used. These have something of the nature of the fantasia, extending the fantasia element *within* movements — far-reaching digressions — to key relationships *among* movements. The remote key can be matched by a strangeness of affect; Haydn, in the Quartet in D major, Op. 76, No. 5, 1797, placed a slow march in a luminous F♯ major, whose texture sustains the sweetness of the distant key in drawn-out chords, between a siciliano and a minuet, both in D major.

Two-movement works automatically remain in the home key — for example, Mozart's Clavier and Violin Sonatas in G major, K. 301, E♭ major, K. 302, and C major, K. 303, all composed in 1778. When all movements of a work remain in the same home tonic, interchange of mode provides harmonic contrast, as in Beethoven's Quartet in C minor, Op. 18, No. 1, 1800, and his Quartet in E minor, Op. 59, No. 2, 1806. As in a single movement, unity of key is the most important single factor for unity in a multimovement cycle.

NUMBER OF MOVEMENTS

The purpose for which a work was written had some bearing upon the number of movements it contained. Entertainment music generally offered the listener material that was immediately accessible, well trimmed, and rather brief. This purpose could be served either by a two-movement work or one that contained a series of short movements, three or more. In a two-movement work, contrast of affect was made by differences in tempo and meter, but a slow movement was rarely incorporated. The quality of a slow movement was achieved by a slow introduction to a finale (Viotti, Duo in D major, 1784), a slow variation in a quick set, or an episode in a rondo. Serenades and divertimenti had as many as six or seven movements, the first and last of which were comparable to opening movements and finales of sonatas, symphonies, etc. Middle movements were optional arrangements of slow movements and dances, often two minuets.

Works of serious import contained three or four movements, somewhat longer than those of entertainment music, and their material, especially in the works of the masters, is much more intensively worked out.

STRUCTURAL LINKS

Ordinarily, affect and key provide sufficient coherence among classic movements. In some cases, links exist to create stronger connections. These include

(1) harmonic links; (2) thematic links — recall of material; (3) a grand plan for a group of movements, involving both melodic and harmonic factors.

Harmonic Links

The most familiar harmonic link is the half cadence that ends an introduction, prepares a coda, or connects movements. It was expected that an introduction pause upon a half cadence; Mozart observed this convention in the first movement of his *Prague* Symphony, 1786, but added a stronger link by delaying the establishment of the tonic until the cadence of the first period of the Allegro. Beethoven connected the second movement of the *Appassionata* Sonata, Op. 57, 1804, to the finale by a deceptive cadence upon the VII^7 of F minor, carrying the dominant tension well into the Allegro. He uses the same kind of dominant carry-over to begin the coda of his overture to *Egmont*, Op. 84, 1810.

A striking, remote key relationship between movements engages the attention of the listener more powerfully than a usual shift. The Eb major–E major–Eb major relationship in Haydn's Eb major Sonata, H.V. XVI, No. 52, 1794–1795, is discussed in Ch. 23. One of the most striking such relationships is that of Beethoven's C minor Concerto, Op. 37, 1800 — C minor–E major–C minor. The connection here would appear to be a melodic one, rather than functional; that is, each tone of the C minor triad, by sideslipping a semi-tone, can proceed to a tone of the E major triad. The return to C minor at the finale is achieved by a lightning-quick interchange of mode, where the G♯ of the E major triad is lowered a half step, then raised again to become Ab in the dominant minor ninth chord in C minor. The Db major–G major relationship between the third and fourth movements of Beethoven's Bb major Quartet, Op. 130, 1825, is an abrupt separation, the tritone between the keys reflecting the parodistic, often patch-work-like style of this quartet.

Thematic Links

Thematic links appear occasionally in classic music. Haydn applied what would later be called thematic transformation to the opening subject in the introduction of his Symphony No. 103 in Eb major, 1795, so that it became a thematic member of the second key area of the Allegro; later, the introduction is quoted just before the closing rhyme of the recapitulation. Mozart, in the D major Quintet, K. 593, 1790, recalls the introduction at the end of the first movement, interlocking two sections of markedly different affect; Beethoven does the same in the first movement of the *Pathétique* Sonata, Op. 13, 1798, framing all principal sections of the Allegro with recall of the introduction material. Occasionally, Beethoven used what might be called a *motto*. Each movement of the *Hammerklavier* Sonata, 1819, begins with a rising major third. The *pathetic* motive (see Ch. 15) appears frequently throughout the last quartets. In each of these instances, the melodic material has a striking profile so that it can fulfill its function as a motto.

Grand Plan

In several of his mature works Beethoven promoted overall unity through a grand plan involving all movements. The links between the succeeding movements in his F major Quartet, Op. 59, No. 1, 1806, are increasingly strong:

1. First to second movement: F major–B♭ major as V–I.

2. Second to third movement: B♭ major as IV of F, followed by a single tone C to begin the third movement as V of F; then the open fifth, F-C, to indicate F as I without definition of major or minor mode; finally, E♭, D♭, and A♭ to define F minor as the key. With a minimum harmonic gesture, the leap from B♭ major to F minor is accomplished.

3. Third to fourth movement: a physical connection by means of a cadenza that dissolves the pathetic style of the third movement; the cadenza gradually neutralizes its patterns, narrowing to a trill on C, erasing the adagio tempo; the trill continues into the fourth movement above the theme in the violoncello. Confirmation of F major is delayed until m. 35 of the finale.

In the C♯ minor Quartet, Op. 131, 1826, traditionally performed without pauses between movements, actual links occur only between movements 3 and 4, half cadence; 6 and 7, half cadence; and 5 and 6, *attacca*. Between movements 1 and 2 and movements 2 and 3, the melodic configuration carries over so that the beginning of one movement is the counterstatement to the preceding. The grand plan for this quartet, however, is *harmonic*.

Movements 1–4 have a strong orientation toward the subdominant, initiated by the subject of the fugue (see Ch. 15). This sets a path, harmonic and rhetorical, that traverses the entire work, as Ex. 19-1 outlines.

Ex. 19-1. *Grand plan.* Beethoven, Quartet in C♯ minor, Op. 131, 1826.

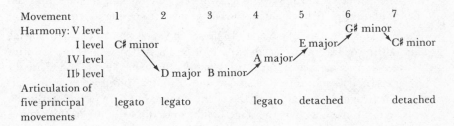

The keys of the successive movements trace a cadential path; the rhythmic progression from *legato* with ambiguous scansion to *detached* with symmetrical scansion gives the effect of a grand iambic meter. *Compatibility of key has become a dialectic of relationships; compatibility of affect has become a dialectic of rhythm*; together, these create an organic unity for this work that is unique in music literature.

COMPOSITE FORMS

Composite forms are created when individual sections within a movement have a high degree of autonomy. This is the obverse of the tendency to link separate movements; the two trends run parallel and often join in operatic ensemble numbers and in the fantasia, completely interpenetrating each other in Beethoven's *Grosse Fuge*, Op. 133, 1826, and, later, in Liszt's B minor Sonata, 1853.

For instrumental music, the fantasia, composed of a number of contrasted sections, is the prototype of this trend, as in the C minor Fantasia of Mozart, K. 475, 1785 (see Ch. 18). The rondo and the variation, with their couplet layouts, create separate small pieces, and, as we have seen, classic composers would sometimes join these in a continuous flow without obscuring their individual character.

Two aspects of sonata form occasionally embodied a well-defined inner articulation. (1) When the X section borrows the form of the *da capo* aria and is set as an autonomous episode, as in the overture to Mozart's *Abduction from the Seraglio*, K. 384, 1781-1782, or in the finale of Beethoven's F minor Sonata, Op. 2, No. 1, 1795, the organic unity of the form yields in favor of a striking affective contrast. (2) The opening, middle, and closing sections of the *exposition* of Beethoven's *Appassionata* Sonata, Op. 57, 1804, are markedly different in style — pathetic in F minor, lyric in A♭ major, agitated in A♭ minor — giving the impression of fragments taken from three larger works and juxtaposed by the thinnest of connections. This is a plan used later by Schubert, Brahms, and Tchaikowsky, well suited to the color and intensity of romantic expression.

Beethoven, who so often found unique solutions to problems of form by modifying or expanding conventional 18th-century layouts, created a form within a form in some movements:

F major Quartet, Op. 18, No. 1, 1800, finale. This contains a rondo within a rondo. The second episode of this sonata-rondo movement has an A B A B A arrangement, the refrain being a wild fugato, the B a sing-song tune. This movement, one of Beethoven's longer finales, generates its momentum from the whiplash triplet 16th-notes at the beginning of the principal theme.

F major Quartet, Op. 59, No. 1, 1806, second movement. This movement, laid out in sonata form, has an exposition in an A B A C A D rondo form, where A represents solid returns to B♭ major, the home key, B and C are digressions, and D stands for the second key, a short two-reprise tune in F minor. The fragmentary nature of the opening material, with its odd harmonic and textural tangents, sets the stage for the episodic structure of this exposition, unique in its layout of sections and its very brief second key area in the dominant minor.

The ideal habitat for a composite form is a section of a vocal work in which an extended text is set. Operatic ensembles, and the "Gloria" and "Credo" of the Mass often have a number of separate sections unified principally by key relationships.

Four of the six sections of Haydn's *Theresienmesse*, 1799, are composite forms — the "Kyrie," "Gloria," "Credo," and "Agnus Dei." Although the entire work is unified by its ruling key, B♭ major, and the individual sections are all in B♭ major except for the "Benedictus," there is no counterstatement of thematic material between subsections of a movement. Still, some subtle unifying elements are present: the quick polonaise rhythm of the first and last movements, the recurrence of drum-like figures in the "Gloria," "Benedictus," and "Agnus Dei," the bass figure of the "Credo," and the subject of the "E vitam" fugue.

The "Credo" contains four major subsections, the incipits of which are quoted in Ex. 19-2.

Ex. 19-2. *Composite-form incipits.* Haydn, *Theresienmesse,* 1799, "Credo."

1. "I believe in one God." I-V, X-I; B♭ major. Quick march-like tempo, continuo-bass and vocal texture reminiscent of Handel. Forty-seven measures.

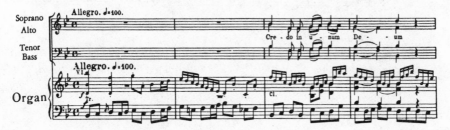

2. "And became incarnate." I-III, X-I; B♭ minor. Three parts beginning respectively "And became incarnate," "And was made man," "He was crucified." No melodic recall or rhyme. Forty-eight measures.

Ex. 19-2, cont'd.

3. "And was resurrected." Three separate parts. Part I, "And was resurrected," in G minor and D minor; a vigorous allegro with continuo-type bass. Part II, "To judge," in B♭ major, in a small I-V, X-I form; a combination of brilliant style and portamento-*alla breve*. Part III, "And in the Holy Spirit," with statements in B♭ major, F minor, C minor, and B♭ major culminating in a pedal on F leading to the fugue, "Et vitam"; tutti-solo layout in *aria cantabile* style. Sixty-three measures.

4. "And the life of the world to come." Fugue, many closely spaced entries; gigue time. Sixty-two measures.

Broude Bros.

Composite numbers show much more latitude in recall and rhyme of melodic material than is the case in key-area and rondo forms. Haydn's "Credo" does not look back at all. Conversely, Mozart, in the "Sanctus" and "Benedictus" of his *Coronation* Mass, 1779, uses both melodic and structural devices to bind these two sections, ordinarily separate; and in the "Agnus Dei" the material of the "Kyrie" is recalled as well as the style of the opening of the "Credo" to establish elements of unity for the entire Mass. An outline of the "Sanctus" and "Benedictus" (Ex. 19-3) shows the ingenuity of Mozart's plan.

Ex. 19-3.   Mozart, *Coronation* Mass, K. 317, 1779, outline of "Sanctus" and "Benedictus."

"Sanctus"

I to V Andante maestoso. "Holy, holy, holy." C major opening leading to a half cadence on G. The style and the bass line are very similar to the beginning of the *"Kyrie."* This section could be a first reprise of a small key-area form. Rhythm of the sarabande.

X to I Allegro assai. "Hosanna in the highest." This section begins on an extended pedal on G (*Ponte*), leading eventually to C major, with three short periods in C major to end the movement. (see Ex. 10-20). These two sections of the "Sanctus" make up a small key-area form without melodic recall. Minuet style.

"Benedictus"

I to V Allegretto. "Blessed." This is a complete small two-reprise form with a coda that makes a cadence on the dominant (see Ex. 10-19). Contredanse, C major.

X Allegro assai. "Hosanna." Recall of the X section of the "Sanctus," with a cadence on the dominant, G.

to I Allegretto. "Blessed." Recall of the first section of the "Benedictus."

I Allegro assai. Recall of the final section of the *"Sanctus."*

In these two movements, Mozart has interwoven two small galant dance forms, except that the minuet has no first reprise. These two styles complement each other. The minuet is bold and decisive, proper for the exultant sentiment of the "Hosanna," while the contredanse is set more gently, suitable for the invocation of a blessing.

The finale to Act II of Mozart's *The Marriage of Figaro*, 1785–1786, is probably the most celebrated example of a composite form in opera. The dramatic events—anger, accusation, surprise, discomfiture, apology, each colored by the noble, capricious, naive, or querulous character of each person involved—move back and forth in an increasing excitement through eight different sections, *each of which is a complete form.* Mozart carefully adds a new element to each succeeding section—a change of key, a new character, a change of tempo. The principal idea—the effort of the Count to gain the upper hand, first by discrediting the Countess, then eventually by putting Figaro on the defensive—undergoes a number of shifts in color as one complication after another enters to change the firmness in stance of the various parties. This principal idea, in which the Count is victorious at the end of the act, is represented by the key of E♭ major, which opens the finale and which prevails at the end. The entire finale is set as a key-area plan in analogy to the boudoir battle. The first section is in E♭ major; the second and third are in B♭ major. Suddenly there is a shift to G major, a point of furthest harmonic remove, as Figaro enters to shatter the temporary victory of the Countess and Susanna. Then the keys run down the circle of fifths to the initial E♭ major as the dénouement runs its course. A point-by-point examination of this masterpiece, correlating text, character, key, figure, and topic, opens a world of incredible subtlety to the listener as we watch Mozart playing his complicated yet ever-delightful games.

NOTE

1. Sulzer, *Allgemeine Theorie,* p. 1122.

Conclusion to Part III

The preceding survey has demonstrated the role of classic rhetoric in shaping form. Rhetorical elements — topic, periodicity, cadential harmony, key definition and contrast, rhythmic scansion, layout of melodic figures — are clear in their functions and sufficiently flexible in their arrangements to be organized into such widely different patterns as the couplet rondo and the fantasia. Moreover, each version of a standard plan has its unique configuration; individual movements can be seen often as paraphrases of each other, as the spirit of the *Ars Combinatoria* produces new and fresh examples of the old familiar continuity.

While *expression* in classic music places its sharpest focus at the *beginning* of a line of action, thus defining the ruling sentiment, *form* makes its strongest point at the *end*, securing the structure by decisive cadences. Expression is thus *fore-accented*; form is *end-accented*. The sense of structural precision and inevitability that is one of the greatest pleasures we take from classic music comes from this deployment of cadential action, often on a very broad scale, to bring whatever rhetorical trajectory may have preceded it to a proper and satisfying conclusion.

The interplay of opening and closing phases of action, coordinated with the often very complex chain of middle events, cannot easily be grasped immediately. A retrospective view is necessary; classic forms furnish the opportunity for review by repetitions of reprises.

The apogee of formal excellence and scope was reached in the great sonata forms, rondos, concertos, and variations of Haydn, Mozart, and Beethoven. We can trace their growth in the works of these composers; these three are largely responsible for the subtleties of nuance, power and declamation and expression, and breadth of scope we associate with the great classic forms. The roots of these forms reached far back into the 18th century and earlier, but the magnificence that commands our attention and wonder was created by these masters alone.

IV Stylistic Perspectives

Expression, rhetoric, and form in the classic style have been interpreted in this book as manifestations of a language common to all 18th-century music, a language with diverse branches. Stylistic distinctions thus far observed — between the old and the new, the strict and the free, the chamber, church, and theater styles — have been read as variants of this language.

The musical criticism of the 18th century was deeply concerned with style. In addition to the distinctions listed above, considerable attention was given to styles of various genres, regional schools, and individual composers. In part IV of this book three points of stylistic perspective are taken to supplement the broad categories already explored. These are:

1. *National schools* — Italian, French, and German, categories widely discussed in 18th-century musical criticism

2. *The high and the low styles* — a distinction that was also a central point of discussion and controversy, and one of the chief contrasts in classic music

3. *Individual styles* — represented by characteristic mature works of the three classic masters, Haydn, Mozart, and Beethoven.

20 National Styles

Three major national styles were recognized during the 18th century—Italian, French, and German. Türk's description, 1789, is quoted here:

The Italian style is pleasant, singing, full (often overladen), brilliant, varied, and very expressive. At least it has been so characterized heretofore. Presently, one finds much that is aimless, often stale, unimportant, shallow, etc. in the works of various Italian composers; still, they must be given credit for melody that has a captivating suppleness.

The French style would be, according to Rousseau's opinion, "insipid, flat, hard, poorly-articulated and monotonous." This is a judgement that is certainly too harsh and betrays the writer's preference for the Italian style. [At this point Türk appends a footnote to say that Walther, Scheibe, and Quantz had better opinions of the French style.] Apart from the fact that French composers sometimes write in a somewhat empty and dry fashion, or that they neglect harmony a bit, one, nevertheless, must give more credit to their taste. There is no doubt, however, that they have long had an eminent position as composers for the clavier and in this consideration deserve much more preference than the Italians.

The German style was not known to Rousseau in any favourable light. It is jumpy, choppy, but harmonic, he says. If this had been the case formerly in clavier pieces, it is certainly no longer true today. I believe that our style expresses itself through careful working out, throughness, and powerful harmony. Moreover, we have taken much from the French and Italians, and perhaps not always the worst. Also, we can match the foreigners with many of our own masters of composition in instrumental as well as vocal music. Meanwhile, we might let the Italians keep something of their music; because I believe that our excellent powerful style has begun lately to degenerate into light frivolity.[1]

See also p. 196.

ITALIAN STYLE

Of the three major national styles, the Italian was by far the leader. Italian was the language of opera, both comic and serious, except at some Parisian theaters; Italians invented many of the figures, textures, and phrase structures that we associate with classic music; their performers were skilled and numerous; many manuals of composition show a strong orientation to the Italian style.

Italian music was hotly debated, embraced, or rejected. When in 1715 de Freneuse complained that the Italians "change the key too frequently and use the same passage too often,"[2] he nevertheless described the layout that established the structural basis for a vast amount of 18th-century music—one idea or

affection, systematically maintained through changes of key. Rousseau's preference for Italian music and his arguments to support this view are well known
from articles in his *Dictionaire,* 1768, and his *Lettre sur la musique française,*
1753.[3] The following excerpts from a letter sent by a German traveler in Italy,
published in Cramer, 1783, show the same bias:

> . . . the Italian actually prefers learning to sing rather than to play an in-
> strument. He knows, only too well, that a beautifully-trained voice, singing
> in such a sweet harmonic language, touches the heart more than do sona-
> tas, even when they are performed by the hand of a Bach [presumably
> C.P.E. Bach] upon a Silbermann clavier. . . . Can the Germans have their
> own original style, when they have cultivated their taste in vocal music ac-
> cording to the Italians, as for example, Hasse, Graun, Telemann, Hiller,
> Schweitzer, etc.; when, in the greatest German cities it is not the Germans
> but the Italians that sing and are represented as models? The Italians have,
> from time immemorial, had their original style in opera, as well as their
> original taste in song. The Germans import their taste from Italy, or they
> permit it to be imported by castrati. . . .[4]

At the end of the century Daube, 1797, in his defense of German music, bears
witness to the prominence of the Italians at that time:

> Does not Germany have great men in composition and instrumental per-
> formance who compete with the Italians for precedence?[5]

The aspects of the Italian style that made it so persuasive are discussed below.

Declamation

The suitability of the Italian language for musical setting was universally recognized (see pp. 345–346). Its rich clear vowel sounds, crisp consonants, essentially
regular rhythm, and tendency to end syllables with vowels or soft consonants
("La ci da-rem la ma-no") promoted beauty and elegance of vocal delivery.
These qualities also provided scope for many nuances of declamation. Rousseau
praises the Italian language for the "variety of expressions in its accents . . . to
which the musician owes the force and grace of his melody."[6] The regular flow of
syllables promotes the *aria cantabile* style (Ex. 4-15); the open vowels can be
carried through *bravura* passages (Ex. 16-1); they also support the *portamento*
(Ex. 10-11); the crisp, even syllables provide an ideal framework for *parlando*
(Ex. 22-4).

Melody

The "captivating suppleness" of Italian melody praised by Türk is probably the
most attractive feature of both vocal and instrumental Italian music. Ex. 20-1,
taken from an early 18th-century work, illustrates the suppleness that characterizes Italian melody throughout the 18th century. The clarity and attractiveness
of this melody arise from its overall contour — a graceful descent, wave-like, followed by a balancing rise to the apex, B, in m. 10; its neat articulation into two-

measure phrases shaped by complementary melodic figures and given an added dimension by the simple imitation in the bass; from its clear and bright embodiment of the key, G major, by a symmetrical alternation of tonic, dominant, and subdominant harmonies; and from the constant use of thirds and sixths between the soprano and bass, imparting a sweetness to the sound (note especially the rising parallel thirds, mm. 5–13, in which the stepwise rising line gives a strong sense of direction to the period). The cadential section, mm. 13–23, reinforces the sense of symmetry, with a subtle slight disturbance, mm. 17–19, caused by the interpolation of a three-measure phrase. This ritornello, cast in a graceful, rather quick siciliano rhythm, represents what Chastellux praised in Italian melody — its clarity of period structure (see p. 35).

Ex. 20-1. *Italian melody.* "Pupillette vezzosette" ("Enchanting eyes"), from Crotch, *Specimens,* vol. III, p. 18, 1806.

Italian melody gained much expressiveness through the use of appoggiaturas. Professional singers, trained from childhood, were skilled in adding appoggiaturas to a simple melody; amateur instrumentalists were generally guided by notated appoggiaturas, either as *agréments* or essential notes. Ex. 20-2a illustrates

Mozart's addition of appoggiaturas in *alla zoppa* rhythm to a simple melody; had this been a vocal piece, it might have been notated as a straightforward bourrée tune, as given in Ex. 20-2b. The poignancy and sweetness of the appoggiatura are increased by chromatic alteration, especially when the *agrément* resolves upward. The double appoggiaturas in the opening measure of the second movement of Mozart's D minor Concerto, K. 466, 1785, represent an Italianism found often in classic music.

Ex. 20-2.   *Alla zoppa and appoggiaturas.* Mozart, Sonata in B♭ major, K. 333, 1778, 1st movt.

a. *Instrumental.*

b. *Vocal.*

Italians had a special knack for drawing attractive melodic figures from the harmony. In their *allegros* they created well-anchored, pleasing patterns often in arpeggios for salient themes, and exuberant mechanical figurations in rapid notes for brilliant passage work (see Ex. 17-2, p. 285). In their *adagios* they had a tradition of florid ornamentation—trills, appoggiaturas, mordents, tiratas—arranged in irregular patterns. This free floridity is underpinned by regularity of punctuation and a steady bass that fixes the pace. Ex. 20-3 illustrates this procedure, described by Rousseau, 1753:

> The Italians are more adroit in their *Adagios,* for when the time is so slow that there is any danger of weakening the sense of rhythm, they make their bass proceed by notes of equal value which mark the movement. . . .[7]

Ex. 20-3.   Zuccari, *The True Method of Playing an Adagio,* ca. 1762, Adagio I.

In Ex. 20-3 the bass line moves in steady quarter-notes by sequence to a cadence in m. 5. The melody does not reflect the action of the bass, covering its cadence with elaborate figuration; its complementary moment, mm. 3–4, occurs when the bass relinquishes its sequential action. Despite the floridity and irregularity, we can sense the firmness of the underlying structure. The Adagio of Mozart's D major Quartet, K. 499, 1786, makes lavish use of this style of ornamentation over a slow sarabande rhythm; a similar instance occurs in the second movement of Beethoven's G major Quartet, Op. 18, No. 2, 1800.

The tradition of the ornamentation of an Adagio had a long life; it was a standard practice in the early 18th century and was maintained in the Italian style of singing and the French violin discipline in the mid-19th century. Florid ornamentation was an important topic in performance practice manuals.[8]

Italian melodic exuberance, fed from a collection of familiar clichés, often led to works put together in chains of variegated figures, an effect that offended the sensibilities of some French and German observers with respect to unity. As Kirnberger, 1771–1779, says:

> We often hear compositions in the new Italian style; often there are passages containing note values that do not appear elsewhere in the entire piece. This destroys the unity of expression completely so that we do not know, by the end of the piece, what we have heard.[9]

Goudar, in his *Brigandage,* 1778, a vitriolic attack on Italian music, says the following concerning an aria of Paisiello:

> I have analyzed an aria of the famous Paisiello. I found a great and fiery imagination in the first phrase; in the second, this cooled noticeably; in the third he introduced a disorderly, jangling noise; in the fourth, he made an unpleasant modulation; and the fifth was entirely from another world; the rest was in the usual Italian fashion, and upon a very fine text by Metastasio.[10]

No doubt this shallow facility, working within simple and familiar structural recipes and abetted by paraphrase and direct plagiarism, was largely responsible for the enormous number of Italian-style compositions produced in the later 18th century. But the same mixture and play of contrasted figures, fashioned with elegance and linked felicitously, lies at the heart of Mozart's rhetoric, which he learned from the Italians.

Harmony

Italian melody drew its sweetness and clarity from slow and regular chord changes, hinging upon the reciprocal action of I, IV, and V, creating a neat trim of cadential formulas. Simple or florid, Italian melody rarely disturbed the luminous effect created by this regular procession of simple harmonies.

Apart from its cadential function, IV provided a characteristic nuance as an ornament to I, particularly at the beginning of a phrase. Ex. 20-4 illustrates this typically Italian turn, where IV occurs in the $\frac{6}{4}$ position over a tonic pedal *à la musette.* J. C. Bach and Mozart favored this progression, as in Bach's G major Sonata, Op. 17, No. 4, 1773, first movement, and Mozart's C major Sonata, K. 309, 1777, finale.

Another familiar Italian cliché was the series of cadences closing a movement or major section. In these bass moves

and the cadential $^6_4$ adds to the Italianate flavor with its particularly ingratiating sound. Ex. 20-5 illustrates this cadential peroration. Beethoven caricatured this conventional cadential formula in the 2nd movement of his Symphony No. 8, Op. 93, 1812, where he cramped it into a stretto instead of allowing it to expand in its normal way. Riepel, 1755, recommends that cadences be repeated, pointing to their special effect in opera arias.[11]

Ex. 20-4.   Galuppi, *L'Olimpiade*, 1747, "Piu non si trovano" ("One can no longer discover").

Ex. 20-5.   Guglielmi, *Le Pazzie d'Orlando,* 1771, "Fra tiranni" ("Among tyrants").

"My valor in bondage, my courage lost.'

Texture

Texture in late 18th-century Italian music was thin, to highlight melody, support lively rhythms, and allow long chains of cadential formulas to retain freshness. Rousseau, 1753, praises the lightness of Italian texture:

> . . . the great art of the composer consists no less in knowing on occasion which notes to leave out than knowing which to use. It is by studying and continually turning the pages of the masterpieces of Italy that he will know how to make that delicate choice. . . .[12]

> "What!" said I to myself, "the complete harmony has less effect than the harmony mutilated, and our accompanists, filling out all the chords, produce only a confused sound, while this one, with fewer notes, creates more harmony, or at least makes his harmony more distinct and pleasant!"[13]

The two-part basic texture of classic music (see Ch. 7) and the three-part harmony recommended by Daube, 1773 (see p. 123), are taken from Italian scoring.

The clarity of Italian texture was critically important to the "exactness of time" that Rousseau admired.[14] This rhythmic precision also contributed to the clarity of period structure, noted by Chastellux. French texture, full-voiced and loaded with *agréments*, undoubtedly contributed to the lack of rhythmic precision about which Rousseau and Chastellux complained.

The Italians developed a number of devices that served to maintain the rhythmic pulse, imparting some profile to the accompaniment without interfering with the prominence of the melody:

1. *Repeated notes.* The harmony, moving slowly in whole- or half-notes, was activated by the division into eighths. This could take place in the bass (Ex. 20-5) or in middle voices (Ex. 9-5).

2. *Alberti bass.* The accompaniment plays a broken chord figure in close position. See p. 135.

3. *Punctuating bass.* The bass merely provides accents on strong beats, giving minimum support to a slowly changing harmony (Ex. 9-5).

4. *Figured accompaniment.* One mark of a skillful composer was his ability to give figures with some character to supporting voices. Charles Burney, 1789, mentions an accompaniment of Galuppi:

> ANTIGONO, set by Galuppi. . . . In the charming air "A torto spergiuro," we see the first time, perhaps, when the base was struck *after* the treble, of which Emanuel Bach and Haydn have often made happy use. The accompaniment of "Giá che morir deggio," in slow triplets, has been the model of many subsequent songs. . . .[15]

> Some admirable songs of Galuppi's composition . . . in a new and fine style of dramatic Music, in which the accompaniments, in two of three slow triplets after each note in the base, has a new and fine effect.[16]

Ex. 20-6, in running 16th-notes, illustrates the lively Italian style of accompaniment, also employed frequently by Mozart.

A counterpart to active accompaniment was *reinforcement* of the principal melody; this might be (1) exact doubling of the voice, (2) a simplified version of the solo part in the treble, (3) a more elaborate version of the solo, (4) unison for the entire ensemble, (5) reinforcement by parallel thirds or sixths. Rousseau, 1753, noted this feature of Italian texture:

> This unity of melody seems to me to be an indispensable rule. . . . It is in this great rule that one must seek the cause of the frequent accompaniments in unison which are observed in Italian music. . . .[17]

Exs. 7-2, 10-9, 10-10, and 10-11 illustrate various doublings or reinforcements of the melody.

Ex. 20-6.   Guglielmi, *Le Pazzie d'Orlando*, 1771, "Fra tiranni" ("Among tyrants").

Vocal Superiority

Italian vocal art was acknowledged the finest in the 18th century. Schubart, 1785, said, "Without question singing has attained the finest flowering in Italy of all nations."[18] This advantage was ascribed to two causes: (1) the natural bent of the Italians toward song; (2) the superb training of Italian singers.

Most of the noted singers of the time were Italian — Farinelli, Senesino, Faustina, Mingotti, Cuzzoni, Pacchirotti; these were not only celebrated for their vocalism but notorious for the enormous fees they charged and their professional aggressiveness.

Except for *buffa* roles, very little Italian music was written for bass voice. Noted singers were sopranos, altos, and tenors. One circumstance contributed immensely to Italian vocal superiority — the spectacular preeminence in beauty of tone and power of delivery possessed by the great *castrati* of that age. All accounts testify to the compelling nature of their performance. Burney, 1789, wrote of Carlo Broschi Farinelli, by far the greatest castrato:

> No vocal performance of the present century has been more unanimously allowed by professional critics, as well as general celebrity to have been gifted with a voice of such uncommon power, sweetness, extent, and agility as Carlo Broschi detto Farinelli . . . [he] enchanted and astonished his hearers by the force, extent, and mellifluous tones of the mere organ, when he had nothing to execute, articulate, or express."[19]

The instruments of the 18th century, with their softer and less bright tones, could not approach the extraordinary brilliance of the *castrati*, probably greater than anything we hear today. This circumstance alone can account for much of the superiority of 18th-century vocal music, and Italian vocalism in particular.

Pedagogy

Italian methods of teaching were also considered superior to those of other countries. Conservatories in Venice and Naples produced most of the great Italian composers and singers of the 17th and 18th centuries. Koch, 1802, comments on performances at these conservatories:

> On afternoons of Sundays and feast days, these young ladies perform oratorios accompanied by all the standard instruments, led by the musical director of the institution . . . thanks to their excellent performance and the many beautiful voices, these performances are attended by many amateurs and connoisseurs.[20]

In addition to furnishing some of the most ingratiating music of the 18th century and providing standards for vocal performance, the Italians also contributed to music in the strict style, thanks to their traditional maintenance of the 16th-century *stile antico*. The majority of Italian treatises deal with *canto fermo* and the forms based upon it. Cramer, 1783, in a sketch of the Italian *Capellmeister* at Bonn, Andrea Lucchesi, speaks of his early training in theater and church styles, clearly implying that these constituted the two formal branches of Italian compositional pedagogy.[21] The theater style, incorporating the chamber, was taught informally, from master to pupil; there are no instruction manuals in this style comparable to those which give detailed tutelage in the church style.

Italian contributions to pedagogy include Tosi, *Opinioni de'Cantori antiche e moderna*, 1723, probably the most celebrated treatise on singing in the 18th century, translated by Galliard into English, 1743, and the basis for the treatises by Agricola, *Anleitung zur Singkunst*, 1757, and Hiller, *Musikalisch-zierlichen Gesange*, 1780; Tartini, *Traité des agrémens*, 1782, one of the most valuable sources for ornamentation; Martini, *Esemplare*, 1774–1775, the most important treatise on strict counterpoint of its time.

Thanks to the Italians, the aria, concerto, sonata, and *opera seria* and *buffa* became standard 18th-century genres. Composers of other nations adapted Italian idioms to their own regional and personal styles, but the Italian influence is present in most of classic music.

To conclude, the quotation from Quatremère de Quincy, 1789, indicates how Italian music was regarded in the later 18th century by a sophisticated Parisian:

> . . . one cannot deny, and everyone agrees that Italy, in music, is richer than all other nations combined. She has produced, out of proportion, more great masters than all the rest of Europe has ever produced. She owes this advantage to the harmonious idiom, sonorous and flexible, in which the simple prosody becomes somehow the principle element of the melody; to the nature of a soft and voluptuous climate, which lulls the organs, exalts the passions, embellishes their language, and which provides the imagination with ardent strokes of nature; to all those institutions favorable to the exercise of music; and finally to the excellence of the schools established for the culture of this art.[22]

FRENCH STYLE

France's centralized political structure during the later 17th century and the 18th was reflected in French style and the role music played in French life. French musical activity was centered principally in Paris and Versailles, whereas Italian music was exported throughout the western world. The theater was the center of French artistic life; music was an adjunct to declamation and dancing, heightening the effect of the word and completing the sense of movement in choreography, in contrast to the Italian emphasis upon melody and excellence in vocalism.

During the reigns of Louis XIV, 1643-1715, and Louis XV, 1715-1774, French music—heavily subsidized and strictly regulated—developed a number of highly refined features, many of which reflected the French orientation to drama. While most of these stem from the earlier 18th century, their effect upon the classic style was significant.

Declamation

One of the sharpest points of controversy between Italian and French music was the word-tone relationship, a reflection of the different attitudes held by the Italians and the French toward the relative importance of music and drama in the lyric theater. The Italians regarded the voice as the most beautiful, most perfect musical instrument, a model for all other instruments, and they wrote their music to display the voice in all its richness, sonority, brilliance, and flexibility. Hence the brief stanzas, short lines, frequent repetitions, and elaborations upon a convenient syllable. The French, on the other hand, took the voice to be a vehicle for declaiming an elegant text, full of content; music was used to heighten the expressive nuances of the words. French music was consistently set syllabically, with relatively few florid moments; French vocal pieces were considerably shorter than their Italian counterparts.

Le Pileur d'Apligny, 1779, describes these differences:

. . . the [Italian] musician simply chooses a key and a tempo analogous to each passion which the music can depict . . . while he composes a concerto, being free to give rein to his wandering fantasy to make a bold and agreeable melody . . . this can create an illusion up to a certain point but it is impossible, by this means, to achieve perfect expression. . . .

He then characterizes French declamation:

It is necessary, in order that music express perfectly the passion of a personage, that the composer concern himself with bringing to life all the phrases of the discourse, that he have regard for the character and situation of the personage, that he express the sentiment that moves him and the progress of his passion, by mixtures of short and long notes and by modulations that fit the situations; . . . that he retard or accelerate the pace of his melody. . . . All of this demands an attention that can cool the imagination somewhat and make the melody somewhat less brilliant; but the expression will be truer since it is more detailed. The costraints thus placed upon the composer very much resembles those which rhyme places upon the poet. . . .[23]

Also, from *AMZ* 1801:

The sensuous charm of a tone is inhibited by the word, because the consonants mute the resonance. It is a characteristic of Italian music that this takes place as little as possible, due to the frequency and clarity of vowels in this language. The French, although they do not strangle the tone as much as the Germans do, cannot compete with the Italians insofar as sonority is concerned. . . . In the arts, it is feeling that dominates the Italian, while reason controls the French. Thus, the Italians are concerned more with *tone*, the French with *ideas*. Therefore, according to their nature, the Italians prefer the melismatic style, while the French (for example, Lully and Gluck) prefer the syllabic style. . . .[24]

From *AMZ*, 1800:

The French, whose lively, spirited character has imparted amiability and elegance to their speech, have overused simple declamation in their great masterworks, and, due to the poverty of their pure vocalism, provide too few opportunities for melismatic passages . . . in French, the syllables are only counted; in Italian and German, on the other hand, they are weighed, hence brought closer to musical rhythm.[25]

Le Pileur d'Apligny's comments on the differences between French and Italian declamation are in accord with his distinctions between French and Italian expressive qualities. He finds that a Frenchman will express himself in a more self-contained manner than an Italian:

The elevation of the head, a tone of voice at first more measured and majestic, wherein the inflections become gradually more active and precipitate,

announces, in a Frenchman, an offense to his self-respect, and the sentiment of vengeance. We observe in an Italian (and above all, in a Neapolitan), moved by the same passion, the eyes, the head, and the entire body
affected by a convulsive movement, a piercing vocal sound, irregular, interspersed with inflections that indicate a more quarrelsome tone than that of
offended self-respect. In a word, the Frenchman, in anger, appears more
menacing than quarrelsome. . . . . what I say of anger should be understood
for all the passions. [Le Pileur d'Apligny then links these differences to the
ways in which feelings are expressed in each nation's music.][26]

French recitative was the chief embodiment of the French musical treatment of
declamation. Its principal feature was the change of meter that frequently occurred to accommodate a stressed syllable upon a strong beat. This technique,
employed in French opera from Lully to Rameau, is illustrated in Ex. 20-7.

Six changes of meter are written into the 8 measures quoted, reflecting
changes in scansion. The text has several changes in meaning—a question, an
answer, a poetic simile, and the notions of a fine day, sleep, and singing. In an
Italian recitative, these may well have been highlighted by some expressive turn
or touch of word-painting (see Ch. 18). Here, we find no change in the steady
monochromatic setting. The rate of chord change is frequent, contrary to the
sustained harmonies of Italian recitative, but the harmonic orbit is narrow, lacking any of the striking shifts often heard in the Italian. Shifts of key are carried
out smoothly and unobtrusively, through chords common to both keys. The
mood is coolly objective—an observation rather than a participation. When the
continuo is realized, the voice, as written, becomes the treble in a full chord texture, lacking its prominence in an Italian recitative. Perhaps to avoid being thus
absorbed, French singers loaded their recitative with a heavy burden of ornamentation, according to Rousseau, 1753.[27] In doing so, they obscured the sense
of the text and destroyed its carefully planned scansion.

Ex. 20-7.　Rameau, *Platée*, 1745.

"What do I see? Is it Thespis? Yes, it is he who sleeps, [and] that sweet
moisture on his eyes seems like poppies; should he, on this fine day, allow
himself to sleep, he who sings so well...."

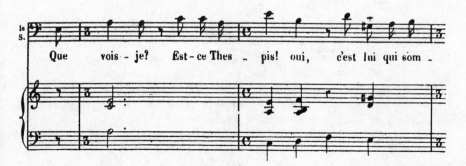

Ex. 20-7, cont'd.

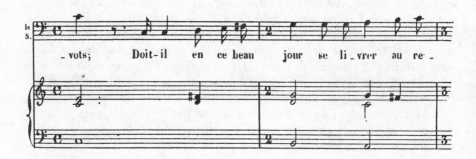

Chef d'Oeuvres

Shifting meters in French recitative disappeared after Rameau, but French declamation had a profound effect upon later 18th-century opera, since it was fitted more closely to the sense and structure of the text than Italian, and therefore promoted dramatic truth. Gluck's *reform* operas adopted elements of French declamation, contributing significantly to the trend toward a closer word-tone relationship. In these operas he simplified musical content and fitted the music more closely to the dramatic action.

Dances

French expertise in dance was developed through centuries of practice and refinement in the courts and salons in Versailles and Paris and in the French theater. Most of the dances current in the 18th century were French in origin or adaptation. By means of French dances, the two-reprise form was standardized; Walther, 1732, specifies two reprises in his descriptions of French dances.[28] These antedate other descriptions of two-reprise form. While the French style of singing was confined principally to French theaters and salons, French dances were exported constantly throughout the 18th century; French dancers and dancing masters traveled throughout Europe much in the way Italian composers and performers did. Jean Georges Noverre, the great French choreographer, worked first in Paris and later in Berlin and London, also for the Duke of Württemburg, and for the Empress Maria Theresa in Vienna, finally returning to Paris to become ballet master of the Paris Opera.

Ballet, the most important dance genre and one in which the French excelled, was constantly incorporated into theatrical productions—plays, comedy-ballets, serious and comic opera. As a theatrical feature, ballet involved *pantomime* as well as choreography, an element stressed by Noverre in his many ballets upon classic themes. Rousseau, 1768, says:

> . . . the theatrical dance should necessarily be the imitation of something else, much as the singing actor represents a speaking person, and the decoration represents places other than that which it occupies.[29]

Rousseau here criticizes the practice of virtuoso dancing which told no story and had no mimetic content. Quatremère de Quincy, 1789, refers to this situation, one which Noverre sought to alter:

> In Paris, where the art of the dance appears to be the most highly developed, it appears often without dramatic interest, free of the impediments of pantomime. . . . One dances in Paris for the sake of dancing, as in Italy one sings for the sake of singing.[30]

(See p. 17.)

Spectacle and Variety

A French theatrical production was a mélange of scenery, airs, recitatives, ballets, and choruses, combined to create a series of tableaux, sometimes organized into a scene complex but often no more than a series of diverting episodes. Algarotti, 1755, says that "a great number of French operas . . . are nothing better than entertainments for the eyes, having more the appearance of a masquerade than of a regular performance."[31]

The French taste for spectacle and variety called for different arrangements within an act than those of Italian opera. For example, Act I of Hasse's *Arminio,* 1745, an *opera seria,* consists of six *da capo* arias and a terzetto in *da capo* form, each preceded by their recitatives. These numbers range in length from 100 to 200 measures. The prologue to Rameau's *Dardanus,* 1739, a *tragédie lyrique,* opens with a relatively short *da capo* aria, the type called *ariette* by the French; subsequently, there are five recitatives, six dances, three choruses, and three *airs* (brief arias) alternating to provide much variety. Hasse includes arias *di strepito, di bravura, cantabile,* and *di portamento* among his set numbers, loading the music heavily with coloratura. Rameau's ariette is in cantabile style; he rarely employs florid figuration. For the listener, Hasse's music fixes the attention as it moves through its broad trajectories; Rameau's listener is led to expect a new turn of events as the short numbers follow each other in diverting contrasts.

Orchestration

Thanks to ballet, the French orchestra in the 17th and 18th centuries enjoyed greater prominence in the theater than the Italian orchestra did. The obligatory five-part French string texture created a massive sound and a heavier, more slowly moving rhythmic effect than the scoring of the Italians for two treble parts and continuo. This fuller texture gave the orchestra a more important presence; the full, stately *grave* or adagio that began the overture called attention to the importance of the occasion — the entry of the dancers and important personages. Throughout a stage piece the orchestra was often heard as pure instrumental music — to accompany dances, to provide entrées, entr'actes, and closing pieces. In contrast, the Italian orchestras came upon the scene with a busy, variegated, often inconsequential string of commonplaces in the opening movement of the *opera sinfonia*. Apart from the ritornellos of arias, the Italian orchestra had little independent work within an opera.

Thus the tradition of an important orchestra arose in France and was firmly established by Lully, both with respect to scope and discipline. France became a pioneer in the history of orchestral concerts, beginning with the *Concerts spirituels* in Paris in 1725.

The French taste for spectacle, the picturesque, and the mimetic — especially strong in the first half of the 18th century — was reflected in the many effects of orchestration that Rameau devised, effects that contributed significantly to the modern concept of orchestration that arose in the later 18th century. Rameau reduced the string parts to four and introduced many striking effects of orchestral color — solo winds, string figurations, sustained winds, the novelty of clarinets (*Zoroastre,* 1749). His "Ramage des oiseaux" ("Chirping of the birds") from *Le Temple de la Gloire,* HAM 276, 1745, is a series of figures imitating bird songs, assigned to strings and flutes in alternation in a typical chamber music texture; the vocal soloist himself participates in these imitations occasionally as an embroidery of the typical French declamation.

French ideas of orchestration and orchestral style had their effect upon composers who came to Paris. Gluck, when he adapted *Orfeo,* first presented in Vienna in 1762, for presentation in Paris in 1774, placed considerably more emphasis on the orchestra to suit the French taste. The first version contains virtually none of the full, agitated effects that are prominent in the second version, as in the music for the Furies. When Mozart composed his Symphony in D major, K. 297, 1778, for the Parisians, he scored the work for pairs of flutes, oboes, clarinets, bassoons, horns, and trumpets, with timpani and strings — the fullest orchestration in all his symphonies.

The Clavecin Style

The French clavecin style, best known from the suites of François Couperin and Rameau, was distinguished by elaborate ornamentation — *agréments* such as the *port de voix* (appoggiatura), *cadence* or *tremblement* (trill), *double cadence* (turn), *pincé* or *mordant* (mordent) etc., that decorated single tones — by short phrases often echoed in various registers, by striking coloristic effects often pictorial in intent, and by the *style brisé*, the "broken" style adapted from French lute music, in which notes of a chord were played in succession instead of simultaneously. This last feature was turned to great advantage, giving rise to a rich variety of figurations. Burney's only comment on Couperin's music, 1789, referred to the fact that "his pieces are so crouded and deformed by beats, trills, and shakes, that no plain note was left."[32]

German composers made use of the French clavecin style frequently; the treatises of Marpurg, 1755, C. P. E. Bach, 1753, and Türk, 1789, show a strong French orientation; Kirnberger's *Recueil*, circa 1783, is largely made up of French dances for clavecin. The French influence is apparent in the B minor Sonata of C. P. E. Bach, *Kenner und Liebhaber*, series I, 1799, quoted in Ex. 7-4a.

The Popular Theater

The style of the short songs, the *brunettes* and *vaudevilles*, of the popular fair theater in France found its way into late 18th-century music by way of the *opéra comique*. These songs, one example of which is given in Ex. 10-1, were interspersed in the action of popular comedies in the early 18th century and in mid-century were standard items in the newly evolved French *opéra comique*. This genre, in turn, became a model for the German *Singspiel*. The following comment on Hiller's *Lisuart und Dariolette*, 1766, an early *Singspiel*, pinpoints the French influence and, in its final remark, indicates the Italian flavor, putting French layout and Italian style into precise conjunction as they appear in this German work:

The poetic setting [of this *Singspiel*] is made according to the presently very fashionable French comic operas or comedies interspersed with ariettes *(comédies mêlées des ariettes)*. One can object that song in drama is unnatural; here we shall not deal with this objection since it is perhaps not necessary; but the French poets would like to believe, as they persuade us, that it is more natural to hear a piece half sung and half spoken, as that knight who rides with one leg in the stirrup and the other on the ground. As long as it is stylish in France, we [Germans] copy it. The author of *Lisuart* had originally prepared his work as an afterpiece without music, and the present taste of fashion led him then to clothe it in a French cloak; but in fact he gave it more of an Italian cut than a French.[33]

Mozart's early *Singspiel* entitled *Bastien und Bastienne*, K. 50, 1768, was partly modeled upon Rousseau's *Le Devin du Village*, 1751, one of the earliest and most celebrated *opéras comiques*. Late in the century, Johann Reichardt was sufficiently impressed with the French vaudeville that he transplanted the genre, eliminating its comic and satiric texts to conform with a more sober bourgeois German taste, and thus created a form called the *Liederspiel*.[34]

Rapprochement of Italian and French Styles

Throughout the first half of the 18th century heated controversies raged about the relative merits of French and Italian music.[35] Paris, a magnet that drew hundreds of Italian musicians to seek their fortunes, was the center of the confrontation of the two styles. In 1752 an Italian company came to Paris and had a great success with Pergolesi's *opera buffa, La Serva Padrona.* This event touched off the famous *querelle des bouffons* (war of the buffoons), a heated conflict of taste in which political as well as musical issues were involved. The Italian style, representing an international taste, was favored by Queen Marie and her intellectual circle, which included Rousseau, Diderot, and Alembert. The French style, of which Rameau was the chief representative, was endorsed by the conservative, nationalistic faction, led by King Louis XV and his friends and advisers.

To be sure, Italian elements had been incorporated into French music from time to time in the early part of the century. Manfred Bukofzer, in *Music in the Baroque Era,* quotes an excerpt from Clerambault's *Pigmalion,* 1716, which is cast in a typically Italian brilliant style.[36] But the full rapprochement of the two styles was accomplished in the period following the death of Rameau in 1764, the year which according to Daval, *La musique en France,* marks the end of the epoch in which a genuine French style existed. Philidor, in his *Ernelinde,* 1767, wrote a *tragédie lyrique* consisting principally of arias preceded by recitative in 4/4 time. Piccinni adapted his Italian idiom to French protocol (see Ch. 21). French and Italian elements are present in Gluck's *reform* operas (Ch. 21). Another significant figure was Viotti, who fused Italian and French violin styles. The cantabile passages in his concertos often have a French flavor, with broad and simple declamation (see Ex. 20-8) sharing attention with brilliant Italianate figurations. This manner, a hallmark of the French violin concertos of Viotti and his disciples Rode, Baillot, and Kreutzer, was emulated by Beethoven in his D major Violin Concerto, Op. 61. 1806 (see Ch. 17).

Ex. 20-8.   Viotti, Concerto for Violin and Orchestra in G major, No. 23, 1793.

The rapprochement of Italian and French styles was probably accomplished most successfully by Grétry, the most celebrated French composer of his time, popular and admired everywhere. Momigny, 1806, considered him to be a paragon of French musical virtues:

> . . . the Opéra-Comique, then called the Comédie Italienne, shone with the genius and spirit of Grétry, who surpassed Philidor in grace and luster and Monsigny in sparkle and dramatic truth, and who, above all, refined its prosody. One can say that whenever this celebrated composer has had a proper text, he has shown that music also had its Molière.[37]

Schubart, 1785, noted the mixture of styles in Grétry's music:

> The golden strands of the Italian style are intertwined in his music with the colored silken threads of the French taste.[38]

Grétry's comic operas follow the format of the *théâtre italien*; arias and songs are interspersed with spoken dialogue, eliminating completely the French recitative. Dances and pantomimes are included to satisfy the French taste for ballet. But his music has strong Italian color; Ex. 20-9, from his *Aucassin et Nicolette*, 1782, is a brilliant military aria accompanied by horns, trumpets, oboes, and timpani, in addition to strings. The two-measure phrases, paired in question-answer form, the large melodic leaps, and the busy orchestra identify the Italian style. The formal turn to the dominant in mm. 20–21 is another Italian touch. Only the scansion, syllabic, without *fioritura*, represents the French element.

Ex. 20-9.   Grétry, *Aucassin et Nicolette*, 1782, "Allez, allez."

"Go, go, bring me my weapons, approach, my friends. Aucassin is the victor, banish fear and alarms."

Ex. 20-9, cont'd.

The French sense for protocol — precision, clarity, balance, hierarchy — was embodied in every aspect of French musical style. The scansion of recitative and air was precisely geared to the accents reflecting the length of syllables in French speech; the accents and phrasing of ensemble music mirrored the steps of the ballet. Declaimed speech was sharply distinguished from the chordal style of instrumental music, and these two were nicely balanced throughout a French theater presentation. In contrast, the Italians drew material for both instrumental and vocal music from the same sources—the brilliant and the cantabile styles.

When the French used the Italian style in the earlier 18th century, it was clearly marked off from their own idioms. French music in the 18th century should be viewed from the perspective of the total theater and the contribution each element made to the great spectacle, much as French social and political life was organized around the absolutisms of Louis XIV and his successors. On the other hand, Italian music should be viewed in the light of its characteristic details of composition, those elements that created a characteristic flavor wherever they appeared in any genre. For this reason, Italian elements were susceptible to expansion, manipulation, and modification, and so contributed significantly to the structural growth and individualization of the great classic forms.

GERMAN STYLE

Germany's contribution to 18th-century music was the talent of its composers, rather than a distinctive national idiom. The Germans themselves realized that their role was to adapt Italian and French styles to their own taste. Quantz, 1752, said that the aim of the Germans had been and should continue to be a pleasant and tasteful mixture of the styles of various nations:

> . . . they [the Germans] are the more capable of adopting a style from the outside, whichever they please, and they know how to profit by the good side of foreign music, whatever its kind.[39]

> . . . the operas which the Italians find most tasteful, and rightly so, are actually the products of a German pen.[40]

Quantz was referring to Hasse, the most famous composer of Italian operas in his time. After Schütz, who carried the Italian style of his teacher, Gabrieli, to Germany, German composers looked to France and Italy for their stylistic directions. J. S. Bach's music is saturated with elements of the two styles; Handel's music is entirely Italian in flavor; the clavier styles of C. P. E. Bach and his father were taken from the French; Gluck's declamation comes from the French, while, apart from his *reform* operas, his dramatic style is Italian; Italianate elements appear on every page of Mozart. Yet apart from its adaptation of French and Italian styles, German music had its own characteristic features.

Declamation

Setting a German text involved some basic questions of inflection and syllable construction, as explained in Hiller, 1766:

> One of the greatest inconveniences of our language is that so many syllables end, not with vowels, but with consonants; however, cannot a tasteful singer, with a flexible tongue and easy manner of expression, compensate for these drawbacks by pronouncing the vowels clearly and broadly, and in contrast, bringing out the compound consonants more quickly? In short, he

should imagine that all syllables end with vowels, and thereby all following consonants will belong to the following syllables. The pampered and corrupt ears of the listeners can assist toward this improvement, if they demand less of brilliance and glitter in the music, and will accept more quiet and expressive qualities. This latter is entirely feasible in our musical language; the former not so much, as in the Italian style. It is true, we lose thereby now and then something of beauty; but we will hear less musical nonsense.[41]

Since most Italian syllables begin with consonants and end with vowels, the singer can trail off slightly at the end of a syllable without loss of intelligibility, maintaining a crispness of delivery even in rapid patter songs. German declamation, according to Hiller, should connect consonants to following vowels; it would seem that such a delivery would best be suited to a gentle sing-song style, where the sentimental content of the text would be enhanced by a simple, pretty melody, a legato declamation, and symmetrical phrase structure. Hiller's song "Die Jagd" ("The Hunt") (Ex. 21-16) has 26 syllables in the first eight measures, the same number as in "Là ci darem" ("There we'll take each other's hands") from Mozart's Don Giovanni. Twenty of Hiller's syllables end in consonants; only four of Mozart's. Mozart's melody has four articulations, Hiller's two; the sing-song effect of Hiller's melody has no counterpart in Mozart's.

A comparison of the music for the Italian and German texts in Hiller's Musikalisch-zierlichen Gesange, 1780, demonstrates the different techniques. The German texts are in a simpler syllabic style than the florid settings of the Italian; only the final aria in German, illustrating arbitrary ornamentation, incorporates Italian melisma upon convenient syllables.[42]

Application of the Learned Style

Türk's characterization of the German style as being carefully worked out indicates the direction German composers took in adapting foreign styles. A long-standing tradition of composition in the strict and learned styles, from the chorales and keyboard preludes and fugues of the 17th and early 18th centuries, conditioned German versions of French and Italian music. J. S. Bach's A minor Concerto for Four Harpsichords, BWV 1056, 1730-1733, paraphrases the B minor Concerto for Four Violins by Vivaldi, Op. 3, No. 10, circa 1715. Vivaldi's figuration is simple, clear, transparent, and symmetrical — a minimum texture that relies upon sheer momentum to carry its meaning. Bach adds luxuriant elaboration — complex arpeggio figures, unexpected tiratas, trills — and he inserts additional motives. Not only does the texture become richer, but the regular pulse of Vivaldi is often complicated by counterrhythms in Bach, where the additional figures themselves are Italianate.

The bourrée dance tune in Ex. 20-10 would ordinarily be set with a punctuating bass and unobtrusive inner voices. Haydn, however, creates a complex texture, using imitations, countertime, and a quick harmonic rhythm to produce an effect of compression and greater substance.

Ex. 20-10. *Complex setting of a dance tune.* Haydn, Quartet in B♭ major, Op. 76, No. 4, 1797, finale.

Fantasia

While elements of fantasia appeared in all the international styles, the Germans seemed to be drawn to it more strongly than others. The fantasia element was present in the fantasias, preludes, and toccatas that preceded fugues; it was represented in separate compositions entitled *Fantasia*; it also broke into fugues themselves and into concertos and sonatas, and it became assimilated with regular period structure to create the extended periods without which the larger forms of the classic style could not have evolved. The purest examples of this style are found in the keyboard works of C. P. E. Bach, but the element is strong in the music of Haydn, Mozart, and Beethoven. Mozart was criticized for his "luxuriant fantasy" and his "bizarreries" in *AMZ*, 1801.[43] Haydn and Beethoven were also censured for similar qualities, which the late 18th century associated with the term *baroque*, as described by Koch, 1802:

> *Baroque.* One uses this term to describe a work which has many difficult intervals, tangled harmony, and is overloaded with many dissonances and unusual modulations.[44]

This description would fit the opening of Mozart's E♭ major Quartet, K. 428, 1783, as well as many of Beethoven's works.

Sentiment and Simplicity

If the great works of the classic style represent the complex, speculative aspect of German musical style, the growing literature of social music takes the opposite direction. Early 18th-century German songs, as in the collection *Sperontes Singende Muse an der Pleisse,* Leipzig, 1736, set didactic, humorous, sentimen-

tal, religious texts to French and Italian music—sarabandes, minuets, polonaises, marches, murkies, arias, etc. In the late 18th century a characteristic
German flavor—simple tunes, ingratiating and regular in structure, syllabic in
setting—emerged in the songs of the Berlin composers Reichardt, Schulz, and
Hiller. (See Exs. 10-4, 10-7, 10-8, 10-15.) The popular flavor, expressing simple
sentiments, is notably present in Mozart's *The Magic Flute*, 1791, in both
Papageno's and Sarastro's music.

The ultimate in simplicity was achieved in Hiller's adaptation of the German
chorale repertory, (see Ex. 10-13). At the same time that Hiller was *simplifying*,
other church musicians were following another fashion—introducing a *galant*
flavor into their music (see Ch. 10). Ex. 20-11 shows the "contamination" of the
chorale with elements from Italian opera. The tune is "Werde munter mein
Gemüthe," the same as quoted in Ex. 10-13, but the settings are very different.
Hiller's setting reinforces the sense of sturdy simplicity associated with the German chorale; Vierling's elaborate ornamentation, his galant turns of phrase,
and his cadences come directly from opera. Koch, 1795, could well have been referring to compositions of this type when he wrote:

> Hopefully we shall be . . . assured that the introductions to church songs
> will not be profaned by preludes that are patched together from dances,
> rondos, and comic opera arias.[45]

Vierling's prelude is a cavatina *en rondeau* in moderate minuet time. It has a
striking similarity to Leporello's "Nella bionda" ("With fair ones") from *Don Giovanni*, Act I.

Ex. 20-11. *Italianate elements in the chorale.* Vierling, "Werde munter
mein Gemüthe" ("Be cheerful my soul"), 1789.

Germans as Observers

As the Germans imported and adapted other styles, they became sharp observers of the international music scene; they described, criticized, and taught the international styles. This was especially true of north Germany, where important trends in criticism and pedagogy were developed through a great number of theoretical and critical publications. Hamburg, Dresden, Leipzig, Berlin — the names of these cities and of towns nearby appear frequently upon the title pages of didactic and critical works. The active commerce of north Germany, a heritage of the Hanseatic League, encouraged musical trade. A composer like Telemann reflected the business-like attitude of his milieu, producing enormous quantities of music, all useful and all made from the same general kind of raw material, as if his works were musical transactions rather than compositions. Being distant from the wellsprings of 18th-century style, the Germans had a broader perspective on the international scene. In their music they coordinated and synthesized; in their writings they clarified and summarized what was essentially a Franco-Italian galant style.

REGIONAL STYLES

While Italian, French, and German music occupied a central position in the classic era, regional styles contributed much in the field of popular and folk music. Songs and dances of many nations were published in various arrangements and sometimes furnished topics for the concert and theater music of the time. Beethoven's settings of songs of the British Isles — England, Wales, Scotland, Ireland — are elaborate arrangements with independent instrumental accompaniments. Rousseau quotes examples of Canadian and Persian dances.[46] William Crotch, in vol. I of his *Specimens*, 1807, compiled a large collection of national airs, among which are Arabian, North American, Chinese, Danish, East Indian, Greek, Hottentot, Hungarian, Jewish, Moorish, Norwegian, Polish, Persian, Russian, Spanish, Slavonian, and Turkish songs and dances, in addition to those of the British Isles. Crotch precedes this collection with an extended account of his sources and with some critical comment on many of the pieces.

Most of the dances in vogue during the 18th century had specific local color or origin. Between these and the great styles and genres there was a lively interchange; characteristic local and exotic music was incorporated into theater and chamber music; in turn, popular music took much of its repertory from the melodies of art music.

A counterpart to the interest in local and exotic musical styles was the interest in music of the ancients — part of the general growth of archeological science that characterized western culture during the 18th century. In their histories Burney, Hawkins, and La Borde give considerable space to Greek, Roman, and Biblical music — principally information gleaned from traditional sources. Koch's *Lexikon* has many articles dealing with music of the ancients, their instruments, their modes, and their legends. Then, as now, there was little or no music to examine. In the mainstream of 18th-century music, the ancients furnished elements for operatic plots, not musical topics.

MUSICAL CENTERS

The leading musical centers in later 18th-century Europe are listed below, with comments on their special features and the names of some of the principal composers who resided there. Above all, it must be remembered that Italian opera was the chief item in the musical repertory of the private and public theaters of these centers, as well as dozens of lesser musical establishments throughout Europe.

Paris.   The leading musical center of Europe; vigorous publication activity. After the Revolution a grandiose operatic style evolved, featuring a large and colorful orchestra, massive effects, and melodramatic plots.

Cherubini, 1788–1842

Gluck, visits in 1764, 1773, 1774, 1776, 1778–1779

Gossec, 1751–1829

Grétry, 1768–1813

Le Seuer, 1784–1837

Méhul, 1778–1817

Monsigny, 1754–1817

Philidor, 1756–1795[?]

Piccini, 1776–1800

Sacchini, 1772–1782

Salieri, 1784, 1786

Viotti, 1782–1791

Vienna.   The center of the classic style in the last years of the century, principally because the leading composers were resident there. Before that time, Vienna had a strong orientation to Italian music, with conservative tendencies in church music.

Beethoven, 1787, 1792–1827

Cimarosa, 1792

Gluck, 1754–1787, interrupted by short visits to Paris and other centers

Haydn, 1790–1809

Mozart, 1781–1791

Salieri, 1766–1784, 1788–1818

London.   Principally a major importer of continental musicians, with a strong preference for Italian style. Much publication of music, fine orchestras.

Abel, 1759–1787

J. C. Bach, 1762–1782

Clementi, 1782–1802, 1810–1832

Haydn, visits in 1791–1792, 1794–1795

Sacchini, 1772–1782

Mannheim.   A leading center for the new orchestral style; one of the finest orchestras in Europe, featuring novel effects—crescendo and decrescendo, tutti sound, prominence of wind scoring, thanks to excellent wind players.

Cannabich, 1758–1798[?]

Filtz, 1754–1760

Holzbauer, 1753–1783

Richter, 1747–1769

Johann Stamitz, 1745–1757

Karl Stamitz, 1762–1770

Berlin.   Under the sponsorship of Frederick the Great, himself a fine flautist and composer, Berlin became an important north German music center, with a strong leaning toward French taste in chamber music. In the last years of the century, Berlin was a leading song school.

C. P. E. Bach, 1738–1767

Boccherini, 1786–1797

K. H. Graun, 1740–1759

Kirnberger, 1751–1783

Marpurg, 175[?]–1795

Quantz, 1740–1773

Reichardt, 1775–1785, 1786–1797

Other important centers included:

Dresden, where Hasse was court composer from 1739 to 1760

Stuttgart, where Jommelli resided from 1753 to 1769

Madrid, where Boccherini lived from 1769 to 1786

St. Petersburg, visited by Cimarosa, Paisiello, Traetta, Manfredini, Galuppi, and Karl Stamitz

Venice, where Galuppi was resident to 1785, interrupted by visits elsewhere

Milan, where Sammartini resided permanently to 1775

Bologna, where Martini resided permanently to 1784

A factor that probably contributed to the wide dissemination of the Italian style throughout Europe was the short term of residence available in the great Italian opera centers, Venice and Naples. Once trained in their national style, Italian composers sought their fortunes in northern and western Europe, thus spreading the style that became the basis of the international musical language of the 18th century.

NOTES

1. Türk, *Klavierschule*, pp. 404-405.
2. Quoted in Hawkins, *History*, p. 834.
3. Rousseau, *Dictionnaire*, pp. 179, 227, 345, 385; Rousseau, *Lettre*, in Strunk, *Source Readings*, p. 636ff.
4. Cramer, *Magazin*, 1783, p. 347.
5. Daube, *Melodie*, p. 57.
6. Rousseau, *Dictionnaire*, p. 3.
7. Rousseau, *Lettre*, in Strunk, *Source Readings*, p. 650.
8. Tartini, *Traité des Agrémens*; Hiller, *Musikalisch-zierlichen Gesange*; Martini, *Melopée*; Zuccari, *The True Method of Playing an Adagio*; Türk, *Klaverschule*; Wolf, *Unterricht*; Quantz, *Versuch*; etc.
9. Kirnberger, *Kunst*, II, pt. 1, p. 152.
10. Quoted in Cramer, *Magazin*, 1783, pp. 434-435.
11. Riepel, *Grundregeln*, p. 58.
12. Rousseau, *Lettre*, in Strunk, *Source Readings*, p. 647.
13. Ibid., p. 645.
14. Ibid., p. 641; see also p. 338 of the present work.
15. Burney, *History*, p. 845.
16. Ibid. p. 859.
17. Rousseau, *Lettre*, in Strunk, *Source Readings*, p. 643.
18. Schubart, *Ideen*, p. 53.
19. Burney, *History*, p. 789; see also Le Pileur d'Apligny, *Traité*, p. 143ff.
20. Koch, *Lexikon*, p. 360.
21. Cramer, *Magazin*, p. 378.
22. Quatremère de Quincy, *Dissertation*, p. 7.
23. Le Pileur d'Apligny, *Traité*, p. 141ff.
24. *AMZ*, 1801, pp. 243-244.
25. Ibid., 1800, p. 242.
26. Le Pileur d'Apligny, *Traité*, pp. 139-140.
27. Rousseau, *Lettre*, in Strunk, *Source Readings*, p. 652.
28. Walther, *Lexikon*, pp. 28, 110, 188, 274, 281, 398, 542.
29. Rousseau, *Dictionnaire*, p. 39.
30. Quatremère de Quincy, *Dissertation*, p. 38.
31. Algarotti, *Saggio*, in Strunk, *Source Readings*, p. 660.
32. Burney, *History*, p. 976.
33. Hiller, *Nachrichten*, I, p. 255.
34. Koch, *Lexikon*, p. 904ff.
35. Strunk, *Source Readings*, pp. 471-531, 619-683, quotes a number of 18th-century comments on this topic.
36. Bukofzer, *Music in the Baroque Era*, p. 258.
37. Momigny, *Cours complet*, pp. 17-18.

38. Schubart, *Ideen*, p. 266.
39. Quantz, *Versuch*, in Strunk, *Source Readings*, p. 595.
40. Ibid., p. 596.
41. Hiller, *Nachrichten*, I, p. 254.
42. Hiller, *Musikalisch-zierlichen Gesange*, passim.
43. *AMZ*, 1801, pp. 392, 393.
44. Koch, *Lexikon*, p. 214.
45. Koch, *Journal*, p. 142.
46. Rousseau, *Dictionnaire*, examples.

21 High and Low Styles; Serious and Comic

All the stylistic distinctions thus far discussed—local, free versus strict, national, and personal—were geared to what was probably the most profound stylistic opposition—the high versus the low. Dignity of musical style reflected the consciousness of *status* in 18th-century life, the fundamental principle in a social order organized according to clergy, nobility, bourgeois, and peasant and their internal rankings.

Scheibe's description of the high, middle, and low styles, 1745, cited on pp. 7–8, remained valid throughout the classic era. Ernst Gerber, in *AMZ*, 1799, rejected other classifications in favor of this distinction:

> To clarify the idea of style, the best division is: the *high*, the *middle* or *moderate*, and the *low* or *comic*. The high style encompasses all great, exalted, dreadful feelings, and violent passions. The middle style includes softer and milder feelings, such as love, calmness, satisfaction, cheerfulness, and joy, and in the low style we include that which is more popular and obvious than genteel, more trifling and merry than clever, and particularly, everything that pertains to caricature and comedy. Instrumental music, which is an echo of the feelings that vocal music expresses, is also classified accordingly; except that instrumental music, in addition, tries to arouse wonder by means of brilliant passages proper to the virtuoso technique of the instrument.[1]

The opposite ends of the spectrum—high and low—represent the clearest definitions of musical status and the sharpest mutual contrasts, those of the serious and the comic. The middle was flexible and could be oriented to either style.

HIGH STYLE

Expressive and Rhetorical Features

The high style in 18th-century music had its own degrees of dignity. The highest rank was represented by the *alla breve*, the descendant of plainsong, itself the musical counterpart of a liturgical text. *Alla breve* was the setting for the most serious, grave sentiments; it is illustrated in *stile famigliare* in Ex. 10-3, in a chorale in Ex. 10-13, in motet style in Ex. 10-14. Ex. 21-2 below illustrates a fugal application of the *alla breve*. The cited examples express respectively a statement of faith, a prayer for the lifting of the spirit, a cry for pity, and a moral message.

Figured music was incorporated into the high style; this represents the influence of opera and chamber music. The great passions of drama—fear, pride,

364

hate, patriotism, anger, noble love, conflicts of love and duty, ambition — were expressed by means of musical topics and procedures associated with the upper classes — military figures, high-style dances, recitative *obligé*, and *arioso*.

A pointed comment on the trend toward figured music was made in Koch's *Journal*, 1795, concerning an oratorio by Paisiello:

> Paisiello has set the *Passion of Jesus Christ* of Metastasio almost entirely in the same way he has composed his operas. A famous composer and critic has characterized this composition very well in the following comment: "I can discover here all the passions, saving that of Jesus Christ."[2]

Ex. 21-1 quotes an excerpt from this work illustrating the operatic flavor — the florid figuration that pictures the restless sea, and the pathetic cries of the fearful passenger. *Strepito* and *cantabile* elements are coordinated here.

Ex. 21-1.   Paisiello, *Passione di Gesu Cristo*, n.d., "Torbido mar."

"Restless sea that rages."

a. Opening solo *(strepito)*. In addition to the sketched parts, there are second violins, viola, bassoon, and horn.

b. Contrasting phrase *(cantabile)*. Oboes and bassoons double the voice, adding parallel thirds below the melody.

"At the cries and prayers of the fearful passenger."

In general, high-style expression called for maintenance of the ruling sentiment, with limited contrast throughout a principal section. The pace is deliberate, even in allegro tempos, the vocal style alternating between portamento and brilliant styles. For classic music, the high style was a heritage from the earlier 18th century, when one of the main objects of this style was to celebrate authority.

Locales of Performance

Church. The principal habitat of the high style was the church, where the gravity and importance of the religious sentiment could be expressed by *alla breve*, fugue, and motet. Still, there was a considerable range of dignity and status, as described in Ch. 10. Allegri's *Miserere* and other works in the *stile antico* were sung by trained soloists and chorus in the great Catholic cathedrals; they represented the highest level of dignity. Mozart's *Coronation* Mass, K. 317, 1779, was clearly marked by elements of entertainment music; it too had a trained ensemble for performance. The chorale was sung in Protestant churches by the congregation, representing middle- and lower-class status but standing at the highest level of dignity for a popular style. The versions of the chorale melody in Exs. 10-13 and 20-11 embody learned, popular, and galant treatments.

Concert and Chamber Music. Until the last quarter of the 18th century, very few chamber and orchestral works would have qualified in the high style. Neither their expressive stances nor the degree to which they incorporated elements of the learned style matched the dignity of the noblest church and theater works. But as concert activity grew, taking over much of the function of theater and church, orchestral and chamber music works achieved greater scope and dignity and drew the attention of critics as major works of the art. Mozart's *Jupiter* Symphony, 1788, his *Symphonie Concertante*, K. 364, 1779, Haydn's London symphonies, 1791-1795, Boccherini's *Sinfonia* in D minor, *La Casa del Diavolo*, 1771—these represent the highest level of orchestral music, comparable in this genre to the great works for church and theater. Classic string quartets, thanks to their careful and imaginative *Ausarbeitung* (Ch. 8), were given the highest rank in dignity: the first movement of Beethoven's F major Quartet, Op. 59, No. 1, 1806, exemplifies this turn-of-the-century view (see Ch. 24).

High style was also proper to the *oratorio*, a concert genre that combined features of church music (chorus, sacred subject matter) with those of opera (recitative, aria, story line). Johann Forkel, quoted in Cramer, 1783, places the oratorio on the highest level of dignity in his comments on types of performance:

> The word *concert* is not intended here to mean the well-known instrumental composition . . . but a group of performing people. . . . When such a group performs publicly, they are called a *Collegium musicum* or a musical academy, as one finds in Italy, France, and occasionally in Germany. They are, in their way, the counterparts of the scientific academies and societies.
>
> When church music stood in its full glory, and theater music had not been degraded, church and theater could rightly have been considered as fitting or suitable for such academies. . . . With the undeniable decline of church and theater music, the concert remains the only means by which taste can be developed and the ideals of music achieved. . . . It is a question now as to what type of music is most important for reaching these goals. . . .
>
> Experience and other reasons prove that vocal music serves this purpose best. The union of poetry and music, touching both mind and heart, is so advantageous that undeniably herein do we have the full power of expression. . . .
>
> . . . it follows therefore that only such compositions, among them especially the oratorios with sacred or moralistic content, deserve the first and most important place in our concerts.[3]

High style in the oratorio was exemplified for later 18th-century listeners by Carl Heinrich Graun's *Der Tod Jesu*, 1755. This work remained in the repertory for many years; Crotch quotes from it in his *Specimens*; years after it was written, Schubart, 1785, expressed his admiration for the work:

> His *Tod Jesu* caused the entire world to gaze in wonder, even though one can say, justifiably, that it has too worldly an aspect. But Graun did this with serious intention; the Angel takes on a pilgrim's manner, in order to speak with those who live in a lowly state—God! who has ever composed a fugue such as "Christ has given us a model. . . ."[4]

Of the 18 numbers in this work, only three move out of the orbit of the home key, E♭ major; all others are in closely related keys, conforming to the harmonic schemes of early 18th-century choral and theater works. There is even distribution in the settings—six chorales, five choruses (two fugal), six solos; all solos and the final chorus are set as *da capo* forms. Some pictorialism is present, but the principal expressive treatment is that of early 18th-century opera—one principal idea carried through an entire number. The fugue mentioned by Schubart exemplifies Graun's treatment of text; the people follow in Christ's footsteps, as the *comes* follows the *dux* in a fugue. Ex. 21-2 quotes the beginning of the fugue; the stepwise descent of the structural line from A to E, the suspensions, the announcement of the subject in the bass contribute to the air of gravity that made this fugue a "model" for Schubart. Oddly enough, this subject has much the same melodic and harmonic outline as the finale of Haydn's A major Quartet, Op. 20, No. 6, 1772, which is in the style of a galant contredanse.

Theater: Gluck and 18th-century operatic style. High style in 18th-century opera supported plots in which heroes, demigods, and gods engaged in grand conflicts of love and duty, the individual against fate, good against evil. These stories provided opportunities for the protagonists to display noble virtues and violent passions, qualities proper to those of high status, and especially flattering to the noble patron of serious opera.

Ex. 21-2.   Graun, *Der Tod Jesu* (*The Death of Jesus*), 1775.

Ex. 21-2, cont'd.

Novello

Early in the century, the protocol of opera reflected the ceremonial formalism of the court. Italian opera had its rigid prescriptions for the distribution of arias, their style, and their degree of brilliance, based upon the relative importance of the various singers. The breadth and magnificence of the great *da capo* aria set not only the affective stance but also the grand scope that established the gravity of the high style. Plots themselves were constructed in a highly formalized manner, adapting Greek and Roman models. French *tragédie lyrique* also had its long-established rules concerning plot, declamation, and distribution of numbers.

Around 1760–1770 a trend toward a more flexible musical drama developed. Jommelli, Traetta, and other Italians abandoned the rule of recitative-aria to some degree. But it was Gluck who created the most convincing changes in serious opera. In the 1780s, a knowledgeable musician would probably single out Gluck as the finest representative of the high or serious style in music.

Gluck arrived on the scene at an opportune time, when both Italian and French opera showed signs of bogging down. Daval, in the epilogue of *La musique en France*, pictures Gluck coming from Bohemia to teach Paris what should be good French taste:

Soon, his operas *Orfeo* and *Iphigenia in Aulis* eclipsed, with their rigid and ungraceful lines, *Castor and Pollux* and *Dardanus*. As the massive colonnade of the Madeleine—of which the first stone was laid in that year 1764— obliterated for the centuries, in the perspective of the Rue Royale, the exquisite, delicate, and spiritual design of the palace of Gabriel.[5]

Feelings ran high, for and against Gluck. The bitterest antagonist was Forkel, who published a lengthy anti-Gluck article in his *Musikalisch-kritische Bibliothek*, 1778-1779. Grétry, in his *Mémoires*, 1797, praised Gluck for his dramatic genius. Burney, 1789, whose taste ran to Italian opera, granted that Gluck's style added something to the French theater:

> . . . the simplifying dramatic Music in Gluck's manner, in favour of the poet, at the expense of the composer and singer, is certainly very rational, where an opera is performed in the language of the country, and the singers have no great abilities to display, as in France; but in England, where we have frequently singers of uncommon talents, and where so small a part of an opera audience understands Italian, by abridging the symphonies, and prohibiting divisions and final cadences, in favour of an unintelligible drama, we should lose more than we should gain.[6]

Notwithstanding the differing views of Gluck's music, which formed part of the notorious Gluck-Piccinni rivalry in Paris, it was Gluck's sense of musical theater that brought his later operas to the fore. Burney recognized this quality:

> Gluck's music is so truly dramatic, that the airs and scenes, which have the greatest effect on the stage, are cold and rude, in a concert. The situation, context, and interest, gradually excited in the audience, give them their force and energy.[7]

To illustrate some features of Gluck's style, excerpts from *Iphigenia in Tauris*, 1779, will be discussed, and some comparisons will be drawn with Piccinni's opera of the same name, produced in 1781.

The plot is essentially the same for both operas. Iphigenia, saved by the goddess Diana from being sacrificed to speed the Greeks to Troy, has been taken to Tauris to become a priestess for the Scythians, led by Thoas. Orestes, Iphigenia's brother, and his friend, Pylades, have come to Tauris to find Iphigenia. They are shipwrecked and captured. One must be sacrificed, and each wishes to stand in place of the other. Orestes is chosen to die and Pylades is sent to Greece by Iphigenia with the message that she is a captive in Tauris. At the moment before the sacrifice, Iphigenia and Orestes recognize each other as sister and brother; the Greeks enter, Thoas is killed, and the goddess Diana appears to reclaim her image from the Scythians and to ordain peace.

Gluck's libretto, by Guillard, is almost twice the length of Piccinni's, by Roland. This greater length arises from the expressive stance, as the characters convey their feelings openly and directly. The text in the Piccinni version retains the conventional *opera seria* stylization, elevated in tone but static and sketchy.

These differences are paralleled in the music. Piccinni begins with a typical *sinfonia* with its busy and noisy simplicity. Gluck's version, unlike other 18th-century operas, sets us *in medias res*; the first music is a calm pastoral, a dance of the priestesses, replacing the conventional overture. Before this dance can complete its usual two-reprise course, it is interrupted, four measures before the cadence, by the storm music that is the principal topic of the opening scene.[8] This extended storm scene, with its brilliant and furious orchestral action, gives the spectator the substance of an overture, incorporated into the drama itself. It forms the background to the prayers of Iphigenia and her sister priestesses. Exs. 21-3 and 21-4 illustrate the opening sections of the two operas.

Gluck set the prayers of Iphigenia and the other priestesses simply, in sharply defined anapest meter, contrasting the long notes of the stressed syllables effectively with the hurly-burly of the orchestra. Gluck here epitomized the French music-text relationship, keeping each in its place, not transferring idioms.

It takes Piccinni some time to reach a peak of dramatic intensity comparable to that which Gluck achieves in the first prayer. Piccinni's storm comes at the end of Act I; Gluck's storm is the opening curtain for the whole opera. Thus Orestes and Pylades have entered Gluck's drama by implication at the very beginning, and their actual appearance, in a climactic scene at the end of Act I, is a counterstatement to the opening mood. In Piccinni's version, Orestes and Pylades appear only at the beginning of Act II, although a continuity is maintained by no change of scene, no intermission between acts, and a carryover of the storm.

The principal subject of Iphigenia's distress, for Piccinni, seems to be her forthcoming marriage to Thoas, which the Scythians celebrate with a wedding ballet. For Gluck, the storm and Iphigenia's dream of her father, recalling her

Ex. 21-3.   Piccinni, *Iphigenia in Tauris,* 1779, overture.

home, rule Act I; the Scythians first appear to honor a blood sacrifice. Exs. 21-5 and 21-6 illustrate the contrast between these two numbers; Piccinni first introduces the Scythians in a ballet with a pompous highly flourished wedding march that rings out the changes on tonic and dominant harmonies; Gluck has them announce their bloodthirsty intentions chorally, with low-pitched texture and deceptive cadences to suggest the dark menace of the scene.

Despite the pathos that rules the mood of Act I, Piccinni, unlike Gluck, does not introduce a strong pathetic accent until he is well into Scene 2, where a recitative of Iphigenia introduces a sustained chord of the diminished seventh. All the music preceding is in a conventional style—brilliant and active for parts I and III of the overture, a deliberate dance for part II, an ornate Italian-style march for Iphigenia's opening arioso, and a French, minuet-like dance for the song of the priestesses.

Another point that distinguishes the two versions is the reference to a momen-

Ex. 21-4.   Gluck, *Iphigenia in Tauris*, 1779.

a. Introduction.

Ex. 21-4, cont'd.

b. Storm music.

Gewitter von ferne
Tempête de loin

Eulenburg No. 917

tary sense of calm felt by Iphigenia following her dream. Piccinni sets this as the principal solo of Act I, comprising first an arioso in which the orchestral phrases themselves would link together as a small two-reprise form, typically Italian in flavor, then an ariette in the French style. Gluck, on the other hand, reads this moment of calm as a brief turn of feeling that highlights the mood of pathos through contrast. Exs. 21-7 and 21-8 give the opening measures of Piccinni's arioso and ariette and Gluck's setting.

Ex. 21-5.   Piccinni, *Iphigenia in Tauris*, Act I, wedding ballet.

The first acts of both these versions carry out the protocol of the *tragédie ly-rique* as huge scene complexes, with many shifts of scene, few arias, relatively short numbers, chorus, and ballet. The comparison of these two opening acts shows Piccinni's version to be attractive and decorative, the work of a gifted practitioner; Gluck's version is a powerfully affecting dramatic action where music and story reinforce each other tightly.

Other telling strokes in Gluck's version include the famous ariette of Orestes, Act III, just before the pursuing Furies confront him. Gluck devised a subtle *contresense*; Orestes sings that peace has come once more to him, but the music belies this. The accompaniment is agitated, suggesting a hidden anxiety; on the word "calme" Orestes sings F♮, a pathetic nuance. The resultant augmented second, F to G♯, hints that the path to peace is rough. Upon the word "coeur" ("heart") the note A is reached, but in this context it is an unstable dominant, not a firm tonic. This ariette serves as a dramatic counterstatement to the words and music of Iphigenia's solo after the storm creating a link between the two characters.

Gluck's melodic style is ideal for the musical theater he creates. It is simple, free from elaborate ornaments, well turned, flexible, with a sense of elevation, a hint of grand manner that commands the respect of the listener. The opening measures typify the melodic style. Arias are short, as a rule, with two-reprise layouts used often. Iphigenia's first aria, "O toi, qui prolongas mes jours" (Oh you, who prolonged my days"), Act I, addressed to the goddess Diana, who saved her from the sacrifice, is *en rondeau* or, if we ascribe Italian influence to it, in a brief *da capo* form in a gavotte rhythm. A broader layout is used in "Je t'implore" ("I

Ex. 21-6. Gluck, *Iphigenia in Tauris*, Act I, chorus of Scythians.

"We needed blood to expiate our crimes; the captives are in irons."

Note. Strings double the voices with accompaniment of triangle and drum, a "Turkish" touch.

Ex. 21-7. Piccinni, *Iphigenia in Tauris*, Act I, Iphigenia's solo.

"But suddenly the sky is without clouds, the sun shines in the sky, calm reigns on the seas."

a. Arioso.

Ex. 21-7, cont'd.

b. Ariette.

"Ah, may I hope that fate is no longer implacable."

Ex. 21-8.   Gluck, *Iphigenia in Tauris*, Act I, Iphigenia's solo following the storm.

"Calm returns, but in the depths of my heart, alas, the storm still lives."

Note the *contresense* (music and text contradicting each other) as the bass remains on an unstable dominant pedal and the resolution is deceptive. Compare this passage to Piccinni's setting in Ex. 21-7, anchored on the tonic.

Ex. 21-9.   Gluck, *Iphigenia in Tauris,* Act II, Orestes.

"Calm returns to my heart."

Eulenburg No. 917

implore you"), Act IV, when Iphigenia implores Diana to save her from having to sacrifice Orestes. It is the most Italianate and most grandiose aria in the opera (see Ex. 21-10). It reaches the dimensions of a sonata form with bipartite melodic layout

A   B   A   B
I   V   V   I

but the most striking feature, not entirely assimilated into the rest of the opera, is the grand cadential peroration at the end of both principal sections. Mozart and his Italian contemporaries rely heavily upon this kind of cadential rhetoric, but it is not a sound we generally associate with Gluck.

Iphigenia's aria in Act II "Ô malheureuse Iphigénie" (see Ex. 21-11) has one of the most poignantly beautiful melodies in all opera; its setting, luminous and transparent, with oboes, bassoons, horns, and strings, provides a gently pulsating background to the simple yet exquisite tune that floats above. The melody itself scans the poetry syllabically, in a constant stream of iambs and anapests with some slight elaboration. At the end Gluck, in a masterful dramatic stroke, brings in the priestesses with the words "Mêlons nos cris plaintifs" ("Let us join our plaintive cries") to sing first in unison with Iphigenia, then in three-part har-

Ex. 21-10.   Gluck, *Iphigenia in Tauris*, Act IV, "Je t'implore."

"I obey, and my heart is prey to remorse."

Ex. 21-10, cont'd.

Eulenburg No. 917

mony with her, and finally to take over the last measures of the number by themselves. He thus adds a dimension of dramatic depth to a musical picture that seemed already perfect.

Gluck was at his best in the late operas, the *reform* works. He synthesized elements from his Italian apprenticeship—*cantilena*, clarity of scoring, neatness of phrase structure—with the French procedure for which he had personal affinity —ballet, chorus, flow of action, fidelity to poetic scansion, and brevity in set forms. He fused them with his sense of theater, his genius for doing the right thing at the right time. His late works display the full scope of his personal style, with its simple, powerful, and direct manner, now and then elegant but always elevated, in the high style.

In his Italian operas and his instrumental music he falls short, lacking the vivacity and ease of invention of the best Italian composers of his generation— Jommelli, Traetta, Piccinni, Paisiello—and the discursive skills of Haydn and Mozart. Very rarely do we find the large-scale blocking out of key areas, the tug-and-pull of part-writing, and the sprung scansions that build the powerful periodicity of the mature classic style.

Boccherini, in his Sinfonia in D minor, *La Casa del Diavolo*, 1771, paraphased Gluck's "Dance of the Furies," used both in *Don Juan*, 1761, and *Orphée*, 1774. A comparison shows Gluck's orientation to theatrical, mimetic effects and Boccherini's characteristic instrumental, discursive treatment.

Gluck's piece is organized as a mid-18th-century fantasia, with the following key scheme: D minor, A minor, E minor, D minor, A minor, D minor. His harmonic directions are not predictable. Boccherini's D minor–F major–X–D minor, a key-area layout, has much clearer shape and stronger rhetorical thrust. Both composers link short figures into two- and four-measure phrases, in a mosaic fashion, but Boccherini builds greater momentum by a clearer symmetry of phrases and a more direct trajectory to points of arrival. The first two measures of each version set their respective directions (see Ex. 21-12). Gluck confirms the 3/4 meter by restating the motive of m. 1 on V in m. 2. Boccherini gathers both

Ex. 21-11.   Gluck, *Iphigenia in Tauris*, Act II, "Ô malheureuse Iphigénie."

a. Iphigenia alone.

"Oh, unhappy Iphigenia, your family is destroyed."

b. Entrance of the priestesses.

Iphigenia: "I have lost my parents."
Priestesses: "Let us join our plaintive cries."

Ex. 21-11, cont'd.

c. Final measures, priestesses alone.

"We have lost everything, no hope remains for us!"

measures into a quasi 6/4 measure (see Ch. 5) by opposing the shapes of his first two figures, setting up a broader and more swinging quality of movement. Thus Gluck's trajectory is shorter than Boccherini's, and he will use this short thrust to change direction abruptly.

Gluck reaches his first *forte* in m. 11 rather suddenly. Boccherini holds back his first *forte* until m. 17, building a strong anticipation for this moment *rhythmically* by maintaining symmetry, *harmonically* by a strong preparation for V. Boccherini's *forte* "rides" on V, while Gluck's "sits" on I.

Gluck's music has the intensity and fury of impact and gesture, while Boccherini's has the excitement of momentum and the elegance of well-shaped phrases. This type of discursiveness, rare in Gluck's mature works, still needs the ballet to fulfill its purpose, and demonstrates why Gluck was not essentially an instrumental sonata or symphony composer.

Ex. 21-12.   Boccherini, Sinfonia in D minor, *La Casa del Diavolo,* 1771, finale, and Gluck, *Don Juan,* 1761, "Dance of the Furies."

These two works represent a facet of the 18th-century high style as they awake feelings of terror and awe by invoking the supernatural and diabolic with appropriate *concitato* figures and plentiful diminished sevenths. Gluck's serious intentions are clear; Boccherini, we might suspect, may have had a parodistic purpose, to demonstrate how Gluck's figures could have been used more felicitously from his point of view; thus his version would not rank as high in style as Gluck's dance.

LOW STYLE; COMEDY

Expressive and Rhetorical Features

High style was the principal point of expressive focus in early 18th-century *opera seria* and church music. The middle, gentler styles emulated the grander manner in polish and elegance. Low style was set apart. It appeared in the intermezzi separating the acts of serious opera, in its own realm of popular theater, or as occasional parodies and grotesqueries ("La vielle" from Telemann's E♭ major *Lyra Suite*, n.d.; pictorial numbers from Vivaldi's *Le Stagione*, circa 1725).

Reflecting political, economic, and social changes in the 18th century, the wheel of musical fashion turned. The middle and low styles were increasingly cultivated, signifying a marked shift toward comedy. This shift has considerable documentation. William Smith, in *The Italian Opera and Ballet in London* lists twice the number of comic operas as tragic presented in London in the last years of the 18th century. Triest, in *AMZ*, 1801, says that "from the North and East Seas, and France's ancient borders to New East Prussia . . . hardly a fair-sized town does not have a wandering comic troupe some weeks of the year."[9] Dictionaries and periodicals begin to devote special articles to the comic in music. Sulzer, 1774–1779, ranks levels of comedy:

> The *low comic* is actually the farcical, which is humorous because of its absurdity. Material, which, by means of its fine wit, and through actions and customs of the genteel world, as is the custom with people of good breeding, and which the Romans call *urbanity*, pleases and delights, belongs to the *middle comedy*. The *high comic* is that comedy which approaches the tragedy in content and mood, and where powerful and serious passions come into play.[10]

Note that this comment ranks comedy from the lowermost level upward, signifying an awareness of the polarity of the low versus the high. This description covers all that does not pertain specifically to the high and tragic styles; thus the greater part of the music discussed in this book would be regarded as having some comic content, since it makes use of the low and middle styles. This mixture, although it pleased the taste of late 18th-century audiences, was deplored by some; Schubart, 1785, has the following to say about Haydn:

> His style is fiery, full, and noble . . . only that sometimes he scatters ornamentations through his masses, out of an inclination to the Austrian taste . . . this tinsel often seems like the spotted costume of a harlequin, and profanes the pathos of the church style. His fugues are worked out with ardor and thoroughness.[11]

Burney, 1789, recognized this strain in Haydn but felt it to be a diversion, a bit of relief from his serious music.[12]

One of the most thorough discussions of comic music, by Daniel Weber, appeared in *AMZ*, 1800.[13] Some of his criteria are used in the following survey of the comic element in classic music. Weber classified comedy as the "non-tragic category." He lists the following types: mimicry, wit, parody, and artful imitations of musical bungling.

Mimicry.   Mimicry, the most obvious type of musical humor, imitates sounds and motions in a precise and localized type of word-painting. The little natural history from Haydn's *Creation*, 1798, part II, pictures the roar of the lion, the leap of the tiger, the gallop of the stag, etc. Beethoven mimicked bird songs in the second movement of his *Pastoral* Symphony, 1807-1808. While relatively few examples of mimicry occur in the greater works of the classic style, the tradition had a long life in western music, reaching back to the descriptive figures of the 14th-century *caccia*.

Wit.   Wit represents the opposite pole from mimicry in respect to subtlety. Weber defines wit in music as follows:

> Just as poetic and descriptive wit depends upon the tasteful connection of one clever idea to another similar idea, so does musical wit depend as well upon the unexpected similarity [perhaps a better word would have been "compatibility"] between two musical ideas and their tasteful and proper connection as delivered by means of surprise. Among our native composers we have many that possess the gift of musical wit, so that it is unnecessary to look for foreign examples. Who would not include, in addition to the above-mentioned Dittersdorf and Mozart, father Haydn, Schubart, Knecht, Rossetti, and Schmittbaur, Naumann and Schuster? It is a pity that musical wit that is present in pure instrumental music almost always requires a commentary, which only the composer himself can provide, and thereby, its object, to surprise and delight, is often not fully attained. When there is a text, everyone has such a commentary without further explanation, and one that is generally clear.[14]

Related to this point is the comment in Sulzer, 1771-1774, on music's effect in the comic theater:

> We must grant that music, which, by its very nature, appears only to be useful for joyful or heart-stirring expression, is most apt in underscoring farce and sharpening the comic, which neither speech, dance, nor pantomime itself can do so well. No comedy, no ballet arouses such laughter as we hear so often in the intermezzo and the operetta.[15]

Both Weber and Sulzer make striking comments on the interaction of music and text, recognizing the potential for wit that lies in music. When Weber refers to the wittiness that is often not recognized in instrumental music, he is describing a condition that is just as valid today as it was in his time. Much of the instrumental music of the classic masters is saturated with comic rhetoric which may be vaguely sensed but is not often fully savored. Haydn's reputation along these lines has already been mentioned; Ex. 21-13 quotes an example of musical wit from Mozart. The first eight measures constitute a period of two four-measure phrases, but the internal arrangement is highly irregular. Each pair of measures has its own figure, highly-contrasted with each of the others. They are forced into close juxtaposition while the harmony is wrenched here and there in a peremptory manner. The fanfare motive begins brightly and simply, but it is suddenly interrupted by the heavy-footed cadential figures on E, which in turn are thrust aside by the fanciful roulade of the first violin, itself pulled up short by the hammer strokes of the cadence. Following this brief but violent mêlée, a graceful singing figure quiets the action and restores innocence for a moment.

Ex. 21-13.   Mozart, Quintet in D major, K. 593, 1790, 1st movt.

Eulenburg No. 50

This rapid succession of military, peasant, brilliant, brusque, and singing manners must have suggested to Mozart's listeners that he was imitating an episode from the *commedia dell'arte*, with its slapstick effects, its darting here and there, and its play of unexpected events. Behind these gestures lies another vein of wit, in which Mozart gives the upbeats of each phrase a different nuance. The first upbeat is *routine*, typical of a bourrée-march; the second forces a *sudden shift* of stress, tempo rubato; the third momentarily *suspends the regular meter*, beginning a phrase that is *nine quarter-notes* in length. The fourth phrase ends with the first violin chord suspended in midair as an *afterbeat*. Then mm. 9-12 sit squarely on the downbeat. The harmony, for all its twists and turns, provides the thread that holds these twelve measures tightly in rein. In Ex. 21-14 note the frequency of V-I progressions in this passage, emphasizing the peremptory rhetoric.

Ex. 21-14.   Mozart, Quintet in D major, K. 593, 1790, 1st movt. Structural line of Allegro, mm. 1-12.

Parody.   According to Weber, parody hardly needs an explanation. He mentions that Hiller sets a comic aria in an old-fashioned style with long passages, sing-song manner, etc., to achieve a masterful humorous effect; this exemplifies the notion of parody—placing a serious topic in a more or less ridiculous light.[16] A parodistic aria from *Il Maestro di Musica*, "Le virtuosi," attributed to Pergolesi, places extravagant versions of figures from the arsenal of the virtuoso in comic juxtaposition.[17] These include "note fermate" (sustained tones), "fulminate" (lightning strokes, i.e., brilliant runs), "trilli" (trills), and "cadenze" (cadenzas). The quick contrasts of highly differentiated figures in this early 18th-century piece represent the type of melodic rhetoric later cultivated by Haydn, Mozart, and their contemporaries. Parody could also be quite subtle, as in the duet between Susanna and Marcellina in Act I of Mozart's *Marriage of Figaro*, 1785-1786; the exaggerated politeness that masks the hostility of these two women is set to a courtly bourrée rhythm, very suave with a hint of the march.

Artful Imitations of Musical Bungling.   This is the last category mentioned by Weber, itself a type of parody. Actually, it is the reverse of parody, in that parody reduces the serious, while this raises the clumsy to an artistic level. Mozart's *Ein musikalischer Spass*, K. 522, 1787, is the most celebrated example of this technique. Apart from its obvious "bloopers"— the ending in five different keys, the whole-tone scale in the cadenza of the third movement, and the chromatic parallel thirds that slip "out of gear" in the minuet—this work has an elegant

gaucherie, in which galant figures and textures are juxtaposed in a totally inconsequential way.

In addition to Weber's categories, comic elements in classic music might include (1) the sentimental manner, (2) the extraordinary, (3) mechanical elements.

The Sentimental Manner. The sentimental manner, referred to above
(p. 357), was a prominent strain in comic opera, songs, and salon pieces, and
sometimes found its way into important works. It must have been quite pervasive, since it drew the fire of a number of critics. Koch, 1795, refers to the artists
and amateurs of musical fashion who reject fugal writing as dry and tasteless
pedantry of humorless composers, who prefer the oversweet melodies of the current vogue, and whose musical digestion is so spoiled by these sweets that they
cannot stomach the stronger musical fare.[18] He also says that modern composers
prefer the lighter sentiments—playfulness, tenderness—to the deeper feelings.[19]
A comment on a symphony of Josef Kraus, *AMZ*, 1798,[20] warns that those who
prefer stylish, sweet, and ear-tickling effects will find little to please them in this
work. William Jackson, 1791, complained that "the Airs we have been lately
used to hear in the middle and last Movements of Symphonies, are, for the most
part, *childish*; and, where they are not so, they are vulgar. . . ."[21] (See also
pp. 27 and 173.)

Ex. 21-15 illustrates a typical sentimental vein in late 18th-century music.
Note the simplicity of the inner strophic layout, both phrases of the text set to
the same tune, reinforcing the sing-song repetitions of the principal figure; the
somewhat stilted quality of the gavotte rhythm; the "back to nature" sentimentality of the text, in which the words are carefully chosen to minimize the harsh-
ness of German consonants; and finally, the hint of yodel in the melody. Bastienne's song "Mein liebster Freund" from Mozart's *Bastien und Bastienne*, K.
50, 1768, also expresses a sweetly sentimental mood, appropriate to the more
sober moments in comic opera.

Ex. 21-15.   Hiller, "Die Jagd" ("The Hunt"), 1776.

"Roses and jasmine are beautiful in spring when, untouched, they are still
blossoming on the twig, and glistening with dew."

The Extraordinary.   This refers to bizarre and exotic topics as well as to special feats of brilliance and dexterity in performance. Turkish and oriental effects, magic, and colorful pictorialism such as battle scenes had the carnival touch that links the extraordinary with the comic, a musicodramatic "hocus-pocus" encouraged by late 18th-century audiences. In Mozart's *The Magic Flute*, 1791, the comic aspect of the extraordinary is represented by the bird pair, Papageno and Papagena, while its serious aspect is represented by the Queen of the Night and Sarastro.

Mechanical Elements.   The 18th-century preoccupation with clockworks as toys and decorations was manifested in music by mechanical musical instruments of many ingenious types, by music written for these instruments, and by imitations of clockwork effects in music for standard instruments.

As a toy or diversion, a mechanical musical instrument serves a need for play; hence it has some comic meaning. Clockwork instruments themselves are parodistic, operating in rather limited registers with tones that lack a sense of human presence, however pretty they may sound. The second movement of Haydn's *Clock* Symphony, 1794, imitates the tick-tock of a timepiece, a background for a wealth of material—florid melody, changing textures, and, in the middle section, a powerful Storm and Stress fantasia. The high register and mechanically regular accompaniment in the first four measures of Mozart's C major Sonata, K. 545, 1788, can easily be heard as imitating a musical clock playing an aria. but in Ex. 21-16, while the clockwise effect is unmistakable, the wheels appear to have a highly eccentric motion, at times running completely wild.

Such effects must have appealed strongly to Beethoven. They appear often in his music, throughout his entire oeuvre: A major Quartet, Op. 18, No. 5, 1800,

Ex. 21-16.   Beethoven, Quartet in B♭ major, Op. 130, 1825-1826, 3rd movt.

Ex. 21-16, cont'd.

Eulenburg No. 9

variation 5 of the third movement; F major Quartet, Op. 59, No. 1, 1806, second movement; Symphony No. 8, Op. 93, 1812, second movement; F major Quartet, Op. 135, 1826, first movement. The hocket texture in these examples can be managed only when different instruments located at different points in space work back and forth, to suggest a living clockwork mechanism. Therefore this texture does not appear notably in Beethoven's keyboard music. While its manner often hints at humor, it was turned to a deeply pathetic statement in the final measures of the *Eroica* Symphony, 1803, where the broken line of rhetoric suggests the final halting steps of the dead march, the faltering heartbeat, the clock of life running down.

COMIC OPERA

The comic theater was the prime mover in the shift toward comedy. Both in subject matter and in techniques of composition, it turned the premises of earlier 18th-century music topsy-turvy. Instead of gods and antique heroes, it portrayed contemporary types—pompous, often hypocritical nobles, sly servants, clever maids, fools, betrayed husbands, dry scholars. In its situations, the underdog won out over authority figures, the servant over the master, the young over the old, the poor over the rich. The heroine of Pergolesi's *La Serva Padrona*, 1733, the maid who became mistress, epitomizes this reversal of status. Many variations were played upon this theme. The heroine of Piccinni's *La Buona Figliola*, 1760, is a baroness, not a servant; that of Gassmann's *La Contesina*, 1770, is a young noblewoman whose betrothed is a commoner. In Mozart's operas, Susanna, Figaro, Zerlina, and Leporello end up in better shape than those above them. King Theodore in Paisiello's opera of that name is a thoroughly ridiculous figure. The principal authority figure in comic opera, a titled or wealthy personage, was often given the basso *buffo* role, easily adapted to caricature.

The plots also have their topsy-turvy. Lightning-quick twists of action, concealed or mistaken identities, double dealings, embarrassment, chagrin—these are the stock-in-trade, taken directly from the *commedia dell'arte*, the ancestor of the comic opera. We also recognize *commedia* types—Pantalon, Harlequin, Columbine, the Doctor, etc.—among the familiar characters in Mozart's comic operas. The following quotation from *AMZ*, 1813, touches upon some of the features of comic opera:

> Concerning comic opera, it appears to open a wide field for both the poet and composer; to the former because it must be easier [in *opera buffa*] for him to discover popular characters to delineate [than in *opera seria*]; to the latter, because he can more easily approach a natural and familiar style [in *opera buffa*]. Nevertheless, it is only recently that this genre has been improved. The characters were all made false and unnatural, because, in every opera, Hollanders, Frenchmen, Spaniards, Germans were introduced in turn wearing masks, as were Truffaldino, Brighella, Pantalon, the Doctor in comedies. According to formula the buffo must wear a large peruke, the mezzo carattere must be the lover of the prima donna. A stupid father, a jealous and betrayed husband, etc. are the points around which the machine of the comic opera turns. Everyone must sing an aria in turn and these arias give place, without the slightest touch of probability, to the finale which ends in the hurly-burly of a battle, an earthquake, or a thunderstorm.[22]

Originally, comic opera was a leaven, an intermezzo to lighten the mood of a serious opera. But it came into its own later in the 18th century, reflecting important social changes. As an autonomous genre it could act as a lens through which the whole world was viewed, and a mask behind which bitter and subversive social comment could be delivered. It was part of the time of "ferment" described as follows by Triest, 1801:

> If one might characterize the last 10 or 20 years of the last century with one word, no better could be found than *ferment*. Virtually all human knowledge and accomplishment has been increasingly involved in this trend . . . formerly, vocal music was dominant, and instrumental music served merely to accompany it, or to imitate it in its pleasing or brilliant qualities. But slowly instrumental music raised itself to a higher level by improving and expanding its techniques. So the ruled one became the ruler, that is, vocal music must accommodate itself to instrumental, and not infrequently is placed in the shadows, where once it shone. Thereby, a struggle of everyone against everyone, as in democracies, developed, which so often charms or bewilders us in our modern operas.[23]

The sense of immediacy in comic opera, the "here and now" ambience, was achieved through a highly volatile musical idiom, of which the following items were typical:

1. A spectrum of affects and topics that ranges from sentimentality at one end to furious effervescence at the other; prevalence of dances, simple songs, mock-military, mock-serious, and rustic styles.

2. Prominence of the bass voice (a rarity in *opera seria*), giving a broader perspective to sonority, sharpening the contrasts of characterization, and introducing a parodistic element when the bass is called upon to leap about melodically with agility.

3. Relatively short phrases, much repetition of figure and phrase giving a bobtailed effect, itself loaded with humor.

4. Quick changes of affect, sharpening the sense of each figure by contrast.

5. Many ensemble numbers, in which we have a tug and pull of comic characters and situations, set up by the features listed in 2, 3 and 4 above.

6. Patter songs, in which a rapid-fire declamation rides upon simple alternations of basic functional harmonies.

7. A transparent, lively, and colorful scoring, often doubling the voice but at other times busy with its own figures.

8. A stock of thoroughly familiar clichés — sighing figures, turns, tremolos, fanfares, pedal points, repeated notes, crescendos, and chains of cadential stereo-types to wind up a number or major section.

9. Relatively short forms — rondo, two-reprise, composite — with some larger key-area numbers, generally in a grander style.

10. Pinpoint word-painting, apt because of the quicksilver play of figure typical of the *buffa* style.

11. Use of coloratura only for extravagant or parodistic effect; in general, the singers of *opera buffa* were less virtuosic than those of *opera seria*.

As long as comedy was presented in good taste, in a style proper to its subject matter, it was considered generally to be a good influence, beneficial to both body and spirit.[24] But to some, there was something very disturbing about the mixtures of the heroic-tragic with the comic that were taking place in the last years of the 18th century. Weber, 1800, comments on this mixture:

> Since the first version of this essay (1792) a hybrid version of the operetta, half heroic, half comic, appears with increasing frequency on the lyric stage. Without condemning or praising this new branch of the lyric theater, I must say that attention must be paid to the clear lines of demarcation, that the heroic character must not descend, nor the comic rise.[25]

The mixture of styles and the crossover from serious to comic is lamented by Koch, 1795, in the following bitter complaint:

> Opera seria . . . is presently banished from the theater because of the general preference for comic opera, and has lost much of its value because of the way that comic opera is composed. So long as the *ariettes* of comic opera retained their own manner, different from the *arias* of opera seria, the comic opera did no harm to the serious. Ever since buffoon ariettes began to take on the broad-scale form of the arias of serious opera, the serious arias began to lose their true value; as soon as the humorous masters the form of the serious, the serious takes on features of the humorous. . . . In general, good sense will reject the style of the comic ariette laid out in the form of the serious aria; because what buffoon can express effectively his humorous ideas with many exlanations and repetitions? The expression of wit is short and apt, and therefore, it is entirely against the nature of the comic ariette to sustain a humorous idea with an elaborate musical statement including frequent repetitions, especially when, in our fashionable comic operas, the humor is so flat that even Hanswurst himself would be ashamed of it.[26]

As is often the case in complaints, we receive a sharper picture of an actual situation than through approval. Koch's remarks tell how much *opera buffa* had taken over musical theater by 1795, and how it had preempted the manner of *opera seria*. We cannot identify the targets of Koch's criticism; hundreds of comic operas were performed in his time. Still, we might wonder whether he had some of Mozart's music in mind, music which displays exactly this intermingling of *seria* and *buffa* elements.

Absorption of *seria* techniques into comic opera indicates that a greater number of fine composers occupied themselves with this genre. The invention, sophistication, high style, and skillful working out required in serious music was being carried over into the comic. The reverse was also true. Comic rhetoric—quick juxtapositions of contrasting ideas, short and lively figures, active interplay of dialogue, light textures, marked articulation, unexpected turns—is found throughout the great instrumental and vocal works of the classic style. Even the monumental first movement of Mozart's *Jupiter* Symphony, 1788, is saturated with the rhetoric that characterizes high comedy—a laughing, not an angry Jupiter.

NOTES

1. *AMZ*, 1799, pp. 295-296.
2. Koch, *Journal*, p. 197.
3. Cramer, *Magazin*, pp. 1065-1070.
4. Schubart, *Ideen*, p. 81.
5. Daval, *La musique*, p. 261.
6. Burney, *History*, pp. 942-943.
7. Ibid., p. 973.
8. Gluck, in his preface to *Alceste*, said that the music should "apprise the spectators of the action to be represented." However, this is the case only in *Iphigenia in Tauris* and *Alceste*.
9. *AMZ*, 1801, p. 373.
10. Sulzer, *Allgemeine Theorie*, pp. 212-213.
11. Schubart, *Ideen*, p. 79.
12. Burney, *History*, pp. 959, 960.
13. *AMZ*, 1800, p. 137ff.
14. Ibid., pp. 141-142.
15. Sulzer, *Allgemeine Theorie*, p. 851.
16. *AMZ*, 1800, p. 142.
17. The aria is reprinted in HAM, II, pp. 225-226.
18. Koch, *Journal*, pp. 95, 96.
19. Ibid., p. 92.
20. *AMZ*, 1798, p. 10.
21. Jackson, *Observations*, p. 19.
22. *AMZ*, 1813, p. 17.
23. Ibid., 1801, p. 369.
24. Sulzer, *Allgemeine Theorie*, p. 851.
25. *AMZ*, 1800, p. 162.
26. Koch, *Journal*, pp. 102-103.

22 Mozart, *Don Giovanni*

During the apogee of the classic era, 1780–1810, it was Mozart who reached his peak earliest, in the 1780s. His personal style, which enabled him to turn every common topic into a fresh statement and to create a strong yet graceful shape in his forms, was perhaps the most decisive factor in synthesizing what we now regard as the mature classic style. With his capacity to coordinate many diverse elements, it was inevitable that opera would offer the richest field for his genius. Among his operas, *Don Giovanni*, 1787, represents the greatest synthesis of all.

The musical and dramatic components of *Don Giovanni* were familiar to Mozart's audience. The styles and forms described above constituted its musical language. The story was known through the dramatizations of Molière, Tirso de Molina, and Goldoni. Gluck and Gazzaniga had composed musical settings. The characters recalled stereotypes from the *opera seria* and the *comedia dell'arte*. Upon this familiar material Mozart and his librettist Da Ponte superimposed refinements, multiple levels of action and meaning that offered something to every segment of their audience.

Compared to the intricacies in *Figaro*, 1786, and the beautiful balance in *Così fan Tutte*, 1790, the plot of *Don Giovanni* hardly progresses between the two decisive confrontations between the Don and the Commandant that frame the story, the first in the opening scene, the second just before the end. The intervening action is a character study of the Don, a life history told in typical situations, almost as flashback, as he engages with the other characters. He is seductive, arrogant, crafty, carousing, a grand host, a gourmet — anything but repentant. Thus, when retribution arrives, his defiance is the logical consequence of his life story. Each incident has a deft turn, contributing to the delineation of the Don's character. The incidents intermingle *seria* and *buffa* elements according to the format of comic opera — short numbers, skillfully contrasted and balanced.

Symmetry distinguishes high-born from low-born characters:

High-born	Low-born
Commandant	Leporello
Donna Anna	Zerlina
Don Ottavio	Masetto

The other two characters, Don Giovanni and Donna Elvira, while noble by birth, depart from the behavior of their class so far as to stand outside it. The Don is a rascal, while Elvira, more than once in the opera is made to look ridiculous, albeit human. Of all the characters, only the Commandant and Masetto retain their conventional *seria* and *buffa* aspects throughout. The others are shaded with nuances that modify their conventional status. We cannot be sure that Anna's hatred for the Don is not colored by a hidden fascination, especially in view of her constant remoteness from Ottavio. Ottavio, a typical heroic tenor, loses much of his manly aspect as he seconds Anna but takes no part in the act of retribution. Even in the lightness of his voice, a tenor, against the four deeper male parts he loses some of the air of authority his role traditionally would have carried. Leporello and Zerlina both have their eyes directed upward, to higher social status. Leporello envies the Don, dreaming of taking his place, while Zerlina is ready to abandon her peasant lover when the Don approaches her.

Some of the broader relationships that organize this opera include Mozart's assignment of values to certain keys. Here he reflects a general 18th-century view that keys could represent affective qualities to color elements of plot and character. Einstein has written at length about Mozart's choice of keys; comments on qualities of keys appear in Koch, 1802, Schubart, published 1806, Kirnberger, 1774–1779, and Galeazzi, 1796.[1] These views reflect a tradition of mean-tone temperment, in which the diatonic scales of major and minor keys vary slightly in the size of their whole and half steps, those closer to C being more "in tune" than the remoter keys.

No intrinsic quality for any key is presumed in the following list, but the association of certain keys with plot situations is so consistent as to suggest that they were part of Mozart's grand plan:

1. *D minor.* We are reminded of the tragic and fateful aspect of the story by D minor. It opens the overture with the *ombra* music; it is the key of the duel, of the revenge duet of Anna and Ottavio; it appears briefly in the "catalogue" aria when Leporello sings of a very young girl (prefiguring Zerlina, who will appear in the next scene); it forms the middle section of Anna's great aria "Or sai" as she recalls the death of her father; it furnishes an episode in the finale of Act I, when the revenge motive is treated afresh; and it is the key of the scene in Act II when Don Giovanni is summoned to hell by the statue of the Commandant.

2. *D major.* If D minor tells of the Don's fate, D major is linked to his worldly aspect—his status, his arrogance, and the brilliance that surrounds him. This key is used as a thread throughout the entire opera, in the Allegro of the overture, in the serenade, and at the beginning of the "supper" scene. While both D major and D minor have strong presence within the opera, the Don himself rarely sings in these keys; others do, as they refer to him—Leporello in the "catalogue" aria, Elvira in "Ah, fuggi," and Anna in "Or sai."

3. *F major.* This is frequently assigned to low-born characters—Leporello in "Notte e giorno" at the start of the opera, Zerlina and Masetto in Act I, and other cases to be described below. The situation creates this association for F major; it does not have the absolute value of the D keys, since it is used once for the minuet in the finale of Act I, as well as for Anna's great aria "Non mi dir" in Act II.

4. *E♭ major.* This is Elvira's principal key, for her entrance, "Ah, chi mi dice mai," her "Mi tradi," Act II, and the sextet, "Sola, sola," which she begins and in which she is one of the focal characters.

5. *A major.* Two numbers are set in A major, one in each act, both involving amorous persuasion. "Là ci darem," Act I, couples the Don and Zerlina, while "Ah taci," Act II, involves Elvira, the Don, and Leporello. The freshness of this

key and the placement of the two numbers creates a long-range factor of harmonic recall.

6. *Bb major*. This key appears in situations involving high-born characters, singly or in ensemble—the struggle between Anna and the Don, the quartet, "Non ti fidar," the "champagne" aria, the trio "Protegga," from Act I; Ottavio's "Il mio tesoro" and Elvira's plea to the Don, "L'ultima prova," Act II.

7. *C major*. This key, often used in 18th-century music for brilliant and gala topics, rules the finale of Act I. Its bright effect, thanks to the purity of its intervals, sets the mood of the grand party Don Giovanni is about to give; this effect is set particularly in the two marches included in the finale (see p. 407). The C major hurly-burly at the end of the finale, when the Don is being pursued after the attack on Zerlina, tells us that all the action will come to naught, since the significant keys for the Don are D major and D minor.

8. *E major*. A striking sound, used only once, when Leporello invites the Commandant to supper.

9. *F minor*. This is heard as an episode after the duel, at the death of the Commandant. F minor and E major appear respectively when the Commandant leaves the scene and when he reappears; their distance from C and hence their strangeness of sound match the horror of both situations.

10. *Bb minor*. Finally, at the return of the Commandant in Act II, Mozart creates a harmonic climate heretofore unexperienced in the opera except for the introduction to the overture. The form is key-area—d-a, X-d; the style is *ombra*-fantasia. The A minor sound is new to our ears, but the most striking sound is that of Bb minor in the X section. Mozart hovers about this key for eleven measures without making a formal cadence. This passage occurs when Don Giovanni sets his defiance to the Commandant; the remote minor hints at the consequences of this desperate bravado.

At three points in the opera Mozart assigns a special meaning to a shift of key from D major or D minor to F major. These changes take place when the focus of attention shifts from Don Giovanni to Leporello; they occur at the end of the overture and in the finales of both Acts I and II.

Four scene complexes frame the action of the opera. The first and last, in D minor, are critical in the plot structure, setting the plot lines and accomplishing the dénouement. The second and third scene complexes, the finale of Act I and the sextet in Act II, represent blind alleys, since in both cases it is Leporello, not the Don, who becomes the object of pursuit and capture. Hence these are in off-center keys, C major and Eb major respectively.

The episodic nature of the plot, the symmetry of the character types, and the wide range of status they represent provide many opportunities for the play of figure and topic, from the most profoundly serious—*ombra* and pathetic—to the carefree and comic—galant and *buffa*. Mozart is at his best in managing these kaleidoscopic changes, often in startling juxtaposition; his sense of timing and his deftness in linking contrasts, as well as his inventiveness in texture and figure, carry us swiftly and surely through these complex shifts. Most numbers are quite short; there are no full *da capo* arias; two-reprise forms of various lengths and composite numbers represent the principal structural layouts. The full key-area plan with X appears four times—in the overture, in the revenge duet, in "Ah taci," and the end of the "supper" scene. In the shorter numbers, dance elements are prominent, offering a strong mimetic color.

Change of identity—an age-old motive in comedy, embodied either in the servant become master or the masks—acquires a greater depth of meaning in the interplay of Don Giovanni and Leporello. Leporello yearns for the life style of the Don, but he becomes his surrogate only when it is to the Don's advantage— before and during the "catalogue" aria, when he is blamed for what the Don has done, finale of Act I; and to replace the Don in the wooing of Elvira, Act II, while the Don seeks fresh conquests. In none of these situations does Leporello *enjoy* his shift of role; rather, he is a buffer, standing in the Don's place momentarily to bear the brunt of an unpleasantness. When the Don sings "Metà di voi" in Act II, he assumes Leporello's identity and also appropriates Leporello's key, F major. But Mozart cleverly tiptoes through F major, both with figure and harmony, so that we are hardly aware of the tonic before it moves to V. This number has the Don misdirecting the search party, so that Mozart's disguise by the use of F major suggests the false Leporello.

Mimetic content is strongly marked in every number. The orchestra often carries the leading role in this respect, with sharply etched figuration. Indeed it would appear at times that the function of the text is to explain what is taking place in the orchestra pit, as in the opening of the "catalogue" aria, where Leporello intones while the orchestra has the principal action. Perhaps Triest, 1801, had this type of scene in mind when he complained about the voice having to accommodate itself to instruments (see p. 394). Among the more sharply drawn mimetic configurations are "Notte e giorno," "Ah, chi mi dice mai," "Là ci darem," the "champagne" aria, "Batti, batti," and "Metà di voi."

With its incredibly rich musical content, mimetic nuances, sharply drawn characterizations, and the direction of its plot, *Don Giovanni* can suffer translation without serious loss of impact. But the final touches, the ultimate subtleties, the perfect matching of word and text with their shades of meaning only emerge when the opera is sung in Italian.

Act I, Scene 1.   Scene 1 is arranged like the four movements of a symphony:

First movement: overture—Andante introduction in *ombra* style, suggesting *sinfonia da chiesa*, then Allegro in galant style. D minor and major, sonata form.

Dance movements: Leporello's "Notte e giorno" and the struggle of Anna and the Don, both in small two-reprise forms, both suggesting march topics. F major, Bb major.

Slow movement: duel, death, and recitative *obligé* in fantasia style. D minor, F minor, shifting keys.

Finale: revenge duet, large-scale I–III, X–I in D minor.

The overture and final duet represent the pillars to the form of Scene 1; the cadence in D minor, averted in the overture, is delivered in grand style at the end of the duet, recalling the high style of Handel and Gluck.

The dramatic intensity of Scene 1 parallels its musical shape:

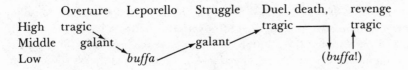

Specific points of topic, style, and structure in this scene include:

1.   The unexpected shift from D major to the V of F major at the end of the overture. This is the first confrontation of D and F, shifting the focus from Don Giovanni to Leporello, and the most arresting, as it engages the listener to prepare for Leporello.

2.   The mimetic touches in Leporello's aria—his foot-march figure, carried a bit too far for properly balanced 18th-century rhetoric (eight times); the cavalier music, a riding march with fanfares when Leporello yearns to be a gentleman; the touch of *agrément* when he speaks of "that dear galant man"; his musical grumble on "no, no, no"; the patter music when he hears someone approaching. Even when Leporello sings about Don Giovanni, he retains his own low style—straight and square—while the orchestra paints the gallant picture with hunting fanfares and French *agréments*. Leporello cannot break out of character even though his dream hovers in the orchestral background.

3.   The acceleration that leads into the struggle; the give-and-take between Anna and the Don, set in a powerful march rhythm; the rising figures to communicate tension, while Leporello sings in typical *buffa* style, maintaining the patter of his opening song. There is a strong ballet-like quality to this struggle, framed by the two-reprise form proper to a march.

4.   The entrance of the Commandant, signaled by a subtle harmonic shift that emphasizes the third of the Bb major chord, a doubling proper to a deceptive resolution in D minor; the notes Bb and F drop out, so that the note D becomes a fulcrum to shift the harmony to D minor, changing the mood from angry struggle to fateful portent. The massive simplicity of the Commandant's portamento declamation, the dark color of his bass voice, and the crackling orchestration build this mood to its climax, the death of the Commandant. A master stroke of vocal color—three deep men's voices—adds to the gravity of the situation. Note the formality of the challenge, during the cadence D-Bb-G-A-D, one of the most powerful in 18th-century music, suggesting that the protocol of punctilious politeness is retained even in moments of mortal combat. The duel itself is frankly pictorial; the thrusts and parries portrayed by rapid scale passages and the diminished seventh at the death blow. As the Commandant dies, the harmonies become chromatic (a typical 18th-century cliché), and melodies descend, with one figure recalled from the struggle. Throughout this entire scene of the duel and death, the *buffa* ensemble texture is maintained, including Leporello's *parlando*. No cadence ends this part, which dissolves into a simple recitative whose humor has a shocking effect coming so close upon the death, a fantastic juxtaposition of tragic and comic. This dip into comedy interrupts the tragic continuity momentarily and hints at the *buffa* events to follow. When Anna returns, she expresses her feelings in a recitative *obligé* that is as high in its

pathos as the preceding was low in its comedy. Exs. 22-1 and 22-2 quote from these recitatives; note the pictorialism in Ex. 22-2.

5.   The duet "Fuggi, crudele" that ends the scene and brings the harmony back to D minor is set as a key-area form with three affects: (1) sorrow and despair, (2) consolation, (3) resolution for revenge. At the beginning the declamation is spasmodic and tentative, reflecting Anna's sorrow; Ottavio's consolation, moving to F major, levels out the movement; the decisive gestures of the X sec-

Ex. 22-1. *Simple recitative: quick buffa parlando, slow chord change.* Mozart, *Don Giovanni,* K. 527, 1787, Act I.

From Ratner, *Music: The Listener's Art.* Copyright 1957, 1966, 1977 by McGraw-Hill Book Company. Used by kind permission of the publisher.

Ex. 22-2. *Recitative obligé: expressive declamation, orchestral participation, shifting harmonies.* Mozart, *Don Giovanni,* Act I.

From Ratner, *Music: The Listener's Art.* Copyright 1957, 1966, 1977 by McGraw-Hill Book Company. Used by kind permission of the publisher.

tion, the recitative *obligé* that sets the decision for revenge, carry forward into a powerful, driving, regular declamation, confirming Anna's tragic affect.

In this duet the harmonic and dramatic forms reinforce each other:

Harmonic		Dramatic
Part I:	D minor	Anna's despair
	F major	Ottavio's consolation
Part II:	X recitative	Vow for revenge
	D minor	Resolution for revenge
	X recitative	Restatement of vow
	D minor	Restatement of resolution, extended and reinforced to provide a cadence for the duet *and* the scene

Apart from the recitative, no long-range recalls or rhymes appear, yet the duet fulfills the harmonic requirements of a classic sonata form.

With the exit of Anna and Ottavio, the *buffa* mood hinted at in Scene 1 comes to the fore, to prevail for a considerable time, touching upon the low styles — humorous, bucolic, sentimental. The tone will rise again to a serious climax in Anna's "Or sai" and in the trio "Protegga il giusto cielo," but the *buffa* quality frames these points, and indeed its format and tone dominate the remainder of the opera except for the end of the "supper" scene. One of Mozart's greatest skills lies in his ability to swing the pendulum of affect from serious to comic and back within the *buffa* framework.

"Ah, chi mi dice mai" (Elvira).   Elvira's impressive entrance has the quality of high style as she strides onto the scene to the accompaniment of an elegant march, stately and ceremonial, yet the weight of the mood is lightened by the ornate figures and the rather "bouncing" motion. She too is bent on revenge after betrayal by the Don. Unlike Anna and Ottavio, who call upon heaven, Elvira intends to see to revenge herself by "carving out his heart," a decidedly human response. Her intense feeling is expressed by her portamento style and the wide leaps in her melodic line, contrasted by the "level" interpolations of the Don toward the end of each reprise of this I-V, I-I trio.

The ruling sentiment "cavare" dominates the closing sections of each reprise; the phrase "I'll carve out his heart" is repeated many times, accumulating intensity until it breaks out into a brilliant coloratura that represents pictorially the turning and twisting of the knife (see Ex. 22-3), a substantive rather than decorative use of coloratura.

"Madamina," the "catalogue" aria (Leporello).   This composite aria, one of the most famous *buffa* numbers in opera, has Leporello speaking for the Don as he informs Elvira of the "facts of life." Part I, as Leporello enumerates where the Don has wooed women and how many, is set in quick duple time, with a steady eighth-note background, as if a counting machine were operating. Part II, in which the qualities of the Don's women are described, is set in a slow minuet

Ex. 22-3. Mozart, *Don Giovanni*, Act I, climax of Elvira's aria "Ah, chi mi dice mai" ("Ah, who will tell me").

"Gli vo' cavare il cor." ("I'll carve out his heart.")

Schirmer

tempo, rounded and somewhat seductive in effect. Many mimetic and pictorial touches appear, including the following:

1.   The orchestra carries the principal action in part I, a duet between treble (woman?) and bass (man?), while Leporello remains the commentator with a simple intonation (see Ex. 22-4).

2.   The diminutive "Madamina" suggests a patronizing attitude that will be explicit at the end of the aria in "You know how it is."

3.   The unison at "a thousand and three" where all join in wonder.

4.   When the harmony moves to V (part I is a key-area reprise), the census changes from numbers to status; each succeeding phrase reaches a higher apex as chambermaids, baronesses, and princesses join the list. Fourteen measures before the end of part I, a merry chase is suggested as the *parlando* runs up and down the scale.

5.   As a stately minuet, part II would normally run its course in 16 to 20 measures; the cut of the opening phrase projects such a layout. But this length would be entirely inadequate to cover what Leporello has to say about the qualities of the Don's women. Therefore, this two-reprise form is masterfully spun out, extended by means of parentheses, deceptive cadences, and cadential reinforcements to a length of 88 measures. The critical points are:

Measure 17, parenthesis to m. 39

Measure 47, deceptive cadence and parenthesis to m. 58

Measure 62, deceptive cadence

Measure 70 et seq., cadential extension to m. 88

6.   Many pictorial touches give a piquant profile to this rhetorical tour de force:

Measure 11, "la costanza" (constancy), a powerful unison arpeggio.

Measure 15, "la dolcezza" (sweetness), parallel chromatic thirds.

Measures 22–31, "la grande maestosa" (the grand majestic one), full texture, driving rhythm, reaching a sustained climax on high D.

Measure 32, "la piccina" (the tiny one), a delicate texture, graceful figures.

Measure 47, "sua passion predominante" (his leading passion), deceptive cadence.

Measure 70 et seq. In the final cadential section, Elvira herself joins the list as Leporello sings the musical equivalent of a sly leer, implying that she knows all about this game of seduction.

Ex. 22-4.   Mozart, *Don Giovanni*, Act I, "Madamina," the "catalogue" aria.

Ex. 22-4, cont'd.

Schirmer

"Là ci darem la mano" (Don Giovanni, Zerlina). This duet, an ingratiating court dance in gavotte rhythm, is a formal play of seduction. The Don and Zerlina shape their figures accordingly—the Don's are strong and direct, Zerlina's are bending, ornate, spun out to express her wavering. The end of this composite number, a pastoral gigue over a drone bass, tells us that Zerlina has really prevailed, that she has captivated the Don.

"Finch'han dal vino," the "champagne" aria (Don Giovanni). This aria, the Don's first solo, is a headlong contredanse, driven breathlessly forward to suggest the reeling motion of an intoxicated spree. Cadence is piled upon cadence to spin out this two-reprise form, with little respite for the Don to catch his breath.

"Batti, batti" (Zerlina). Here again Zerlina's femininity is given a subtle turn. She asks Masetto to beat her, but her music delivers a delicious *contresense.* Her ingratiating tune, in gavotte rhythm, represents a rather courtly middle style not usually sung by peasant girls. This suggests that Zerlina is taking on a more lady-like, upward-looking attitude, especially after the Don has made his advances to her. Ornamentation at the return of the tune reinforces the impression of elegance.

Finale, Act I. If the opening scene is laid out as a *symphony* to frame portentous events, the finale is a *divertimento,* in gala style, with little consequence for the final dénouement of the opera because it is in the "wrong" key, C major. The order of movements is as follows:

Type	Key	Characters
Contredanse	C major	Masetto, Zerlina
March	C major	Giovanni, retainers
Slow minuet	F major	Zerlina, then Giovanni, then Masetto
Contredanse	F major	Zerlina, Giovanni, Masetto
Contredanse	D minor	Elvira, Anna, Ottavio
Minuet	F major	Leporello, Elvira, Anna, Ottavio
Adagio (aria)	B♭ major	Elvira, Anna, Ottavio
Gigue	E♭ major	Giovanni, Leporello, Zerlina, Masetto
March	C major	Above four plus Elvira, Anna, Ottavio
Minuet	G major	Giovanni, Elvira, Leporello, Ottavio, Anna, Masetto
Contredanse	G major	As above, simultaneously with continuing minuet
Gigue	G major	Above six plus Zerlina, simultaneously with preceding two dances
Final ensemble	C major	Ensemble of the seven principals

The final events of Act I hinge upon the Don's efforts to seduce Zerlina — the entire gala has been planned to this end. After the attempt (was it successful?), Leporello ironically is accused by the Don as the seducer, to bear the brunt, the punishment, not the pleasure of what he yearned for in his "Notte e giorno." This brings about the second confrontation of D and F as the switch from the Don to Leporello takes place. The music is headed for D minor, as if retribution were about to fall upon the Don, but suddenly shifts to F major, Leporello's key (see Ex. 22-5).

Ex. 22-5. *Confrontation of D and F.* Mozart, *Don Giovanni*, Act I, finale.

Ex. 22-5, cont'd.

Schirmer

As the music turns via F to C major, we know that the Don will escape his punishment for the time being. The last section of the finale, for all its frenzy, is more like a *buffa* finale than a purposeful dénouement. Despite its high feeling, its threats, it involves only one decisive action—the escape of Don Giovanni and Leporello, signaled by the close in C major instead of D minor.

"Ah taci, ingiusto core", (Elvira, Giovanni, Leporello).   This number is unique in the opera; it is the only fully worked-out compressed *da capo* number. The middle section, linked by both text and melodic figure to the following serenade, adds a special dimension to the play of amorous sentiment and burlesque expressed in the exposition and recapitulation, forecasting the complete reversal in the roles of the Don and Leporello. The give-and-take, as well as the key, forms a counterstatement to similar features in "là ci darem," Act I.

"Sola, sola, in bujo loco" (sextet).   The principal event in this finale-like ensemble is the unmasking of Leporello as a reluctant stand-in for Don Giovanni. The surprise experienced by Anna, Elvira, Zerlina, Ottavio, and Masetto is expressed in the phrase "Che impensata novità" ("What an unexpected novelty," i.e., turn of events). The entire final section is harmonically static—in Eb major—but active texturally, as Mozart juggles about a dozen figures in a kaleidoscopic series of quick changes within the orbit of I and V. After Eb has been drummed in, a series of harmonic and stylistic "novelties," musical puns, reflect the sense of the word "novità." First, the harmony drops bodily and abruptly from Eb major to Db major, while Anna sings a coloratura passage quite out of context with the other material. Later there is a deceptive cadence, and finally,

a truly weird novelty, a bit of motet style furnished with a tiny harmonic labyrinth, like nothing else previously heard (Ex. 22-6).

"Il mio tesoro" (Ottavio).   This aria, in *opera seria* style, displays the sentimental and military qualities of the nobleman. It begins cantabile with one of
Mozart's suavest melodies; later it introduces dotted march rhythms to express
Ottavio's resolve toward Anna. Serious as it is, it serves merely as an entr'acte in
the story line. It is a set piece, generally sung before the curtain, with some of the
coloratura of the *opera seria* aria. Here Mozart has reversed the ancient relationship of *seria* and *buffa* to make an intermezzo of the former. This relationship
reflects Ottavio's role in the opera — decorative rather than substantial.

Yet this aria is one of the opera's most glowing moments, containing some of
Mozart's most exquisite music, and this circumstance throws light upon one of
Mozart's greatest gifts — his ability to justify virtually any turn of musical discourse by the grace of his figures, his felicity of melodic invention. Apt as his
word-painting may be, it is not only the correspondence of music to text and gesture but also the winning turn of phrase that convinces us. Hence the pleasure
his music can give us without our precise knowledge of text or action.

The "supper" scene.   This scene, the climax of the opera, recalls elements
from earlier scenes:

1.   The divertimento style at the beginning — march, minuet, gigue — recalling the finale of Act I.

2.   The entry of Elvira, paralleling the opening of the struggle in Act I, Scene
1. Both numbers are in B♭ major; both involve the Don and Leporello, with an
agitated female character; both involve give-and-take, a textural as well as a
dramatic tug-of-war; both pick up the stylistic quality of the preceding number — a march in the first scene, here a Ländler to maintain a link with the divertimento mood. The sense of the scene is directly opposite to that of Act I, Scene
1 — then it was to capture Don Giovanni for *punishment*, now it is to capture him

Ex. 22-6.   Mozart, *Don Giovanni*, Act II, "Che impensata novità" ("What
an unexpected novelty").

for *rescue*. He will have neither punishment nor redemption as he sings his motto "Vivan le femmine! Viva il buon vino! Sostegno e gloria d'umanità" as a final response to Elvira. The sense of struggle is built into the phrase rhythms—two-measure groups in which the singers and orchestra seem to be at odds with each other; the vocal rhythm is trochaic, but it is forced into an iambic rhythm by the orchestra. Periodically, this imbalance is resolved only to begin its imbroglio anew. Ex. 22-7 quotes the beginning measures.

Ex. 22-7. Mozart, *Don Giovanni*, Act II, entrance of Elvira, "supper" scene.

"The final test of my love."

3. The approach of the Statue, signaled by the harmonic shift from B♭ major to V of D minor with a broad half cadence on A, carries the import of fate; D minor is indicated, but once more F major intervenes, in the third confrontation of these two keys, and again there is a shift from the Don to Leporello, whose *buffa* music, despite its figures suggesting terror, recalls his "Notte e giorno" in Act I, Scene 1, even to the use of similar figures.

4. The final section of the "supper" scene expands the material heard in the introduction to a full-scale key-area fantasia. When the Statue takes the Don's

hand, the duel music is recalled, but now it is a duel of hands, not swords, and the outcome is reversed as the Don is dragged to hell.

Epilogue. The epilogue, closing the opera as though it were a morality play with the homily that evil ends badly, is set as an Italian *opera sinfonia*—two quick movements enclosing a larghetto. Hints of preceding material appear; the 3/4 G major matches the tempo, key, and style of "Eh via, buffone"; the Larghetto is a trio in the same vein and with the same characters as "Protegga il giusto cielo"; the final Presto has some of the same "novità" as the sextet—motet and tiny harmonic labyrinth. The entire epilogue has the lift of a *buffa* scene, leaving us with the same ambivalence we have experienced throughout the opera, the mixture of serious and comic so skillfully blended in this *drama giocoso*. In the final analysis comedy prevails, raised to the highest power of humor—what can man do but laugh as he looks down upon tragedy?

Don Giovanni represents an attitude toward perfection in art opposite to that embodied in works such as the *Art of the Fugue* and the Masses of Palestrina. These latter strive for ultimate refinement and purity of style. *Don Giovanni*, like many other works of Mozart, gathers as many diverse elements as possible into a coordinated structure. In drama, Shakespeare is the epitome of this approach; for classic music, Mozart's *Don Giovanni* achieves this goal.

NOTE

1. Koch, *Lexikon*, p. 1559ff.; Schubart, *Ideen*, p. 377ff.; Kirnberger, *Kunst*, II, pt. 1, p. 70ff.; Galeazzi, *Elementi*, p. 293ff. See also pp. 59-60 of the present work.

23 Haydn, Sonata in E♭ Major

Haydn's music is known principally from his last 12 symphonies, the quartets, Op. 33 to 77, *The Creation, The Seasons*, and the last six Masses—works written during the last years of his Esterházy service, which ended in 1790, and later, as a free agent. These works represent the culmination of a long period of growth in skill, fluency, and fantasy. In the genres listed, the plane of this growth rises steadily; but in the piano sonatas, there is a sharp turn upward after the 49 sonatas written before 1794, and culminating in the E♭ major Sonata, H.V. XVI, No. 52, 1794-1795. The unique character of this work was recognized in a review in *AMZ*, May 1799:

> Grand sonata, rich and complex, both with respect to content and manner. Truly, this reviewer must repeat for the hundredth time what others have said; Haydn is inexhaustible and never grows old. What individuality we again find here! Nothing that echoes his earlier music. Whoever can perform this most excellent sonata, composed for connoisseurs and much more difficult than his earlier works, with precision and mastery of the minute details, such a performer can say that he truly plays.[1]

The first movement stands apart from the rest of Haydn's keyboard music as if it had been composed in another time and place; it is a much more speculative and fantastic movement than any other. Apart from one startling turn of events in the development and a modified recall of thematic material in the recapitulation, this movement, the opening of which is presented in Ex. 23-1, observes the protocol of classic sonata form—the usual presentation, opposition, and confirmation of keys, thematic recall and rhyme, the greater length of the second key area. The distinctive feature of this movement is its handling of rhetoric—its management of topic, its fluid rhythmic scansions, its subtle phrase connections, its quality of fantasia.

Two principal topics are used, both of them taken from the high styles: (1) the *French overture*, announced in the first two measures, restated to begin and close the second key area, and recalled at comparable points in the recapitulation; (2) an ornamented *stile legato* phrase, m. 6, consisting of an elaborated fourth species counterpoint in descending sixth chords with suspension, used first as a foil for the French overture figure but also in the development as a discursive fantasia topic. Against these two Haydn sets the *galanterie* of the horn-fifth figure, always placed in high register to suggest a music-box effect, m. 27. Other topics used are the *brilliant* style, m. 9 and elsewhere; the *empfindsamer* manner, m. 3; the *ombra*, mm. 37, 111; a hint of *Turkish* music, mm. 29, 101; and a little *harmonic labyrinth*, suggested in m. 20, explored more deeply beginning at m. 52.

Within the 117 measures of this movement, topics change frequently, at least three dozen times; no topic is maintained for more than six measures continuously. Very few formal cadences separate topics; they are joined by overlapping or by change of figure within a phrase. Haydn's early training in the short-winded, mosaic-like phrase structure of mid-century galant music is clearly in evidence here, fused by the subtle legerdemain of his wit into a continuous but ever-varied discourse.

The march-like beginning raises a question of tempo. The full voicing in six- and seven-note chords, the ceremonial style that calls for overdotting long lotes, and the low center of sound in both hands suggest a *deliberate* tempo, slower than the allegro specified by Haydn. The lighter, more brilliant topics and the halts in motion that come later tempt the performer to take a *quick* tempo. In view of the subtle twists in rhetoric which would be obscured in a rapid tempo, it seems that the proper tempo for the march should determine the pace for the entire movement, and that any variation in speed should be reconciled to the moderate step of the march.

This sonata was clearly written for fortepiano, as the diminuendo signs in mm. 5 and 16 and the sustained tones in m. 38 indicate. Yet the entire sonata has a strong flavor of harpsichord style. The opening chords would sound magnificently sonorous and percussive played on a harpsichord; the topical effects and the brilliant style would be sharply etched. Perhaps Haydn wished to imitate the harpsichord as a topic in this fortepiano sonata. In any case, a performance on whatever instrument would benefit by the awareness of this textural reference to the crisp sound of the harpsichord.

Haydn's subtle and eccentric rhetoric asserts itself immediately; the first two measures represent a cadence, a complete statement anchored to a tonic pedal point. This is a powerful gesture, but it is very short, too short for even the briefest of normal periods. To extend it, Haydn uses an echo, itself varied and re-echoed again and again until it gathers momentum to become an agent for continuation in m. 5. The melody arrives at the tonic for the first time at m. 6; we could easily imagine a dominant under the descending parallel thirds in the second half of m. 5, so that the tonic of m. 6 could represent an authentic cadence and the end of the period. But Haydn changes the sense of the tonic twice: first, by underpinning it with C so that a deceptive cadence is suggested; second, by completing the chord with an A♭ so that the harmony becomes IV⁶. At this point, the sixth chord is defined as the carrier of the *stile legato* action, continuing the descent that began with the first echo. The period ends with a *Tacterstickung* in m. 9, where the tonic serves a double function—arrival and departure. Again the peremptory brevity of the opening figure, always presented in a two-measure phrase, provides a springboard for contrasting action; this time, the tirata heard in m. 1 becomes a brilliant-style flourish, and the bound style, instead of being the *final* consequence of the echo, enters *early* to rob the cesura of the march figure of its final beat. Throughout the movement, the passage in *stile legato* is treated in a flexible manner; it may enter upon a first, second, third, or fourth beat; it may be 8 to 21 beats in length.

This play of rhetoric, topic, and texture is framed by rhythmic configurations that are at the same time rigidly regular *and* oddly scanned. The regularity lies in the overall measure count; the first eight measures constitute the first period, and the second eight measures form the second period, at the end of which the dominant is established to begin the second key area, m. 17. Also, the opening two measures define an *even* measure count as a basic unit.

The irregularity lies in the grouping of figures, the placement of cadences, the accents provided by long notes. If we take the half measure as a unit, the scansion of the first 16 measures comes out as given on the first line; the measure scansion is given on the second line:

Half measures 123/12/12/123/12/12/12/123/12/12/123/12/12/12
Measures   1 2/ 1 2 3/ 1 2 3/ 1 2/ 1 2 3/ 1 2 3

Once alerted to the play of duple and triple scansions, we can sense the eccentricity and the tightness of the macrorhythm throughout the movement.

Ex. 23-1.   Haydn, Sonata in E♭ major, H.V. XVI, No. 52, 1795, 1st movt.

From Haydn, *Sämtliche Klaviersonaten* (Christa Landon, ed.). Copyright 1964 by Universal Edition A.G. Wien. Used by kind permission of the publisher.

The development of this movement plays a strange and marvelous joke with the point of furthest remove. In the first part of the development, mm. 45–67, the harmony that normally represents the point of furthest remove, G major, is a powerful presence, whose importance is underlined by the fermatas in mm. 45 and 67. During these 23 measures, we hear a very tight and thorough working over of melodic material from the exposition while the harmony drops in a rather irregular manner down the circle of fifths, eventually to reach the dominant of D♭ major in m. 63. At this point an enharmonic switch—G♭ equals F♯— pulls the harmony abruptly back to G major, and the music arrives at this chord, the dominant of VI, with great ceremony, to announce the point of furthest remove. But then, instead of dropping a *major* third, to E♭ major, which he could well have done to accomplish the return, Haydn makes a calculated false step, dropping a *minor* third to begin a new section in E major, at m. 68. Here the point of the joke is sharpened by Haydn's recall of the little music-box hunting figure, the toy music that acted as a foil for the serious French overture and bound styles in the exposition, a scintillating and exotic effect in the remote key of E major. A sketch of the development is given in Ex. 23-2, showing how E major acts as a point of even further remove.

The *stile legato* passage beginning at m. 73 performs its most vital structural function following the E major episode. It leads the harmony chromatically downward to come to rest on the dominant of the home key, m. 77, thus forming the last link in a chain of startling events. The section from the E major episode

Ex. 23-2.   *Extension of the point of furthest remove.* Haydn, Sonata in E♭ major, H.V. XVI, No. 52, 1st movt., development.

to the recapitulation stands as a huge parenthesis, mm. 68–78; the recapitulation could well have begun after m. 68.

Typically, Haydn makes some permutations in the order of recall in the recapitulation. These involve the lengthening of the first period by spinning out the *stile legato* passage and a suppression of one statement of the march figure. The *ombra* is given a strange touch by added chromaticism, mm. 110–111, and is extended by one measure. Otherwise the rhyme, mm. 99–117, is quite literal.

The second movement, like the first, remains within the limits of its conventional form, a *da capo* aria or rondeau. Each section of this movement comprises a small two-reprise form; the style is that of a sarabande, the tempo adagio. The most striking feature is the key, *E major*. The sound of this key was highlighted in the first movement, at the point of furthest remove; the manner in which it was approached in the first movement clearly defined it as E major by the implied descent G, (F), E. As it begins the adagio it is heard as *Fb major*, a deceptive resolution, taking the Eb major of the first movement as a dominant. Again, the texture lends additional color to this striking harmonic juxtaposition; the slow tempo and the chordal texture allow the sound of E major to resonate. The richness of sound here, like the sparkling effect of E major at m. 68 of the first movement, demonstrates how Haydn gave special values of color to this remote key.

The slow, quiet beginning of the second movement creates room, as the movement progresses, for a great deal of florid ornamentation suggesting some modifications of tempo to provide for an arioso-like declamation. Ex. 23-3 gives the opening reprise and its *da capo* to illustrate the typical elaborations specified by Haydn.

Ex. 23-3.   Haydn, Sonata in Eb major, H.V. XVI, No. 52, 2nd movt.

a. Opening reprise.

b. Da capo.

The gravity of this movement is sustained by its dotted rhythms, similar to those of the first movement, but here charged with greater solemnity. Its flexible declamation invites rubato, but its period structure is rigidly regular. The schedule of the small two-reprise form—cadences, shifts of tonal center, return—is maintained (mm. 4, 8). The six-measure reprise in part II, mm. 19-24, and the reinforced cadential sections in part I, mm. 15-18 and 47-54, represent the only departures from the minimal 16-measure groupings of the basic two-reprise form.

As the movement ends, the treble sings G♯, clearly set apart from the rest of the texture. The ear follows this tone, matching it to the E in the bass that supports the E major sound. When the G♮ that begins the finale is heard, an interchange of mode is sensed. Thus the movement that began in F♭ major ends truly in E major—another reading of the E♭-E relationship. The second measure of the finale drops the fifth, E-B, down a chromatic half-step to E♭-B♭, a harmonic sleight-of-hand that brings the home key back into view. Ex. 23-4 sketches these various readings of E major.

Ex. 23-4.   Readings of E major in Haydn, Sonata in E♭ major, H.V. XVI, No. 52.

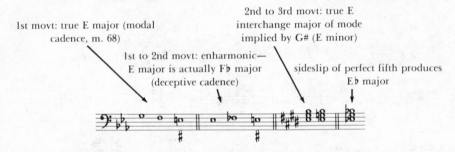

1st movt: true E major (modal cadence, m. 68)

1st to 2nd movt: enharmonic— E major is actually F♭ major (deceptive cadence)

2nd to 3rd movt: true E interchange major of mode implied by G# (E minor)

sideslip of perfect fifth produces E♭ major

If the first movement of this sonata has marked *fantasia* elements and the second movement employs the declamation of the *arioso*, the finale is truly a *capriccio*. Its eccentric stance is set harmonically with the first note, the G that contradicts the G♯ of the second movement, with no chordal support for this shift. The piece is a contredanse. Its tune seems simple and popular enough, a little sing-song figure over a musette bass. But where is its downbeat? The first measure or the second? We could easily hear the first measure as "good" (see p. 70 and p. 191) were it not contradicted by the strong accent of the entering bass in the second measure. The "free" first measure, of course, gives the listener a bit of time to get accustomed to the G♮; its interpretation as the third of the chord of E♭ major is a gratifying surprise, but the entire context throws the regular scansion out of joint. These subtle flickers of meaning suggest that the tempo be moderate enough to convey them to the listener. The same oddness of structure pervades the theme of the Capriccio of Haydn, discussed in Ch. 18; the two themes have a number of similarities.

This contredanse has difficulty in getting under way and in maintaining its momentum throughout the movement. Fermatas at the ends of phrase I and phrase II appear as consequences of the tonic phrase running on too long; the entire theme could easily have been given a proper contredanse form by four measures of tonic, four of subdominant, and eight of dominant, to reach its cadence at m. 16 instead of m. 28. The tonic phrase is pulled up short by the first fermata; it is then answered by a transposition upward by step. The massive sequence (a *rosalia*, sometimes regarded as absurd by 18th-century theorists) has a peremptory, blocked-out effect that disconnects the phases of the cadential action, especially with the help of the fermatas. In these first two phrases there is too much *go* (the overlong phrases) and too much *stop* (the fermatas). Once the dominant is reached the music moves full speed ahead for a while, only to encounter more fermatas that halt the contredanse movement; the most striking of these is a cluster of fermatas just before the recapitulation (this movement is in sonata form) framing a little written-out cadenza in adagio tempo.

The rhythmic pattern of the first two measures (see Ex. 23-5) generates the two principal melodic figures in the movement. In addition to underpinning the opening theme, it frames striking contrasting material, a chromatic scale that enters at m. 29. Both figures are used in various contexts. One of the oddest is the treatment given the repeated-note figure toward the end of both the exposition and recapitulation. After the cadence in the tonic is reached, this figure falls in immediately on the subdominant without chordal support; this fourth degree is eventually rationalized as part of dominant harmony, but not until Haydn's sleight-of-hand has given an eccentric touch to the harmonic sense. Ex. 23-5 quotes the first period and the beginning of the second, as well as a part of the recapitulation that illustrates the juggling of the sense of the subdominant.

Ex. 23-5.   Haydn, Sonata in E♭ major, H.V. XVI, No. 52, finale.

a. Opening section.

Ex. 23-5, cont'd.

*) ℔ möglicherweise ein Irrtum Haydns; vgl. Takt 249.
℔ possibly an error by Haydn; cf. bar 249.

"drum" and chromatic figures combined

b. Closing section.

From Haydn, *Sämtliche Klaviersonaten* (Christa Landon, ed.). Copyright 1964 by Universal Edition A.G. Wien. Used by kind permission of the publisher.

In its way, the finale of the E♭ major Sonata matches the uniqueness of the first movement. Finales of earlier sonatas are attractive closing pieces featuring frankly tuneful melody cast in rondo, variation, or relatively compact sonata form. Only in the E♭ major Sonata did Haydn close with a broadly scaled sonata form in which most of the action is harmonic, rhythmic, and textural, and where melody as tune plays a subordinate role. This finale, therefore, provides a fine balance to the opening movement.

The E♭ major Sonata is the first of three sonatas composed in 1794-1795, the others being in C major, H.V. XVI, No. 50 (the last composed), and D major, H.V. XVI, No. 51. In these, the only movement that truly matches those discussed above is the first movement of the C major Sonata; here Haydn's imagination and subtle humor run wild and free as he sets the opening arpeggio figure in many odd and incredibly varied ways throughout the movement.

C. P. E. Bach's influence appears throughout the E♭ major Sonata, as it does in much of Haydn's other keyboard music. The flavor of fantasia, the stop-and-start effects, the manipulation of figure, and the odd harmonic relationships link this work to Bach's style. The difference — a profound one — lies in Haydn's greater emphasis upon periodicity by means of key-confirming cadences. In contrast, Bach's less emphatic closes frequently convey an impression of suspended action, maintaining the air of wonder and whimsy after the music stops. In both composers the quality of high comedy often appears.

Beyond its deft management of detail and its skillful shaping of large-scale form, the E♭ Sonata handles compatibility and organic unity among its three movements in striking ways (See Ch. 19). Formally, sonata-rondeau-sonata provides clarity and intelligibility for the listener. Topically, the limits of compatibility are reached by the march-fantasia, aria-sarabande, contredanse-capriccio contrasts. The overarching factor for *organic unity* is, paradoxically, the very element that loosens the set forms — the ever-present fantasia treatment *within* each movement, and the startling E♭ major-E major-E♭ major sequence of keys in the sonata. Haydn's firm hold on *both* types of rhetorical flow — the bound and the free — gives this sonata, as well as other of his works in the 1790s, that marvelous combination of directness and subtlety that lies at the heart of his inimitable wit.

NOTE

1. *AMZ*, 1799, p. 520.

24 Beethoven and the Classic Style

The changes in musical style that took place around the turn of the 19th century were so profound that this time might well be considered the beginning of the romantic era. Were it not for Beethoven, this view would be entirely valid; significant trends after 1800 were more consistent with later than with earlier styles. These new trends included the grand orchestral tutti, extension of the range and amplification of the sound of the piano, greater emphasis upon mechanical virtuoso skills, richer tone color due to mechanical improvements in instruments, all resulting in a growing taste for sheer sound effects, and a broader sweep of melodic line. Also, by 1800 the presence of a lyric *middle* theme in a sonata or symphony movement had been fairly well established. These devices tended to focus the listener's attention upon immediate effects, to please quickly; as a consequence, the grand thrust of rhetoric essential to classic sonata form was interrupted.

Beethoven assimilated all these new elements into a line of structure that maintained the periodicity of 18th-century rhetoric. The works of his maturity, in this sense, represent the final embodiment of classic principles, raised to even a higher power than that reached by Haydn and Mozart. This apotheosis of structure was not achieved by any later work, although facets of his style were imitated for more than a century afterwards, so that in retrospect, much of Beethoven's music seems to have a romantic flavor.

Beethoven's contemporaries—among them Cherubini, Viotti, Clementi, Johann Dussek, Grétry, Méhul, Pleyel, Salieri, Steibelt, Krause, Sterkel, Hümmel—all reflect the popular taste of their time more clearly than does Beethoven. Their names appear again and again on programs and in critiques. The taste they represent was a mélange of sentimental, comic, and pathetic elements from the time of Haydn and Mozart alternating with brilliant, bizarre, and colorful effects to arouse the sense of wonder. Another facet, in serious music, was the melodramatic posture already present to a degree in Gluck and Mozart, intense, often violent, as in the opening of the overture to Cherubini's *Medea*, 1797 (see Ex. 9-9); later this was to become an important ingredient in the music of Schubert, Schumann, Berlioz, and Weber. But Beethoven's contemporaries, talented as they were, lacked the grip on rhetoric which was Beethoven's greatest strength, and which enabled him to create the formulations and syntheses that added a final and greater dimension to the classic style.

Many examples already cited have demonstrated that Beethoven drew heavily from the topical and technical resources of the later 18th century; others have exhibited strikingly different and unique formulations. To complete this study of the classic style, we shall investigate one of Beethoven's most characteristic and impressive movements, the first movement of his F major Quartet, Op. 59, No. 1, 1806.

Beethoven's quartets constitute his most comprehensive group of works, embodying a full life history of his mature style, from the sharply topical formalities that often articulate the Op. 18 Quartets, through the breadth and fluidity of the Op. 59 and 74, to the highly-speculative, often elliptical rhetoric of the last quartets. Thanks to the texture of the quartet, a virtually ideal medium in Beethoven's time (see Ch. 8), and a sureness of touch in Beethoven when he wrote for this medium, his quartets have a refinement of texture and a flow of rhetoric more polished than in his sonatas and symphonies.

Texture plays the most important role in setting the character of the first movement of Op. 59, No. 1. The sound of the string quartet—rich, balanced, broad in range, capable of an infinite variety of nuances—is the matrix from which action proceeds.

The opening chord sets the mood; it is set low, with the violoncello taking the melody in a rich tenor range. The chord is ambiguous in meaning—C-A-F—indicating a possible F major, confirmed only at the end of the first measure. To avoid the bold instability of a $^6_4$ sound, Beethoven was careful not to include F in the accompaniment. With C doubled in the outer voices, this chord, lacking firmness, has a floating quality, a plagal rather than authentic effect.

The first four measures appear as an expansion or elaboration of this opening sound, establishing a premise of broadly scaled gestures in which rich, sonorous chords are well sustained, forming a backdrop for floating melodic elaborations. More than half the duration of this movement is given to such a texture, as at mm. 30, 77, 91, 152, 218, 368, and elsewhere. Even the opening violoncello melody, distinctive as it is, evolves as a decoration of the tone C in the first four measures. This movement might be characterized in much the same way as Renaissance polyphony, as a "long drawn-out sweetness," an embodiment of the vocal quality that Beethoven sought to incorporate in his instrumental music, best achieved in the string quartet.

Shadings in the spectrum of sound color the harmony, thereby affecting the shape of the key-area plan Beethoven used in this movement. The most important harmonic presence in the movement is F major, but it is expressed in ways that modify its traditional function as the central point of harmonic reference. The entire movement contains but two authoritative V–I cadences—mm. 18-19 and at the end of the movement. The floating effect set by the violoncello at the beginning is continually explored throughout the movement in light chord positions—inversions of tonic or dominant harmony—that soften the edge of articulation usually present in cadential harmony. Cadential formulas often take the 2-1 or 7-1 path in the bass; this is especially prominent in the drone-like cadences of mm. 374-395. With the exception of the final cadence, the violoncello does not take the role often assigned to it in 18th-century quartets—to provide a strong point of punctuation. It remains as fluid and melodic in its treatment as the upper instruments; this is the critical point that sets the sonority of the movement—the treatment of the violoncello as a melodic instrument or a drone, but rarely as a true bass.

The tone D is given a prominence that adds a flavor of pentatonic modality. On the first page of the score it is a neighbor tone to C, a ninth in dominant harmony, the uppermost note in subdominant harmony, and it adds a strong color to the plagal range of the opening theme. Throughout the movement the sixth degree of the major scale stays with us. When the D minor chord, the firmest crystallization of this sixth-degree sound, appears at m. 396, immediately preceding the final dominant, it recalls an important nuance that has colored some of the most salient material.

Due to this sustained ambience of sound, a single mood dominates the movement—introspective, dark, perhaps melancholy and nostalgic, especially in view of the sing-song phrases and the drones, bittersweet in the touches of sharp dissonance. This mood is articulated by the melodic material. Again we can see the opening measures as a pattern for the entire movement. The melody, as it turns on C, the fifth of the scale, strives upward by step to the tonic, but reaches it only at the fourth beat, to fall back to C. At other times, it will move through the tonic and upward. This uppermost of four notes, melodically the strongest—an apex—but rhythmically the weakest, becomes an object for expressive nuance when it is marked *sfp*, m. 40, or *sf*, m. 348. Since the opening figure is a scale, it can be trimmed to various lengths. It comprises four notes in m. 1; in mm. 42–48 it is extended to a length of 23 notes, to build a long and powerful ascent to one of the most decisive cadences in the movement. It can also be quickened in eighth-notes or triplet eighths, and slowed to half-notes. Clear as it may be, the opening motive has a fluidity that allows it to penetrate and saturate the melodic action, contributing to the broad flow and the unity of mood in the movement. Of the 400 measures, more than one-third incorporate stepwise melodic action related to the opening figure.

The flow is broken by a number of incisive gestures whose melodic material has an angular contour—mm. 20, 52, 73, 85, 144, 185, etc., as well as the final measures of the movement. While these gestures provide the main melodic and rhetorical contrasts in the movement, they do not function as "second" or "subsidiary" themes. The themes representing I and V are very similar in contour and style; the dominant theme is a brief episode, eight measures in length; apart from announcing the dominant in a rather reticent manner, it has nothing to do with the main business of the movement.

Stepwise action covers a wide range of rhetorical gestures, from the ornamentation of a single tone to an enormous sweep, from the straightforward announcement of the opening theme to a completely eccentric spinning out of eighth-notes in the style of a fantasia. Ex. 24-1 illustrates some of these usages.

Ex. 24-1. *Uses of stepwise motion.* Beethoven, Quartet in F major, Op. 59, No. 1, 1806, 1st movt.

a. Extended rise to climax.

b. Simple and ornamented lines.

c. Ornamentation in eighth-notes as countertheme to fugato subject.

Ex. 24-1, cont'd.

d. Fantasia figure.

Eulenburg No. 28

Disjunct action in this movement takes two forms: (1) an angular line; (2) a pulling apart of the generally homogeneous chordal texture. Both are illustrated in Ex. 24-2. Only Ex. 24-2c represents the standard classic manner, where a "vertical" gesture serves as a point of final punctuation.

Ex. 24-2. *Disjunct action.* Beethoven, Quartet in F major, Op. 59, No. 1, 1st movt.

a. Angular line.

b. Dispersion of texture.

c. Final cadence.

Eulenburg No. 28

Formally, this movement follows the layout of the classic sonata—the I–V, X–I plan, the distinctive melodic member for each key, the rhyme in the recapitulation, the tour of keys in the development. Two modifications are striking: (1) a new theme in the development treated as a fugato, (2) a permutation in the order of material at the beginning of the recapitulation. Both of these variants arise from the context of style and form unique to this movement; they will be discussed among the special points of technique described below.

1.   *Length of movement; breadth of periods.* This is by far the longest first movement among the quartets. Its length develops out of the leisurely, spun-out action, the sustained chords, the play of ornamental figures, to suggest a slower rate of time lapse than that of the first movement of the *Eroica* Symphony — also a tremendously long form — where the thrust of the action and the imbroglios release powerful, long-reaching trajectories. In Op. 59, No. 1, the discourse of the first movement is carried out smoothly, with much overlapping of action, resulting in a number of very long periods — mm. 60–93, 112–180, 222–295, 340–400.

2.   *Harmonic contour.* While the general key-area plan is clearly discernible in this movement, in the usual proportions assigned in classic forms, some significant modifications of the standard protocol of key definition occur, consistent with the character of the piece. Instead of a solid statement of the tonic at the beginning, there is the tentative implication of F major discussed above, as if the movement were beginning *in medias res*, some moments after the actual start. The confirming establishment of F takes place at m. 19, well into the piece. Other points of harmonic definition are compromised. One of these is the cadence of the exposition. At m. 83, the normal harmonic grammar calls for a root position of V. Instead the lower strings begin an arpeggio figure on G to obliterate the point of arrival. Later, a cadence in C appears but only in the *middle* of a phrase, so that the punctuating effect of this cadence is reduced to that of a comma instead of a period; melodic and harmonic punctuation here do not coincide, and the effect is to maintain the sense of flow. Both the opening and the close of the exposition, then, contribute to the fluid declamation typical in this movement. Ex. 24-3 quotes the weakened cadence at the end of the exposition.

Ex. 24-3.   *Weakened cadence at end of exposition.* Beethoven, Quartet in F major, Op. 59, No. 1, 1st movt.

Eulenburg No. 28

The blurred focus is even more marked in the vicinity of the recapitulation. Beethoven reversed the order of material, recalling the incisive gestures of m. 20 and the following measures *before* the return of the opening theme. Neither of these points is supported by an authentic cadence in F. We must wait until the rhyme of the second key-area material for such a cadence. When the opening theme returns, it actually appears *in medias res*, as implied at the beginning. Thus we cannot pinpoint the moment of recapitulation, only recognize its dispersal among several gestures. This area of the recapitulation is quoted in Ex. 24-4.

Ex. 24-4. *Dispersal of recapitulation functions.* Beethoven, Quartet in F major, Op. 59, No. 1, 1st movt.

Eulenburg No. 28

By way of compensation for the equivocal harmonic punctuation, the final section of the movement, from m. 348, remains in F. The opening theme is presented in a powerful root position, the only such setting in the movement, and a drone bass is used. But, for all its vehemence, this presentation lacks the stability that Beethoven gave to the final appearance of the opening theme in the first movement of the *Eroica* Symphony (m. 632). In the quartet, the final statement of the theme, m. 348, is approached by eight measures of tonic pedal, instead of the conventional V. Lacking harmonic punctuation, this violent statement of the theme does not act as an effective peroration for the movement, a climactic point of arrival. Moreover, the active bass involving the use of B♮ and inversions in the second phrase also reduces the firmness. The music then, in m. 368, returns to its original qualities—sound and flow—to bring matters to the final cadential arrival. This involves a swing back and forth between I and V, seven times within 23 measures. Even here, the firmness of root position is avoided, as the violoncello consistently takes stepwise motion between V and I. Only at the end do we have root position, a peremptory effect that puts us as much on the alert as it satisfies the needs of harmonic rhetoric, opening the way to the second movement.

If the weakened cadences reflect the smooth quality of movement, the incisions in harmony and texture throw this quality into sharp relief. The incisive gestures mentioned above (p. 424) are not merely local contrasts; they take over the articulation functions normally assigned to cadences, appearing in the *midst* of extended phases of action—for example, m. 20, within the first key area; m. 48, a station en route to V; m. 73, a digression in the second key area; m. 144, in the development, just before the apparent preparation for the return to F; and at m. 185, the fugato. Thus the "vertical" and "horizontal" exchange roles in this movement, to fuse even more strongly the continuous flow.

Superimposed upon the key-area plan, this movement has a harmonic profile that highlights some of its special structural features. The plan of keys is shown in Ex. 24-5. The points included there represent some embodiment of tonic harmony in the keys indicated. The extended and relatively static establishment of F calls for a peremptory gesture to pull the harmony away. This is done by the powerful rise to G and the strong incision at m. 48. From this point the harmony descends, as from a high harmonic plateau, into the deep flat regions, to return, via interchange of mode, to F major. The emphatic and powerful cadence in G acts as a "launching pad" for an enormous harmonic trajectory that will not complete its tour until m. 307, the next authentic cadence in F major. This deep dive into subdominant regions prefigures the plan of the C♯ minor Quartet, Op. 131, 1826 (see Ch. 15).

Ex. 24-5. *Plan of keys.* Beethoven, Quartet in F major, Op. 59, No. 1, 1st movt.

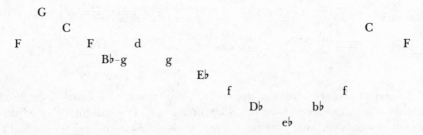

In the course of this trajectory, the harmony passes twice through F, at m. 103 and m. 157. At m. 103, the return to F major and the opening theme could sound either as a feint toward a repeat of the exposition or as a rondo procedure. Thanks to the fluid quality of the theme, the music can slide through F major without a strong harmonic commitment, continuing its path toward the flat keys. At m. 152, the harmony arrives at the dominant of F, resolving to F minor at m. 157. However, the dominant of F is weakened in cadential effect as the violoncello, true to its role, takes the third of the C major chord and moves stepwise into F minor. Thus the arrival at C major in m. 152, which could have signaled the advent of the home key, sidesteps this responsibility through its first-inversion position. Actually, it opens the way to a far-reaching digression.

This digression, mm. 152-222, creates a huge parenthesis in the form, organized as a prelude, fugato, and postlude. The prelude, mm. 152-184, is in fantasia style with scale figures of irregular length in the first violin. This quasi-improvisatory play is underpinned by a steady stepwise rise in the line of the violoncello—E, F, G♭, A♭, B♭, C, D♭, E♭, and F—until finally a cadence in D♭ major is reached, m. 180, to round off the prelude and lead to the fugato, m. 185. The fugato, mm. 185-210, begins in E♭ minor and ends in F minor; it constitutes the area of furthest remove in the form. Of all the major sections in the form of this movement, the fugato is the most regular; its evenly spaced entries and its traditional protocol of imitation stand in bold contrast to the flowing quality of the rest of the material. A short postlude, again with the quality of fantasia, mm. 210-221, returns the harmony to C major at m. 222 to wind up the great parenthesis and begin the preparation for the return to F major. Ex. 24-1d illustrates the prelude figuration; Ex. 24-1c gives the beginning of the fugato. Both subjects of the fugato are variants of the melodic material of the first key area; the eighth-notes ornament a rising scale; the subject in longer notes makes a free permutation of the patterns of the second period. This "enclosed" prelude, fugato, and postlude represent a layout sometimes employed by Beethoven—the form within a form (see Ch. 19).

3.   *Harmonic details*. More than half of this movement involves tonic and dominant harmonies in complementary arrangement; subdominant harmony does not figure prominently or often in these formulas, but occasionally is highlighted to take on an intense expressive nuance, as in Ex. 24-6.

Ex. 24-6.   *Highlighting of the subdominant harmony*. Beethoven, Quartet in F major, Op. 59, No. 1, 1st movt.

355

Against the slowly moving, smooth alternation of I and V in virtually a sing-song manner, certain bold and edgy effects are placed. Ex. 24-2a has a rich chromaticism that acts as a foil to the I–V–I of the first period; Ex. 24-7e displays this chromaticism in reduction. Other parts of Ex. 24-7 quote some of the harmonic details — dissonances, ungrammatical progressions — that interrupt the harmonic flow; Beethoven distorts the texture to give a more substantive and bizarre quality to these moments, especially in the dispersal of chord members over a wide range.

Ex. 24-7.   *Harmonic details.* Beethoven, Quartet in F major, Op. 59, No. 1, 1st movt.

a. Inverted pedal point.

Eulenburg No. 28

b. Reduction of texture to strict style.

c. Legitimation of an ungrammatical progression.

Eulenburg No. 28

d. Reduction of last six measures of c.

e. Reduction of mm. 22-29 (see Ex. 24-2a).

Other points of harmonic interest include the transposition of the musette theme into D♭ major, m. 279, touching the darkest color in the movement when the viola and violoncello echo the violins.

4.   *The opening period.* In this unique movement, the opening period has its own distinction, with features not matched elsewhere in the form. It touches the alpha and omega in defining the key—the merest hint at the beginning and the strongest confirmation in the entire movement at m. 19. It covers a huge melodic ascent, from the low C of the violoncello to the high F of the first violin. In doing so, it builds a tremendous crescendo, increasing the texture from three-note to eight-note chords. This crescendo is negotiated by one of the most common 18th-century devices—the *Trommel-bass*.

To m. 16, the phrase structure is symmetrical, with four equal members; the melody has the broadly singing manner favored in turn-of-the-century Franco-Italian music, where the 4 + 4 symmetry builds expansive gestures. But here the resemblance to the conventional manner ends. The melody cannot end at m. 16 satisfactorily, due to the harmonic rhythm; despite the slow change of harmony—only *two* changes within the first 19 measures—the shift from I to V occurs at an odd point, the middle of m. 7. Therefore the harmony does not arrange itself in the usual classic balance to punctuate the inner structure of this period; instead, mm. 5–7 have a harmonic rhythm of 3/2, rendering the shift to V as uncertain as the opening hint of the tonic, and also as incomplete. The fourfold statement of the rhythm of the first four measures provides none of the rhythmic compression needed to enclose the cadence within the first 16 measures. The cadence can only be reached by extension, resulting in the scansion shown in Ex. 24-8.

Ex. 24-8. *Scansion of first period.* Beethoven, Quartet in F major, Op. 59, No. 1, 1st movt.

```
 1    2   1   2   1   2   1   2   3   1
1 2  1 2  1 2  1 2  1 2  1 2  1 2  1 2  1 2  1
                          or  1 2  3 1  2 3  1
                                           1
```

The scansion by full measures in period 1 provides a foil for an abrupt shift in period 2, matching the sudden change in melodic and textural configuration. Half-notes become the unit, in a sprung pattern as follows: 3 2 2 4 4 2 3 2 (see Ex. 24-2a); the final measure of period 1 becomes the first two beats of this pattern.

Now let us return to the original figure of period 1 and its floating plagal quality. When the first violin takes it, the notes that are stressed over dominant harmony are D as a rising ninth; F as an appoggiatura; G, the fifth of the chord; B♭, the seventh—all notes that maintain the light, suspended quality. Then, in whole notes, C, D, E, F, a firm and conclusive gesture. Here the F achieves its goal finally as the apex of the melodic ascent upon a strong rhythmic point (see p. 000); the final four notes of the period can thus be read as an augmentation of the opening figure and its fulfillment, capping the upward surge with success. Ex. 24-9 quotes the first period.

While this movement lends itself especially well to analysis because of the refinement and intensity of its unique qualities, virtually all of Beethoven's major works incorporate comparable aspects—premises intially stated as problems to be worked out and solved during the course of a movement. At times the musical statement at the beginning of a movement would ordinarily have been considered inadequate or inappropriate for an opening theme. Some instances:

1. An off-center harmony, Sonata in E♭ major, Op. 31, No. 3, 1801–1802, first movement (a II $^6_5$ chord)

2. A sketchy figure, Quartet in F major, Op. 59, No. 1, 1806, second movement (repeated B♭'s in violoncello)

3. An elusive texture, Quartet in F major, Op. 135, 1827, first movement

4. An unconventional treatment of a traditional topic, Quartet in F major, Op. 59, No. 1, 1806, finale (the Russian theme in the violoncello against a trill in the first violin)

Ex. 24-9. *Opening period.* Beethoven, Quartet in F major, Op. 59, No. 1, 1st movt.

Eulenburg No. 28

Such figures create problems for unity and continuity of form, but also they provide leverage in the struggle for their solutions. The solutions reconcile these unique situations with the traditional harmonic and periodic balances of classic music — in each case the result is a victory symphony. In much the same way that Beethoven struggled to achieve the ideal contours of his themes — a process recorded in his sketchbooks — so must he have worked to reach a formal perfection for an entire movement or work; some of the shape and energy of this thrust toward the realization of form is sensed in the finished works themselves.

Conclusion

This book has endeavored to convey some idea of the scope of classic music, the quality of its expression, the nature of its rhetoric, the shape of its forms, its range of style and genre. The basis of this approach was an investigation of premises common to all 18th-century music—stylized affective postures, periodicity, key definition, cadential harmony, hierarchical rhythmic organization, structural and ornamental melody, and polarity of treble and bass. Special attention was given to the classic use of the two-reprise form and its harmonic contours.

Details of arrangement and configuration within these categories were examined and some of the countless options available were described. In this light, the spirit of the *Ars Combinatoria*, the master game, appeared as valid for music as it did for mathematical speculation in the 18th century. The precision with which these options and variants were put together had something in common with the amazing clockwork devices that were produced at that time.

The play of options offered many possibilities for ambiguity—various ways in which a chord could function, shifts of accent, changes of rhythmic grouping, opposition of statement and counterstatement, mixtures of comic and serious components, structural displacements. This thrust in two directions is present in the music itself—a centrifugal motion that departs from a point of reference, and a compensating centripetal motion that returns. These two motions achieve a power of reconciliation unlike that of any other style, encompassing the action of an entire movement.

In handling centrifugal and centripetal forces, classic music stood between the baroque, where the centrifugal action is held firmly in rein by the pull of the tonic, and the romantic, where the centrifugal action becomes too strong for the tonic to act as a regulator of events, and harmony takes on the coloristic value that eventually led to impressionism.

The exquisite balance between the centrifugal and centripetal provided the opportunity for classic composers to enrich the traditional rhetoric of 18th-century music with a wide range of varied and subtle content. In this vein, the speculative classic approach to musical material had full scope—to deal searchingly with familiar topics, or to build a powerful and continuous discourse throughout the length of a sonata movement or rondo. It was precisely this power of speculation that distinguished the great masters of the style from the hundreds of competent practitioners who refined and clarified the basic premises of the style. Upon the base established by their contemporaries and predecessors, the masters built the monuments of the style; we can trace this growth, this rise into sublimity in their works—the early works promising but typical, the later works achieving the transformation in which the classic style par excellence is recognized.

436

The ambiguities and mixtures in classic rhetoric and expression are matched by some striking paradoxes in its image. To the casual listener, the classic style is clear and easy to grasp; yet it contains many subtle and elusive nuances of expression, style, and form that only the connoisseur can detect after careful study. It is ideal for the composition of musical miniatures; yet it has produced masterpieces of the utmost grandeur and power. Historically, the style is visible and important by virtue of these masterpieces; yet the life of the style was lived on a modest level where uncounted works were produced, performed, and laid aside, in innumerable towns, courts, churches, homes, opera houses, and concert halls in Europe, from St. Petersburg to London, from Copenhagen to Naples, and across the Atlantic in both Americas. The style is generally held to be abstract and instrumental, since the greater part of its visible corpus of works is in the chamber music and orchestral genres. Yet vocal music dominated the style in its time, and it is so saturated with theatrical elements, both vocal and mimetic, that any performance of a classic work must be thought of as a kind of stage presentation. From the time it came into prominence in the middle years of the 18th century, the style has had a profound effect upon music to the present day; yet its full flowering occupied but a brief period of no more than 30 or 40 years in the later 18th century.

Above all, it was a language spoken throughout the western world in its time. I have attempted to define its terms and their application in the hope that readers of this book will gain some fresh insights as they hear, study, or perform this music.

Sources Consulted

Author's note: This list comprises works actually consulted in the preparation of this book. Further bibliographic aids will be found below under the heading "Suggested References and Readings."

ADLUNG, JACOB, *Anleitung zur musikalischen Gelahrtheit*. Erfurt, 1758.

AGRICOLA, JOHANN F., *Anleitung zur Singkunst* . . . (Ger. tr. of Tosi, *Observations*). Berlin, 1757.

ALBRECHT, JOHANN L., *Gründliche Einleitung in die Anfangslehren der Tonkunst*. Langensalza, 1761.

ALBRECHTSBERGER, JOHANN G., *Gründliche Anweisung zur Composition*. Leipzig, 1790.

ALEMBERT, JEAN LE ROND D', *Élémens de musique* . . . (*nouvelle* ed.). Lyon, 1766.

ALGAROTTI, FRANCESCO, *Saggio sopra l'opera in musica*. . . . Livorno, 1755.

Allgemeine musikalische Zeitung. Leipzig, 1798-1848.

ANTONIOTTI, GIORGIO, *L'arte armonica* (Eng. tr). London, 1760. 2 vols.

ARTEAGA, STEFANO, *Le rivoluzioni del teatro italiano*. . . . Bologna, 1783-1788.

AVISON, CHARLES, *An Essay on Musical Expression*. London, 1752.

AZOPARDI, FRANCESCO, *Le musicien pratique* . . . (Fr. tr.). Paris, 1786. 2 vols.

BACH, CARL P. E., "Einfall einen doppelten Contrapunct in der Octave von sechs Tacten zu machen. . . ." in *Historisch-kritische Beyträge zur Aufnahme der Musik*, Friedrich W. Marpurg, ed. Berlin, 1754-1758. Vol. III, pt. 1, p. 167ff.

————, *Versuch über die wahre Art das Clavier zu spielen*. Berlin, 1759-1762. (Eng. tr., William J. Mitchell tr. & ed., New York, 1949).

BACH, J. C., & RICCI, FRANCESCO P., *Méthode ou recueil de connoissances élémentaires pour le pianoforte ou clavecin*. . . . Paris, 1786.

BAILLOT, PIERRE, *L'art du violon*. . . . Paris [1834].

BEMETZRIEDER, ANTON, *Nouvelles leçons de clavecin* . . . (Eng. tr.). London, 1782.

BERTON, HENRI-M., *Traité d'harmonie*. Paris, 1815.

BONESI, BONIFACIO, *Traité de la mesure, ou la division du tems dans la musique et dans la poésie*. Paris, 1806.

BONNET, JACQUES, *Historie de la musique et ses effets*. . . . Amsterdam, 1725.

BOLLIOUD-MERMET, LOUIS, *De la corruption du goust dans la musique françoise*. Lyon, 1746.

BOYÉ, *L'expression musicale, mise au range des chimères*. Amsterdam & Paris, 1770.

BREMNER, ROBERT, *The Rudiments of Music*. Edinburgh, 1756.

————, *Some Thoughts on the Performance of Concert Music*. London, 1777.

BROSSARD, SÉBASTIAN DE, *Dictionnaire de musique*. . . . Paris, 1703.

BROWN, JOHN, *Letters upon the Poetry and Music of the Italian Opera*. Edinburgh, 1789.

BURNEY, CHARLES, *A General History of Music*. . . . London, 1776-1789.

BUSBY, THOMAS, *Concert Room and Orchestra Anecdotes of Music and Musicians*. London, 1825. 3 vols.

CALLCOTT, JOHN W., *A Musical Grammar* (3rd ed.). London, 1817.

CALLEGARI, ANTONIO, *L'art de composer la musique sans en connaître les éléments*. Paris, 1803.

CATRUFO, JOSEPH, *Barême musical, ou l'art de composer la musique sans connaître les principes*. Paris, 1811.

CHASTELLUX, FRANÇOIS J., *Essai sur l'union de la poésie et de la musique*. Paris, 1765.

CHORON, ALEXANDRE E., *Principes de composition des écoles d'Italie*. Paris, 1808.

CHRISTMANN, JOHANN F., *Elementarbuch der Tonkunst*. . . . Speyer, 1782-1789.

CLEMENTI, MUZIO, *Clementi's Selection of Practical Harmony*. London, 180[?]. 3 vols.

CONTANT D'ORVILLE, ANDRÉ, *Histoire de l'opéra bouffon*. . . . Paris, 1768.

COOKE, BENJAMIN, *Notes on the Theory of Music*. Ms., n.d. Br. Mus. Add 29298.

CORFE, JOSEPH, *A Treatise on Singing*. . . . London, 1799.

CRAMER, KARL F. (ed.), *Magazin der Musik*. Hamburg, 1783-1787. Copenhagen, 1789.

CROTCH, WILLIAM, *Elements of Musical Composition*. London, 1812.

_____, *Specimens of Various Styles of Music*. London, 1807-1822. 3 vols.

CZERNY, CARL, *School of Practical Composition, Op. 600*. Eng. tr. John Bishop. London: Cooks and Co., 1848. 3 vols.

_____, *Ueber den richtigen Vortrag der sämtlichen Beethoven'schen Klavierwerke* (facsimile). Paul Badura-Skoda ed. Vienna: Universal Edition, 1963.

DAUBE, JOHANN F., *Anleitung zur Erfindung der Melodie*. . . . *Vienna, 1797-1798*.

_____, *Generalbass in drey Accorden*. . . . Leipzig, 1756.

_____, *Der musikalische Dilettant*. Vienna, 1773.

DIBDIN, CHARLES, *Music Epitomized* . . . (4th ed.). London, 1822.

DITTERSDORF, KARL D. VON, *The Autobiography of Karl von Dittersdorf* Eng. tr. A. D. Coleridge. New York, 1970.

DREWIS, F. G., *Freundschaftliche Briefe über die Tonkunst und Composition*. Halle, 1797.

DUBREUIL, JEAN, *Manuel harmonique*. . . . Paris, 1767.

ENGEL, JOHANN J., *Ueber die musikalische Malerey*. Berlin, 1780.

EXIMENO, ANTONIO, *Dell'origine e delle regole della musica*. . . . Rome, 1774.

FORKEL, JOHANN N., *Allgemeine Geschichte der Musik*. . . . Leipzig, 1778.

_____, *Allgemeine Litteratur der Musik*. . . . Leipzig, 1792.

_____, *Musikalischer Almanach für Deutschland*. . . . Leipzig, 1782, 1783, 1784, 1789.

_____, *Musikalisch-kritische Bibliothek*. Gotha, 1778-1779. 3 vols.

FRAMERY, NICHOLAS-E., & GUINGUENÉ, PIERRE-L., *Encyclopédie méthodique*. Vol. I, Paris, 1791. Vol. II, Paris, 1818.

FRICK, JOSEPH, *A Treatise on Thorough Bass*. . . . London, 1786.

FURTADO, JOHN, *An Essay on the Theory and Advancement of Thorough Bass*. London, 1798.

FUX, JOHANN J., *Gradus ad Parnassum* (1725). Eng. tr., subtitled *Practical Rules for Learning Composition*. London [ca. 1768].

GALEAZZI, FRANCESCO, *Elementi teorico-practici di musica*. . . . Rome, 1791-1796. 2 vols.

GASPARINI, FRANCESCO, *L'armonico pratico al cimbalo*. Venice, 1708.

GEMINIANI, FRANCESCO, *The Art of Accompaniment*. . . . London, 1756-1757. 2 vols.

GERBER, ERNST L., *Historisch-biographisches Lexicon der Tonkünstler*. . . . Leipzig, 1790-1792. 2 vols.

_____, *Neues historisch-biographisches Lexikon der Tonkünstler*. Leipzig, 1812-1814. 4 vols.

GERVASONI, CARLO, *La scuola della musica in tre parti divisa*. Piacenza, 1800. 2 vols.

GIANOTTI, PIETRO, *Le guide du compositeur*. . . . Paris, 1759.

GOUDAR, ANGE, *Le brigandage de la musique italienne*. . . . Amsterdam & Paris, 1780.

GRASSINEAU, JAMES, *A Musical Dictionary*. . . . London, 1740.

GRETRY, ANDRÉ. *Mémoires, ou essais sur la musique*. . . . Paris, 1797. 3 vols.

HASTINGS, THOMAS, *Dissertation on Musical Taste*. Albany, N.Y., 1822.

HAWKINS, JOHN, *A General History of the Science and Practice of Music.* London, 1776. 5 vols. (Reprint of 1853 ed., Charles Cudworth ed., New York, 1968.)

HAYDN, JOSEPH, *Gioco filarmonico.* . . . Naples, 1793.

HAYES, WILLIAM, *The Art of Composing Music by a Method Entirely New.* . . . London, 1751.

HECK, JOHANN, *The Art of Playing Thorough Bass.* . . . London [ca. 1777].

HEINICHEN, JOHANN D., *Der General-Bass in der Composition.* . . . Dresden, 1728.

HILLER, JOHANN A., *Anweisung zum musikalisch-richtigen Gesange.* . . . Leipzig, 1774.

————, *Anweisung zum musikalisch-zierlichen Gesange.* Leipzig, 1780.

————, *Anweisung zum Violinspielen.* . . . Leipzig [ca. 1792].

———— (ed.), *Wöchentliche Nachrichten und Anmerkungen die Musik betreffend.* Leipzig, 1766-1770. 4 vols.

HOEGI, PIERRE, *A Tabular System Whereby the Art of Composing Minuets Is Made So Easy.* . . . London [1763].

HOYLE, JOHN, *Dictionarium Musica.* . . . London, 1770.

JACKSON, WILLIAM (of Exeter), *Observations on the Present State of Music in London.* London, 1791.

JONES, WILLIAM, *A Treatise on the Art of Music* . . . Colchester, 1784.

JUNKER, CARL L., *Portefeuille für Musikliebhaber: Charakteristik von 20 Komponisten.* . . . Leipzig, 1792.

KAYE, JOHANN G., *Kleine Clavier-Schule.* Sondershausen, 1822.

KING, MATTHEW P., *A General Treatise on Music.* . . . London, 1800.

KIRCHER, ATHANASIUS, *Musurgia Universalis.* . . . Rome, 1650.

KIRNBERGER, JOHANN P., *Der allezeit fertige Polonoisen- und Menuettencomponist.* Berlin, 1757.

————, *Gedanken über die verschiedenen Lehrarten in der Komposition, als Vorbereitung zur Fugenerkentniss.* . . . Berlin, 1782.

————, *Die Kunst des reinen Satzes in der Musik.* . . . Berlin, 1771-1779.

————, *Methode, Sonaten aus'm Ermel zu schüddeln.* Berlin, 1783.

————, *Recueil d'airs de danse caractéristiques.* . . . Berlin [ca. 1783].

KOCH, HEINRICH C. (ed.), *Journal der Tonkunst.* Erfurt, 1795. 2 vols.

————, *Musikalisches Lexikon.* Frankfurt am Main, 1802.

————, *Versuch einer Anleitung zur Composition.* Leipzig, 1782, 1787, 1793. 3 vols.

KOLLMANN, AUGUST F., *An Essay on Musical Harmony.* . . . London, 1796.

————, *An Essay on Practical Musical Composition.* . . . London, 1799.

KRAUSE, CHRISTIAN G., *Von der musikalischen Poesie.* . . . Berlin, 1752.

KUNZEN, FRIEDRICH L., & REICHARDT, JOHANN F. (eds.), *Musikalisches Wochenblatt.* Berlin, 1791-1792.

Kurzgefasstes musikalisches Lexikon. . . . Chemnitz, 1737.

LAAG, HEINRICH, *Anfangsgründe zum Clavierspielen und Generalbass.* Osnabrück, 1774.

LA BORDE, JEAN-B. DE, *Essai sur la musique ancienne et moderne.* Paris, 1780. 4 vols.

LANGE, HERMANN-F. DE, *Le tôton harmonique ou nouveau jeu de hazard.* . . . Liège [1768].

LANGLÉ, HONORÉ-F., *Traité de la basse sous le chant.* . . . Paris [ca. 1798].

————, *Traité d'harmonie et de modulation.* Paris [ca. 1797].

LE PILEUR D'APLIGNY, *Traité sur la musique.* . . . Paris, 1779.

LEVESQUE, & BÊCHE, *Solfèges d'Italie avec la basse chiffrée composés par Leo, Durante, Scarlatti, etc.* Paris, 1768.

LOGIER, JOHANN B., *System der Musik-Wissenschaft.* . . . Berlin, 1827.

LOBE, JOHANN C., *Lehrbuch der musikalischen Komposition* (2nd ed.). Leipzig, 1858. Vol. 1.

LOHLEIN, GEORG S., *Anweisung zum Violinspielen.* Leipzig & Züllichau, 1774.

———, *Clavier-Schule* (5th ed., rev. Johann G. Witthauer). Leipzig & Züllichau, 1791.

———, *Georg Simon Löhleins Clavier-Schule . . .* (3rd ed.). Leipzig & Züllichau, 1779. Vol. 2, Leipzig & Züllichau, 1781.

Ludus Melothedicus, ou le jeu de dez harmonique. . . . Paris [ca. 1758].

MAJER, JOSEPH F., *Neu-eröffneter theoretisch- und praktischer Music-Saal. . . .* Nürnberg, 1741.

MANCINI, GIAMBÁTTISTA, *Practical Reflections on Figured Singing* (1774, 1777 eds.). Tr. & ed. Edward Foreman. Champaign, Ill., 1967.

MANFREDINI, VINCENZO, *Difesa della musica moderna e de' suoi celebri esecutori. . . .* Bologna, 1788.

———, *Regole armoniche. . . .* Venice, 1775.

MARCELLO, BENEDETTO, *Il teatro alla moda. . . .* Venice [ca. 1720]. (Tr. Reinhard Pauly, *MQ*, April, July, 1948, pp. 222-233, 371-403.)

MARMONTEL, JEAN-F., *Essai sur les révolutions de la musique en France.* Paris, 1777.

MARPURG, FRIEDRICH, *Abhandlung von der Fuge. . . .* Berlin, 1753[-1754]. 2 vols.

———, *Anleitung zum Clavierspielen. . . .* Berlin, 1755.

———, *Anleitung zur Singcomposition.* Berlin, 1758.

———, *Clavierstücke mit einem practischen Unterricht für Anfänger und Geübtere.* Berlin, 1762-1763. 3 vols.

——— (ed.), *Der critische Musicus an der Spree.* Berlin, 1750.

———, *Handbuch bey dem Generalbasse und der Composition. . . .* Berlin, 1755-1758.

——— (ed.), *Historisch-kritische Beyträge zur Aufnahme der Musik.* Berlin, 1754-1758. 5 vols.

——— (ed.), *Kritische Briefe über die Tonkunst. . . .* Berlin [1759-1764]. 3 vols.

MARSH, JOHN, "A Comparison between the Ancient and Modern Styles of Music." *The Monthly Magazine,* vol. II, 1796, p. 981, (See Charles Cudworth, "An Essay by John Marsh." *ML*, XXXVI, 1955, pp. 155-164.)

———, *Hints to Young Composers of Instrumental Music. . . .* London, 1800.

MARTINI, GIAMBATTISTA, *Esemplare a sia saggio fondamentale di contrappunto sopra il canto fermo. . . .* Bologna, 1774.

———, *Saggio fondamentale pratico di contrapunto fugato.* Bologna, 1775.

MARTINI, JEAN-P., *Melopée moderne ou l'art du chant. . . .* Paris [1792].

MARX, ADOLPH B., *Die Lehre von der musikalischen Komposition* (2nd ed.). Leipzig, 1841-1851. 4 vols.

MATTHESON, JOHANN, *Exemplarische Organisten-Probe. . . .* Hamburg, 1719.

———, *Johann Matthesons Grosse General-Bass-Schule. . . .* Hamburg, 1731.

———, *Grundlage einer Ehrenpforte,* Hamburg, 1740.

———, *Der vollkommene Capellmeister. . . .* Hamburg, 1739.

MERBACH, GEORG F., *Clavierschule für Kinder.* Leipzig, 1782.

MERSENNE, MARIN, *Harmonie universelle. . . .* Paris, 1636.

MEUDE-MONPAS, J. J. O., *Dictionnaire de musique. . . .* Paris, 1787.

MILLER, EDWARD, *Elements of Thorough Bass and Composition. . . .* London, 1787.

MIZLER VON KOLOF, LORENZ C., *. . . Neu eröffnete musikalische Bibliothek. . . .* Leipzig, 1739-1754. 4 vols.

MOMIGNY, JEROME J. DE, *Cours complet d'harmonie et de composition.* Paris, 1806.

MOZART, LEOPOLD, *Versuch einer gründlichen Violinschule.* Augsburg, 1756.

MOZART, WOLFGANG A., *Anleitung zum componieren von Walzern. . . .* Berlin [ca. 1793].

Musikalische Charlatanerei. Berlin, 1792.

Musikalisches Handwörterbuch. . . . Weimar, 1786.

NICHELMANN, CHRISTOPH, *Die Melodie nach ihrem Wesen. . . .* Danzig, 1755.

PAISIELLO, GIOVANNI, *Regole per bene accompagnare il partimento.* . . . St. Petersburg, 1782.

PASQUALI, NICOLO, *Thorough-Bass Made Easy.* . . . Edinburgh, 1757.

PETRI, JOHANN S., *Anleitung zur praktischen Musik* . . . (2nd ed.). Leipzig, 1782.

PLANELLI, ANTONIO, *Dell'opera in musica.* . . . Naples, 1772.

PORTMANN, JOHANN G., *Leichtes Lehrbuch der Harmonie, Composition, und des General-basses.* . . . Darmstadt, 1789.

PRAETORIUS, MICHAEL, *Syntagma Musicum.* Wolfenbüttel, 1619.

PRINTZ, WOLFGANG C., *Phrynis Mitilenaeus.* . . . Dresden, 1696.

QUANTZ, JOHANN J., *Versuch einer Anweisung die Flöte traversiere zu spielen.* Berlin, 1752. (3rd ed. Breslau, 1789.)

QUATREMÈRE DE QUINCY, ANTOINE C., *Dissertation sur les opéras bouffons italiens.* Paris, 1789.

RAGUENET, FRANÇOIS, *Parallèle des Italiens et des François* . . . (Eng. tr.). London, 1709.

RAMEAU, JEAN P., *Génération harmonique.* . . . Paris, 1737.

———, *Traité de l'harmonie.* Paris, 1722.

Recueil de romances (compiled by Ch. de Lusse). Paris, 1767–1774. 2 vols.

REICHA, ANTON, *Traité de mélodie.* Paris, 1814.

RELLSTAB, JOHANN C., *Versuch über die Vereinigung der musikalischen und oratorischen Declamation.* . . . Berlin, 1786.

RICCI, FRANCESCO P., *Au plus heureux jeux harmoniques pour composer des minuets ou des contredanses au sort d'un dez.* N.d.

——— (with J. C. Bach), *Méthode ou recueil de connoissances élémentaires pour le pianoforte ou clavecin.* . . . Paris, 1786.

RIEPEL, JOSEPH, *Anfangsgründe zur musikalischen Setzkunst.* . . . Regensburg & Vienna, 1752.

———, *Gründliche Erklärung der Tonordnung insbesondere.* . . . Frankfurt & Leipzig, 1757.

———, *Grundregeln zur Tonordnung insgemein.* Frankfurt & Leipzig, 1755.

ROUSSEAU, JEAN-J., *Dictionnaire de musique.* Paris, 1768.

———, *Lettre sur la musique française.* Paris [1753]. (Eng. tr. in Oliver Strunk, *Source Readings in Music History*, New York, 1950, p. 636ff.)

SCHEIBE, JOHANN A., *Der critische Musikus* (2nd ed.). Leipzig, 1745.

———, *Über die musikalische Composition. Erster Theil: Die Theorie der Melodie und Harmonie.* Leipzig, 1773.

———, *Zweyter Theil: Die Harmonie oder die Zusammensetzung der Töne an und für sich selbst.* Ms., 1777. Royal Library, Copenhagen.

SCHUBART, CHRISTIAN F. D., *Ideen zu einer Aesthetik der Tonkunst* (completed 1785). Vienna, 1806.

SHIELD, WILLIAM, *An Introduction to Harmony.* London, 1800.

SORGE, GEORG A., *Anleitung zur Fantasie.* . . . Lobenstein, 1767.

SPIESS, MEINRAD, *Tractatus Musicus compositorio-practicus.* Augsburg, 1746.

[STADLER, MAXIMILIAN], *Table pour composer des menuets et des trios à l'infinie.* Paris [ca. 1780].

STEINBART, GOTTHILF S., *Grundbegriffe zur Philosophie über den Geschmack.* Züllichau, 1785.

SULZER, JOHANN G., *Allgemeine Theorie der schönen Künste.* Leipzig, 1771–1774. 2 vols.

TARTINI, GUISEPPE, *Traité des agrémens.* . . . Fr. tr. P. Denis. Paris [1771]. (Eng. tr. Cuthbert Girdlestone, Celle & New York, 1961.)

TOSI, PIER F., *Observations on the Florid Song* . . . (1723). Eng. tr. [John] Galliard, 2nd ed. London, 1743.

TRIEST, ROBERT, "Bemerkungen über die Ausbildung der Tonkunst in Deutschland im achtzehnten Jahrhundert." *AMZ*, vol. III, no. 14, Leipzig, 1801.

TÜRK, DANIEL G., *Klavierschule*. . . . Leipzig & Halle, 1789. (2nd ed. 1802.)

_____, *Kurze Anweisung zum Generalbassspielen*. . . . Hamburg, 1791.

VIERLING, JOHANN G., *Versuch einer Anleitung zum Präludiren für Ungeübtere*. . . . Leipzig [1794].

VOGLER, GEORG J., *Kuhrpfälzische Tonschule*. Mannheim, 1778.

_____, *System für den Fugenbau*. . . . Offenbach, 1811.

Vriendenzangen tot gezellige Vreugd. Haarlem, 1801.

WALTHER, JOHANN, G., *Musikalisches Lexikon*. . . . Leipzig, 1732.

WEBER, DANIEL, "Ueber komische Characteristik und Karikatur in praktischen Musikwerken." *AMZ*, vol. III, no. 9, Leipzig, 1800.

WEBER, GOTTFRIED, *Versuch einer geordneten Theorie der Tonsetzkunst*. Mainz, 1830.

WIEDEBURG, MICHAEL, *Der sich selbst informirende Clavierspieler*. . . . Halle & Leipzig, 1765-1775. 3 vols.

_____, *Musikalisches Chartenspiel ex G dur*. . . . Aurich, 1788.

WOLF, ERNST, W., *Musikalischer Unterricht*. Dresden, 1788.

WOLF, GEORG F., *Kurzer aber deutlicher Unterricht im Klavier-spielen* (3rd ed.). Halle, 1789. 2 vols.

ZARLINO, GIOSEFFO, *Le istitutioni harmoniche*. . . . Venice, 1558.

ZIEGLER, CHRISTIAN G., *Anleitung zur musikalischen Composition*. Ms., 1739. Drexel Collection, New York Public Library.

ZUCCARI, CARLO, *The True Method of Playing an Adagio Made Easy by Twelve Examples*. . . . London [ca. 1762].

Suggested References and Readings

COMPOSERS (BIOGRAPHICAL)

ABERT, HERMANN, *W. A. Mozart* (revision of Otto Jahn, *Mozart*). Leipzig: Breitkopf & Härtel, 1923-1924.

ANDERSON, EMILY, *Letters of Beethoven*. New York: St. Martin's Press, 1961. 2 vols.

_____, *The Letters of Mozart and His Family* (2nd ed.). Prepared by A. Hyatt King & Monica Carolan. London: Macmillan, 1966. 2 vols.

DEUTSCH, OTTO ERICH, *Mozart: A Documentary Biography*. Tr. Jeremy Noble & Peter Branscombe. Stanford: Stanford University Press, 1965.

EINSTEIN, ALFRED, *Gluck*. Tr. Eric Blom. New York: Collier Books, 1962.

_____, *Mozart: His Character and Work*. Tr. Arthur Mendel & Nathan Broder. New York: W. W. Norton, 1945.

GEIRINGER, KARL, *Haydn: A Creative Life in Music*. Berkeley & Los Angeles: University of California Press, 1968.

GIAZOTTO, REMO, *Giovan Battista Viotti*. Milan: Curci, 1956.

GOTWALS, VERNON (tr. & ed.), *Joseph Haydn, Eighteenth-Century Gentleman and Genius* (tr. of Georg August Griesinger, *Biographische Notizen über Joseph Haydn*, and Albert Dies, *Biographische Nachrichten von Joseph Haydn*). Madison: University of Wisconsin Press, 1963.

LANDON, H.C.R., *Haydn: Chronicle and Works*. Bloomington, Indiana University Press, 1976.

ROTHSCHILD, GERMAINE, *Luigi Boccherini: His Life and Work*. Tr. Norbert Dufourcq. London & New York: Oxford University Press, 1965.

ST. FOIX, GEORGES DE & WYZEWA, THEODORE DE, *Mozart*. Paris: Desclée de Brouwer, 1912-1946. 5 vols.

SCHENCK, ERICH, *Mozart and His Times*. Ed. & tr. Richard & Clara Winston. London: Secker & Warburg, 1960.

SCHINDLER, ANTON, *Beethoven as I Knew Him*. Ed. Donald MacArdle, tr. Constance Jolly. Chapel Hill: University of North Carolina Press, 1966.

SCHOLES, PERCY, *The Great Dr. Burney*. London & New York: Oxford University Press, 1948. 2 vols.

SOLOMON, MAYNARD, *Beethoven*. New York, Schirmer Books, 1977.

TERRY, CHARLES SANFORD, *John Christian Bach* (2nd ed.). London & New York: Oxford University Press, 1967.

PERFORMANCE

ALDRICH, PUTNAM, *The Principal Agréments of the 17th and 18th Centuries*. Dissertation, Harvard University, 1942.

ARNOLD, FRANCK T., *The Art of Accompaniment from a Thorough-Bass*. London: Oxford University Press, 1931. 2 vols.

BABITZ, SOL, "Differences between Eighteenth-Century and Modern Violin Bowing." *The Score*, no. 19, March 1957, pp. 34–55.

BADURA-SKODA, PAUL & EVA, *Interpreting Mozart on the Keyboard*. Eng tr. Leo Black. New York: St. Martin's Press, 1962.

BOYDEN, DAVID, "Dynamics in Seventeenth- and Eighteenth-Century Music." In *Essays on Music in Honor of Archibald Thompson Davison*. Harvard University Press, 1957. Pp. 185–194.

———, *The History of Violin Playing from Its Origins to 1761*. London & New York: Oxford University Press, 1965.

BRODER, NATHAN, "Mozart and the Clavier." *MQ*, XXVII, 1941, pp. 422–432.

CARSE, ADAM, *The History of Orchestration*. London: K. Paul, Trench, Trubner, 1925.

———, *The Orchestra in the XVIIIth Century*. Cambridge, England: W. Heffer, 1951. New York: Broude Bros., 1969.

DART, THURSTON, *The Interpretation of Music*. New York: Harper & Row, 1963.

DONINGTON, ROBERT, *The Interpretation of Early Music*. New version. New York: St. Martin's Press, 1974.

HARDING, ROSAMUND, *Origins of Musical Time and Expression*. London & New York: Oxford University Press, 1938.

KIRKPATRICK, RALPH, "Eighteenth-Century Metronomic Indications." *PAMS*, 1938, pp. 30–50.

OBERDÖRFFER, FRITZ, *Der Generalbass in der Instrumentalmusik des ausgehenden achtzehnten Jahrhunderts*. Kassel: Bärenreiter, 1939.

PARRISH, CARL, "Criticisms of the Piano When It Was New." *MQ*, XXX, 1944, pp. 428–440.

———, "Haydn and the Piano." *JAMS*, I, 1948, pp. 27–44.

SMILES, JOAN, *Improvised Ornamentation in Late Eighteenth-Century Music*. Dissertation, Stanford University, 1975.

SNOOK, SUSAN PAULINE, *J.F. Daube's Der musikalische Dilettant, Translation and Commentary*. Dissertation, Stanford University, 1978.

ZASLAW, NEAL, & VINQUIST, MARY, *Performance Practice: A Bibliography*. New York: W.W. Norton, 1971.

STYLE, FORM, GENRES

ABRAHAM, GERALD, *Beethoven's Second Period Quartets*. London: Oxford University Press, 1942.

ALLANBROOK, WYE JAMISON, *Dance as Expression in Mozart Opera*. Dissertation, Stanford University, 1974.

BARFORD, PHILIP, "The Sonata Principle: A Study of Musical Thought in the Eighteenth Century." *MR*, XIII, 1952, pp. 255–263.

BENARY, PETER, *Die deutsche Kompositionslehre des achtzehnten Jahrhunderts*. Leipzig: Breitkopf & Härtel, 1961.

BRODER, NATHAN, "Mozart and the Clavier." *MQ*, XXVII, 1941, pp. 422–432.

BROOK, BARRY, "The Symphonie Concertante: An Interim Report." *MQ*, XLVII, 1961, pp. 493–516.

———, *La symphonie française dans la seconde moitié du XVIII° siécle*. Paris: Publications de l'Institut de Musicologie de l'Université de Paris, 1962. 3 vols.

CHURGIN, BATHIA, "Francesco Galeazzi's Description [1796] of Sonata Form." *JAMS*, XXI, 1968, pp. 181–199.

———, (ed.), *The Symphonies of G. B. Sammartini*. Vol. 1, *The Early Symphonies*. Cambridge, Mass.: Harvard University Press, 1968.

Cockshoot, John, *The Fugue in Beethoven's Piano Music.* London: Routledge & K. Paul, 1959.

Cole, Malcolm, "The Vogue of the Instrumental Rondo in the Late Eighteenth Century." *JAMS*, XXII, 1969, pp. 425-455.

Cudworth, Charles, "Cadence Galante: The Story of a Cliché." *MMR*, LXXIX, 1949, pp. 176-178.

_____, "An Essay by John Marsh." *ML*, XXXVI, 1955, pp. 155-164.

Dent, Edward J., "Italian Opera in the Eighteenth Century and Its Influence upon Music of the Classical Period." *SIM*, XIV, 1912-1913, pp. 500-509.

_____, *Mozart's Operas: A Critical Study.* London: Oxford University Press, 1913. (2nd eds. 1947, 1960.)

Engel, Hans, "Die Quellen des klassischen Stils." In *Report of the Eighth Congress of the International Musicological Society.* Kassel: Bärenreiter, 1961. Pp. 285-304.

Feil, Arnold, *Satztechnische Fragen in den Kompositionslehren von F. E. Niedt, J. Riepel, und Heinrich Christoph Koch.* Dissertation, Heidelberg University, 1954.

Fischer, Wilhelm, "Instrumentalmusik von 1750-1828." In Guido Adler, *Handbuch der Musikgeschichte,* II (2nd ed.) Berlin: H. Keller, 1930.

_____, "Zur Entwicklungsgeschichte des Wiener klassischen Stils." *StM*, III, 1915, pp. 24-84.

Girdlestone, Cuthbert, *Mozart's Piano Concertos.* London: Cassell, 1948.

Gradenwitz, Peter, "Mid-Eighteenth-Century Transformations of Style." *ML*, XVIII, 1937, pp. 265-275.

_____, "The Symphonies of Johann Stamitz." *MR*, I, 1940, pp. 354-363.

Helfert, Vladimir, "Zur Entwicklungsgeschichte der Sonatenform." *AMW*, VII, 1925, pp. 117-146.

Hertzmann, Erich, "Mozart's Creative Process." *MQ*, XLIII, 1957, pp. 187-200.

Horsley, Imogene, *Fugue.* New York: The Free Press, 1966.

Kerman, Joseph, *The Beethoven Quartets.* New York: Alfred A. Knopf, 1967.

King, Alexander Hyatt, *Mozart in Retrospect.* London: Oxford University Press, 1955.

Kirkendale, Warren, *Fuge und Fugato in der Kammermusik des Rokoko und der Klassik.* Tutzing: Hans Schneider. 1966.

La Laurencie, Lionel de, *L'école française de violon de Lully à Viotti.* Paris: Delagrave, 1922-1924. 3 vols.

_____, & St. Foix, Georges de, "La symphonie française vers 1750." *L'année musicale,* 1911, pp. 1-123.

La Rue, Jan, "Significant and Coincidental Resemblance between Classical Themes." *JAMS*, vol. XIV, 1961, pp. 224-234.

Landon, H.C.R., *Essays on the Viennese Classical Style. . . .* London, Barrie & Rockliff, 1970.

_____, *The Symphonies of Joseph Haydn.* London: Universal Edition & Rockliff, 1955. Supplement 1961.

_____, & Chapman, Roger (eds.), *Studies in Eighteenth-Century Music.* London: George Allen & Unwin, 1970.

_____, & Mitchell, Donald, *The Mozart Companion.* London: Rockliff, 1956.

Lang, Paul Henry, *The Creative World of Mozart.* New York: W. W. Norton, 1963.

_____, "Mozart after Two Hundred Years." *JAMS*, XIII, 1960, pp. 197-205.

Lenneberg, Hans, "Johann Mattheson on Rhetoric and Affect." *JMT*, II, nos. 1, 2, 1958, pp. 47-84, 193-236.

Levy, Janet, *The Quatuor Concertant in Paris in the Latter Half of the Eighteenth Century.* Dissertation, Stanford University, 1971.

Loesser, Arthur, *Men, Women, and Pianos.* New York: Simon & Schuster, 1954.

Mann, Alfred, *The Study of Fugue.* New York: W. W. Norton, 1965.

MASON, DANIEL GREGORY, *The Quartets of Beethoven*. New York: Oxford University Press, 1947.

MIES, PAUL, *Beethoven's Sketches*. Tr. Doris L. Mackinnon. London: Oxford University Press, 1929.

MISCH, LUDWIG, *Beethoven Studies*. Norman: University of Oklahoma Press, 1953.

MOZART-JAHRBUCH, Salzburg: Internationale Stiftung Mozarteum, 1950-.

NETTL, PAUL, *The Dance in Classical Music*. New York: The Philosophical Library, 1963.

NEWMAN, WILLIAM, "Concerning the Accompanied Clavier Sonata." *MQ*, XXXIII, 1947, pp. 327-349.

_____, "Kirnberger's 'Method for Tossing Off Sonatas.'" *MQ*, XLVII, pp. 517-525.

_____, "The Recognition of Sonata Form by Theorists of the 18th and 19th Centuries." *PAMS*, 1941 (printed 1946), pp. 21-29.

_____, *The Sonata in the Classic Era*. Chapel Hill: University of North Carolina Press, 1963.

NOSKE, FRITS, "Le principe structural-génétique dans l'oeuvre instrumental de Joseph Haydn." *RBM*, XII, 1958, pp. 35-39.

NOTTEBOHM, GUSTAV, *Beethoveniana: Aufsätze und Mittheilungen*. Leipzig: C. F. Peters, 1872.

_____, *Ein Skizzenbuch von Beethoven*. Leipzig: Breitkopf & Härtel, 1865.

_____, *Ein Skizzenbuch von Beethoven aus dem Jahre 1803*. Leipzig: Breitkopf & Härtel, 1880.

RATNER, LEONARD, "Ars Combinatoria . . ." in *Studies in Eighteenth-Century Music*, H. C. Robbins Landon & Roger Chapman, eds. London: George Allen & Unwin, 1970, pp. 343-363.

_____, "Eighteenth-Century Theories of Musical Period Structure." *MQ*, XLII, 1956, pp. 439-454.

_____, "Harmonic Aspects of Classic Form." *JAMS*, II, 1949, pp. 159-168.

_____, "Key Definition: A Structural Issue in Beethoven's Music." *JAMS*, XXIII, 1970, pp. 472-483.

_____, *Music: The Listener's Art*. (2nd ed.). New York: McGraw-Hill, 1966.

RINGER, ALEXANDER L., "The Chasse as a Musical Topic of the 18th Century." *JAMS*, VI, 1953, pp. 148-159.

_____, "Clementi and the Eroica," *MQ*, XLVII, 1961, pp. 454-468.

ROBINSON, MICHAEL, *Opera before Mozart*. New York: William Morrow & Co., 1967.

ROWEN, RUTH HALLE, *Early Chamber Music*. New York: Da Capo Press, 1974.

_____, "Some 18th-Century Classifications of Musical Style." *MQ*, XXXIII, 1947, pp. 90-101.

ST. FOIX, GEORGES DE, *The Symphonies of Mozart*. Tr. Leslie Orrey. London: Dennis Dobson, 1947.

SCHWARZ, BORIS, "Beethoven and the French Violin School." *MQ*, XLIV, 1958, pp. 431-447.

SCHWARZMAIER, ERNST, *Die Takt- und Tonordnung Josef Riepels*. Munich: Verlag für Musikalische Kultur und Wissenschaft, 1934.

SIMON, EDWIN J., "Sonata into Concerto: A Study of Mozart's First Seven Concertos." *AM*, XXXI, 1959, pp. 170-185.

SONDHEIMER, ROBERT, *Haydn: A Historical and Psychological Study Based on His Quartets*. London: Bernoulli, 1951.

_____, *Die Theorie der Sinfonie und die Beurteilung einzelner Sinfonie-komponisten bei der Musikschriftstellern des 18. Jahrhunderts*. Leipzig: Breitkopf & Härtel, 1925.

STRUNK, OLIVER, "Haydn's Divertimenti for Baryton, Viola, and Bass." *MQ,* XVIII, 1932, pp. 216-251.

TOBEL, RUDOLF VON, *Die Formenwelt der klassischen Instrumentalmusik.* Bern & Leipzig: Paul Haupt, 1935.

TORREFRANCA, FAUSTO, *Le origine italiane del romanticismo musicale.* Turin: Fratelli Bocca, 1930.

TOVEY, DONALD F., *Essays in Musical Analysis.* London: Oxford University Press, 1935-1939, 1944, 1946.

_____, *Musical Articles from the Encyclopedia Britannica.* London: Oxford University Press, 1944.

TUTENBERG, FRITZ, *Die Sinfonik Johann Christian Bachs.* Berlin: Georg Kallmeyer, 1928.

TWITTENHOF, WILHELM, *Die musiktheoretischen Schriften Joseph Riepels.* . . . Halle: Buchdruckerei des Waisenhauses, 1934.

UNGER, HANS HEINRICH, *Die Beziehungen zwischen Musik und Rhetorik im 16-18. Jahrhundert.* Würzburg: K. Triltsch, 1941.

VEINUS, ABRAHAM, *The Concerto.* New York: Dover, 1964.

SURVEYS, HISTORIES, DICTIONARIES

APEL, WILLI, *Harvard Dictionary of Music.* Cambridge, Mass.: Harvard University Press, 1944, 1969.

BLUME, FRIEDRICH, *Classic and Romantic Music: A Comprehensive Survey.* Tr. M. D. Herter Norton. New York: W. W. Norton, 1970.

BÜCKEN, ERNST, *Die Musik des Rokokos und der Klassik. Handbuch der Musikwissenschaft* series, vol. 4. Potsdam: Akademische Verlagsgesellschaft Athenaion, 1927.

BUKOFZER, MANFRED, *Music in the Baroque Era.* New York: W. W. Norton, 1947.

_____, *Music of the Classic Era.* Berkeley: University of California Press, 1944, 1955.

COBBETT, WALTER W. (ed.), *Cobbett's Cyclopedic Survey of Chamber Music.* London: Humphrey Milford, 1929; Oxford University Press, 1963. 2 vols.

DAVAL, PIERRE, *La musique en France au XVIII siècle.* Paris: Payot, 1961.

FÉTIS, FRANÇOIS-J., *Biographie universelle des musiciens* . . . (2nd ed.). Paris: Firmin Didot, 1860-1880. 8 vols., 2 supplements.

FREYSTÄTTER, WILHELM, *Die musikalischen Zeitschriften seit ihrer Entstehungen* . . . Munich, T. Riedel, 1884.

GROUT, DONALD J., *A History of Western Music.* New York: W. W. Norton, 1960, 1973.

HELM, ERNEST E., *Music at the Court of Frederick the Great.* Norman: University of Oklahoma Press, 1960.

LANG, PAUL H., *Music in Western Civilization.* New York: W. W. Norton, 1941.

Die Musik in Geschichte und Gegenwart. Kassel: Bärenreiter, 1949- 10 vols. & revisions.

The New Oxford History of Music. New York & London: Oxford University Press, 1954-.

The Oxford History of Music (2nd ed.). London: Humphrey Milford, 1929-1934. 7 vols.

PAULY, REINHARD, *Music in the Classic Period.* Englewood Cliffs, N. J.: Prentice-Hall, 1965, 1973.

PREUSSNER, EBERHARD, *Die bürgerliche Musikkultur* . . . (2nd ed.). Kassel: Bärenreiter, 1954.

ROSEN, CHARLES, *The Classical Style.* New York: Viking Press, 1971.

SLONIMSKY, NICHOLAS (ed.), *Baker's Biographical Dictionary of Musicians* (6th ed.). New York: Schirmer Books, 1978.

STRUNK, OLIVER, *Source Readings in Music History.* New York: W. W. Norton, 1950, 1965.

BIBLIOGRAPHIES, SOURCES

The Breitkofp Thematic Catalogue . . . 1762–1787. Barry Brook ed., New York: Dover, 1966.

DUCKLES, VINCENT, *Music Reference and Research Materials* (2nd ed.). New York: The Free Press, 1967.

———, & MINNIE ELMER, *Thematic Catalogue of a Manuscript Collection of Eighteenth-Century Italian Instrumental Music.* Berkeley & Los Angeles: University of California Press, 1963.

EITNER, ROBERT, *Biographisch-bibliographisches Quellen-Lexikon. . . .* Leipzig: Breitkopf & Härtel, 1900–1904. 10 vols. (Reprint New York: Musurgia, 1947.)

JOHANSSON, CARI, *French Music Publishers' Catalogues of the Second Half of the Eighteenth Century.* Stockholm: Publications of the Royal Swedish Academy of Music, II, 1955. 2 vols.

KIRKENDALE, WARREN, *Fuge und Fugato in der Kammermusik des Rokoko und der Klassik.* Tutzing: Hans Schneider, 1966. (Bibliography pp. 339–357.)

KROHN, ERNST CHRISTOPHER, *The History of Music.* St. Louis, Washington University Press, 1952.

LA LAURENCIE, LIONEL DE, *Inventaire critique du Fonds Blancheton. . . .* Paris: Librairie E. Droz, 1930–1931. 2 vols.

LARSEN, JENS P., *Drei Haydn Kataloge in Faksimile.* Copenhagen: Einar Munksgaard, 1941.

LESURE, FRANÇOIS (ed.), *Écrits imprimés concernant la musique.* (*International Inventory of Musical Sources*, series B, VI, 1–2.) Munich: Henle [ca. 1971]. 2 vols.

———, *Einzeldrücke vor 1800.* (*International Inventory of Musical Sources*, series AI, 1–5.) Kassel: Bärenreiter, 1971–1975. 5 vols.

Library of Congress, *Catalogue of Early Books on Music.* Julia Gregory, ed. Washington: Government Printing Office, 1913. Supplement, Hazel Bartlett ed., 1944.

NEWMAN, WILLIAM S., *The Sonata in the Classic Era.* Chapel Hill: University of North Carolina Press, 1963. (Extensive bibliography pp. 810–869.)

SCHNAPPER, EDITH (ed.), *The British Union Catalogue of Early Music, Printed before the Year 1801.* London: Butterworth, 1957.

UNVERRICHT, HUBERT, *Geschichte des Streichtrios.* Tutzing: Hans Schneider, 1969. Pp. 301–338.

THEMATIC CATALOGUES

GÉRARD, YVES, *Thematic, Bibliographical, and Critical Catalogue of the Works of Luigi Boccherini.* (Tr. Andreas Mayor.) London, New York: Oxford University Press, 1969.

GIAZOTTO, REMO, *Giovan Battista Viotti.* Milan: Curci, 1956. Pp. 289–368.

HOBOKEN, ANTHONY VAN, *Joseph Haydn: Thematisch-bibliographisches Werkverzeichnis.* Vol. 1, *Instrumentalwerke.* Vol. 2, *Vokalwerke.* Mainz: B. Schotts Söhne, 1957–.

KINSKY, GEORG, *Das Werk Beethovens. . . .* Completed by Hans Halm. Munich: Henle, 1955.

KÖCHEL, LUDWIG RITTER VON, *Chronologisch-thematisches Verzeichnis sämtlicher Tonwerke Wolfgang Amade Mozarts* (6th ed.). Wiesbaden, 1964.

TERRY, CHARLES SANFORD, *John Christian Bach* (2nd ed.). London & New York: Oxford University Press, 1967. Pp. 193–361.

WOTQUENNE, ALFRED, *Thematisches Verzeichnis der Werke von Carl Philipp Emanuel Bach.* Leipzig: Breitkopf & Härtel, 1905.

———, *Catalogue thématique des oeuvres de Chr. W. von Gluck.* Leipzig: Breitkopf & Härtel, 1904.

Name Index

Subject Index